P. F. M. FONTAINE

THE LIGHT
AND
THE DARK

A CULTURAL HISTORY OF DUALISM

VOLUME IV

J.C. GIEBEN, PUBLISHER
AMSTERDAM

THE LIGHT AND THE DARK

THE LIGHT AND THE DARK
A CULTURAL HISTORY OF DUALISM

VOLUME IV

DUALISM IN THE ANCIENT MIDDLE EAST

J.C. GIEBEN, PUBLISHER
AMSTERDAM 1989

To my joyous, original,
and self-reliant daughters,
Bernadette and Relinde

No part of this book may be translated or reproduced in any form, by print, photoprint, microfilm, or any other means, without written permission from the publisher.

© by P.F.M. Fontaine / ISBN 90 5063 032 4 / Printed in The Netherlands

"For all things are called
light and darkness"

Parmenides

CONTENTS

Preface   xi

I   EGYPTIACA   1

1. The Red Land and the Black   1
   a. Seeing the desert blossoming   1
   b. Retreat to the Nile   3
   c. The 'lotus plant'   4
   d. A definite margin   5
   e. The Fiend and the Master   6
2. The Reed and the Bee   7
   a. The Egyptian composite   7
   b. The unifying concept   9
   c. Pharaoh as the bearer of the national duality   10
   d. The Two Ladies   12
   e. A case of dualism   13
3. The 'true men' and the lesser breeds   15
   a. Splendid isolation   15
   b. The fine feeling isolation gives   16
   c. Successful propaganda   19
   d. A blast of God   21
   e. Egypt's public enemy   23
4. Pharaohs and mortals   24
5. The deviant king   28
   a. A dualistic revolution   28
   b. From 'Re' to 'Aten'   30
   c. The 'heresy'   31
   d. Pathological traits   34
   e. 'Back to normalcy'   35
6. Between Chaos and Order   36
   a. The nearness of Chaos   36
   b. The cosmogony of Heliopolis   37
   c. The Theban cosmology   39
   d. The Memphite theology   40
7. The Egyptians and Death   41
   a. Life and Death contrasted   41
   b. 'Ka'   43
   c. Presentations of life after death   46
   d. Denial of death   47

Notes to Chapter I   52

II   ISRAELITICA   58

1. The Bible   58
2. The sources of the Pentateuch   60

3.	The 'creation stories'	62
4.	A non-dualistic religion	64
5.	A biblical anthropology	66
6.	Biblical chronology	67
	a. The creation of time	67
	b. The need of a definite beginning	69
	c. The Bible's preference for a 'short chronology'	70
	d. The 'Great Year'	71
	e. Times-cycles	72
	f. Summing up	74
7.	Apocalyptic dualism	75
	a. The Messianic future	75
	b. The kernel of Jewish apocalyptic writing	77
	c. The Book of Daniel	79
	d. Daniel's four beasts and the Son of Man	81
	e. Salvation in the future	83
8.	The biblical notion of God	84
	a. Israel's exclusive monotheism	85
	b. Anthropomorphism or theomorphism	87
9.	The zealous god and the other gods	90
	a. The lure of idolatry	90
	b. Do idols exist?	94
10.	Dark powers	96
	a. The 'waters'	96
	b. Magic	99
	c. The 'nomadic ideal'	103
11.	The origin of evil	105
	a. The tree and the snake	105
	b. Another origin of evil?	107
	c. The role of the devil	110
12.	Relationships of man	110
	a. 'In the image of God'	110
	b. Death as an anomaly	113
	c. No blessing for sinners?	115
	d. Job between good and evil	117
	e. A vision of the afterlife	121
	f. 'The tenacious inconvenience'	122
	g. The magic circle around marriage	125
	h. Rifts in the building	126
	i. The anthropological kernel of the question	128
	j. Why there are men and women	131
	k. Man and women as 'Adam and Eve'	135
	l. A prey to anxiety	138
	m. 'The joy of Israel'	144
	n. Why God is male	147
	o. Man in his relation to nature	151
	p. God's identity	154
13.	Jahve and the king	156
	a. The Gilgal-tradition	156
	b. Theocracy and 'normalcy'	158
14.	The antagonism of north and south	160
	a. Precarious unity	160

		b. Two separate kingdoms	162
		c. Jews and Samaritans	165
15.	Israel and the Gentiles		167
		a. The Covenant	167
		b. The idea of election	169
		c. 'Never pitying them'	171
		d. Wholesale destruction as a metaphor	173
		e. From the ideal to practice	175
		f. An inconsistency in the biblical presentation	177
		g. 'The tears of Esau'	180
16.	The wholeness of the world		185
		a. The way of the Messiah	185
		b. Holiness and wholeness	186
Notes to Chapter II			191

III	MESOPOTAMICA AND ANATOLICA		204
1.	The dualism of universal states		204
2.	Sumer		205
3.	Akkad		208
4.	Sumer and Akkad		209
5.	Hammurabi's Babylonian Empire		212
	a. The first master of all Mesopotamia		212
	b. Conquest divinely sanctioned		213
	c. The aftermath		215
6.	The Hittites		216
	a. The Old Hittite Empire		216
	b. The New Hittite Empire		219
7.	The Assyrians		221
	a. The beginnings of Assyria's greatness		222
	b. The great Assyrian conquests		223
	c. Immense cruelty		226
	d. Assyria's greatest days		229
8.	The New Babylonian Empire		232
9.	Kingship		234
	a. The Hittite kings		234
	b. Legendary kings of Sumer		236
	c. The historical Mesopotamian kings		237
10.	Dualistic aspects of Mesopotamian and Anatolian religion		241
	a. The Sumerian religion		241
	b. The Hittite religion		244
	c. Babylonian religion		247
Notes to Chapter III			253

IV	PERSICA		257
1.	The coming of the Persians		257
2.	The Median Empire		258
3.	The Persian Empire		259
	a. The founding of the Empire by Cyrus		259
	b. Cambyses conquers Egypt		262

		c.	Darius I and the Scythian menace	263
		d.	The Great Kings and the Greeks	265
		e.	Alexander's campaign	267
	4.		The origins of dualism	271
	5.		Dualistic aspects of non-Zoroastrian religion	274
		a.	The three great gods: Vayu, Mithra, and Zervan	276
		b.	Ormuzd and Ahriman	279
	6.		Persian kingship	280
	7.		What we know of Zoroaster	282
	8.		Zoroaster's doctrine	286
		a.	The Wise Lord and the Holy Immortals	286
		b.	The Evil Spirit	287
		c.	The dual entities	289
		d.	The need to choose	291
		e.	Ahuras and daevas	293
		f.	Body and soul	295
		g.	Life and Death	296
		h.	The end of the universe	296
	9.		Zoroaster's dualism	297
	10.		Zoroaster's religious community	299
	11.		Prayer and ritual	300
	12.		Syncretism and heresy	301
Appendix to Chapter IV				304
Notes to Chapter IV				306
Bibliography				311
General Index				321

Map I	Egypt	opposite p.	4
Map II	Israel	opposite p.	64
Map III	The Empire of Sumer and Akkad	opposite p.	208
Map IV	Hammurabi's Empire	opposite p.	212
Map V	The Hittite Empire	opposite p.	216
Map VI	The Assyrian Empire	opposite p.	222
Map VII	The New Babylonian Empire	opposite p.	232
Map VIII	The Median Empire	opposite p.	258
Map IX	The Persian Empire	opposite p.	260

PREFACE

In Karen Blixen's magnificent book 'Out of Africa' (1937) I stumbled on a phrase that could serve as a Leitmotiv for the whole series of which this volume is the fourth instalment. She wrote that "the world, after all, is not a regular or calculable place". This is an utterly un-Hellenic idea. To the Greeks the world was a well-ordered and essentially homogeneous whole, a real cosmos. But as Volumes I-III abundantly proved, their religion, their ideology, as well as their mode of existence, contained many irregularities and contradictions. Perhaps, indeed, individual and communal life might have been easier for the Greeks, had they been able to accept the fact that life, and their own lives too, is made up of anomalies which, in their civilization, were of a very basic kind. Instead, they doggedly clung to the notion that the Greek polis, in which their individual existences were embedded, was the reflexion of the cosmic order - in spite of all the horrifying things that occurred in the poleis and in spite of all the atrocities that the Greek cities inflicted on each other.

The Bible takes a far more realistic stand. "Our human thoughts are hesitating, our conjectures hazardous ... It is hard enough to read the riddle of our own life here, with laborious search, ascertaining what lies so close to hand". This is what the Book of Wisdom says (9:14 and 16). Now the Old Testament concurs with the Greek point of view in so far that it too starts from the premise that, at least, the world is meant to be homogeneous and was created as such. That it did not remain in a harmonious state is, it avers, the consequence of the Fall. Rifts and fissures have appeared at many points in our existence; it has become difficult for us to reconcile the contradictions and to bridge the oppositions with which mankind is confronted.

This does not mean at all that the world is totally divided against itself. What people long for, always and everywhere, is peace, harmony, and togetherness. Often enough this ideal is realized, in happy families, in harmonious and contented lives, in peaceful national existence, in fruitful collaboration between nations. But only too frequently the wrongs means are employed and the general state of things deteriorates; then it all ends in divorce, strife, war, and utter alienation. Speaking in the terms of this series, I might state that, although dualism is not the original, the anthropological human condition - I mean that of the human race in its present, historical state -, the world is so shaped that it easily gives rise to dualistic tendencies, even to sheer dualism.

I see as yet no reason for changing the wording of my definition of dualism that I presented already in the preface of Volume I. Dualism denotes the existence of two utterly opposed conceptions, systems, principles, groups of people, or even worlds, without any intermediate link between them. They cannot be reduced to one another; in some cases they are not even dependent on each other. The opposites are considered to be of a different quality - so much so that one of them is seen as distinctly inferior and hence must be repudiated or even destroyed. This definition also implies that there is no reason at all why dualism should be supposed to occur only in the realms of philosophy or religion. Unbridgeable oppositions are equally to be found in history and politics, in the arts, and in personal and communal life.

Dualism is a rather intricate subject; it is possible to define it more subtly by creating a number of subdivisions. For this I may refer to the afterword of Volume I. One of these subdivisions occurs in this volume too, that of absolute (or radical) and relative dualism. In radical dualism the two principles or worlds are absolutely coeval, they are both from eternity, and there is no interdependence whatsoever between them. In relative dualism the two systems or groups of persons are dependent on each other. However strongly opposed they may be, they can, nevertheless, not do without each other. (I am quoting myself verbatim from the prefaces of Volumes II and III.)

This volume can be read independently of Volumes I-III. I wrote it directly in English, which saved me the long detour over the Dutch language, my vernacular. As in the foregoing volumes, Dr. J.R.Dove, associate professor of English literature at the University of Oulu in Finland, has corrected my English carefully and conscientiously; I also feel grateful to him for the sensible advice he gave me with regard to the contents and the composition of this book.

My two 'general readers' have remained faithful to me throughout this work too. My daughter Resianne, now a doctor of pihilosophy with her thesis happily behind her, supplied me with much good advice and interesting insights - in spite of the fact that she has little time to spare since, in addition to her responsibilities as a wife and mother of four children, she is also engaged part-time on a scholarly project. The second reader was, again, Dr. A.Budé, a classical scholar, who provided me with many valuable comments. Both of them may rely on my deeply felt gratitude.

Chapter I of this volume I submitted to the critical judgment of Dr. M.Heerma van Voss, professor of ancient religions at the University of Amsterdam. The sections on the Hittites in Chapter III were read by Dr. Ph.Houwink ten Cate, professor of Ancient Near Eastern history and of Hittite and related languages; another expert was kind enough to peruse the Mesopotamian sections of the same chapter. Chapter IV, on Persia, was assessed by Dr. W.Skalmowski, professor of Iranian studies at the Catholic University of Louvain in Belgium. I feel deeply indebted to these scholars who, although having no lack of work, readily invested their time in this volume. I always feel gratified by the way the publisher, Mr. J.C.Gieben, is taking care of my brain-children.

For Chapter II, on Israel, I trusted to my own lights and to those of my daughter, a semitologist and philosopher, wo discussed several sections with me. True enough, I am not a biblical scholar myself but, to a certain extent, I feel entitled to rely on the fact that I have now read the whole book, Old and New Testament, eleven times from cover to cover, without even omitting a tittle or iota. I say nothing of the innumerable times I have read individual books, like Isaiah, the

Song of Songs, the Letter to the Hebrews, or the Revelation of John, and, in particular, my best-loved book, that of Genesis, which I have read over and over again, in Hebrew, Greek, and Latin, in Dutch and in English. The main ideas I bring forward in this chapter are wholly my own, the result of decades of meditating on the Bible. Nevertheless, I do not offer what I wrote as a personal religious testimony. I do not want to be misunderstood on this point. Although I am, of course, not able to dissociate what I expressed in this part of my book from my religious insights, I present it as an essay on the religion of Israel that must be studied and judged on the same grounds as all the others, that is to say, as an attempt to find out and to present the dualistic elements in this religion.

My son Filip, an electrotechnical engineer-to-be, deserves my thanks for drawing the nine maps so neatly. This time the task of my dear wife Anneke was somewhat easier than that with respect to Volumes I-III, since there is no original Dutch version in this case. However, as accurately as ever she corrected the camera-ready typescript of this volume, which requires a measure of dexterity I myself cannot boast of. I cannot thank her enough. I wish to stress that the sole responsibility for this work rests with me, not only with respect to its contents but also regarding the translation and the typography. The main part of Chapter I was written between September 1986 and February 1987, the rest of it in October 1987, and the Chapters II-IV between January and October 1988, the manuscript having been completed on October 28. If all goes well, the series will be continued with a volume on dualism in the Ancient Far East.

Piet F.M.Fontaine
Amsterdam NL

CHAPTER I
EGYPTIACA

1. The Red Land and the Black

a. Seeing the desert blossoming

To an air-passenger flying over the Sahara, or to a motorist crossing it in his car, it may seem hardly imaginable that all this enormous expanse of land, parched by a pitiless sun, once was green. Yet we have to go back at least half a million years to see the desert blossoming. In Northern Africa the climate was then somewhat cooler than it is now, and rainfall was more abundant. The wadis and wells which went dry long ago were full at that time and watered the land. What later became an ochre coloured desert was still a savannah grown over with trees like the tamarisk and all kinds of shrubs. There was food and water enough even for larger animals like the elephant and the hippopotamus.

At the eastern edge of this green land flowed the Nile. It was already there in the Lower Tertiary; German geologists give the Nile of those days the mythically sounding name of 'Urnil' [1]. It is doubtful whether it already possessed a connection with the Ethiopian highlands where the heavy rains fall; probably it was still fed by numerous tributaries which has long since dried up. "The fruitful valley of the Nile was not there in distant geological times", says Wilson [2]. It was an uninhabitable region of endless marshes, much broader than the present Nile and, in Southern Egypt, lying considerably higher than what is now the bed of the river [3].

Through century after century the Nile scoured out its bed in the hard rock-bottom, depositing gravel and mud in the trough it made, while, at its many mouths, it patiently filled up with sediments the immense swamp of its Delta, which was later to become known as Lower Egypt. This age-long process ended with the formation of the modern Nile, only 'a relatively puny descendant', however, of the 'Ur-nil' [4], at least with regard to its width. What it lost here it recovered in length. In the period when the rainfall in Northern Africa began to diminish dangerously the Nile became connected with the East African lake district by means of the White Nile, and with the Ethiopian highlands throught the Atbara or Blue Nile.

In consequence of this every spring-time enormous masses of water are transported to Egypt where, before the construction of the barrages in Upper Egypt, they used to cause the annual inundation of the Nile valley. Without this connection with the Ethiopian tableland the Nile would have disappeared completely, for in the dessication period all its tributaries dried up; on a stretch of more than 1300 miles southward from the sea not a single one is left. Nevertheless, in spite of its reliance on the tropical rainfall, the river, between Aswân and Cairo, loses much of its majesty [5].

Hayes gives an alluring description of life in the savannah that is now the Sahara, including the Egyptian western desert; for, in those far distant days, it was inhabited not only by a varied fauna but also by human beings. This is what he says : "Here then, for the time being, was a portion of the earth's surface affording every advantage to primitive man in his early struggles for existence ... an adequate but not excessive rainfall ... choice camp sites in protected river alleys and lake basins ... Here, too, was a land over most of which animals could roam with almost complete freedom ... Small wonder that Egypt, because of its natural endowments, its accessibility, and its central position in the ancient world, was an area much frequented by earliest Man" [6].

From this idyllic scene we must, however, except the Nile valley; it was at once too boggy and too humid to carry a human population, not to speak of conditions in the Delta. Only on the spurs of the present desert, above the Nile valley, was human life possible; buried tree-stumps testify that once there was abundant vegetation here [7].

b. Retreat to the Nile

There was as yet no agriculture; the small groups roaming the territory of the present Sahara were nomads. They too were dependent on the rainfall for their existence. Then, some ten or twelve thousand years ago, at the end of the fourth and last glacial period, a profound change in the climate occurred : the rainfall began to diminish till, at least in the southern part of the Sahara, it almost reached cessation point. At the same time it grew considerably hotter. Finally, the condition was reached that is still prevailing in Upper Egypt, where a shower of rain is a rarity occurring perhaps once in every three years. Even a cloud in the sky is seldom seen there; at noon the temperature rises to 40° C. in the shade.

The inevitable result of this climatic change was dessication. The wadis and rivulets started to dry up, the lakes evaporated, the wells disappeared. First, the trees got the worst of it; then the bushes; finally the grass. The animals large and small emigrated southward to Central Africa, leaving behind them jackals, snakes and scorpions. The nomads retreated eastward, clinging to the shrinking patches of green land, till they finally reached the Nile valley. Here, along the rims of the desert the oldest cultures of Egypt have been discovered.

Ten thousand years ago the river valley was still no place where man could live comfortably. To put it in the words of Wilson : "Each summer the inundation must have rushed through without restraint ... The two banks must have been a thicket of reeds and brush ... a thick, jungle-like tangle of marsh at the edge of the stream" [8]. This was certainly not an inviting habitat but prehistoric man was simply driven into it. "Trapped" - to go on quoting Wilson - "between the encroaching desert sands and the riotous riverine jungle ... he had to drain and to root out the jungle, and he had annually to thrust and to hold the water out against the greedy desert sands" [9]. Yet from century to century the industrious Egyptian turned the Nile valley into the land we know. The aquatic and agricultural situation remained unchanged for the last five thousand years, at least till the construction of the great dams. Perhaps there always remained, rooted in the soul of the

Egyptian, an atavistic fear that the desert is his mortal enemy. But certainly he must have been proud of his achievement. For the habitable part of Egypt is really a man-made country.

c. The 'lotus plant'

Between the fringe of the deserts on either side of the Nile banks runs a long-stretched belt of land, 750 miles in length along a south-north axis. The southern part of it, southward from Aswân, has sometimes been described as 'a land two hundred miles long, and five yards broad'; here "the desert sands and the commanding cliffs come up right to the riverside" [10]. A large part of the land in this region has disappeared now under the waters of Lake Nasser, the reservoir above the Aswân dams. North of Aswân the river runs for four four hundred miles through densely populated areas; the width of the valley varies but nowhere does it exceed thirteen miles. There are places, however, in particular on the eastern bank, where the rocks approach the river so closely that there is no room for agriculture. Finally, there is the Delta, Lower Egypt, one hundred and fifty miles long and about as broad at the largest diameter, half of it still 'being occupied by shallow lakes and low-lying salty ground not yet reclaimed' [11].

Egypt, at least the fertile part of it, is sometimes said to resemble 'a lotus plant with the Nile valley as the stake, the Delta as the flower, and the depression of the Fayyûm (a large swampy area south of the Delta) as a bud' [12]. Now the most conspicuous feature of this 'lotus plant' is its very clear partition from the surrounding desert. The outer borders of the Nile valley lie where the fruitful soil ends, at the utmost edge of the inundation, and the desert begins. Many visitors to Egypt have noticed that one can put - literally! - 'one foot on the gleaming sand and the other on the corn-carrying soil' [13]. Thus the Nile valley is held 'vice-like between two deserts (the eastern and the western)', utterly dependent on the yearly inundation of the river [14]. To be held 'vice-like' is not a comfortable position, and this may have influenced the mentality of the Egyptians and their outlook on life. Indeed, on the surface at least, the separation of valley and desert would seem to suggest a dualistic opposition. Let us explore this more deeply.

d. A definite margin

Perhaps we may start with a quotation from Wilson's book where he speaks of the 'definite margin' between 'the fertile black land and the red desert sands'. This difference is not simply one between two different types of country but rather between life and death. "As one looks inward", Wilson continues, "to the river valley, one is conscious of bustling and teeming life. As one looks outwards toward the sandstone hills, one is aware of vast desolate stretches where no life is possible" [15]. If we take into account the great interest the ancient Egyptians took in matters of life and death, then we must not exclude beforehand the possibility that their ideology had something to do with their ecological situation. In any case, the western desert where the sun went down was the home of the dead, literally so because they were buried there. Baikie is undoubtedly right in asserting that "the alluvium of the valley was too much needed by the living to be spared, in general, for the dead" [16]. But couldn't they have burned their deceased as was the custom in so many other cultures?

Of course, there was also the accident, as Wilson calls it, that the dry desert sand preserves all materials incomparably better and indefinitely longer that the fertile alluvial soil [17]. This must surely have weighed with the ancient Egyptians when they chose the desert as 'the eternal habitat of the dead'. At the same time, they may have turned the chance discovery that corpses found in the sand were preserved intact, into an ideology and a ritual, only after they had decided that, for some reason or other, corpses had to remain intact. Baikie phrases it like this : "The alluvium would not have served that purpose of age-long preservation of the body which was the main object that was sought in accordance with the Egyptian crave for immortality" [18].

The ancient Egyptian needed two specific names to distinguish the two parts of the sharply divided world in which he found himself. He referred to 'the Red Land' - the Sahara glowing reddish in the sun -

and the 'Black Land', after the darkly coloured mud that the Nile inundations spread over the valley. The Egyptian name for the Red Land was 'drt' and that for the Black Land 'kmt', vocalized in Coptic respectively as 'kêmi' (or 'kême') and 'dashre' [19]. The opposition between them both is not absolute in so far as in the hieroglyphic texts Pharaoh is often called Master of the Black Land and of the Red Land [20]; thus both regions were more or less united in the person of the king. Nevertheless, it is perfectly allowable to state that this opposition is relatively dualistic, to say the least. For the first time in our enquiry we meet here the dualism of two geographical, or perhaps better, ecological systems; on the one hand, the desert where no life is possible; on the other, the valley teeming with life. The ancient Egyptians must have been afraid of the desert. Perhaps there lingered in the depth of their souls the fear that the desert from which they had escaped providentially in prehistoric days would prevail over them once again. In the years in which the Nile inundations remained far below their average level, this danger seemed very real.

e. The Fiend and the Master

The idea of the distinction between the Black Land and the Red was carried over into Egyptian mythology. For here we find the terrible enmity of 'Seth, the Red Fiend, against Osiris, the beneficient Master of the Black Soil and the growing corn' [21]. Like many other Egyptian gods Seth too is represented as an animal, although it is difficult to say what kind of animal. The ancient Egyptians did not deem it necessary to portray him in a realistic way but provided him with unnatural traits to make him all the more horrifying. Thus he became a doglike beast that roamed the desert at night [22]. He was a god of the desert who symbolized a host of natural ills that the dwellers in the valley attributed to the Red Land : thunderstorms, hail, the black clouds, the fine desert dust that made the eyes sore. In this way, as Kees says, Seth became connected 'with all those elementary forces that, to the Egyptians, seemed to originate from the caves in the desert mountains' [23].

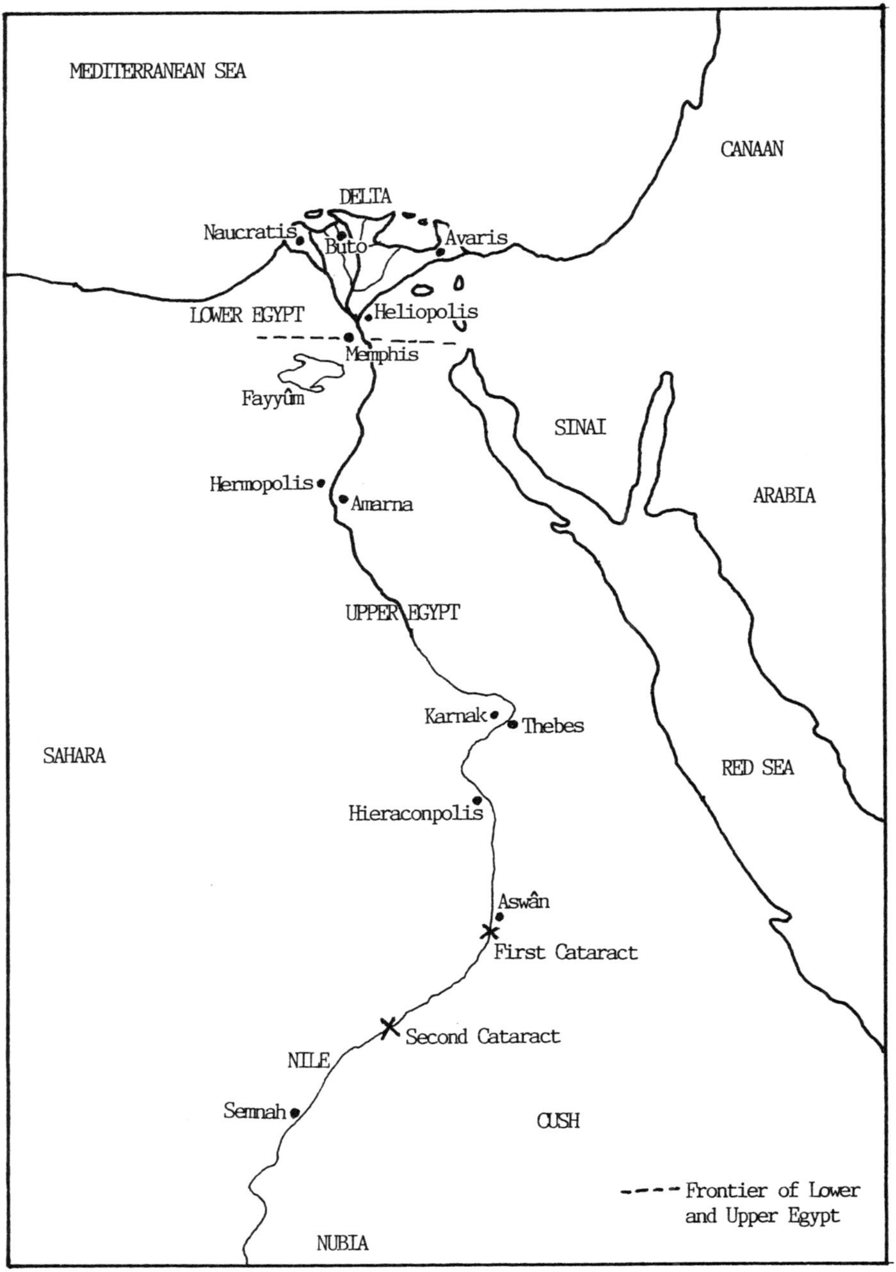
MEDITERRANEAN SEA
CANAAN
DELTA
Naucratis
Buto
Avaris
LOWER EGYPT
Heliopolis
Memphis
Fayyûm
SINAI
ARABIA
Hermopolis
Amarna
UPPER EGYPT
Karnak
Thebes
SAHARA
RED SEA
Hieraconpolis
Aswân
First Cataract
Second Cataract
NILE
Semnah
CUSH
Frontier of Lower and Upper Egypt
NUBIA

In early Egyptian mythology Seth is the sworn enemy of Horus; they fight one another with the possession of Egypt at stake. Seth turned out to be the loser and as a kind of indemnification Egyptian myth left the foreign parts to him [24]. Later, however, Seth became the opponent and counterpart of Osiris, the god of fertility and growth, of vegetation and harvest, and also the life-giving god of the realm of the dead. Seth was accused of his murder.

As the god of natural phenomena Seth was also the god of the sky, although in this capacity he was considered, paradoxically enough, as the enemy of the light. His real domain was darkness and night; what he loved was obscurity and most of all 'darkness at noon' when the sandstorms whirl over the Nile valley. In line with the development of Egyptian ethics, he was later seen as the god of moral evil and as the very essence of evil itself [25]. In spite of all this Seth succeeded in keeping his place in the Egyptian pantheon for a very long time. It proved not easy to ban him completely, perhaps because he was still needed. For, since he was the god of the western desert, the sun set in his domain, and it was he who assisted the sun to rise again in the morning [26]. But he slowly but certainly lost ground. When King Seti I (1305-1290) designed his big rock-tomb, the name of Seth, the murderer of Osiris, was not mentioned, although the king wore a 'sethic' name himself. And finally it was to come to a point when, in many places, the name of this god was hacked away from the reliefs in the temples. Then he had become, as Ermann says, 'the devil, the enemy of all the gods' [27].

2. The Reed and the Bee

a. The Egyptian composite

Between Upper and Lower Egypt there has always existed a considerable ecological difference. Lower Egypt, the Nile Delta, is a wide expanse of more or less flat land. Being near to the sea its climate is cooler, and it has a regular rainfall during the winter period. Originally one big swamp. It has been reclaimed slowly and patiently, a process that is still going on. The interminable Nile valley, on the other hand, lies hemmed in between desert and rocks, there is very little rainfall, and the closer we approach the south, the more suffocating the heat becomes. The difference between these areas is so great that even in the most ancient times the Egyptians used to speak of 'the Two Lands'. These two lands were indicated by two different hieroglyphic signs, a reed (sut) for Upper and a bee (bit) for Lower Egypt.

The contrast between the Two Lands and their different ecological and agricultural possibilities must also have influenced the attitude of the inhabitants to their surroundings and to each other. In fact, as Wilson says, the two populations have always 'been conscious of their distinction - anciently and modernly the two regions spoke markedly different dialects and had different outlooks on life' [28].

Historically we should not think of the ancient Egyptian population as having originated from two different ethnic groups. It was originally constituted of varied ethnic groups that included Semitic as well as Hamitic, African and Asiatic elements, and, in addition, nomads; these groups embraced cattle-breeders as well as peasants [29]. Admittedly up to now anthropology has not succeeded in classifying this variety of elements or their original locations with any degree of certainty. But what is really important for our theme is that they, although originally a mixed lot, reduced the elements of their population structure to two only.

In doing this they were guided by two powerful factors, the first of these being, of course, the twofold division of the country as it was given by nature. The second is of quite another order. Experts on Egyptian history and culture agree among themselves that the Egyptians mastered the multiplicity of the phenomena around them by bringing them back to two, to dualities that is - this being the most simple, or should we say, the most abstract form of the multiple [30]. Whether this meant that the opposition between the Two Lands was dualistic, instead of a duality, is another question. But one thing is certain : all through their incredibly long history, until way into the Ptolemaic period, the Egyptians were of the opinion - and they expressed this opinion incessantly in the most varied forms - that their country was a composite of two different lands.

b. The unifying concept

Ca. 3000 B.C. a certain King Menes unified the Two Lands into one single kingdom; at least, this is what most of us will have learned at school. Manetho, the priest who about 300 B.C. composed the Egyptian royal registers, put this King Menes at the head of them, as the first king of the first dynasty. With the unification of the country Egyptian history proper is supposed to begin. We need not pry too deeply into the difficult question who this 'Menes' really was. Perhaps 'Menes' is not a name but a title; in that case his real name may have been 'Aha'. Sometimes he is associated with Narmer, a king of the Late Predynastic Period and somewhat earlier in time. We may also leave aside the tricky question whether the unification was a triumph of the (southern) Hamitic or African element over the (northern) Semitic or Asiatic one. The present state of our knowledge does not warrant such a rough distinction between the Two Lands. We may, however, state as a historical fact that the unifying movement started from the south.

In the temple of Nekhbet, in Narmer's capital Hieraconpolis, far to the south, a slate palette was discovered depicting, on both sides, a victory of the king. On the one side the king threatens a kneeling prisoner, much smaller than himself, whom he holds by the hair. The falcon god Horus brings him a prisoner, tied on a rope; on a strip unerneath bearded enemies flee. On the other side we see the king, again twice as big as all the others, in front of his enemies whose heads are lying between their feet; on the strip underneath the royal bull (= the king himself) breaks the backbone of a downtrodden enemy with his leg. This representation became the model for the iconography of Egyptian victories : the king always triumphs, the enemy is always annihilated. But the important thing here is that this palette, with its clearly dualistic manner of picturing the event, describes a victory of Egyptians over Egyptians. And although they did not yet consider one another as compatriots at that time, one may surmise that, even after they had lived together as citizens of one kingdom for centuries, perhaps something of a nasty after-taste still lingered in the deep recesses of the Egyptian soul : in the south a sentiment of haughty superiority based on an assumption of greater strength and culture, in the north distrust of the aggressive south.

In order to express and to fortify the newly established unity a new capital was founded just south of the Delta, that is to say, on the spot where Lower and Upper Egypt adjoin. Its foundation is traditionally ascribed to King Menes, and although this is not absolutely sure, it is not improbable either. This city that was the capital during the whole history of the Old Kingdom (ca. 3000-2134) but is now lying in ruins near the village of Mit-Rahineh, eighteen miles south of Cairo, was called Memphis, or 'the White Wall'. This capital city had a special significance for the unification of the two parts, since it was 'the granary ... where the sustenance of the Two Lands is taken care of', as it is expressed in a very old document, the so-called 'Memphite theology', perhaps dating back to the beginning of Pharaonic times. That a city could be so fruitful was, as Frankfort says, 'explained by the presence on its soil of the interred body of Osiris'. Theologically this was a somewhat artificial construction - like Memphis itself - since this god was buried somewhere else. Anyhow, to quote Frankfort again, "the statement that Osiris was buried at the new capital proclaimed it the new centre from which the vitalizing forces radiated"[31]. In the long course of Egyptian history the unity of the country got lost several times but every time it was restored. The unifying concept always proved stronger than the dividing tendencies right until the present [32].

c. Pharaoh as the bearer of the national duality

What is more important than the historical background is the ideological fact that the political construction of the Two Lands mirrors the Egyptians' general conception of duality rather than a specific historical event. They arranged the phenomena of this world in pairs of opposites, and, as one would expect, the idea they had of their own country reflected this basic conception. The notion of its duality was kept carefully intact during the whole of Egyptian history; it is, furthermore, present in every aspect of their concept of kingship.

The complete title of a king consists of five component parts, the last two of which are written in cartouches. The fourth part, the first in a cartouche, contains a reference to the sun-god Re in his relationship to the king. For instance, 'Menkhepure' = Re is manifesting himself constantly'. This cartouche is preceded by the signs for Upper and Lower Egypt, the Reed and the Bee respectively. It is notable that the Reed always precedes the Bee; very probably this order indicates the old precedence of the Valley over the Delta. The word for 'reed' is also the usual term for 'king'. This means that the all-Egyptian king is indicated by the symbol for Upper Egypt.

Egyptian Pharaohs have many crowns but the most important of them are the white and the red ones. The white crown, a high conical cap rather than what we understand by a crown, is the headdress of the king of Upper Egypt; the lower red one he wears as king of Lower Egypt. Often he is represented as wearing the two crowns together, artfully worked into each other, in order to express the unity of the country. But for the Egyptians it was only possible to express this unity by means of a duality. We find this dualistic conception of the Egyptian political entity already on Narmer's palette. During the coronation ceremony both crowns were placed in the Dual Shrines, a sanctuary that symbolized Upper and Lower Egypt. The Pyramid Texts, however, only inform us of the passage of events in the Lower Egyptian Shrine. When the king approached the shrine, its doors were opened and he beheld the crown. He then recited a litany, after which it was placed on his head. There is no doubt that this ceremony was repeated in the Upper Egyptian Shrine [33]. Again, there is no ritual to enthrone the king as ruler of all Egypt. The twofold coronation was seen as the 'the union of the Two Lands'.

There existed, in the rituals of kingship, a curious ceremony called the 'Sed festival'. It was understood that the king, after having reigned for a long period, lost much of his potency. As his potency, his force of life, was of crucial importance for the existence of Egypt, it was necessary to revitalize the king, or rather to revive him. It is often said that the Sed festival had to be performed after a thirty years' reign but in fact there was no fixed term. That the king presented himself for this ritual need not mean that he was actually ill or debilitated or in danger of dying; it was rather a precautionary measure. Some Pharaohs went through this ritual twice. It was a very long, very elaborate and very intricate ceremony but it will be clear by now that the final act, the re-enthronement, again was dual. Even "the gods who came to participate in the feast were housed according to their origin from Upper and Lower Egypt" [34]. The people of Egypt were also present but only symbolically, for they were represented by a council called 'The Great Ones of Upper and Lower Egypt', consisting, it seems, of ten members for each area [35].

The throne on which the king was seated is actually a pair of thrones. In its hieroglyph we see it as such, two empty thrones, 'in two pavilions placed back to back. This may be a graphic way of combining the two royal seats which in reality stood side by side. The dual pavilions allow Pharaoh to appear as king of Upper or Lower Egypt according to the requirements of the ritual' [36]. The last stage of the festival was the re-enthronement consisting of two sequences, one for Upper and one for Lower Egypt, which were by no means similar to each other.

d. The Two Ladies

This concept of the duality of the country was carried over into the mythological sphere. The second of the royal names was that of 'the Two Ladies'. One of these Ladies was Nekhbet, the protecting deity of Upper Egypt; the other was Uto or Wadjet, the goddess of Lower Egypt [37]. Their temples stood respectively in Hieraconpolis in the far south, and in Buto in the Delta [38], thus connecting the extreme ends of the country [39]. Both deities had their symbol, Nekhbet the vulture, and Uto the cobra or uraeus. It is in terms of these symbols that they are represented in the second royal name and on the crowns, the prying bird and the angrily hissing snake with head erected. Yet the word 'symbol' is, perhaps, inappropriate, since the goddesses were conceived as actually present in these animal forms and conferring, by their presence, power and life force on the king.

e. A case of dualism

In my opinion we are allowed to view this political construction of 'the Two Lands', of the duality of Egypt, as a case of dualism. Here are two political entities that never became one single entity, neither in theory nor in praxis. For thousands of years the distinction was kept intact with meticulous care. The Two Lands could not become one entity because they were opposed to one another. Although we may not speak of a permanent antagonism, we must not forget that they had not come together of their own volition or grown into a unity organically but had been united by force. Their symbols and signs always remained different. There was even a difference in quality, for the Valley seems to have had a kind of precedence over the Delta. Anyhow, the populations themselves never forgot that they differed.

But what kind of dualism was this? Or to put it in another way, where was the focus of unity to be found? For behind or prior to all dualism there is always some focus of unity. Nobody may say 'two' who did not first say 'one'. The ancient Greek philosophers, like Pythagoras and the Presocratics, were right to deduce the 'Dyad' from the 'Monad'. We may express this also in the words of Aristotle : " 'The One', then, is the starting-point of what is knowable in respect of every particular thing" [40]. This is plainly logical : for the human mind two apples are this one apple and that one apple, and two boys are the boy here and that boy yonder. Even in the most radical dualisms, as for instance that of the Cathars, there is always a point of unity : the two worlds of the good and the bad may be thought of as utterly opposed and incompatible but they are seen as such by the one and undivided person who is thinking them.

Egyptian dualism was formulated by Otto in these words : "Every existing whole consists of two complementary opposite pairs; in them the essence of existence resides. Against this, pre-existence is characterized by the still undivided one" [41]. 'Complementary' means that the

the elements of the pair are dependent on each other, and this notion is thoroughly applicable to the dual construction of Egypt. Thus we have here a case of relative dualism. Could it be that the king was the focus of unity? Yet, if we were to say, with Frankfort, that the Two Lands are 'united in the single person of the ruler' [42], we would lay ourselves open to a serious misunderstanding. For what is meant by 'the person of the king'? The king as a human being? But as such he is totally unimportant in the ideology of kingship. He is solely and exclusively presented as king, this means, as a divine being. And in this capacity he personifies two kings. The focus of unity must, therefore, be found somewhere beyond the human person as well as beyond the political dual aspects of kingship, somewhere in the realm of universal divinity.

An Egyptian king is a god, in particular he is Horus [43]. Of course, Horus as a god is himself one of a pair, that of Horus and Seth. Most of the time - but not always - Horus stood for Lower and Seth for Upper Egypt. But as we have already noted Seth was gradually pushed out and made into the god of the desert and later also of the non-Egyptian lands. As such he remained combined with Horus in the person of the king who was seen as a universal ruler. But in the fruitful and habitable parts of Egypt, in the Delta as well as in the Valley, Horus gained the upper hand; he was the first of the Egyptian gods, writes Wolfgang Schenkel [44], to gain more than regional significance and to become 'widely recognized as a supreme god' [45]. As the god of heaven, of the firmament that is, he is represented as a falcon. "His out-stretched wings are the sky, his fierce eyes sun and moon" [46].

In this context it is important to observe that in the very early 'Memphite theology' "Horus, in contrast to Seth, seems not to appear as a king in his own right" - that is to say, not specifically as a king of one of the Two Lands, - "but as the legitimate successor to his father Osiris ... Horus assumes kingship over the Two Lands, not as a conqueror, but as rightful heir" [47]. In the five official names of the king this dominance of Horus is also conspicuous. Two of them are dedicated to the falcon god, without any allusion to Seth. The very first of these names is the 'Horus name' proper which was always accompanied by a recitation of the perfection of the god, as, for instance, in the already quoted name of Thutmosis IV : "Horus, mighty bull (the hieroglyphic text gives the sign of a bull after that of a falcon), perfect in glorious appearances". The third name is the 'Golden Horus name' : "Golden Horus, with the strong arm, suppressor of the Nine Bows (= Egypt's enemies)". In the royal names unity and duality alternate. The first and third names express unity, in the person of Horus; the second and fourth names indicate duality by mentioning the Reed and the Bee and the Two Ladies. But there is no common term for duality integrated into unity.

I believe that here, in the identification of the king with Horus, the unity behind the dualistic conception of the Two Lands is to be found. At the same time, however, we must not forget that Horus' shadow, Seth, was not far away and was with difficulty kept at a distance. So the question arises where, beyond Horus as the real unifier of Egypt, that undivided one resided that, in the words of Eberhard Otto, was 'pre-existent'.

3. The 'true men' and the lesser breeds

a. Splendid isolation

Egypt, that interminable Nile oasis, lived in splendid isolation. Nature protected her on all sides with impregnable barriers. To the east and west of the river we find deserts, rocks and even mountains. In the south the First Cataract, in the neighbourhood of present-day Aswân, provided the kingdom with a secure natural frontier, for "it consists of rapids caused by the intervention of great red and black granite mass barring the way" [48]. Sometimes the Egyptian sway reached still farther south, as far as the Second Cataract, where the biblical land of Cush began, in these parts a desolate and sparsely populated region. Although these barriers were not impenetrable there was no great danger of an invasion here. Cultural influences went to and fro and there was trade with the Nubians to the south.

The really weak spot in Egypt's armour was in the north where the Delta bordered on the Mediterranean. Egyptian texts and reliefs show fights with invading foreigners coming from over the sea and for that reason called the 'Sea Peoples'. We must situate their incursions in a period roughly between 1300 and 1150 B.C., the time of the nineteenth and twentieth dynasties and of famous Pharaohs like Ramses II, Merenptah and Ramses III. These Sea Peoples were a mixed bag of Mediterraneans, mainly from the shores of Asia Minor and from the Aegean islands. Since they came with women and children, they probably wanted, with the help of the Libyans, to settle themselves in the Delta. Merenptah beat them back but a considerable number of prisoners actually became colonists in the Delta.

A second wave arrived during the reign of Ramses III (1194-1163) when the Sea Peoples marched on Egypt through Canaan and the Sinai desert. Right through the 'sandy waterless waste' of this desert there runs a road, along the coast. Since this road is only ninety miles long "that distance is insufficient to deter those whom need or greed attracted towards the fleshpots of Egypt" [49]. In a combined sea- and land-battle Ramses III succeeded in halting the threatening invasion just before the gates of Egypt. A great relief in his temple at Medinet Habu shows the victorious king towering high above his own troops and his enemies. Under the hoofs of Ramses' horses the invaders tumble down in heaps. Part of the invaders remained behind in southern Canaan, among them the Philistines who gave this country its name, 'Palestine'.

b. The fine feeling isolation gives

Several modern authors are of the opinion that the ancient Egyptians were quite content with their isolated position. These writers express themselves in nearly identical terms. Wilson speaks of 'a happy position of geographic isolation', and Gardiner says that Egypt was 'about as happily isolated as any continental country could be'. He goes on to state that this situation enabled the Egyptians to develop their own highly individual culture, and Wilson adds that "this relative sense of security bred in the ancient Egyptian an essential optimism about his career in this world and the next" [50].

What is more, this feeling of being secure through isolation gave the Egyptians an unmistakable feeling of superiority over all other peoples in the world. They had a high opinion of themselves, so much so that, in their own eyes, they were the only 'true men'. When Herodotus visited Egyptian Thebes the priests showed him the great inner court of a temple, with 345 wooden figures of former high priests. The priests declared "each figure to be a 'piromis', the son of a 'piromis', that is, in the Greek language, one who is in all respects a good man" [51]. The Greek historian uses the term 'kalos kagathos' here, the nearest equivalent of this word being 'a gentleman'.

The Egyptian word given by Herodotus is 'pi-romis', from 'rome' = (true) man. The others, the non-Egyptian foreigners, are no 'rome', no 'true men'; they are, indeed, somewhat less than human. "Normally she (Egypt) was contemptuous of her nearest neighbours, to whose chieftains she invariably applied the word 'vile' " [52]. On a stele of Sesostris I (1971-1926), at Semnah, in the extreme south, we find this opinion of the Nubians : "They are not people of worth; they are caitiffs broken of heart" [53]. And here is a somewhat earlier judgment on the Asiatics of Southern Palestine" : "The miserable 'caam' (= Asiatic) ... dwells not in any single place, driven abroad by want, and his feet are always on the move" [54]. We detect an authentic dualistic opposition here, between the Egyptians themselves, the only ones fully entitled to the qualification 'human', and all the others who, at all events, were not so completely human as the Egyptians.

How little the Egyptian valued foreigners becomes evident from the way they are usually depicted. On the innumerable reliefs on which foreigners figure there are very few which represent them for their own sake. By far the greater part of the foreigners in Egyptian iconography are those fallen in battle or taken prisoner. We see them being hewed down by the king in person and lying in rows and heaps on the battle-field with the Egyptian chariots riding roughshod over them. We see them prostrate under the royal throne or conducted into Pharaoh's presence bound together with ropes and chains. We find foreigners depicted on the soles of sandals and thus, symbolically, constantly downtrodden. And when they arrive peacefully in Egypt it is most of the time in order to bring tribute [55].

Everywhere and always the Egyptian sentiment of superiority is conspicuous. Even in the after-life prisoners were needed. We find them depicted on the bottom of the sarcophagi under the feet of the deceased or in the shape of figures in the tombs. The defeat of the foreigner was, one might say, a basic condition for an untroubled life after death [56].

Of the many peoples with whom Egypt came into contact during the course of her long history two groups deserve some special attention, the Nubians in the south and the Asiatics in the north-east. Nubia was seen as a country to be feared and to be conquered; numerous Pharaohs had campaigned there. Fortresses were built to keep the population in check; later a policy of Egyptisation was followed [57]. Nubians immigrated into Egypt, not always of their own accord. The men served as soldiers and were not infrequently hired out as mercenaries and also as servants; the women were imported as handmaids and dancers. They were often given Egyptian names to make them seem less foreign.

Asiatics were a still greater problem. The Egyptians were afraid of them, the worst of them being the nomads, the Bedouins, who made forages into the Delta and created havoc there. Although there were long periods of peaceful co-existence, the normal situation was one of warfare. Later Egyptian attempts to gain control of Palestine mainly aimed at keeping off the Asiatics as far as possible. Nevertheless, many of them immigrated into the country of the Nile. Asiatic soldiers were numerous and could even reach high positions. Many more were imported to do menial work; they became stewards in the houses of the rich or skilled workmen in the shops and on the wharfs. A striking number of Asiatic women were imported. This is bound up with the fact that so many Egyptian women died young during childbirth [58]. Often the Asiatics too were given Egyptian names. Although the people of the Nile slowly learned to appreciate the qualities of the

Asiatics their relationship to them was always coloured by prejudice. It was virtually impossible for Egyptians to value other peoples in their own right [59].

This does not mean that foreigners living in Egypt were necessarily badly treated. It will have become clear from the foregoing sections that a great many foreigners were to be found in the Delta and the Valley. Later whole branches of production were in their hands; the eastern part of the Delta became virtually an Asiatic region on account of the immigration of Asiatic cattle-breeders, like for instance the Hebrew family of Jacob. They did not become popular, for "the Egyptians hold all shepherd-folk in abhorrence" [60]. A Greek colony, Naucratis, a daughter of Milete, was founded in the western Delta, ca 600 B.C. [61]. King Amasis (570-526) gave it the monopoly of Greek trade. Large groups of foreigners melted together with the native population; many Egyptians were married to foreign women. Nevertheless, the relationship of the Egyptians with the foreigners in their midst always remained somewhat cool; for instance, they never ate together with foreigners. A well-known example of this aloofness is the following passage from the Book of Genesis : "Food was brought, with separate portions for Joseph, for his brethren, and for the Egyptians who kept them company; the Egyptians are not allowed to eat with men of Hebrew blood, and would think it a foul disgrace to share a meal with them" [62]. The proud inhabitants of the Nile country never got rid of their haughty sense of superiority.

c. Successful propaganda

It is a remarkable thing that the Egyptians succeeded in communicating this feeling to other peoples and to later times. The world seemed - and still seems - to acquiesce readily in what Wenanum the Egyptian said to the king of Byblos : "Wisdom comes from Egypt" [63]. The Hebrews who lived in the Delta for a very long time took much of this wisdom with them when they fled from Egypt; there are marked similarities and analogies between Egyptian maxims and the Book of Proverbs. As Montet says, "the Hebrew sage made no attempt to conceal his debt to his Egyptian predecessor (what is meant is the Book of Wisdom of Amenope, ca. 950 B.C.) or indeed to the Egyptian didactic writers in general". To this he adds that the Bible says that Moses 'was learned in all the wisdom of the Egyptians' [64].

Many well-known Greek scholars paid a shorter or longer visit to Egypt, Pythagoras, Herodotus, Plato, to cite only a few of them. To them a stay in Egypt seems to have been as much 'de rigueur' as was the Grand Tour for a cultured young man of the eighteenth century. The Greeks were very well aware that their civilization owed much to the Egyptians, for instance that they were indebted to them for their alphabet and calendar [65]. Most of their information about Egypt the Greeks of the fifth and fourth centuries got from Herodotus who devoted the whole of his second book to this country. He was there about 450 B.C., visited a great number of towns and sanctuaries, and spoke with many people. His main informants were priests. "On the whole", Montet says, "the classical writers were better informed about the great religious festivals than about the kings. What impressed them most was the very great antiquity of the Egyptian religion. They realized that, long before the Trojan War, the Egyptians had temples and priests, and that for that reason Egypt should be called the mother of gods" [66]. Evidently, the Greeks were imbued with a feeling of awe with regard to the 'wisdom of Egypt'. Plato expresses this very aptly when he makes an Egyptian sage say that compared to the Egyptians the Greeks were like children [67].

This feeling of awe persists until our own time. For instance, there still exists a popular idea that the pyramids contain a secret wisdom expressed in the measures of these edifices. The feeling that the Egyptians knew more than we do about essential things is wide-spread. This is even naively endorsed by certain advertisements that endorse their products by an appeal to ancient Egypt beginning with this incantation : "the ancient Egyptians already knew ..." (e.g. some quality or other of the recommended article). We may, therefore, conclude that the Egyptians did not fail to transmit to posterity the idea that, as a people, they were superior to all others.

d. A blast of God

Underneath this conspicuous sense of superiority there must, however, have lurked a feeling of anxiety. The observant scholar gets the impression that the Egyptian was afraid of the foreigner. True enough, they had some reason for this fright. Isolated as their country was, it had open ends, and as we have already seen, foreigners streamed in and settled comfortably in Delta and Valley. I have already alluded to invasions and incursions by Libyans from the west and Asiatics from the east. In this connection there is a historical period of particular interest, since it was a time when Egypt was, literally, under the control of foreigners. It is known as the Hyksos domination (ca. 1650--1542). This subject is a ground where 'angels fear to tread' but luckily the more detailed arguments that it has inspired are of little importance to my theme. With regard to the ethnic identity of the Hyksos it may be safely stated that there was a strong Semitic element among them, with, probably, a fair number of Hurrites. At any rate, they were Asiatics.

Their name is a Greek transcription of a word meaning 'rulers of foreign parts'; probably this name originally only referred to their kings. It is a hotly debated question whether there was really a full-scale armed Hyksos invasion or rather a massive wave of immigration. Anyhow, wether the coming of this people was peaceful or not, a number of Pharaohs in this period were Hyksos. The grip of the Hyksos kings on the south was always less strong than it was on the north, understandably enough since their centre of power was in the north; it was from the south that the national reaction started. It was, finally, King Ahmosis I (1550-1525) of Thebes who made an end of the Hyksos domination [68].

Cyril Aldred is certainly correct when he writes that "the Hyksos seizure of power (was) one of the great fertilizing influences in Egyptian civilization, bringing fresh blood, new ideas, and different techniques into the Valley" [69]. This is not, however, how the Egyptians themselves felt about it. "Ahmosis was regarded by the Egyptians as ... the founder of a new and glorious era in Egyptian history", says

Aldred. From now on "the Hyksos were dismissed as foreigners and the several native loyalists (i.e. Egyptians serving the Hyksos kings - there must have been many of them - F.) as rebels, and it must have been the official narrative of the triumphant Thebans that Manetho drew up for his picture of the Hyksos as a horde of infidel oppressors" 70).

This is how the Manetho version of events ran. "A blast of God smote us, and unexpectedly, from the regions of the East, invaders of obscure race marched in confidence of victory against our land. By main force they easily seized it without striking a blow; and having overpowered the rulers of the land, they then burned our cities ruthlessly, razed to the ground the temples of the gods, and treated all the natives with a cruel hostility, massacring some and leading into slavery the wives and children of others" [71]. This tendentious passage reflects the hard feelings of the Egyptians about what they considered to be a humiliating period of foreign domination, and expresses at the same time their fear of these uncouth Asiatics. It is no accident, I think, that just at this juncture the Pharaohs in their turn began to invade Asia. Already Ahmosis I had campaigned in Asia, and soon afterwards Egyptian expansion reached its acme when Thutmosis I (1504-1492) planted his standard on the Euphrates.

But in the long run the Egyptian kingdom proved unable to ward off foreign intruders definitively. From 950 B.C. onwards there were no longer native Egyptian kings. The kings were Libyans, Kushites or Nubians, although they were still viewed as real Egyptians by their subjects [72]. This was not, however, the case with the Assyrian conquerors who invaded Egypt in 671 B.C., to be succeeded subsequently by the Persians, the Macedonians and the Romans : their kings were hated as foreigners. Egypt remained under foreign influence or domination - Arab, Turkish or English - till in 1952 the Naguib revolution made the country really independent. For a proud people a long period of subjugation!

e. Egypt's public enemy

We must now turn our attention to the ideological and mythological side of the question. The non-Egyptian world - in fact everything outside the Delta and the Valley - seemed to the Egyptians a world of chaos, of darkness, of non-existence, of evil. Consequently they saw some resemblance between the notions of 'foreigner' and 'evil'. When somebody died outside Egypt the family had his corpse transported home, in order to make sure of his survival in the after-life. They could only accept a foreigner as one of their own when they had given him an Egyptian name - like Moses the Hebrew [73]. Attempts to take a more humane view of the world outside were smothered in the growing hatred of foreigners after the Hyksos period [74].

In that outlandish world of chaos everything was wrong, even nature. For there the land was not fructified by a river but by rain. The Egyptians called the Euphrates 'the wrong river' because it did not flow, like the Nile, from south to north. The foreign enemy had to be destroyed utterly, belonging as he did to the realm of death. Most of the time the destruction was executed pictorially; we find, for instance, foreigners as enemies of the gods in presentations of hell. We even observe in the iconography that bound enemies are sacrificed on an altar to the gods. Was this only a symbolic presentation or did it correspond to a really existing religious practice? It seems certain that human sacrifices were not a common feature of Egyptian religion but, nevertheless, they sometimes occurred. The victims - Nubians or other foreigners - were seen as followers of Seth [75].

More generally, actual human sacrifice was replaced by destruction rites. They were extremely frequent, executed as they were on a great number of occasions : the New Year festival, the Sed festival, the coronation and burial of the king, and so on. It seems that the Egyptians felt a constant need to ward off the world outside. Destruction rituals consisted of anathema's and sacrifices. The king is pictured as a great hunter who captures hordes of foreign enemies and subsequently destroys them. Generally speaking, in the course of time the ritual sacrifice becomes more and more identical with the destruction ritual; it is a means of annihilating everyone and everything that was not approved by the Egyptians [76].

We saw already that Seth was the god of the desert and of the threatening sky. He was also to become, and ever increasingly, the god of everything that was alien and inimical to the Egyptians. He was identified as a foreign god, the god from abroad. This idea was strongly confirmed by the long and painful Hyksos domination when these foreigners made 'Seth of Avaris' into the protecting deity of their reign [77]. In the periods of the Assyrian and Persian domination he became the hated personification of all that was alien and, therefore, wrong; he was, we might say, the 'public enemy of Egypt' [78]. All the animals that were unpopular with the Egyptians belong to the retinue of Seth : the ass, the crocodile, the hippopotamus, the tortoise, the pig [79]. There even exists a curse to be used in all the temples of the country : "They chase you (Seth), evil minded as you are, into the country of the Asiatics ... Egypt, dedicated to Horus, wants to see you slaughtered ... You will be delivered to the devourer (= the 'uraeus', the royal snake)" [80].

In all these rituals one idea is abundantly plain. The order of the cosmos, the 'Maat', incorporated in the kingdom of Egypt, is constantly threatened by disorder, by Chaos, as exemplified in foreign countries and by foreigners. It was the duty of all Egyptians, but most especially that of the king, to defend Maat and to fight Chaos. Behind the rampant dualism between Egyptians and foreigners we find, therefore, a still more virulent and fundamental one, that between Order and Chaos.

4. Pharaohs and mortals [81]

The most striking element in the ideology of Egyptian kingship is that Pharaoh was a god. We find this difficult to understand. The family of the king, in particular the royal consort, his servants and his privileged counselors, must have encountered a Pharaoh who was only too human. How was it possible at the same time to consider him divine? The ancient Egyptians must have been aware of the difficulties involved in this dual, even dualistic, conception of monarchy. It constituted, according to Kemp, 'a major intellectual problem for the Egyptians' [82].

This problem did not grow less but rather more acute in the course of time. During the Old Kingdom, when the unification of the country had created a stable situation and the great pyramids became the stone witnesses of royal power, it was perhaps not so difficult to believe in divine kingship. But then the First Intermediate Period (2134-2040) intervened, a century of civil war, of a broken down administration, of unity lost. For now there two kings, one at Thebes in the south, and one at Heracleopolis far more to the north. How could these kings who succeeded one another often after very short intervals be both of them really divine? This is a question that many a thoughtful Egyptian of that time must have put to himself. Finally a powerful Theban king, Nebhepetre Mentuhotep I (2061-2010), made an end of confusion and anarchy and reinstated a stable form of government. It is probably no accident that this prince who later was called one of the founders of Egypt had himself pictured on his reliefs in a godlike shape far more often than his predecessors had done.

To the Egyptians of the Middle and the New Kingdom the Old Kingdom must have appeared 'in an impressionistic way as an heroic age of absolute royal power'. They themselves, however, were plagued 'with doubts and cares'. "It is hard to avoid the conclusion that the ... First Intermediate Period had a disturbing effect" [83]. It would, indeed, be very illuminating if we only knew how the Pharaohs themselves regarded this duality but they were certainly not the persons to leave 'ego-documents' behind them!

That Pharaoh was divine should not make us jump at the conclusion that he was allowed to do everything he wanted to do. First of all, the king was a servant of the goddess Maat who personified 'the ideal state of the universe and of society'. It was the first duty of the king to establish and to preserve Maat, and this acted as a constraint on the arbitrary exercise of power' [84]. Second, however divine Egyptian kingship might be in theory, it was, nevertheless, a political institution, and this meant that the king had to fulfil normal political, administrative and military functions. A text of Sesostris I (1971-1926) clearly indicates this political level of kingship : "He (the god Hor-akhty) appointed me herdsman of this land, for he knew who would keep order for him" [85]. 'Keeping order' has always been the main preoccupation of all governments on earth, divine or not.

An Egyptian king possessed a number of special qualities. While some of these were peculiar to himself, others he shared with common mortals, although in his case they were greatly intensified. A deep insight into human character is ascribed to him and a great wisdom. "He is in the possession of a wisdom that knows his subjects ... He is wise already when he issues forth from the womb" [86]. He is the protector of his people, "a shelter for everyone ..., a rampart with walls of brass ..., a defender who saves the fearful one from the hand of his enemy ..., a shade over the whole country ..., a cool room which enables everyone to sleep in the glaring day, ... a mountain that wards off the storm when the heavens are raging" [87]. From epithets such as these it becomes evident how different the king is from common man, particularly in the instance where we find him exercising a mythological function, that of defending Egypt against the powers of Chaos.

The difference is even more pronounced when the emphasis falls on his indispensability. "What would this land be without him, that excellent god", somebody said of Amenemhet I. "No succesful life is possible without you", said this king himself to his son Sesostris I. Another royal text asseverates : "The collectivity can bring nothing to an end without you. Your majesty ... is surely everyone's pair of eyes". The conclusion is now obvious : "Life is his" [88]. All this results in the idea of the absolute uniqueness of the king. "You are the only one whom the god gave", this too is said of Sesostris I.

The (dualistic) opposition between Pharaoh and his people is very clearly expressed in this eulogy addressed to Sesostris III (1878-ca.1841) : "You are the only one of millions. All those other thousands are small" [89]. The use of the expression 'the only one' is all the more remarkable because it was originally only applied to gods. Blumenthal concludes that it is primarily on account of his uniqueness and indispensability that the king is set apart from his people as a superior person. "As such he does not only appear in comparison with his contemporaries, he also towers over the past" [90].

Hence Blumenthal can say that Pharaoh, and the monarchy as an institution, appear as the coordinates of the system of values. Every subject was essentially less than the king. The high dignitaries of the state, however, became somewhat exalted - although they never became the equals of the king! - by Pharaoh's personal favour. "Even the virtues of a private person become more accentuated by his relationship to his lord" [91]. The king even acts as the supreme judge of morality : "I (the prison governor Antef declares) trust to it that I am upright before my lord" [92] - something that in the Old Testament is only said in relation to God.

It will be abundantly clear by now that the king occupies the supreme and central position in Egyptian society. His people is, so to speak, incorporated in him; in its relation to the gods he is their deputy [93]. He is the son of a god, even of all the gods; so to the gods he says 'my father'. But he may also say 'my mother' for all the gods are at the same time his father and his mother [94]. The most direct relationship of Pharaoh, however, is that to Horus, the god of heaven. The king represents this god on earth. As a divine person the king also enacts, inaugurates and presides over all the rituals. The fact that the king is divine and a partner of the gods does not make him their absolute equal. He is a god but a subordinate god. He executes their commands, he has to pray [95].

In his public appearances the king in no way resembled a modern democratic ruler like Christian X (1912-1947) of Denmark, who, unaccompanied, made a tour on horseback through the inner city of Copenhague every morning. When Pharaoh left his palace it was always a highly ceremonial affair. Its aim was to impress his high status on the people and to keep the commoners at an appropriate distance. In public he appeared like the sun rising above the horizon. Sometimes we see him magnificently attired, carried in a sedan-chair by twelve soldiers while servants with enormous fans wave coolness to him. Another time we meet him proceeding on a chariot while servants armed with canes thrash the populace backwards. On both sides of the chariot his guards manage to keep the pace at a double. Many glittering cars follow, with the queen, the royal children, the dignitaries. The spectators stand back in religious awe praying, perhaps, in these words : "Show me your face, you rising sun, that illuminates both our countries with your beauty, you sun for humanity who dispels darkness from Egypt" [96].

5. The deviant king

Only a few of the innumerable Egyptian Pharaohs are more than just a name to the general public of to-day. First there is Cheops (2551-2528), the builder of the Great Pyramid; many centuries later came Thutmosis III (1479-1425), the famous conqueror. Ramses II (1290-1224) still speaks to the imagination of modern Egypt; his statue on the square in front of the main railway station at Cairo proves that he is a source of inspiration for the Egyptian rulers even now. Tut-ankh-Amun (1333-1323) did not earn fame because of his imperial deeds, but because his tomb, discovered by Howard Carter in 1922 in a virtually undisturbed state, is by far the richest ever found. And finally there is Akhenaten, the monotheist.

a. A dualistic revolution

The original name of Akhenaten was Amenophis IV. He was born a son of Amenophis III (1391-1353), a Pharaoh of the Eighteenth Dynasty, one of the ablest rulers of ancient Egypt. We do not know the date of Akhenaten's birth nor much of his life as prince royal. Contrary to custom he did not marry his sister but a non-royal woman, to become famous as Queen Nefertiti. In this he followed the example of his father whose wife Teje, Akhenaten's mother, was not a royal princess either. Very probably there was a co-regency of father and son during a period of eleven or twelve years. Akhenaten became king in his own right at his father's death in 1353 B.C. and reigned for seventeen years [97].

Soon after his ascension to the throne Amenophis IV began to effectuate radical changes in the existing fabric of Egyptian religion. He strove to establish monotheism which was, up to then, utterly unknown in Egypt - with the exception of a few impulses during the reign of Amenophis III. Henceforward, the sole object of veneration had to be the sun-god, Re-Horakthy, the sun rising above the horizon, and in particular the light radiating from the solar disc called 'Aten'. In order to prove that he meant a radical breach with the past the king changed his name into 'Akhenaten' which may be rendered as '(the king is) agreeable to Aten'. In the fourth or fifth year of his personal rule he broke away from his residence at Memphis - and from all that it meant to him and his people; he founded a new royal capital in the desert, now called, with an Arabic name, 'Amarna'. There he officiated as the high priest of the new solar cult. He and Nefertiti had six daughters, two of whom were already born in Memphis, four others at Amarna. This remarkable king died in 1335 B.C. in the new capital where he was also buried.

The crucial question from our point of view is whether we are confronted here with a dualistic episode in the history of Egypt and Egyptian religion. I have already spoken of 'a radical breach with the past', and in my opinion it will not be difficult to prove that my definition of dualism is fully applicable here. We are, indeed, confronted with two totally opposed religious systems with no intermediate links between them; one of these systems, the old one, was considered utterly inferior to the new cult, so much so that it had to disappear completely.

b. From 'Re' to 'Aten'

The prevailing religious system was a thoroughly polytheistic one. There was, of course, a hierarchy among the gods, with Amun, in the time of the Eighteenth Dynasty identified with the sun-god Re, as the most important. Since Amun-Re was also the personal patron of the reigning king, he incurred the special enmity of Akhenaten with whom kingship began anew and who, therefore, did not want to be associated with his predecessors nor with their god. Apart from Amun-Re there were countless other lesser and greater gods who had to be venerated; many of them had their own temples and shrines, their cults, festivals and priest colleges. Akhenaten swept all this away by proposing Aten as the unique object of veneration, to the exclusion of all other cults.

Several factors may have made Re (not Amun-Re) attractive to Akhenaten. First of all, he was seen as a cosmic god, a universal god, male and female at the same time. He was also 'self-produced', pre-existent before the cosmos and the other gods. As such he was the creator and the supreme ruler of gods and men, and also of the dead. Finally, he was the 'Lord of Maat', of order, justice and right [98]. However, all these imposing qualities were not those in which Akhenaten was especially interested because he was primarily fascinated by the 'Aten-side' of Re, the light emanating from the divine sun-disc.

In fact, it is precisely as sun-god that Re is the creator of the world, for it is by his appearance above the horizon that all life has a new beginning. The anniversary of his birthday was also the Egyptian New Year's Day [99]. The climactic moment of every day was that in which Re rose above the eastern horizon - as 'Herakhty', that is -, for then the Egyptians knew that the god was born again from the primordial waters. The rising sun, climbing higher into the sky from hour to hour, was either Re himself or his eye, or rather the cobra snake, the uraeus, that, as his diadem, adorns the god's head. The fieriness of this eye may easily grow dangerous, even to the gods [100].

The intimate connection of Re with Pharaoh is an old one; the texts bear witness to this since the Fourth Dynasty (2775-2645), that of Cheops. Since the Fourth Dynasty (2645-2323) the kings, apart from their birth-name, assumed a throne-name', more often than not with the name 'Re' as part of it. The god then became the official state-god of Egypt. In the Middle Kingdom, and already as far back as the Fourth Dynasty, the king was seen as the son of Re. Still later, in the New Kingdom, the connection between god and Pharaoh developed into an identification. The king may say of himself "I am Re", and is often addressed with "you are Re" [101]. The throne of the king is identical with that of the god; even the royal statues represent Re, rather than Pharaoh. That the reign of Re was essential to Egypt as a political entity is proved by the fact that the abhorred Hyksos were said to have ruled 'without Re' [102]. So we may agree with Barta that Amenophis IV based his Aten-doctrine on an existing theology of Re. In the beginning this king described his great god still as 'Re-Herakhty', before he definitely became 'Aten' [103]. What was fundamentally new, however, was that this king did away with all the other gods.

c. The 'heresy'

The Aten-doctrine was the personal creation of King Amenophis IV, or rather of Akhenaten. It is highly probable that veneration of Aten existed before this memorable reign. We must make a careful distinction between the word 'Aten' (jtn), signifying the sun as a celestial body, and the god 'Aten', who uses the sun as his seat or as his attribute, as Assmann formulates it [104]. When the king broke with the religious past of his country, his dumb-founded subjects began to experience what Aldred dubs 'the heresy' [105]. Suddenly there was a new god, the 'radiant Aten', represented as a sun-disc, with the royal cobra right under it, and with the 'ankh'-sign - the symbol of life - underneath. Twelve or more long rays emerge from it; all of them end in hands, one of which holds an 'ankh'-symbol just before the eyes of the king [106]. The new image had a revolutionary impact since it was more suggestive and dramatic than the images it was to replace such as, for instance, that of the sun-disc carried by the enormously long wings of a falcon.

Assmann says that the introduction of this new symbol really signified the introduction of a new religion. Two years later the court moved to Amarna, the 'luminous city of Aten'. It was there that the Aten-cult was fully realized. From now on there was only one god, and the strictest monotheism became the rule. Here the dualistic character of this period became fully apparent. The old religion - the element of the dualistic opposition that was considered inferior - was not only abolished, but even, as far as possible, destroyed. All the temples of the country were closed down - with the exception, of course, of the Great Temple at Amarna. Very probably no Aten-temples were built [107] (but perhaps plans to do this were never executed). On all possible monuments the names of the old gods were hammered out by royal order; in particular the name of Amun had to pay for its former glory. In several places the word 'gods', as a plural, was also cut out. The religious zeal of the king even went so far that he sent his workmen to the tops of the obelisks to hack away the hated names even there [108].

None of the old gods were any longer entitled to sacrifices and offerings. The existing priest colleges lost their raison d'être, in particular those of Amun. The only place where sacrifices were countenanced was the Aten-sanctuary at Amarna. Aldred mentions a 'positive forest of brick altars' here that were 'heaped each day with fresh offerings'; he adds that "such lavish provision could only have been made at the expense of other cults". The disappearance of the Amun priesthood was, in fact, so complete that Tut-ankh-Amun, the (second) successor of Akhenaten, did not succeed in finding a sufficient number of priests for the re-established cult of Amun [109].

Once all Egypt had been the domain of the gods, and their temples and altars were to be found everywhere; now the new cult was severely restricted to the territory of Amarna and carefully and jealously marked off by boundary-posts from the outer world. Inside this magic circle the new cult was celebrated, with the king as its pontiff. The rest of the population, hardly understanding what was happening, cannot have participated in it, deprived as it was of all cult-places, old or new. It was as though an interdict was laid upon the country. Thus it is far from surprising that there is evidence of an opposition between a privileged and initiated religious caste - a small minority only - and the non-comprehending and non-partaking mass of the people.

We find the theology of this singular king mainly in the Great Hymn to Aten; it adorns the walls of the tombs of several courtiers at Amarna. Aldred is of the opinion that the version in the tomb of Ay, Akenaten's private secretary, is the fully authorized edition. The poem, says this scholar, does not differ from hymns to other gods, especially those to Amun, either in its manner of address or in its general formulas. However, and let us quote Aldred once again, "its novelty lies not in what it expresses, but in what it leaves unsaid" [110]. The crucial omission is that all the other gods, without exception, are passed over in the deepest silence. There is no mention at all of a godhead as popular (and indispensable) as Osiris, the god of the dead. Everything that even schoolchildren take for granted to-day of the Egyptian conception of life after death, was completely ignored by Atenist theology. There is no journey of the departed soul to the other world, no Last Judgment with the weighing of the heart of the deceased, no miraculously fruitful Elysian Fields. This does not mean that the king and his adherents did not believe in an after-life - the contrary was the case. But they, probably harking back to much older notions, seem to have believed that the souls of the dead rose every morning with the sun [111].

The Egyptians tended to conceive of their divinities as dual in nature, as at once male and female. With the advent of the New Kingdom a kind of trinitarian theology had developed, for now combinations of gods were venerated, consisting of Father, Mother and Son. Aldred says that this strongly appealed to the Egyptians with their love of family life [112]. One of the curious features of the new religion, however, is the absence of the female element. In the new theology Aten was the father, the king was his son, but there is no mother. I believe that this is one of the means to make the idea of god more abstract.

d. Pathological traits

Akhenaten appreciated domestic life no less than his compatriots. We still possess many scenes in which the royal family, consisting of the king, his queen Nefertiti, and their six daughters (there was no son and heir), are pictured. We see the king fondling children on his lap, we see him smelling the flowers which the queen holds to his nose, we even see how the queen is suckling a baby or how the little princesses are eating [113]. Such intimate scenes of royal life were uncommon in Egyptian iconography. The fact that the queen and her daughters were often represented in the nude or only covered with light, transparent veils, would have profoundly shocked the Egyptians.

This conspicuous exhibitionism, however, had a theological purpose. It is not improbable that such scenes represent the royal couple with their children as a kind of 'Holy Family'. Contrary to Egyptian tradition, Akhenaten and his wife formed a pair of divine sovereigns. Nefertiti takes part in the cult; she is often shown sacrificing together with the king. Aldred says that she enjoyed 'quasi-Pharaonic status', emphasized by the fact that somewhere she is pictured as a warrior: she holds an enemy soldier by his hair and kills him with her mace [114]. Her elevated position became accentuated still more by the fact that she added the name of Aten to her own name : her epithet was 'Nefer-nefere-Aten' = 'Fair is the goodness of Aten' [115].

The Amarna society was situated at a considerable distance from normal Egyptian life, not only measured in terms of miles, but even more so psychologically. To use a German expression, it was a 'Fremdkörper' in the whole of Egyptian history, and as such it was considered by Akhenaten's contemporaries. Nonetheless, Akhenaten and his theological revolution enjoy considerable popularity in modern historiography and public opinion. Christian believers sometimes have hailed him as a lonely monotheist in an utterly pagan society, even as a kind of pre-Christian. Liberals saw him as a courageous innovator who triumphed over outworn traditional conceptions. Marxists even succeeded in turning him into an early socialist who overthrew the exploiting classes in the name of the exploited [116]. Interpretations of this kind tell us, of course, more about those who invented them than about Akhenaten himself. Moreover, his modern admirers tend to overlook one thing, namely that there is something very strange in the whole affair, so strange that it prompts Aldred to speak of 'the pathology of Akhenaten' [117]. Not without reason I said a few lines back that Amarna was far removed from normal Egyptian life.

The royal family evidently shows pathological traits. The portraits of the king show such prominent feminine characteristics that they are sometimes easily confused with those of the queen. His neck is that of a graceful woman, his hips are wide, his breasts are nearly female; often he wears the long gown of the women. It is supposed that Akhenaten's physical deformity was the result of an illness known as 'Fröhlich's syndrome' [118]. Possessing no medical knowledge whatsoever - and not wanting to possess it either -, I pass on this information just as I found it, without forming any judgment. In addition the little princesses also exhibit traces of physical deformity, since their occiputs are extremely long and protracted; they seem to suffer from hydrocephalus [119]. The outward appearance of the members of the royal family must have made an unpleasant impression on the Egyptian population and will have alienated them still more from their strange rulers. The fact that Queen Nefertiti, at least in our view, was a really beautiful woman, will not have offset these feelings of distaste [120].

e. 'Back to normalcy'

Right after the death of Akhenaten this whole dualistic situation, as I have sketched it in the foregoing paragraphs, disappeared as snow in the sun. As rapidly as possible Egypt veered 'back to normalcy'. Akhenaten had nominated a co-regent, Smenkh-ka-Re [121], who succeeded him as Pharaoh at his death (Nefertiti was already dead by then). This reign lasted a bare three years (1335-1333) and saw the beginning of a return to the old Amun-cult. At his death Smenkh-ka-Re was succeeded by Tut-ankh-Amun who certainly was cosanguineous with Amenophis III and Akhenaten, although it never became clear whose son he really was [122]. His claim to the throne was fortified by his marriage with Ankhes-en-pa-Aten, one of the royal princesses and the oldest of the children of Akhenaten still living. That the restoration was rapidly gathering momentum is proved by the fact that the new king originally was called 'Tut-ankh-Aten' but replaced Aten by Amun, while his queen was renamed 'Ankhes-en-pa-Amun'.

In the second year of this reign the court left Amarna and returned to Memphis. Due to the circumstance that the king was still very young and in bad health (he died after a reign of nine years without issue) the old establishment was able to reassert itself inexorably. Since the Aten-religion had never gained a firm foothold in Egypt, it proved easy enough to abolish it. Akhenaten the iconoclast now became the victim of iconoclasm himself. His name was chiselled away wherever it was found; in the king-lists it was omitted together with those of his two immediate successors. And when the painful necessity arose to mention Aten's great servant, he was invariably referred to as 'that criminal' [123].

6. Between Chaos and Order

a. The nearness of Chaos

According to Egyptian texts there once was a time when heaven and earth did not exist. There was no mankind, there were no gods, there was not even death. Animals were not yet to be found, and because the sun was not yet created, all was dark and cold. Another text states explicitly that there were no cows and bulls meaning by this that there were no sexes and no sexuality. Yet another coffin text says, in a more general way, that there were 'not yet two things'. This is extremely important for, as I have already pointed out, the Egyptian mode of thought was marked by thinking in dualities, in pairs of opposites, that is. Since there were no dualities, then, according to this logic, there was nothing at all. Everything begins with 'not yet', with non-existence, to be depicted only in negative terms, as Assmann remarked [124]. In a later period the Egyptians were able to indicate four categories of non-existence : there were no limits, there were no roads (this means that it is not possible to explore non-existence), everything was wrapped in darkness, and the only 'element', the most shapeless one, was water. In short, we might say that in the beginning there was chaos, and that an ordered cosmos had not yet originated.

The absence of limits in the primeval situation implies that the primordial waters stretched out endlessly in all directions. These waters were motionless, 'tired and inert'. It is important, however, to realize that, in the process of creation, the chaotic waters of the primeval ocean never wholly disappeared. At its rims the cosmos is based precisely on that primeval ocean. At sunset the sun disappears into these waters which stretch under the (flat) earth; there it is rejuvenated, to rise gloriously again in the morning. The Nile, the great element of cosmic regularity in Egypt, springs somewhere, far to the south, from the primordial waters.

So two great principles of order, the sun and the river, were somehow connected with the principle of Chaos; in fact, they were unable to exist without it. What is more, the Egyptians were not too sure that the world would exist eternally. There were theories that, at the end, it would sink back again into the original ocean from where it came [125]. A dangerous moment in the life of the nation was the death of the king. For Pharaoh was a third great principle of order; without him the Egyptian state would return to chaos [126]. It will be clear that a dualistic division between Chaos and cosmic Order dominated the Egyptian vision of the world. Order reigned but Chaos always seemed near.

b. The cosmogony of Heliopolis

The four great cultic centres, Heliopolis, Hermopolis, Thebes and Memphis, differed in their renderings of the cosmogonic process. But they all agreed in the notion that water was the primary element; to them it was a god called 'Nun'. The primeval waters receded somewhat and a dry island began to rise above the waters, the 'primeval hill'. The course of the Nile inundations can be recognized in this receding of water and the appearance of dry land. All the four cultic centres claimed that their city was built on this hill; the pyramids too can be seen as symbolic representations of it. It was feared that once this hill would sink again into the ocean.

In the cosmogony of Heliopolis, known to us from the Pyramid Texts of the Fifth Dynasty (2465-2323), the creation process begins with the emergence of Atum. This god either created himself or he was born from Nun; he either raised the primeval hill or he was this hill himself. The Egyptians were liberal with regard to what they saw as details. "As Atum had by the time of the Pyramid Texts become identified with the god Ra (Re), his emergence on the primeval hill was also interpreted as the coming of light to disperse the chaotic darkness of Nun" [127]. What is really important here is that Atum is the principle of unity. He is the one 'who created himself and out of himself' [128]. The Egyptians interpreted his name as 'he who is complete' or 'he who is a totality'. He is 'the father of all the gods', the only one to be present in the primeval waters. He is, therefore, 'the original unity of the cosmos from whom multiplicity sprang'; at the same time he is eternal and will survive the final catastrophe of the universe [129].

In Atum, as the principle of totality, masculinity and femininity were united. In order to generate his children, his son Shu, the god of the air or the life principle, and his daughter Tefnut, he did not need to consort with a goddess. The Heliopolitan priests identified Tefnut with Maat, Order. Originally, however, her function was that of constituting a female complement to the male Shu. For the Egyptians, dual sexuality in gods probably suggested an answer to the question why there are men and women, males and females. It was just their clear recognition of the biological division of mankind and the animal world into two that prompted them, we might argue, to think in dualities.

But this mythological description is also an attempt to cope with the age-old problem of the One and the Many, of unity and multiplicity. The act by which Atum begot his children was masturbation, or perhaps rather 'self-fertilization'. Anyhow, it is described in a crudely biological way : "He took his phallus in his fist and caused lust thereby [130]. An expression such as this one indicates in my opinion that Heliopolitan theology was somewhat at a loss when asked to explain how the Multiple originated from the One. There certainly is an opposition here, one with dualistic characteristics. It is a relative dualism since the Multiple is dependent on the One, although it is not at all clear what exactly the relationship is. There is a difference in quality too, for the one is homogeneous, consistent and eternal, while the Multiple is dual or manifold, variegated and finite.

c. The Theban cosmology

The cosmogony of Thebes comes from a considerably later period, that of the New Kingdom (1546-1085), the capital of which was Thebes. It bears a certain resemblance to the much older Heliopolitan cosmology - on the understanding that the main god was now Amun. His great cult centre was the famous temple of Karnak. In Theban mythology Amun is the original godhead, he has no parents, he has created himself. There is no telling how he did this; it is a secret divulged to no one. "He was there at the beginning of all times, Amun the first created, whose original shape nobody knows. No god was before him ... He has no mother after whom he was called, no father who begot him" [131]. Even the Nun of the Heliopolitan priests was now absorbed by Amun; according to Morenz this means that, at this relatively late stage, Egyptian cosmogony began to accept the idea of creation [132]. To the believer, he continues, this idea was more important than the question what could have been the original substance. This mysterious substance produced an egg out of which the sun-god came in the shape of a falcon [133]. Later this egg was shown and venerated at Hermopolis as a relic.

In Egyptian mythology Amun became more and more the creator-god. He it was who had started the creative process and from whom all the other gods came; he was seen as the universal god, as 'he who is present in all things' [134]; he was the principle of unity behind the multitude of gods. Many qualities and predicates that originally belonged to other gods were assigned to him until, finally, in the New Kingdom, he had become the official state-god and the special protector of Pharaoh. "King of the gods, original god, who came into being in the beginning, divine god who generated himself ..., who made what is" [135]. However great and powerful this god may have become, he was, nevertheless, no god from eternity, he has a beginning, and this beginning was in and from Chaos. It does not seem improbable to me that he protected Pharaoh and his people from this original Chaos that was always lurking in the background.

d. The Memphite theology

In the already mentioned Memphite theology the creator-god was Ptah. Although undoubtedly a prominent god, somehow he never acquired pride of place in all Egypt. He differed from nearly all other gods in having an anthropomorphic shape. Not improbably he was of a late date; for this reason it is sometimes surmised that Memphite theology was much younger than the Old Kingdom and possibly dates from the period of the Ramesside kings (12th century B.C.). Since the Middle Kingdom, Ptah was seen as 'a divine artist or craftsman', a skilful god with a great artistic ability. He created not only all other gods but also all good things of life [136]. But he too had an origin, a beginning. In Egypt everything had an origin in time; this even applies to the creator-god who, far from existing from all eternity, did not even create himself.

The problem of the relationship of Ptah to the primeval substance was solved by the Memphite theologians in a peculiar way. Ptah was identified with Nun as 'Ptah-Nun'. This means, says Morenz, that Ptah absorbed the potencies of primeval matter and incorporated them in his own being. In doing so he made the primordial power of pre-existent chaos part of himself. It is, however, impossible to get rid of Chaos completely. "The price Egypt had to pay for following this road", Morenz goes on, "is that Chaos continues to exist around the ordered regions of creation" [137]. For in Egyptian thought the concept 'creation' must always be seen as dualistically opposed to that other concept 'Chaos' (= shapeless primeval matter). The creator-god uses this substance for creating the world but is not able to use all of it. There remains a quantity of matter surrounding the ordered cosmos.

7. The Egyptians and Death

I don't believe that there has ever existed another civilization in world-history that was so much obsessed with Death as the Egyptian. In fact, nearly everything we know of this culture comes from Egyptian burial-places of every kind, from the great pyramids to the modest grave-pits in the desert. All these tombs testify to a general and sincere belief in an after-life since nearly every one of them contains gifts of objects, often very sumptuous ones to be used by the deceased after death. Everyone also knows that the Egyptians tried to preserve the corpses of their dead by 'mummifying' them. There are even modest museums that boast the possession of the mummy of an Egyptian dead for thousands of years. I remember reading in my schooldays a (Dutch) novel by a certain Mr. Feith, called 'The Living Mummy'. It was about a boy who bought a mummy at an auction. In some way or other he succeeded in bringing it back to life again. Thus he became the friend of an Egyptian boy who told him (and the youthful readers too) lots of interesting things about the life of these ancient Egyptians. It would facilitate the task of Egyptology enormously if such fancies really could become true; such a person would also be able to tell us significant things about the after-life he had been so carefully prepared for. As it is, however, we have to rely on the scrapes and pieces of information that the Egyptians have left us.

a. Life and Death contrasted

Death was an ever present reality. So, of course, it is for us. But far more than the ancient Egyptians we are able to put the idea of death as far as possible from us because our life-expectations are so much longer, and because we are so much better protected against illnesses of every kind. During the whole of Antiquity people were deeply convinced of the uncertainty and shortness of life; death was always near, very many people died young. Cult and veneration of the dead were important ingredients of many ancient religions; perhaps religion as such even began with this. Moreover, there was always some sort of an

First of all, we must remember that the Egyptians loved to think in dualities; they had a predilection for contrasts. A very dominating contrast in their existence was that between the Nile valley where they all lived, and the surrounding desert. The contrast between the green, fertile and densely populated valley and the arid, red glowing, completely empty desert must have seemed to them the contrast between the principles of life and death, if not between life and death themselves. No contrast will have seemed stronger and more fierce to them than this utterly dualistic one.

Two texts, presented by Serge Sauneron, will picture vividly how the Egyptians felt about this contrast. The first is an epitaph for a boy. "I was a young child and was abducted by force; my years were cut off when I was still among the young. I was suddenly torn away from my youth, like somebody who is carried off by sleep. I was still a youth when death ravished me to the eternal city, and I appeared before the master of the gods, without having had my due share on earth. I had many friends but no one could defend me ... Everyone in my town burst into tears seeing what happened to me; all my friends lamented. My father, my mother implored death, my brothers were prostrated with grief." This text presents death as a treacherous and pitiless enemy against whom human beings are utterly powerless.

Now all commentators agree that the Egyptians were by no means a dejected and sombre people. On the contrary, they enjoyed life. But perhaps they tried to make as much of it as possible, precisely because death was always at the back of their minds. The second text may make this clear. "Follow your heart's desire and the pleasures you long for. Do what you like on earth, don't constrain your heart. It will come for you too, the day of lamentation, but cries will not redeem a man from the other world. Make your days happy and be tireless in this. Pay attention to this : nobody can take his goods with him, and nobody did ever return from where he went to" [138].

It is a basic tenet of Egyptian theology that death does not make a definitive end of human existence. At the end of his life man is not thrown into Chaos but he remains inside the ordered world of

Maat. Death itself is part of it and not the beginning of 'non-being'. What happens when a mortal dies is that the nature of his existence is changed. However, the deceased remains the same person he or she was during life on earth, an individual recognizable by his or her body. So the difference is not between existence and non-existence but between two modes of existence. In ancient Egypt too 'vita mutatur, non tollitur'. In order to gauge exactly what the difference was between these two modes we can do no better than to turn to Hegel. He writes : "In death man is presented as shorn of all casualness and only in his original being" [139]. And he goes on to say : "The notion that the spirit is immortal entails that the human individual as such has an infinite value. What is simply natural appears as fragmented; it is wholly dependent on something else. But what immortality really means is that the spirit as such is immortal" [140].

Of course, these phrases are couched in unmistakably Hegelian terms like 'der Geist' and 'in sich'. Nonetheless, I feel that Hegel is laying bare the core of the whole question in this passage. The Egyptians must have taken such endless pains to secure their survival after death because they realized, however vaguely, that the after-life would be the more real, the more authentic and unified existence. Freed of the contingencies of natural, earthly life it would bring out the essentiality of every person, which was not possible during life on earth, variegated and fragmented as it is. Borrowing some later terms the Egyptians themselves did not use we could say : the after-life was something like absolute being to them, infinitely more valuable than life this side of death. It will be clear that if Hegel's interpretation is right we are speaking here of a dualistic contrast, akin to that of being and seeming.

b. 'Ka'

A very important concept of the Egyptian theology of death is 'Ka'. When I was still a young and inexperienced teacher I used to tell my pupils that 'Ka' is the soul of man. This is precisely what it isn't; the idea of soul was totally alien to the Egyptians. I am afraid that our modern idioms do not possess the adequate terms that may render the notion of 'Ka' faithfully; there are, indeed, nearly as many explanations of it as there are Egyptologists. Anyhow, we must start from the fact that, although a Ka belongs to every human person, it is not identical with this person. This is proved by the fact that one can have more than one Ka at the same time; this, however, is exceptional, a kind of privilege reserved for the gods of creation, like Re and, on earth, for Pharaoh alone [141]. The hieroglyph of Ka shows two uplifted and open arms. This image may mean that Ka is able to stave off evil; therefore, it has a protective function which has led some scholars to see in it a tutelary spirit, a kind of genius [142].

Ka is something that can be transferred, which is probably also indicated by the outstretched arms. The creator-god gave it to the other gods, gods may give it to men. The first human being entitled to receive Ka is, of course, Pharaoh; in his turn he endows his people with it, first the state employees and then his subjects. In this way the Egyptians were both dependent on the king and organically connected with him.

If Ka is transferable, we may well ask what was being transferred. This was 'nourishment', with which is meant the capability of sustaining oneself, or the faculty of living. The transferability of Ka points to the continuity of life, especially in the family but also in the life of the whole nation. Kaplony says that Ka is not the individual person but rather the hereditary factor [143]. As such it determines the fate of men. It is a symbol of continuity and a sign of uninterrupted vital force. What Ka really is becomes apparent at the moments of birth and death.

We possess a charming picture of how the god Khnum, the personification of creative power, is modelling a royal child [144]. We can see that the king is still an infant since he puts his finger into his mouth. Behind him stands his Ka that, at first sight, is completely similar to him. Presentations like these led Maspero to assume that the Ka is the 'double' of a person, a being of the same substance and the same nature as man [145]. Maspero's view was strongly combated but, nevertheless, not a few scholars accept it as an obviously adequate description of Ka. We must, however, not overlook a small detail : the Ka of the child does not make the same gesture as the infant. This seemingly insignificant detail speaks volumes, for it says that Ka is not of the same nature as a human being. Whereas man is subject to development and growth, to decay and even to death, Ka is something constant, identical with itself and not going through phases of life.

So Ka and the individual person are two different substances, not one, but they are closely connected in some form of co-existence. If this is not outright dualism, it is doubtless a marked duality. What pleads against dualism is that the Ka and its bearer are not at all opposed; on the contrary, they belong together, everyone has even his personal Ka [146]. What, however, suggests some form of dualism is the difference in quality. The Ka has a higher origin and a more solid, powerful and valuable substance than mortal man.

What Ka gives to man and first of all to Pharoah, is a share in the essential faculties of the gods [147]. Expressions like 'Re is my Ka' or 'Ptah is my Ka' prove that deities are sometimes identified with Ka. For a people that was so much future directed as the Egyptian one, the most significant function of Ka did not become apparent at man's entry in life but at his departure from it. Standing before a body rapidly becoming cold and stiff, never to move and speak again, they saw clearly that the vital force had left the deceased person. But the Egyptians were incapable of assuming that this life-force was wholly spent now and was utterly extinguished. According to this view the vital force subsisted after death; accompanied by Ka it continued to exist, or rather, it returned to its Ka. To avoid the hateful word 'death' we sometimes say that somebody 'passed away'; the Egyptians too had their euphemism : somebody had 'fled to his Ka' [148].

This expression 'fleeing to one's Ka' indicates that, whereas during life on earth there exists some distance between a person and his Ka, this gap becomes much narrower after death and is even completely bridged. In Egyptian eyes the difference in quality between life on earth, and the after-life was immensely great. In the Pyramid Texts the dead are often called 'the living'; a coffin may be dubbed 'lord of life'. Obviously life on earth, in the body, is not the real, the full life; the fulness of life is reached only in the after-life. This is one of the many indications that, to the Egyptians, the opposition between life and death had a dualistic character.

Perhaps this may become still more evident by introducing one of the most difficult Egyptian concepts, the idea of 'akh'. Its hieroglyph is the sign for 'ibis', although whether 'akh' was really believed to be a bird is another question [149]. 'Akh' is not a faculty but a mode of existence, namely that of the deceased, in particular of privileged persons. It is, therefore, not a property of a living person, still less of his corpse. 'Akh to the sky, corpse into the earth', states a pyramid text [150]. It is only the existence in the after-life that is designated as 'akh'. This applies equally to kings and commoners. The use of a special term for existence after death is another clear indication that the two modes of existence, before and after death, were seen as opposed and qualitatively different. This is what Frankfort says of it : "... the change caused by death translated man from the sphere of the insignificant to that of the significant, from an ephemeral and singular form of existence to one which was lasting and changeless" [151]. If the Egyptians had been conversant with Greek philosophy - and had been of a philosophical turn of mind, which they weren't -, they would probably have couched their view in terms of 'seeing' and 'being'.

c. Presentations of life after death

Egyptian presentations of the after-life were not uniform; there was no conception of it common to all. The dead might become united with the sun and follow the solar course, or the circumpolar stars might be their abode; others thought they might be united with Osiris, and even merge into his life. I do not believe that these shades of opinion are important for our subject since they all boil down to the same thing : the dead, as Frankfort says, were 'absorbed in the great rythm of the universe' [152]. "The essential unity of the different images", he goes on to say, "... is well expressed in the following blessing addressed by a god to a king : 'I grant thee, that thou mayest rise like the sun, rejuvenate thyself like the moon, repeat life like the flood of the Nile' ". This again presents us with dualistic oppositions in the Egyptian conceptions of death and the after-life. To go on quoting Frankfort, "the Egyptians, who conceived the world a static, conceived their future condition as perennial movement" [153] In the Egyptian theology of death the idea of a fixed abode for the dead, like the Island of the Blessed or the Valhalla, was not so important. Although their tomb retained a great significance for them, "their real happiness lay beyond the earth and the tomb" [154].

For the ancient Egyptians, as for many other peoples, the dead body presents a problem. If one assumes that there is an after-life, he may well ask : what is going to happen to the corpse? Is the deceased reunited with the body in the after-life or is he not? The problem, of course, is that the dead body is not taken away to heaven but remains on earth and is buried or burnt. First of all, where is the abode of the dead? Is it the tomb, with its preserved corpse, or is it Ka, presumably still present in the grave? Are the possibilities of man's continued existence - I am following Morenz here - dependent on the state of preservation of his corpse [155]? According to this scholar the real dwelling-place of the deceased is not his tomb but heaven. The first one to claim access to it was, of course, the king, but as a consequence of the ensuing 'democratization' common people too were expected to go there. Yet a precondition for an existence after death was that the corpse remained uncorrupted in the tomb. "For you the folding-doors of heaven are opened, ... you seat yourself on the great throne and you command the spirits" [156].

d. Denial of death

For our theme it is a very important fact that in the Pyramid Texts the fact of death is often denied without much ado. "Stand up, you shall not die", [157], "My father did not die a death, my father became a spirit" [158], "You did not pass away, you departed living" [159]. These are adjurations to be found in the royal tombs, but later private persons too denied death. "Rise up living, you did not die. Stand up to live, you did not die" [160]. Denying death is attempting to destroy it. Since both life and death are hard facts, an attempt to destroy death means the elimination of something that is only too real. This, of course, is not easy; hence the conjurations, and the peremptory tone which characterizes them. Hence also the constantly recurring sign of Ankh = Life ($\female$) that is omnipresent in Egypt where on all coffins, in all tombs, on the walls of many pyramids and temples, it is encountered in endless repetition. We are in the presence of radical dualism here. We are, indeed, confronted with two opposites, life and death, one of which is considered not only as inferior but even as simply non-existent.

In his illuminating pages [161] Morenz makes it clear that there are two points of view in the funerary texts. According to the first body and spirit are separated and only the spirit ascends to heaven. This is stated categorically in these words : "The spirit belongs to heaven, the body to the nether world" [162]. The second viewpoint is formulated as a wish : "May your spirit not separate itself from the body" [163]. In this case the spirit or life-principle is often represented as a bird. In both lines of thought, there is no dualistic separation of body and 'soul'; the tomb is seen as a kind of anti-chamber of heaven, as is proved by the stars pictured on the ceiling of the sepulchral chamber [164].

There is, however, yet another line of thought in which the realm of the dead has pride of place. This means that the important god is not the sun-god but rather Osiris. According to this way of thinking the dead depart for the nether world. It is unclear where the realm of the dead is to be located. It is associated with the western desert at the edge of which the cemeteries lie, and also with sunset and night. More and more this realm was thought of as situated under the earth; most tombs are, therefore, sunk into the earth; even the sepulchral rooms of the pyramids are not in them but under them. Because of the association with sunset and night the graves are dark. But during the night, when the sun is travelling from the west to the east underneath the earth, it sheds its light on the dead [165].

On the surface this trend of thought may be considered as more definitive than the former, the Heliopolitan one. But in fact this is not correct. For here the dead have a crucial relationship with Osiris who, we must never forget, is not only the god of the dead but also of resurrection, the god who triumphed over death. In this view too death is circumvented. Death is not denied so categorically as in the Heliopolitan doctrine. Osiris really died but, as Sander-Hausen puts it, "the prospect of deliverance from destructive death is held out because of the mystery of Osiris' return to life" [166].

We are in the presence of a more relative dualism here because the fact of death is not utterly denied but is denoted as 'sleep', and the deceased as 'sleeper'. The 'sleeper' par excellence is, of course, Osiris. But we must never lose sight of the fact that he will wake up again. Contrary to the 'dogmatic' denial of death in Heliopolitan doctrine [167], death, according to this viewpoint, is an actual fact. It is, however, only a transitory event, a short disturbance; in his relationship with the god every dead person is capable of winning back his former condition, which is that of being alive. There are innumerable ceremonies surrounding a deceased which intend to restore life to him : "May you do now what you used to do" [168]. Perhaps we may conclude that death is not so much denied as rather lightly slipped over.

Hence what the adherents of Osiris feared is not really actual death, the 'first death', but the 'second death'. In the first death only the body dies, in the second, however, the soul dies, and then all is over. In the realm of the dead the deceased person must appear before a tribunal, organized just like an earthly one. The Egyptians did not find this strange, for to them the after-life was essentially a continuation of life on earth. This doctrine has an ethical background : whoever lived up to moral norms is to be united with Osiris, but the evildoers are assigned to the 'devourer', a monster with the head and the jaws of a crocodile that will quickly make a (definite) end of him or her. This does not mean that the second death was accepted willy-nilly or in a philosophical mood. On the contrary, it proved perfectly possible to escape from the second death. In order to do this the dead were provided with magical texts which could turn the scales in their favour [169]. It will be clear that, as Spiegel stated, such magical practices annul the meaning of the judgment [170]. Here again death, this time the second one, is spirited away by (from the modern point of view) cheating. However, to the Egyptians the combination of fulfulling ethical norms and using magic did not seem incompatible at all.

I have already called the Egyptian attitude to death dualistic [171]. Many texts prove that the Egyptians hated death; it is seen as sudden, inexorable, pitiless; it can not be bought off or bribed, like their officials. It was for this reason that my compatriot Zandee was able to call his doctoral thesis 'Death as an enemy' [172]. The attitude of this people is succinctly summed up in a greeting that often occurs on the outside walls of tombs so that the passers-by may ponder it and feel happy that they are not yet inside : "You who love life and hate death" [173].

e. 'Sub specie aternitatis'

Many representations on the walls of the tombs show us that the Egyptians knew very well how to enjoy life. Nevertheless, it is also evident that they lived 'sub specie aeternitatis'. The thought of death always accompanied them, they were constantly preparing for it. These sentiments might have led to ascetism and contemplation, but the Egyptians were not given to attitudes such as these. The manner in which the tension between life and death took shape in their country was the modelling of that grandiose civilization, the splendour that was Egypt [174]. It was in this way that they tried to triumph over death and to introduce eternity into their existence.

To do them justice, the greater part of their fine civilization stands, after so many thousands of years. Its rediscovery about 1800 became one of the major cultural events of the modern era. In fact, if we assume that one of the central characteristics of modernity is the extension of historical perspective, it can even be argued that this rediscovery, expanding as it did, our historical consciousnous enormously, did much to inaugurate the modern era. And is it purely accidental that this existential encounter with the Egyptian hankering after eternity coincided with the beginning of the process of secularization that brought in its wake the waning, even the disappearance, of belief in an after-life? And is it only superficial sensationalism, a despicable aspect of modern 'mass culture', when 'ancient Egypt' is constantly recurring in popular periodicals, even in the tabloid press, or on TV?

It is true, however, as Morenz remarks, that art, even great art, is not able to triumph over death. What it does is to make 'the attempts to triumph over it more meaningful'. The real need is for 'a foundation of human life based on religion, that makes it really independent of death'. And he goes on to say that Egyptian belief always succeeded in finding new ways of securing the eternity of existence 175).

I need not describe these ways here; everyone is more or less conversant with them. We know how the Egyptians tried to preserve the body by mummifying it; we know how they stuffed the tombs with everything the dead could require in the after-life; we know how they covered coffins and sepulchral chambers with ritual and magical texts, to secure livelihood for the deceased in case posterity no longer cared for them. We also know how they were provided with a 'Book of the Dead' containing minute instructions for the voyage to eternity and texts enabling them to pass the judgment of the tribunal. However, there remains still another aspect to which I want to draw the attention of the reader. This aspect is the fact of mummification. Of course, the aim of this process is to prevent destruction of the body which would mean that there was no longer a 'basis' - perhaps we might say a reason - for existence in the after-life. But there is something more to it.

It is at this point that Hegel's dictum becomes true that "in death man is presented shorn of all casualness and only according to his essential being". In a mummy, rigid and wrapped up as it is, the physical aspects of man are reduced to a definite state, to a 'model' of physical existence as it were. Often, standing in a museum before a mummy, we experience an inexplicable sentiment. Could it be that we, although still living and breathing, feel awed by the stillness of this body that has survived innumerable centuries? What we experience then is the difference between the fortuity and fleetingness of our own lives and the essentiality and eternity of this Egyptian.

NOTES TO CHAPTER I
1) Hayes 3.
2) Wilson 18.
3) Kees, Alte Äg. 1.
4) Hayes 4.
5) Métin 27/28.
6) Hayes 29.
7) Baumgartner I 3.
8) Wilson 9.
9) Wilson 10.
10) Gardiner 27.
11) Gardiner 28.
12) Gardiner 27.
13) Gardiner 27.
14) Wilson 8.
15) Wilson 8.
16) Baikie I 14.
17) Wilson 15.
18) Baikie I 14.
19) Gardiner 27; Montet, Géographie I 4.
20) Montet I 4.
21) Baikie I 17.
22) Kees, Götterglaube 22/23.
23) Kees, Götterglaube 24.
24) Kees, Götterglaube 411.
25) Kees, Götterglaube 411.
26) Moret 78/79.
27) Ermann, 317/318.
28) Wilson 18/19.
29) Hornung 5.
30) Hornung 5. In Lex.d.Äg. 34, 210, Peter Behrens supposes that the difference in the nature of the two lands is already a sufficient explanation.
31) Frankfort 30/31.

32) Frankfort says categorically : "The dualistic forms of Egyptian kingship did not result from historical incidents". His opinion is that, in predynastic times, Egypt was politically amorphous to a degree' (20), so that we cannot speak of two separate kingdoms then. He derives the idea of 'the Two Lands' from "the deeply rooted Egyptian tendency to understand the world in dualistic terms ... The universe as a whole was referred to as 'heaven and earth'. Within this concept 'earth' was again referred to as 'north and south', the 'portions of Horus and Seth', 'the two lands' ... They belong to cosmology, not to history or politics."
I can hardly believe that such a clearcut distinction as that of the Two Lands, kept intact for thousands of years, and as old as Egypt herself, originated solely from a piece of abstract thinking about the construction of the cosmos. It must have some firm foundation in earthly reality. In my opinion, Frankfort demonstrates here the omnipresent proclivity of scholars to limit dualistic phenomena to the realms of religion and philosophy and not to recognize them, however apparent they may be, in history and social life.
I fully admit that this dualism of the Two Lands found its expression in mythology too. This mythological presentation of a political and historical duality of course had its impact on Egyptian thought. We may be sure that this presentation of Egypt as a twofold entity - in every aspect of the royal image - became deeply ingrained in the mind of the Egyptian people - so much so that at last Egypt ever more became a dual monarchy, whatever the historical origin may have been.
This is what what Arnold Toynbee (II 113) has to say of it : "The polarization of political power at the two extremities of the Egyptiac domain was an early as well as a persistent phenomenon of Egyptiac history ..., and after this dualism had been converted into unity by the triumph of the Southern over the Northern power, the memory of it was still kept alive in the symbolism of the double crown." 116 "In the post-imperial age, the old Northern and the new Southern march both failed to attain oecumenical power in the end; and the resultant political dualism persisted during the remainder of Egyptiac history." 117 "Thus the political history of the Egyptiac World, from beginning to end, may be read as a tension between two poles of political power which, in every age, were located in the Southern and the Northern march of the day."
33) Frankfort 107-109.
34) Frankfort 81.
35) Frankfort 81.
36) Frankfort 85.
37) Wadjet = 'the green one', euphemistically for the red crown, 'red' being considered too dangerous, Helck s.v. Uto, Lex.d.Äg. 46, 906/907.
38) Now Tell-el-Farain.
39) Helck. Vorstellung 11 : "In der Vorstellungswelt des frühen Ägypters ... werden diese beiden Orte zu Exponenten der beiden Landes-

hälften und zu Kristallisationspunkten für diese ... Dualitätspaare".
40) Ar., Met. VI 6.17.
41) Otto s.v. Dualismus. Lex.d.Äg. 8, 1148.
42) Frankfort 19.
43) Brunner s.v. Gott-König-Verhältnis. Lex.d.Äg. 19, 462.
44) Schenkel s.v. Horus. Lex.d.Äg. 17, 14.
45) Frankfort 39.
46) Frankfort 37.
47) Frankfort 26.
48) Gardiner 33.
49) Gardiner 36.
50) Wilson 12/13; Gardiner 37.
51) Her. II 143.
52) Gardiner in his Grammar.
53) Gardiner 37, citing from the Journal of Egyptian Archaeology I 30.
55) Helck, s.v. Fremdvölkerdarstellung. Lex.d.Äg. 10/11, 315-321.
56) Wildung s.v. Feindsymbolik. Lex.d.Äg. 9, 146-148.
57) Wennig s.v. Nubien. Lex.d.Äg. 28, 526-532.
58) It is a medically ascertained fact that native women had too narrow a pelvis; this made childbirth dangerous for them. Helck s.v. Fremde in Ägypten. Lex.d.Äg. 10, 307.
59) Giveon s.v. Asiaten. Lex.d.Äg. 3, 462-471.
60) Gen. 46:34.
61) The colony itself has disappeared but its name perhaps lives on in that of the nearby village of El Nikrash.
62) Gen. 43:32.
63) Ca. 1000 B.C., edited by Montet, Eternal Egypt, see p. 280.
64) Act.Ap. 7:32.
65) Morenz, Begegnung 31.
66) Montet 283.
67) Plato, Tim. 22B.
68) Bietak s.v. Hyksos. Lex.d.Äg. 17, 93-103.
69) Aldred, Egyptians 126.
70) Aldred, Egyptians 131.
71) Van Seters 121. Translation taken from W.G.Waddell, Manetho. London, 1940, 79-83.
72) Von Berckenrath s.v. Fremdherrschaft. Lex.d.Äg. 10, 313.
73) The name of 'Moses' is very likely derived from the Egyptian verb 'msi' = to give birth. Cf. the authentically Egyptian names 'Thutmosis' and 'Ram(e)ses'.
74) Helck s.v. Verhältnis zur Fremde. Lex.d.Äg. 10, 311-312. See also Wildung's article 'Feindsymbolik' in Lex.d.Äg. 9.
75) Griffiths s.v. Menschenopfer. Lex.d.Äg. 25, 1009-1012.
76) Schoske s.v. Vernichtungsritual. Lex.d.Äg. 47, 1009-1012.
77) Kees in PW IIA 1905/1906. Stuttgart, 1921.
78) Kees, Götterglaube 411.
79) Wildung, Feindsymbolik. Lex.d.Äg. 9, 147/148.
80) Kees, Götterglaube, citing from Urk. VI 12/13.

81) Title of a book by Torgny Säve-Söderbergh, 'Pharaohs and Mortals'. London (1963). Translated from the Swedish (1958) by Richard E. Oldenburg.
82) Kemp 76.
83) Kemp 76.
84) Kemp 74.
85) Kemp 74.
86) Blumenthal, Untersuchungen 268-274.
87) Blumenthal, Untersuchungen 271-274.
88) Blumenthal, Untersuchungen 265/266.
89) Blumenthal, Untersuchungen 264.
90) Blumenthal, Untersuchungen 281.
91) Blumenthal, Untersuchungen 311.
92) Blumenthal, Untersuchungen 298.
93) Von Beckenrath s.v. König. Lex.d.Äg. 19, 461.
94) Brunner s.v. Gott-König-Verhältnis. Lex.d.Äg. 19, 462.
95) Blumenthal s.v. Königsideologie. Lex.d.Äg. 19, 528.
96) Ermann, Aegypten 67-72.
97) Details in Aldred's book on Akhenaten, Ch. IV and V. The difficult question of a possible co-regency is treated at length in his Ch. VII. See also Wenig s.v. Akhenaten. Lex.d.Äg. 2, 210-221.
98) Barta s.v. Re. Lex.d.Äg. 33 and 34.
99) Barta s.v. Re. Lex.d.Äg. 34, 159.
100) Barta s.v. Re. Lex.d.Äg. 33, 159/160 and 34, 167.
101) For instance in the tomb of a high official of Amenophis II, of the dynasty of Akhenaten, the eighteenth, a certain Kn-ʾImn, who was buried near Thebes. Urk.Buch.d.18.Dyn. IV 1386.13 and 1389.2.
102) Barta s.v. Re. Lex.d.Äg. 34, 162.
103) Barta s.v. Re. Lex.d.Äg. 34, 162/163.
104) Assmann s.v. Aton. Lex.d.Äg. 4, 526.
105) Title of Aldred's 'Akhenaten', Ch. X.
106) Aldred, Akhenaten 168.
107) There may have been exceptions in Memphis and Heliopolis, Assmann s.v. Aton. Lex.d.Äg. 4, 527.
108) Brunner-Traut s.v. Namenstilgung. Lex.d.Äg. 27, 339.
109) Aldred, Akhenaten 194.
110) Aldred, Akhenaten 187 and 190. He prints this hymn in his book 187/190. It is often compared to Psalm 104.
111) Aldred, Akhenaten 191.
112) Aldred, Akhenaten 186.
113) Wenig s.v. Amarna-Kunst. Lex.d.Äg. 2, 174-181.
114) Aldred, Akhenaten 186; relief on two stone blocks coming from Hermopolis.
115) Aldred, Akhenaten 186.
116) See the intriguing and critical Epilogue in Aldred's Akhenaten, 'Akhenaten and the Historians'.
117) Ch. VII of Aldred's Akhenaten.
118) Aldred, Akhenaten 134.
119) Aldred, Akhenaten 135.

120) Her bust, excavated at Amarna in 1912, shows that she would have made furore in modern saloons.
121) Helck s.v. Semenchkare. Lex.d.Äg. 38, 837-841.
122) Eaton-Krauss s.v. Tutanchamun. Lex.d.Äg. 46, 812-816.
123) Aldred, Akhenaten 256.
124) Assmann s.v. Schöpfung. Lex.d.Äg. 37, 678.
125) Barta s.v. Urgewässer. Lex.d.Äg. 46, 868/870
126) Westendorf s.v. Urgott. Lex.d.Äg. 46, 870.
127) Ions, Eg.Myth. 24.
128) Pyr.Text 301, cited by Spiegel, Werden 317.
129) Kákosy s.v. Atun. Lex.d.Äg. 4, 551.
130) Pyr.Text 1248, cit. Kees, Götterglaube 219/220.
131) Amon Hymn, cit. Spiegel, Werden 337.
132) Morenz, Äg.Rel. 186.
133) Morenz, Äg.Rel. 187.
134) Text on a stele from Abydos, Kees, Götterglaube 4.
135) Äg.Götterwelt 257-261.
136) Te Velde s.v. Ptah. Lex.d.Äg. 32, 1178.
137) Morenz, Äg.Rel. 181/182.
138) Sauneron in Dict.Civ.Eg. 177; he does not give his sources.
139) Hegel, Vorlesungen 310.
140) Hegel, Vorlesungen 310/311.
141) Kaplony s.v. Ka. Lex.d.Äg. 18, 276.
142) Kees, Totenglauben 67.
143) Kaplony s.v. Ka. Lex.d.Äg. 18, 276/277.
144) We find it on a wall of the mortuary temple of Queen Hatshepsut (1473-1458) in Dêr-el-Bahri.
145) Kees, Totenglaube 69.
146) The Ka of an individual person has no pre-existence (neither has the human person). The Egyptians did not know the migration of souls either.
147) Kees, Totenglaube 74.
148) Kees, Totenglaube 77.
149) For 'akh' see Otto s.v. Ach. Lex.d.Äg. 1, 49-52.
150) Pyr.Text 474a, quoted Frankfort, Anc.Eg.Rel. 100.
151) Frankfort, Ancient Eg.Rel. 101.
152) Frankfort, Anc.Eg.Rel. 106.
153) Frankfort, Anc.Eg.Rel. 107.
154) Frankfort, Anc.Eg.Rel. 110.
155) Morenz, Äg.Rel. 214/215.
156) Pyr.Text 355.
157) Pyr.Text 657e.
158) Pyr.Text 1385b/c.
159) Pyr.Text 134a.
160) Coffin Texts I 190a/b.
161) Morenz, Äg.Rel. 215/216.
162) Urk.d.Äg.Alt. IV 481.
163) Urk.d.Äg.Alt. IV 114.
164) Morenz, Äg.Rel. 217.
165) Morenz, Äg.Rel. 217.

166) Sander-Hausen, Begriff 12.
167) Sander-Hausen, Begriff 18/19.
168) Sander-Hausen, Begriff 31.
169) Morenz, Äg.Rel. 138.
170) Spiegel, Idee 46.
171) In an important essay the Norwegian historian of religion Kristensen stressed that there is also a monistic Egyptian view of death. From this viewpoint death is considered the necessary condition for eternal life. This is of course true - the idea of an afterlife presupposes death - but I for one would not call this 'monistic'. If this trend of thought were really monistic, there would be either only death or only life; life would be one with death, or death with life. But this is not at all the case. Even in this more rosy view death remains a fact in itself, and very different from life. It is only found acceptable since it leads to a new existence. Moreover, Kristensen himself readily admits that this viewpoint is a subordinated one; the primary conception of life and death is, according to him too, 'dualistic', with death seen as the (literally) mortal enemy of life. Kristensen 7.
172) Zandee, Death as an enemy. His book is an annotated and elaborated collection of funerary texts.
173) Zandee 1. Text cited by Sander-Hausen, Begriff 22, n. 8.
174) See also Morenz, Äg.Rel. 206.
175) Morenz, Äg.rel. 221.

CHAPTER II

ISRAELITICA

1. The Bible

"It is a strange thing that the Bible is so little read ... I dare say that there are many people of distinction in London who know nothing about it." Thus James Boswell in 1763 [1]. Admittedly the Boswell who reveals himself to us both in his Journals and in his masterpiece, 'The Life of Samuel Johnson', was neither a fervent Bible-reader himself nor a particularly devout man. This makes it all the more interesting that he should confess himself puzzled by the curious apathy of his contemporaries who, officially at least, were all of them members of a religious community. One cannot help wondering how he would react to our own day and age. What comment would he pass on a society in which indifference to religion is the rule rather than the exception?

But in spite of widespread irreligiosity or rather, perhaps, of indifference to organized and established forms of religion, the Bible is still frequently quoted. Sometimes this is done to support a religious or theological opinion. Sometimes, and perhaps more frequently, some biblical text is cited only to reject it as outlived, rendered out of date by modern science, or even as downright dangerous. What strikes me about biblical quotations is that they are often misquotations; sometimes, indeed, they cannot even be found in the book. This reminds me of a pupil of mine who confidently stated in a discussion that God created the world because he was bored; he was sincerely convinced that this curious piece of biblical theology was based on an authentic Bible-text. The things one reads in the papers or hears on television, are as often as not equally misguided.

The first great misunderstanding is that the Bible is a 'book', that is to say a continuous and coherent treatise or story that may be read from cover to cover. The fact that the Greek word 'biblos' from which our 'Bible' is derived indeed means 'book' plays into the hands of this misconception. However, the Bible is a collection of books; how many of them there are depends on the canon one prefers. 'Canon' means 'list of books'; a biblical canon contains those books that, by Jewish and Christian orthodoxy, are considered divinely inspired, and, moreover, are acknowledged as such (by some ecclesiastical authority or body). There exist, however, several canons.

The most comprehensive of these is the Roman-Catholic canon, adopted by the Council of Trent on April 8, 1546, confirmed by a decree of the First Vatican Council of April 24, 1870, and still in force. It contains 44 or 45 books (depending on whether one takes respectively Ezra-Nehemiah and 1 and 2 Maccabees as one or two books) for the Old Testament and 27 for the New Testament. Between Roman-Catholics and Protestants there is no real difference of opinion with regard to the number of books in the New Testament, although early Reformers had their doubts respecting some of these (Luther, for instance, used to call the Letter of James the 'straw letter'). The Jews, of course, do not recognize the New Testament as canonical. In the Jewish canon of the Old Testament that is generally accepted to-day several books are omitted that are to be found in the Roman-Catholic list : Baruch, Tobiah, Judith, 1 and 2 Maccabees, Wisdom and Ecclesiasticus. Since the Lamentations of Jeremiah is counted as a separate book, as distinct from Jeremiah's prophecy, the Jewish total of Old Testament books is 39. The seven books mentioned above are called 'deutero-canonical' by Roman-Catholics, and 'apocryphal' by Protestants - although some Protestant Bibles print them [2]. The final result of all this is that the Roman-Catholic canon counts 72 Bible books in all, the Protestant 66, and the Jewish 39. Finally, the shortest canon by far, that of the Samaritans, counts only the five books of Moses, the so-called 'Pentateuch' [3].

No matter which canon we choose, the diversity of the books is enormous. Almost every kind of literary genre is represented. Thus we encounter, apud alia, history, poetry, short stories, proverbs, prayers, pedigrees, even a land register. The style changes from terse enumerations to deeply felt lamentations, from highly factual historical descriptions to glowing love poetry, and from trite maxims concerned with good behaviour to prophetic fervour. Many of the authors of these books are anonymous, others are known only by name; of a few only we know some biographical details. One of the best known, Luke, author of one of the Gospels and of the Acts of the Apostles, was not even a Jew but a pagan Greek by origin, and, in later life, a convert to Christianity [4]. Some of the books are collections of texts - the prophecy of Isaiah, for instance, consists of three different sections. Most of the Old Testament books are written in biblical Hebrew, but some of the later ones wholly or partly in Greek or Aramaic. All the New Testament writings are in Greek [5]. However, in this chapter I shall restrict myself to the Old Testament.

Another common and widely accepted misunderstanding is that the biblical books are arranged in chronological order with the Book of Genesis being the oldest and the Revelation of John the youngest. This is not correct. Since the Book of Genesis is in itself a collection of older texts, the version we possess must be considered the result of a final redaction. Who the editor was may only be guessed. In its present form the book dates from c. 500 B.C., perhaps even a few decades later. The Book of Revelation, on the other hand, was composed in the last years of the Roman Emperor Domitian who reigned from 80 till 96; the Gospel of John, its final redaction dating, perhaps, as late as 110, in every probability postdates it.

2. The sources of the Pentateuch

Since the Book of Genesis, and in particular the 'creation stories' with which it opens, will form the prop and mainstay of much of the argument of this chapter, we must submit it to a careful scrutiny - the more so because its contents are the subject of many profound misunderstandings. It has always been known to biblical scholars that Chapters 1 and 2 of Genesis show considerable differences; for instance, that famous 'seven-days story' of Genesis 1 is conspicuously absent in Genesis 2. In the seventeenth century systematic lists of such differences were drafted. A scholarly explanation had to wait, however, till 1753, when Jean Astruc, the personal physician of King Louis XV of France, drew attention to the fact that the Hebrew text of Genesis uses two different names for God, 'Elohim' and 'Jahve'. On the basis of this he concluded that the author of Genesis (Moses according to him) had made use of older documents [6].

The upshot of Astruc's suggestion is that Genesis is a book composed from older sources. His theory that is now known is the 'document theory' or the 'source theory', has become accepted by exegetes of every denomination. However, in the two centuries that have elapsed since the appearance of Astruc's book, this theory has undergone some important modifications. First, we now know that not only Genesis but also the four other books of the Pentateuch (Exodus, Leviticus, Numbers and Deuteronomy) are compilations. Then, Astruc's two sources, the 'Jahvist' and the 'Elohist', have grown to four with the addition of the 'Priestly Code' and the 'Deuteronomist'. Some passages may even derive from other sources.

Finally, it was long assumed that these 'documents' existed in a written form, so that the editor had four books lying before him when he composed the definitive version of the Pentateuch. Most scholars, however, now believe that the sources of the Pentateuch were really 'oral traditions'. Yet even if this was the case, the editor obviously felt himself committed to fixed texts, whether oral or scriptural, since he did not trouble to eliminate certain minor contradictions between the several sources. His editing was, nevertheless, the reverse of a run-of-the-mill job. We must not think of him working, so to speak, 'with glue-pot and scissors', cutting out passages that appealed to him and arranging them in a certain order. His arrangement, rather, must be seen as a creative act of great importance since he carefully selected certain parts from the sources and combined them into an original sequence, according to a theological vision that was wholly his own.

With regard to Genesis we may leave aside the source that is called the 'Deuteronomist', or 'D', as biblical scholars dub it. It originated about 622 B.C. in the time of the religious reformation of King Josiah of Judah. D is especially concerned with lawgiving and religious ritual. Texts from the 'Elohist', or 'E', are inserted into Genesis but not into the 'creation stories'. It originated in the northern kingdom, Israel, at some time in the eighth century B.C. It usually employs the name 'Elohim' for God. Its idea of God is more sublime than that of the 'Jahvist'; it contains fewer anthropomorphisms. But at the same time its style is more monotonous and less poetical. The 'J' of the 'Jahvist' stands either for 'Jahve', the name of God it prefers, or for 'Judah', the southern kingdom where it originated. It is older than E and dates from the tenth or ninth century B.C. The Jahvist, whosoever he was, is a very good story-teller; many of the finest and best-known biblical stories are by J.

Finally, there is the 'Priestly Code', abbreviated to 'P'; it very probably is a compilation of three older sources which need not occupy us further. Its authors must have had strong connections with the priestly colleges of the Jerusalem temple or may even have been members of it. They are highly intrigued by cultic laws, ritual purity, sacrifices, religious festivals, priesthood, and, of course, the Temple and its forerunner, the Tabernacle. Stylistically, P's prose is terse and 'technical'. The Code was composed somewhen between 570 and 445, that is to say, during or shortly after the Babylonian Captivity. Chapters 1-3 of Genesis are a compilation of P and J.

3. The 'creation stories'

So far I have put the term 'creation stories' between inverted commas for the very good reason that there is not one creation story but two. The first, Gen.1:1-2:4a comes from P; the second, Gen. 2:4b-25, comes from J. This means that Chapter 2 is older by several centuries than

Chapter 1! Gen. 3, with the stories of Paradise and Fall, is also from J. The two narratives differ strongly from each other, quite apart from the fact that Ch. 1 calls God 'Elohim', while Ch. 2 uses 'Jahve Elohim' (= the Lord God) [7]. Ch. 1 circumstantially relates the cosmogonical phases of the creation, from primeval chaos to the creation of man; C. 2 omits all this and starts immediately with the creation of the male. In Ch. 1 plants and animals are prior to man; in Ch. 2, however, the male comes first, then the animals, and, finally, the female. Since in Ch. 1 'the waters' are mentioned so often, it is called 'the wet creation'; because in Ch. 2 the male is made of the dust of the steppe, this story bears the name of 'the dry creation'.

Nearly all modern people, Christians not excluded, have the greatest possible difficulties with these stories because they so evidently conflict with the results of the evolution theory. A creation 'in six days' (not in seven, as people often say erroneously) has become utterly impossible; fundamentalists who still defend its literal meaning disqualify themselves as rationally thinking people by doing so. It must be understood that I am writing neither as a biblical apologist nor as an exegete. Since, however, misconceptions may obstruct comprehension of what I have to say on my subject, a few preliminary remarks are indispensable.

First of all, the fact that the editor of Genesis employs two different versions of the creation that, to some extent, contradict each other - without bothering to iron them out -, proves that the actual course of cosmogonic events was of no importance to him. Obviously he had no intention of relating how the universe, the world and mankind had come about; his overriding aim was to state that God is the sole creator of all that exists. I am even tempted to say that, even if the evolution theory had been known to the author of P, he would have disregarded it and would have written the story in the same vein as it stands at present, because his object was so utterly different.

4. A non-dualistic religion

Now, if we assume that the authors did not intend at all to present us with a factual, let alone a scientifically correct report of the cosmogonical course of events, and if we further assume that their main priority was, perhaps, not the process of creation itself, we may well ask ourselves what prompted them to avail themselves so freely of creational material. The solution to this problem will help us considerably in answering the questions that dominate this chapter. I shall start from the hypothesis that the religion of Israel was utterly non-dualistic. This demands our careful attention since it will help us to explain more adequately the dualistic traits of other religions. Since some of the most important of these religions are closely related to the Judaeo-Christian religion, this is all the more necessary. We may, indeed, think of the Israelite religion, like the Christian one later, as a helpful contrast. In particular this contradistinction will be serviceable once we reach the period of the Gnosis, the alternative religion that nearly succeeded in supplanting the Judaeo-Christian one as the principal religion of the western world.

How should we define a non-dualistic religion - 'non-dualistic' being, of course, only a negative description? Could we say it is monistic? But a monistic religion would be a pantheistic one in which God and creation merge into one another. In the Bible this is evidently not the case. Shall we consider it 'holistic'? But apart from the fact that this term is not wholly free from modern ideological connotations, as a succinct indication or as a key-word it is too vague. The Bible surely presents a 'whole' in which God, world, nature, man, belong together. The German philosopher Wilhelm Schapp would call what the Bible has to tell us, an 'All-Geschichte', a 'story of all and everything' [8]. But the 'whole' of the Bible is a structured whole in which we must make a careful distinction between the several autonomous entities (like mankind) and between autonomous and sovereign (like God) entities. And even if the Bible, doubtless, offers us a 'whole', it is, nevertheless, more intrigued by the relations between these entities.

THE COUNTRY OF THE BIBLE

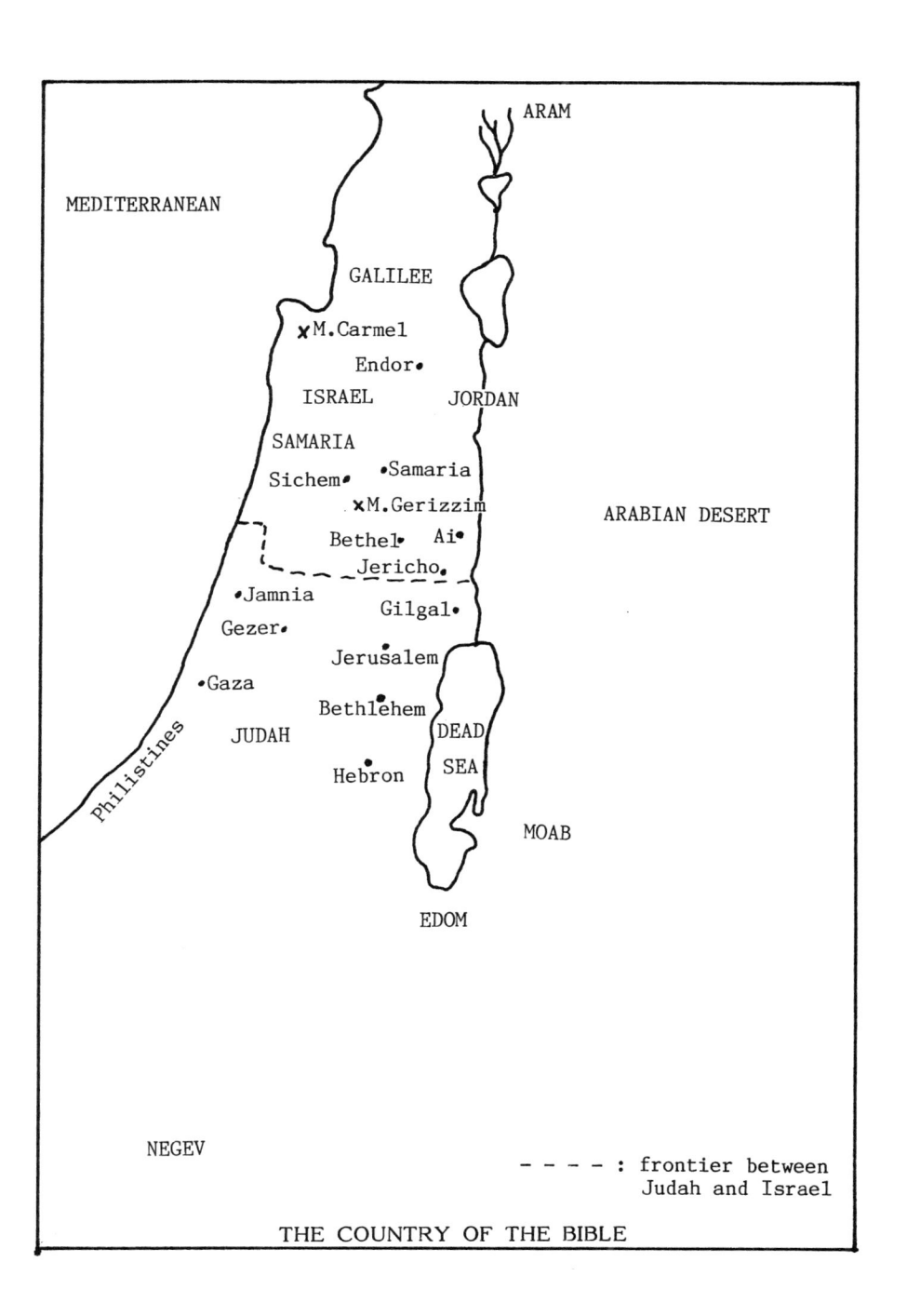

In my opinion, the relationships between the entities of the biblical 'whole' should be referred to by the term 'analogy'. This word is not very popular with philosophers; what they prefer is 'identity' or 'sameness', instead of 'analogy' or 'similarity'. As a philosophical term it is, in their view, not abstract enough. However, the Bible is not a philosophical treatise; there is little or no philosophy in it. And religion is not the same as philosophy. So there is no reason why religious explanation should not make good use of a term that is not approved of by philosophers. In fact, one of the greatest thinkers of mankind, Thomas of Aquinas, made 'analogy' in the form of 'analogia entis' or the 'Analogy of Being', into one of the pivots of his theological system. By 'Analogy of Being' he meant a close relationship, a similarity (although not an identity) between God and creation, in particular between God and man. In this connection he referred to the Bible, especially to Gen. 1, where it is said that God created man 'in his image and likeness'. Therefore I conclude that we must describe the biblical non-dualistic religion as one based on an analogy between Creator and creature. It is precisely this analogy that prevents it from being dualistic.

There is, however, yet another question. If the biblical religion is fundamentally non-dualistic, does this mean that it is, in consequence, wholly free of all dualistic elements? This amounts to the problem whether a profoundly non-dualistic system, of whatever kind, is possible. In the foregoing volumes of this work, I reviewed dualistic systems of many kinds, and we discovered that a radically dualistic system is almost inconceivable. In the last resort there always remains a connecting link in the mind of the person who thinks dualistically. For this person, finally, is not two persons but one. Perhaps the reverse is also true. Could we surmise that a non-dualistic system can exist without any form of dualism? If we assume that every non-dualistic system shows at least a few dualistic traits, we must now see whether this conjecture will be corroborated with regard to the religion of Israel.

5. A biblical anthropology

Genesis starts from the fact that there is a created world, and then goes on to ask what the relationship is between God and man. The essence of Gen. 1-3 is an anthropology, for it speaks of the place of man in the created order and of the general nature of mankind. At the same time, and still more, it is a biblical anthropology, since its speculations involve the relationship of God with man.

Now there are many kinds of anthropology. There is philosophical anthropology, cultural anthropology, religious anthropology, and still others. I don't believe subdivisions of disciplines, such as these, are really very helpful, particularly not in our case. They tend to turn into watertight compartments so that communication between them becomes difficult. Quite simply what I mean by 'biblical anthropology' is a speculation on the human condition as it is typical for the Bible. This means that it has a religious or theological character; it adds, therefore, a dimension that is lacking in other anthropologies, even in the anthropology of religion.

This is not to say that it contradicts or opposes other (scientific) doctrines; it is not even at loggerheads with the evolution theory. It does not clash either with modern prehistoric anthropology that defines man as a being who is capable of making fire, or who lacks the cleft in the lower jaw that is typical for apes. It does not reject definitions of this type, but prefers to define man as a being who is capable of knowing God. With regard to evolutionism there is also no problem about the time of origination of homo sapiens. Genesis does not consider this a fundamental question since it employs another criterion, that of the knowledge of God. This criterion distinguishes man from all other created works and beings, and endows him with a special place in creation; at the same time, this place involves special responsibilities.

We may now enumerate the features that characterize the ideal human condition - keeping in mind that they were not abolished all and sundry at the Fall. All that exists, man not excluded, is created by God, and, therefore, dependent on him. Possessing a likeness to God, man is capable of knowing him and will, naturally, venerate him. Man is God's lieutenant on earth; nature and the animals are subject to him. However, in this capacity he is responsible to the Creator. His likeness to God means that he is gifted with reason and free will; this gives him a rank higher than the animals. Man is created a duality, male and female; man and woman are absolutely equal. The duty of mankind to adore God is expressed by the fact that he must regularly set aside a day on which he does not work but, instead, occupies himself directly with God. Most important of all, there was no sin, and, consequently, no death. This original situation of mankind is usually called 'Paradise', or, as the theologians dub it, 'iustitia originalis'. As a picture of an ideal human condition it serves as a frame of reference for the rest of Scripture.

We can now understand why the authors used so much creational material in their narratives, and why they situated this description in a context of cosmic coming to be. By doing so they wanted to express and to stress the idea that man is not an isolated being, an accident in the whole of nature; he has an essential relationship not only to God but also to nature and the animals. Finally, this description relates to mankind in general, in every period of history, to all peoples, and to every civilization.

6. Biblical chronology

a. The creation of time

It is often overlooked that time belongs to the very first works of creation. On the first day 'the light and the dark' are separated from each other. They are called 'day and night', and with them the most natural chronological rotation has begun [9]. Somewhat later, on the fourth day, God creates the sun, the moon and the stars. It is expressly said that they are there to 'mark the fixed times, the days and the years' [10], even before their function as givers of light is mentioned [11]. It will strike the attentive reader that this passage about the celestial bodies is rather long as compared to the description of the other works of creation. This is because this statement has a polemical character - wholly in accordance with the theological flavour of Chapter 1 which comes from the Priestly Code.

The author is arguing here against (Babylonian) astrology and is combating the superstition that human fate is dependent on the course of the stars; at the same time he is setting his face against worship of sun and moon [12]. He even abhors the names of sun and moon to such a degree that he dares not pronounce them but says instead 'the great lights'. In a terse and matter-of-fact way he tells them what their task is : to regulate the rotation of the seasons, to form the basis of chronology, and to serve as an illumination during the day and the night. But nothing more! The author is also fastidious in his choice of words. The Hebrew verb he uses in Chapter 1 for 'to create' is 'bara', a word that is exclusively used with God as its subject. However, when he arrives at the passage on the celestial bodies, he changes over to 'asah', a verb that means 'to make' (with the hands). By using 'asah' instead of 'bara' the author wants to accentuate that celestial bodies, sun and moon in particular, are 'made' or 'fashioned', and that they are, therefore, no sovereign rulers but humble servants. We may also conclude that we meet here the first clear-cut distinction between Israel's creed and that of all other ancient religions. This already has a distinctly dualistic flavour.

The idea of a creation of time is intimated in the opening words of Genesis 1. Scripture has one of those fine, rustling first sentences that suggest great things to come : "In the beginning God created heaven and earth" [13]. The word 'bereshit' = in the beginning, means that time not only 'has a stop' but also a start. The end will come when "the heavens are rolled up like a bookscroll" [14]. Between these two points the line stretches along which the story of mankind, in its relationship to God, develops. This story contains three great divisions : the time of preparation, the time of the Messiah, and the Final Fulfilment, when time is dissolved into eternity. Then "the Lord God will illumine them (the Blessed), and they shall reign for ever and ever" [15].

b. The need of a definite beginning

The Bible shows a tendency towards a definite beginning that is lacking in other ancient religions. The Greeks counted back to the first Olympiad, 776 B.C., but they did so only from the second century B.C. [16]. The Romans counted from 'the foundation of Rome' - 'ab urbe condita' - in 753 B.C. They began dating in this way not earlier than the first century A.D.; before that date, and later too, they used the years of the annual consulates as the fixed points of their chronology [17]. In both cases we have a chronology that reaches back not very far, and certainly not to the beginning of the world. Moreover, Greeks and Romans use a time-table that is, so to speak, 'nationalistic', for it depends on an event in their own national history. The Jews, however, date back to the creation of the world which, according to Jewish orthodoxy, took place on October 7, 3761 B.C., a date that still determines the official chronology of the modern state of Israel [18].

Adherents as they are of the evolution theory many modern people may find this ridiculous. But apart from the fact that the exact number of 3761 years, or any other total, is nowhere to be found in the Bible - it is a rabbinical calculation -, let us not forget that such a chronological fixation signifies a worldwide view of human destiny that is absent in all other civilizations of Antiquity. The Israelites did not hark back to some event of their own national history, not to King David's reign, not to the conquest of Canaan, not to the Exodus from Egypt, not even to Abraham their father, but to the creation of the world. In doing so they created the first universal view of history. They might even be considered the originators of world-history. Far more than the Greeks, and even more than the Romans with their Empire, they attempted to develop a historical perspective in which all other peoples have a place. The words of Jesus at the end of the Gospel of Matthew : "Go and make disciples of all nations and baptize them" [19], and the vision of John in the Book of Revelation of "the great host whom no one could count, from every nation and tribe and people and tongue, standing before the throne of God and before the Lamb" [20], are a logical consequence of this.

c. The Bible's preference for a 'short chronology'

If we keep ourselves from recoiling in disgust from the rabbinical calculation of the period B.C. as being utterly unscientific, we can detect a marked preference in the Bible for what might be called a 'short chronology'. This is very important since Scripture situates all events in time - contrary to myth -, in order to make them 'historical', even 'chronological'. The biblical vision, therefore, essentially includes a time fundament. In choosing for a short chronology the Bible proves firmly opposed to all kinds of 'long chronologies'. In the interests of a sound discussion between 'science and creed' it cannot be stressed often enough that Holy Writ does not, even by implication, reject the evolution theory. This theory entirely falls outside its scope.

Nevertheless, the scriptural author criticizes, implicitly and avant la lettre, some important consequences of evolutionism. According to this ideology man is seen as the outcome of a natural process that also gives rise to concepts like soul, spirit, consciousness, intelligence, notions of God and religion. By giving man a distinct beginning in time, within a yet intelligible chronological distance, the Bible posits man as a 'historical' being'. In doing so it raises him above sheer naturalness and endows him with an essential freedom regarding natural processes, that is, with a responsibility all his own and with a special place in the order of creation. In consideration of this it does not really matter that homo sapiens actually originated much earlier than ca. 4000 B.C. nor that he must have had hominid forefathers. What is really decisive is that the process was not gradual since at a given moment soul and its faculties were bestowed on him.

The 'historicity' of mankind sets it apart from all other natural genera. Whereas the animals, as we know them, may be the final result of an evolutionary process, whereas even homo sapiens, with respect to his bodily development, may be the finished product of evolution, as 'man', that is, as a rational being, he is essentially different from all other natural beings. This is what biblical anthropology, with the help of its short chronology, wants to tell us. However, we must note here that this special human position could lead to a dualistic opposition between man and nature, between man and animal [21].

d. The 'Great Year'

In its preference for a long chronology the evolution theory concurs with ancient conceptions of time which also show a marked predilection for incredibly extended time-tables. Everywhere in Antiquity the idea of a 'perfect year' or the 'Great Year' was well-known. The 'Great Year' is the exact distance in time between two identical positions of all signs of the Zodiac including sun, moon and planets. The exact length of the Great Year depends on the method of calculation and on the number of signs to be included. But none of them is shorter than ten thousand years; 36.000 years is already more common. In Indian cosmology we find cosmic cycles, for instance 'Brahma-days' and 'Brahma-years', of an incredible length, up to 4.320.000 years, 4.32×10^9 years, or 3.110×10^{14} years [22]. In ancient Greece Heraclitus was an adherent of the Great Year; at the end of each Great Year the world would be destroyed by fire (the essential element of his philosophy), and begin anew. The length of the Heraclitean Great Year is given differently : sometimes it is 18.000 years, sometimes 10.800. Censorinus who sticks to 10.800 years derives this number "by taking a generation of thirty years as a day and multiplying it by 360 as the number of days in a year" [23].

Although the Pythagoreans did not hold the idea of a periodical destruction of the world, they too were adherents of the Great Year [24]. We find this idea also in Plato who was influenced by Pythagoreanism. In his 'Timaeus' he speaks of the 'Complete Year'. The length of his Great Year was perhaps ten thousand years since he tells us, in 'Phaedrus', that "ten thousand years must elapse before the soul of each can return to the place from where he came" [25].

Modern chronology does not know of a Great Year. But it has made us conversant with inconceivably long stretches of time exceeding biblical chronology by far. Evolution theory has pushed the time frontier back into an unimaginable past. The idea of creation has been superseded by gradual origination. Since the changes occur only on a small scale and, moreover, not too often - being only possible in some special conjunction of circumstances -, the process of evolution needs enormous stretches of time. This has accustomed us to thinking in millions and billions of years. Let us add to this that, since evolution is a continuous process, it is not to be supposed that it has stopped in the present age; from the viewpoint of the evolutionists there is really no reason why it should not go on indefinitely.

Furthermore, in the course of the past few centuries the historians had adopted an ever more refined time-table. Modern chronology has assumed a conspicuously arithmetic character so that it is now possible to indicate every moment with the help of a series of numbers. For instance, I am writing this on 26.1.1988 at 11.17 hrs (even the number of seconds after 11.17 sharp might be added!). This exactitude undeniably has great advantages. But at the same time, it also signifies the reduction of time to arithmetics. One of the seductive aspects of counting in year dates is that a new date always can be added to the former one. The row of numbers is endless, and time is, therefore, infinite. This method ignores the idea of the end of the world. This is also expressed by the time-lines and time-charts of which history teachers are so fond as an educational device. A time-line does not represent time but space; the line may be extended endlessly. Here again, the idea of infinity crops up. This means that modern secular thought has replaced the biblical notion of eternity by that of infinity which is something quite different.

e. Time-cycles

The idea of the Great Year necessarily entails its constant repetition. For, to quote Cairns, "there is an intimate connection between astronomical and earthly events", and, therefore, "the events and persons of each world cycle repeat exactly, numerically, the events of the preceding one". This means that time is permanently following a cyclical course; it proceeds in cycle after cycle, each cycle being identical with all the former ones. According to this theory I would be writing this volume again and again as though it had not yet been written, and the reader would be condemned to read it over and over again. Many Greeks actually believed that, in times to come, Socrates would drink the hemlock cup again and again.

This cyclical theory is in fact a deeply pessimistic one, since there never will be any improvement, let alone the final abolishment of evil. The cyclical pattern as well as the concept of infinite time also imply that individual man is a mere speck in the ocean of time. Having no knowledge of a concrete beginning nor of a passage into eternity he is whirled around and around only to arrive at exactly the same spot. Although modern evolution theory does not operate with time-cycles, it nevertheless impresses on man that, apart from having no 'roots', he is only a gradual transition between one phase of development and the next.

Cairns calls the Hebrew-Christian concept of time a 'one-cycle view' [26]. The history of mankind will end where it started : in Paradise. Now this author is an adherent of a cyclical view of history herself, and perhaps therefore she is showing a slight tendency to detect cycles everywhere. In my opinion the biblical conception of time is linear and not circular; there is no time-cycle because time does not end where it started. Nevertheless, Cairns is quite right in drawing our attention to a form of circularity, although this is not chronological. The whole Bible is circular from a thematic point of view, that is to say, in a literary respect. This kind of circularity it shares with many great novels : they end where they began. In this context I only need to remind the reader of the greatest novel, in my opinion, of the twentieth century, Marcel Proust's 'A la recherche du temps perdu', a book that, with some justification, might be called the secular Bible of the modern age. This novel, of which the main character is Time, alludes to time in the famous opening sentence : "For a long time (longtemps) I used to go to bed early", and ends with the great evocation of Time recovered that closes with the phrase 'in Time' ('dans le Temps', with a capital).

Genesis situates the first stage of human history in Paradise; then Paradise is lost - to mankind that is, for it remains in existence as a security for the future. That the serpent will not triumph indefinitely becomes evident from the mysterious words delivered by Jahve : "I will plant enmity between you (the serpent) and the woman, and between your offspring and hers; they shall strike at your head, and you shall strike at their heel; she is to crush your head" [27]. This theme of a brighter future for mankind is later adopted by Jewish apocalyptic writers, especially by the author of the Book of Daniel. "And the kingdom and the power and the glory of the kingdoms under the whole heaven shall be given to the people of the saints of the Most High" [28].

This optimistic eschatological thinking is brought to its final fulfilment in the Book of Revelation. The blissful life of the elect is depicted here by means of the image of the Heavenly City that appealed so much to later prophetic movements [29]. Then Paradise has returned, or rather, the City proves to be Paradise. For its streets are watered by the water of the river of Life; on both sides of it grow the trees of Life bearing fruit every month. There the elect will reign for ever and ever [30]. Perhaps I might indulge at this point in a musical metaphor. Gen. 1 and 2 are set in C major, but from Gen. 3 onward all sorts of keys are heard, even the most sombre ones, till, at the end of the New Testament, we hear the initial C major-theme again.

f. Summing up

Summing up we must conclude that the biblical time-concept in every respect differs from all others in Antiquity - so much so that we are allowed to speak of a dualistic opposition. Genesis opposes a linear time-concept to a cyclical one; history happens only once, there is no eternal return. Over against the expansive chronology of the Great Year stands the short chronology of the Bible. Instead of being suspended somewhere in infinity mankind has a fixed beginning in time and a definite end; therefore, time is finite. Finally, time is not a sovereign entity, not a divine being, but a creature made by God and at the end returning into his hands. There are no points of reference between the biblical time-concept and those of other civilizations. Although the authors must have been conversant with them, at least with the Mesopotamian ideas on time, they completely ignored them. In this way they expressed their deep abhorrence of an ideology that they considered utterly pagan.

7. Apocalyptic dualism?

What 'apocalyptic dualism' is was defined succinctly by Goodrich-Clarke (in a non-biblical setting) : it is the absolute difference between the present age and the future [31]. It is self-evident that, in this view, the present age is utterly bad; the sooner it is disposed of the better, even if it has to be destroyed. But the future will be the time of the greatest bliss and the uttermost felicity. The expectation of a glorious time-to-come, with the simultaneous rejection of the present age, has always been an important ingredient of esoteric movements - so much so that we are entitled to speak of a 'prophetic future'. Many of these 'prophets' appealed to biblical apocalyptic visions. The question now is whether they were justified in doing this, in other words, whether the Bible, in this context the Old Testament in particular, gives rise to such expectations.

a. The Messianic future

If it is true that the biblical time-concept is an uninterrupted line finally dissolving into eternity, there still remains a shadow of a doubt with regard to the scriptural form of historical consciousness. Are past, present and future always seen as succeeding each other continuously and following on one another without a break? At first sight this seems to be the case. In other ancient civilizations there never is a real end of time because, in cyclical concepts, the end always becomes a new start. There may be a final destruction at the close of a cycle but never a last fulfilment. Israel, however, with its linear time-concept, fostered an 'Enderwartung', a hopeful expectation of the end, when, with time, all imperfection would disappear and human destiny would be fulfilled. Then the 'Messiah' would appear and become the real ruler of the future.

'Messiah' - in Hebrew the 'Mashiach' [32] - is originally a neutral word meaning 'anointed'; in the kingdom of Judah the kings were anointed. Here the word is already assuming a new significance, for these kings were called 'the Anointed of Jahve', the chosen servants of God. It is only in the New Testament that the word 'Messiah' comes to mean an eschatological Saviour [33]; it is then applied to Jesus of Nazareth.

That the specific term 'Messiah' for the ideal ruler of the future does not occur in the Old Testament does not mean that the notion itself is not there. On the contrary! The idea of kingship already got a special significance with the divine promise to David [34] : "I will prolong for ever his royal dynasty ... I will not cancel my merciful promise to him ... Through the ages, far as your thought can reach, dynasty and royalty both shall endure; your throne shall be for ever unshaken" [35]. Several passages in the psalms refer to a king of the future : "Victory your mercy grants to the King you have anointed, to David and to David's line for ever" [36]. Although the word 'anointed' is often connected with the name of David, it is obvious that not the historical king is meant, but a future king as great as he or even greater. However, David's name always remained attached to the Anointed, so that in the Gospels Jesus could be denoted as the 'Son of David'.

Around 730 B.C. Isaiah prophesied a Messianic future in a famous passage beginning with these words : "A people that went about in darkness has seen a great light". The yoke on the shoulders and the rod of the tyrant will be broken. "To us a child is born, to our race a son is given whose shoulder will bear the sceptre of princely power. What name shall be given him? Peerless among counsellors, the mighty God, Father of the world to come, the Prince of Peace" [37]. Here we find one line of eschatological prophecy that we might call the peaceful line. The great figure of the future is a 'Prince of Peace' who seems to be divine. Somewhat further the prophet says that the spirit of the Lord will rest on him; he will give the poor redress and will right the wrongs of the defenceless. And then we read that hopeful announcement of the return of paradisiacal bliss : "Wolf shall live at peace with lamb, ... calf and lion and sheep in one dwelling-place, with a little child to herd them. All over this mountain, my sanctuary, no hurt shall be done, no life taken" [38].

b. The kernel of Jewish apocalyptic writing

Towards the end of the eighth century B.C. terrible catastrophes were to overwhelm the people of Israel. In the year 722/721 the northern kingdom, Israel, was destroyed by the Assyrian king Sargon II who deported its population to Mesopotamia. In this way ten of the twelve tribes of Israel virtually disappeared from history. In 587/586 came the turn of Judah, the southern kingdom. It was overrun by the Babylonians, and a large part of its population wandered into exile in Mesopotamia. In the midst of a pagan world the exiles of course needed a Messianic future more than ever. But now we can detect a different tone.

This becomes apparent when we turn to the second part of Isaiah prophecy, the so-called 'Deutero-Isaiah', beginning with the famous line : "Comfort ye, my people!" [39]. Its author was an anonymous prophet, probably living among the exiles around 540 B.C. His prophecy contains the four 'Songs of the Servant of Jahve' [40]. It is not at all clear who is meant by this 'Servant', but, anyhow, he is indicated as somebody on whom God's spirit rests [41]. He too is a very peaceful person, no lover of faction : "None shall hear his voice in the streets" [42]. But at the same time he is called 'an arrow' and his word is 'a sword' [43]. The third song says that he will come to grief : "I offered my body defenceless to all who would smite me" [44]. The deeply moving fourth song, that of the 'suffering servant of Jahve', makes it clear that he can only triumph by means of pain and sorrow. "Was ever a human form so mishandled, human beauty so defaced? Yet it is he that will purify a multitude" [45]. It is obvious here that the passage from the present age to the future will not be as smooth as it had been imagined in happier days. There is something profoundly wrong with this world, for the Servant will bear on his shoulders the guilt of all men and atone for it with his life [46].

With the end of the Babylonian Captivity in 538 B.C. the people of Israel, now reduced to the two tribes of Juda and Benjamin, did not regain its independence. The old kingdom of Judah was not restored; its territory remained first part of the Persian Empire, and then, after 323 B.C., of the Hellenistic kingdom of the Ptolemies of Egypt. The rule of the Persians was benevolent and the Egyptian kings did not bother the Jews in their religious beliefs. But around 210 B.C. the Seleucid kings of Syria began extending their sway southward into the Egyptian sphere of power; they even hoped to be able to conquer Egypt herself. In 200 B.C. (or perhaps it was 198) King Antiochus III the Great routed the Egyptians at Panium [47]. From then on the Jews were ruled by the kings of Syria. Only too soon they were to feel the hard hand of an oppressor. Bad days came when Antiochus IV Epiphanes mounted the throne of Syria, for he wanted to hellenize the Jews. To them, however, Hellenism was synonymous with paganism. And indeed, by imperial decree Antiochus forbade the customary sacrifices, the keeping of the Sabbath, and circumcision; the temple was rededicated to Zeus Olympios, the imperial god, and his altar erected there [48]. Protesters and transgressors suffered cruel forms of death [49].

Many Jews proved ready to sacrifice to the idols but others rose in revolt. The famous Judas the Maccabee initiated a guerilla war against the Syrians that soon developed into open warfare. After years of bitter fighting independence was won. It lasted until the arrival of the Romans in 63 B.C. The long period of subjugation, however, with its cruel persecution and ferocious warfare left its traces on the Jewish mind. Their outlook on present history and the future became dramatic and fierce; their interest shifted from the intolerable present to a glorious future. This is the kernel of what is called Jewish apocalyptic. This growing contrast between present and future is forcibly illustrated in the Book of Daniel.

c. The Book of Daniel

The Book of Daniel is a composite text written partly in Hebrew, partly in Aramaic. The main body of the text can be dated reasonably well, between 167 and 163 [50]. This means that, as a prophecy, Daniel is a 'vaticinium ex eventu', a prophecy made after the events that are prophesied. For obvious reasons in a time of persecution, the author did not speak openly of what was happening in his own days but situated his story several centuries back in the Babylonia of King Nabuchodonosor II. His readers will have experienced no difficulty in recognizing Antiochus IV in this godforsaken tyrant! This backdating also means that the titular hero of the book is not its author. The real author will, very likely, remain for ever anonymous; probably he had every reason to hide his identity.

Only half the contents of the book, chapters 7-12, may be called 'apocalyptic'. This word is derived from the Greek verb 'apokaluptein' which means 'to reveal'. An 'apocalypse' is, therefore, not in the first place a final catastrophe but a revelation. However, a 'revelation' is something different from an 'explanation'; we might say that, in a revelation, a veil is drawn from a secret. Consequently, an apocalyptic author is not a common teacher but a prophet, somebody who is initiated into this secret. It is revealed to him by, for instance, an angel, or in visions and dreams. What he hears or sees are mysteries - told in images and symbolic numbers. Thus he is able to describe the situation of his own days in such a way that, at first sight, it apparently contains no reference whatsoever to actual persons and events. This genre strongly reminds us of the productions of esoteric movements that were mentioned in Volume I.

Its visionary character is stressed in the very beginning of the apocalyptic part of Daniel : "Night came, and brought with it a vision for my seeing" [51]. However, in a foregoing chapter a dream had already played a crucial role. It was a nightmare of Nabuchodonosor, and Daniel came to interpret it after its secret had been revealed to him in a nightly vision [52]. The author of this story will not have realized that his interpretation was going to have a worldwide significance! The king had dreamt, as Daniel explained to him, 'of future times', so that 'the pattern of those (coming) times' would be revealed to him [53]. In his vision the Babylonian king had seen a great statue, the head of which was of gold, the chest and arms of silver, the belly and thighs of bronze, the legs of iron, while the feet were a mixture of iron and earthenware - the proverbial 'colossus on feet of clay'. Then a stone, rolling down from the mountain-side, shattered the whole statue [54].

Daniel reveals to the terrified king that with the golden head his own reign is meant. But this will be followed by three other reigns of diminishing quality. The last empire, divided against itself, will be very easily destroyed [55]. The view of history that prevails in this section is a pessimistic one, comparable with Hesiod's steadily deteriorating generations of mankind. Esoteric movements usually are utterly pessimistic about the course of history. The author supplies no further information about the actual meaning of these realms. The commonly accepted exegetic explanation is that they signify : a. the Babylonian Empire; b. the Median Empire; c. the Persian Empire; d. the Macedonian Empire. This last empire was divided into the several kingdoms of the Diadochi. When the author wrote this, already three of the four empires had disappeared. What he wanted to tell his dejected readers was that the Macedonian-Seleucid rule would collapse too in the twinkling of an eye.

Later generations of Christian historians took this to be a real prophecy and a godgiven interpretation of history. It gave birth, indeed, to the 'doctrine of the four world-empires' that was to dominate historiography till way into the eighteenth century. However, this scheme was not practicable without some important modifications that are not warranted by the biblical text itself. First, the Median and Persian Empires had to be merged into one in order to make room for the Roman Empire - which, very likely, the author did not have in mind. Second, it was assumed that the (Western) Roman Empire survived its downfall in 476 by living on as the medieval Holy Roman

Empire 'deutscher Nation'. I do not believe it accidental that the slow invalidation of the four empires-doctrine coincided with the waning of this last empire.

But what historians, Christians and others, always forget is that there are not four empires but five. "Another empire the God of heaven will bring into being, never to be destroyed, never to be superseded; conqueror of all these others, itself unconquerable" [56]. This fifth empire is, therefore, eternal and imperishable.

d. Daniel's four beasts and the Son of Man

In the truly apocalyptic part of Daniel we find first of all the horrifying picture of the four beasts. The four beasts too are kingdoms. They come out of the great sea. This sea is identical with 'tehom', the primeval waters of Chaos. The obvious intention of the author is to pass sentence on these kingdoms as the offspring of chaotic and disorderly powers; as such they are dualistically opposed to God who countered the 'tehom' with his spirit. With these beasts Daniel doubtless meant all earthly powers since their number of four corresponds with the four corners of the earth [57]. He intends very clearly to intensify his already dualistic stand by condemning earthly powers all and sundry as opposed to the reign of God himself. I don't believe we have yet met such a wholesale rejection of political power. This was certainly not the case with the Greeks who venerated the polis (although there was subcutaneous dissatisfaction), nor with the Egyptians to whom Pharaoh was the embodiment, even in a mythological sense, of their whole national life. This anti-political ideology of Daniel was to have a great career in history.

The first three beasts are animals that Israel found dangerous : the lion, the leopard, and the bear. To the fourth animal no label is attached. The lion, who is winged [58], is to all intents and purposes the Neo-Babylonian Empire, for the winged lion often occurs in Mesopotamian art. The bear is probably the Median Empire, represented as particularly cruel and insatiable, 'with three rows of teeth' [59]. The leopard, or panther, symbolizes Persia. There has been some doubt regarding the identity of the unspecified fourth beast [60], but it can be hardly anything else than the Macedonian Empire. It originally had ten horns but a small horn grew up in the midst of the others plucking three of them away to make room for itself; it had 'a mouth that talked very boastfully' [61]. It is not difficult to identify this small horn with the arrogant Antiochus IV, the great persecutor of the Jews.

While commenting very adversely on the first three beasts Daniel's aversion reaches a culmination-point in his description of the fourth, 'the greatest of them all, to crush and trample down a whole world' [62]. This term reminds us of the third empire, the Persian one, that was called 'wide as the world' [63]. What the author intends to say is that the Seleucid Empire has the same pretensions (but with less effect, of course) as the Persian King of kings. The arrogance of the Seleucids, in particular the incredible pride of Antiochus IV, is signified by the image of the horns. This image represents force in the first place, like that of the bull, and then, secondly, power, especially the overwheening political pretensions of earthly kings. In Mesopotamia the horn was a symbol of divinity, her gods often wearing a headgear adorned with bull's horns; sometimes even earthly kings arrogate this to themselves. We still possess coins of Seleucid kings with this same headdress. What blasphemous arrogance, the author suggests, for kings who are in fact so much less powerful than the great Babylonian conquerors.

Continuing in this dualistic vein the author again puts, over against these earthly kingdoms, a celestial realm. This is ruled by one 'crowned with age'; his garments are white as snow, his throne all of flame; he has millions of angels to serve him [64]. It is an image of purity, spiritual force and divine power, wholly different from all earthly rule. The 'beasts' will wield power only as long as the Judge, as the divine ruler is called, will permit them [65]. At this point the author introduces a new figure, the 'Son of Man'. He comes 'riding on the clouds of heaven'; the Judge then hands over to him 'the power and the glory and the kingdom'. Everybody must obey him and his rule will last for ever [66].

Of course, there has been much discussion who this 'Son of Man' is and what he represents. In our context this will later become an issue since several dualistic sects, like the Manichaeans, claimed the Son of Man as their 'First Man'. I am not going to bring up this discussion but shall, instead, point out some differences. First of all, whereas the earthly kingdoms are symbolized by animals, the celestial kingdom is represented by a human being - since man, and not the animals, has been created 'in the image and likeness of God'. But at the same time this Son of Man differs from all other human beings, for he is 'riding on the clouds'. In biblical imagery a cloud is not so much a natural phenomenon as a symbol of divinity - for instance, the cloud that preceded the Israelites in the desert signifies Jahve acting as their guide [67], while the cloud filling the inner sanctuary of the Temple signifies thereby the presence of God [68]. The cloud is never seen in connection with ordinary human beings, kings included. The conclusion from this is that the Son of Man is not an ordinary human being either.

It is not said in as many words that the Son of Man is a human being; he is said to be somebody 'like a Son of Man'. Apocalyptic authors often want to stress that they are talking of beings and objects that bear a resemblance to their earthly counterparts but in reality belong to another world [69]. That the Son of Man is, so to speak, 'commissioned' by the Judge means that his realm is divine (although he is not God himself), and as such the perfect contrast with the antidivine 'beastly' powers - an opposition that is truly dualistic. Finally, it will be obvious that the Messianic tendencies found a concrete expression in the image of the Son of Man, and were fortified by it. Jesus preferably referred to himself as the 'Son of Man'.

e. Salvation in the future

Stressing again that the dualistic opposition between the actual situation and the expectation of a blissful future is the real meaning of apocalyptic biblical literature, I can do nothing better than to refer to what Wendorff wrote. Mystical religions, he said, prefer the eternal return of the same, and have, therefore, no authentic relationship to real history; for the prophets of Israel, however, salvation is lying in the future. The road to it is linear history - the basic line being that along which the story of salvation develops. What Daniel sets out to describe in a visionary manner is that God is the Lord of history; he is conducting mankind along the path of time to the final fulfilment. All events of history, of past, present and future, owe their real significance to this ultimate aim. Time will have a stop although God does not reveal when.

To a people living in a time of persecution by a powerful tyrant, it was obvious enough that there could be no easy triumph over an earthly power like that. Hence the final victory is projected into the future - not in a few years or decades - for then the prognosis would be falsified again and again - but in an 'eschaton', in a last and concluding age of history. Then, with one stroke, all terrestrial, antidivine, political powers will be dethroned and be replaced by God's own radiant and eternal kingdom [70].

8. The biblical notion of God

Volumes I-III have been exclusively concerned with polytheistic religions. Biblical religion, the subject of this chapter, presents us, however, with the strongest imaginable contrast, since scriptural monotheism is of the most uncompromising sort. The third word of the first sentence of Genesis is 'God'. This name, in its different forms, is repeated thousands of times in the Old and the New Testament; it is hard to turn to a page on which the holy name does not occur at least once. But nowhere is the existence of God proved; the overriding modern, rationalistic urge to have cogent proofs of his existence was completely lacking in ancient Israel. The existence of God simply seemed self-evident. In place of logical proof, there was the testimony of action. He was the Jahve of the Book of Exodus who led his people out of Egypt, the 'house of bondage' [71]. This pure und undiluted monotheism makes Israel unique in the history of religions. At the same time this article of faith constitued its most vital legacy to Christianity.

a. Israel's exclusive monotheism

Of course, it is a problem how and when Israel arrived at this dogmatic belief in one God. It is often believed that, in this respect, the Israelites obeyed a general human urge towards monotheism. Assuming that such a tendency really exists, we may well ask why, in Antiquity, the cult of the one God flourished only in Israel, and nowhere else. In other ancient religions it may be the case that only one God of the pantheon is venerated (= 'monolatry'), or that one of the gods is the supreme god, but even so polytheism is presupposed. It should also be pointed out that all other Semitic tribes and peoples, in the midst of whom the (likewise Semitic) Israelites lived, were polytheistic to the core. The comparison with the monotheism of Akhenaten, that is sometimes brought forward, carries very little weight either, since this king's god, Aten, is, like every other Egyptian god, part of nature.

There is also a tendency, in the wake of modern evolutionism, to view Israelite monotheism as the result of a process of development, that begins with animism and then passes from polytheism to monotheism. As proof of a polytheistic phase the two names of God in Genesis, Jahve and Elohim, are adduced. In particular the combined name 'Jahve-Elohim' appeals to adherents of this theory, and still more, the idea that since 'Elohim' is grammatically a plural, it must originally have stood for 'gods'. However, the word 'Elohim', as a name of God, occurs in Gen. 1, of which P is the source. Wouldn't it have been very strange if the author or authors of the Priestly Code, the most 'theological' of the four sources of the Pentateuch, had been careless enough to allow an utterly pagan term to slip into the solemn introduction, of all places?

We must not forget, furthermore, that P had undergone the influence of biblical prophetism with its fervent veneration of the one God. Very likely, moreover, 'Elohim' is not even a plural, for, in this context, it is usually declined as a singular, as is the case in Gen. 1 too. When 'Elohim' means 'divine beings', for instance 'the gods of Egypt', then the plural is used, and in such a plural Jahve is never included [72]. The difference between the names of Elohim and Jahve is that the first is a general name, and the second a proper name. In any case it is impossible to construe 'a residue of polytheism' from biblical terminology. In conclusion we may say that there exists no human explanation of the mystery of Israel's monotheism.

This exclusive monotheism makes Jahve into what Renckens called 'a lonely God'. The discovery of the Ancient Middle East since 1798 makes this very clear. There was never any Israelite pantheon like the Canaanite one assembled round Baal and Astarte. Jahve never had, like so many gods of the ancients, a female companion, a 'paredros' [73]. This, however, does not mean that the Israelites themselves, from king to peasant, were as fervently monotheistic as their prophets or their holy books. Time and again whole sections of the population defected from Jahve and succumbed to the seductions of idolatry. But also time and again an inspired prophet or a holy king succeeded in bringing about a conversion. Finally monotheism became firmly anchored in the mind of Israel. When Jesus came, he did not deem it necessary, like the prophets before him, to fulminate against 'foreign gods'.

Jahve is unique in this respect too that he is the only transcendent god of Antiquity. All the other gods of this period were part of nature, often even personifications of natural forces. Israel's God, however, exists outside nature, he is no part of it, he can and did exist without nature. This dogma is clearly expressed by the very first words of Genesis : "In the beginning God created heaven and earth". This signifies that God already existed before that beginning.

The absolute transcendence of God is stressed by the prohibition to make images or statues of him. Even the inner sanctuary of the Temple did not contain a statue. This was very unusual and put Israel apart from all other peoples. In all other temples of Antiquity there stood statues of gods, like Phidias' giant statue of Zeus in the temple of Olympia. Images great and small, on all kinds of buildings and objects, were to be found all over the ancient world; only Israel was wholly devoid of them. The slightest suggestion that God could be similar to a human being was scrupulously avoided.

b. Anthropomorphism or theomorphism?

This statement will perhaps be countered by some with the asseveration that the Old Testament presents God in anthropomorphic terms. If this were correct it would, indeed, lessen the distance between God and man considerably since God would be in this case not so very different from man after all. Patterson (who is not a scriptural scholar but a philosopher) puts the case like this : "(God) is an anthropomorphic deity with a nature that stands in sharp contrast with the conceptions of a later period" [74]. These later concepts are those of the Priestly Code where we find 'an exalted and spiritual concept' [75].

If this author were right, we would, indeed, be confronted with two conceptions of God - in such a marked contrast that we even might speak of dualism. The anthropomorphic God is to be found in J and is utterly different from the 'exalted and spiritual' one of P; he "possesses some of the characteristics as human beings. He has a physical body and he talks with individuals face to face. He is a jealous God and will not tolerate the worship of any rivals. He is also a war god and one whose interests are narrow enough to include only the welfare of his own people" [76]. It seems that J's deity is guilty of not conforming to the modern liberal ideal of tolerance (and religious indifference).

Other biblical scholars take an intermediary position. Sellin, for one, freely admits that there is much anthropomorphism in the Bible but, he says, this conflicts with real Mosaic belief. This conception of God is, indeed, primitive, but it was so widespread and so popular that the Jahvist did not succeed in weeding out all of it. He took care, therefore, that expressions of this kind only refer to some manifestations of God without, however, impinging on his real nature [77].

Now, first of all, no human being is capable of speaking of God in other than human terms; we simply do not possess the appropriate 'divine' terms. Even P, who is more 'theological' than J, makes God 'speak', as though he had a mouth. And if it is true that his creative activity in Gen. 1 is indicated with 'bara', a verb exclusively used in connection with God, P nevertheless also employs the verb 'ja'as'

= to make (with the hands). If this is anthropomorphism, it is unavoidable, and if the Bible is truly God's word, this way of speaking of him is warranted by himself. Second, the Bible never presents God as an abstraction, as a god 'of philosophers'; he is always and ever a real person, a personality, which is not at all the same as being human. In order to describe God's 'concreteness' and 'nearness', the Bible uses anthropomorphic terms [78]. The authors obviously did not entertain fears that their readers would misunderstand or misuse such terms, or perhaps even compare Jahve to Greek gods with their human shapes and all too human nature. Perhaps in the final redaction the cruder expressions were eliminated, but we shall never be able to ascertain this since not a word of the older texts has been handed down to us.

Nowhere, not even in the oldest texts of Scripture, is there any indication that God has a physical body. Passages in which parts of the body are mentioned, like 'God's hand', are clearly metaphors that relate to his activity. Even a famous pericope like that of Gen. 18 does not prove that God has a physical appearance. True enough, three men appear there to Abraham who is sitting before his tent and eat with him as his guests; the author plainly reveals what he really means when he goes on to speak of 'the Lord God' as one of the three guests [79]. To Israel it was inconceivable that mortal beings could endure the actual presence of God; Abraham would have died had he seen God in his glory. The text, therefore, does not say that God has a human body but that he appeared to his host in the guise of a man. Only some time later Abraham perceives that he must have been dealing with God.

How badly we misunderstand the real intentions of the Old Testament when we speak loosely of 'anthropomorphism', will appear clearly from the mysterious passage in which Moses, on the Sinai, sees God 'from behind' [80], which is often cited as a proof of God's corporality since he apparently has a back. Even the great Moses is not allowed to see God's 'face', that is, his real being. God himself covers Moses' eyes 'with his right hand', until he passed before him, and "then you shall follow me with your eyes". What can this mean other than that human beings - even a prophet like Moses - are not able to have a direct, a personal encounter with God; we can only meet him 'historically', in retrospect ('from behind'), in the unfolding of the biblical tale [81]. In my opinion, this is a total refutation of all kinds of anthropomorphism. A solemn utterance like 'the Lord is one' [82], must make an end of all suggestions that Israel has cherished two (dualistically opposed) ideas of God.

When I now go on to describe the close relationship between God and man in the Old Testament as 'theomorphic', this is no subtle play on words nor a dexterous inversion of the argument but, instead, an honest attempt to come as near as possible to the real intentions of the biblical authors. To the prophet Ezekiel a vision of God in heaven was granted. There he saw something that had 'the form of a throne', and on this throne somebody was seated with 'a likeness of a man' [83]. It is remarkable how often in this theophany the words 'like' and 'shape' ('demût') are used. Obviously the author is making it painstakingly clear that God, indeed, is not a man and that he does not possess a human shape. Nevertheless, in contemplating God, man is, in a mysterious way, reminded of himself.

Now the Hebrew words employed in this passage - 'adam' for 'man', and 'demût' for 'likeness' - are exactly the same as those used in Gen. 1 : 26-27 where the creation of man is related. There can be no reasonable doubt that P is harking back to this Ezekiel text (this being considerably older than Gen. 1). According to Humbert, P formulates what Ezekiel said 'more concisely, more didactically, and more fundamentally'; he goes on to say that this author (P, that is) confers 'an anthropological (not 'anthropomorphic'! - F.) as well as a theological significance on it' [84]. Ezekiel, says Von Rad, inspired P to look for the model of man outside the sphere of creation; man resembles God. Although the difference between man and God is enormous, we are, nevertheless, entitled to view man as 'theomorphic' [85]. Thus there is no real anthropomorphism to be found in the Bible.

9. The zealous god and the other gods

Israel's Jahve was surely 'jealous', in the respect that he did not tolerate other gods beside him. But probably the best translation of the Hebrew word used in this connection ('qannah') is not 'jealousy' but 'zeal'. Jahve is zealous for his own unique position which he does not want to share with another deity. But his zeal has also something to do with love, since God is 'jealous in his love' [86]; he wants his people all to himself [87]. In this claim Jahve is absolutely unique. All other peoples had their pantheons, and most of them were very generous in permitting foreign gods to have a place in them. Often they 'nationalized' the outlandish gods somewhat by giving them a name proper to their own language. Later the Romans could not understand why the Jews refused to equate Jahve with Juppiter. But the Jews knew Jahve's solemn injunction : "You shall have no other gods before you" [88].

a. The lure of idolatry

The stand Israel's religion took regarding the 'other gods' is dualistic to a degree. There is no intercourse whatsoever between Jahve and the gods of other peoples; there may also be no religious commerce of his people with the creeds and cults of other nations. Foreign gods are idols; they are constantly and endlessly vilified. We encounter a vigorous polemic against them throughout the Old Testament, but it reaches its peak with the great prophets, perhaps beginning at full blast in Deutero-Isaiah. He, and also Jeremiah, love to point out that idols are nothing but products of handicraft, nothing but 'a stump of wood'. "And the fool falls down before it, goes on worshipping and cannot free his soul from bondage" [89]. Those that fashion idols have 'empty minds' [90].

The theological stance of the age of the prophets is that idols simply do not exist. They are non-beings, 'non-gods'. "Gods indeed they were not", says Jeremiah [91]. "How sorry a thing is a carver's workmanship, after all his pains. Fond imaginations, phantastic figures ..." [92]. "There are no powers that rival me (Jahve)", says Deutero-Isaiah

[93], "there is no other god" [94], "there is no god where I am not" [95]. Jeremiah expressly says that the foreign gods are 'things of nought', "those vanities of the nations" [96]; who "walks after them becomes 'nought' himself" [97]. The Israelites were not a philosophical people, and their prophets were no philosophers. Otherwise a man like Jeremiah perhaps would have talked, dualistically, of Being and Non-Being, in terms dear to Parmenides, of 'Being' (Jahve) and 'Seeming' (the foreign gods who to 'fools' seem to be but in reality are not).

If we would compare these outbursts against alien gods, it would strike us how repetitive they are. Vituperation against idols is simply one of the great preoccupations of biblical authors. What strikes us is how fierce, how denigrating, how insulting such utterances are in a truly dualistic vein. The authors obviously want to slate the idols, to make them disappear without leaving a trace, to destroy them completely. One is sometimes tempted to suspect that this fierceness betrays a certain fear - a fear that such gods might, after all, really exist, and that they might even succeed in taking Jahve's place in the hearts of his people, perhaps even in the hearts of the prophets themselves. We find this fear also expressed in the stipulation of Jewish law that "he who offers sacrifice to other gods must be put to death" [98]. Not only the idols are threatened with destruction but also their adherents.

Superstition is never far from us, not even from modern rationalists, atheists and agnostics. As Goethe once put it : "Superstition belongs to the nature of man; even when one believes that he is able to suppress it utterly it flees into the most curious corners from where it suddenly returns, when one thinks to be relatively safe" [99]. This is even the case with those who, like orthodox Christians, Jews and Islamites, take a purely monotheistic stand. With regard to the Old Testament religion, however, 'monotheism' hardly is the proper word. Modern -isms, what they connote, and the train of thought that produces them, were wholly alien to ancient peoples, even to Israel which, in modern parlance, was the sole monotheistic people of the ancient world.

The people of Israel often succumbed to the lure of idolatry. Sometimes the great mass seemed to have forsaken the cult of Jahve so that there only remained 'seven thousand that did not bend their knee to Baal' [100]. Many kings were idolators and seduced their subjects to idol-worship. Even the great Solomon, in his old age, became a victim of it. The author blames the outlandish women of his harem for it : "He was enticed by women into the worship of alien gods, and his heart was not true to the Lord, his own God, like his father David's before him" [101]. Many a king of Judah and Israel is dispatched with this short notice : "he disobeyed the Lord's will" [102]. Others are expressly praised because they 'obeyed the Lord's will', for instance Osee who 'scattered the hill-shrines and overturned the images' [103].

The most telling episode in the struggle between the Jahve-cult and idolatry is the reign of the horrible King Ahab who ruled Israel, the northern kingdom, from 875 to 854. He married the still more repellent Jezebel, daughter of the Phoenician king Ethbaal, whose name speaks volumes. Jezebel converted her husband into a worshipper of Baal; he built a temple with an altar for this foreign god. And in doing so "he did more to earn the Lord's displeasure than any king of Israel in earlier times" [104]. He had, however, reckoned without the dauntless prophet Elijah. This man sternly reproached the apostate king and challenged the Baal-priests to enter upon a contest with him [105].

The biblical author situates this struggle in a magnificent setting on the top of Mount Carmel which, with its height of 540 m, offers a grandiose view over the Mediterranean and the coastal plain. Elijah takes command and orders the four hundred and fifty prophets of Baal to bring a sacrifice to their god - on the condition, that is, that this god must light the sacrificial wood himself. Although the Baal-priests stand crying around the altar all day long, they don't succeed. In the evening Elijah has his own altar built, with a bull cut to joints on top of a pile of wood. Then he orders his servants to drench altar and wood with water. He now prays, and fire from heaven falls on the altar consuming not only the sacrifice but even the stones of which the altar was built. The aftermath was bloody : all the prophets of Baal were caught and put to death by the prophet [106]. This is a truly dualistic story. There are two opposing loyalties, and Elijah tells 'the whole of Israel' not to waver between them [107]. Finally Baal is proved to be non-existent, while Jahve manifests himself in the most imposing way. Then destruction is dealt out to the priests of the false god.

A still more telling example, because the two gods are directly involved, is the struggle between Jahve and Pharaoh - the Egyptian king being, if not a full deity, then at least a divinized human being. What is at stake is the possession of Israel itself, still living in bondage in Egypt. At first Pharaoh seems to be the more powerful of the two gods. When Moses and Aaron, having obtained an audience with him, ask him, in the name of Jahve : "Let my people go!", he disdainfully retorts : "And who, then, is this Jahve that I must obey his command, and let Israel go free? I know nothing of Jahve". When the two men explain to him that Jahve is 'the god of the Hebrews', he dismisses them saying coolly : "O no! It is only you, Moses and Aaron, who entice the people away from their work" [108]. Thus Pharaoh reduces Jahve to non-existence and presents himself as the sole divine ruler of Egypt.

But then the ten plagues, the one still worse than the other, rain down on him and his people, and slowly and reluctantly he grows ready to admit that Jahve is a redoutable opponent. However, it is only when all the first-born of Egypt die, including even the prince royal, that Pharaoh relents, seeing his dynasty as well as his people threatened in their continued existence. "Up, out of my kingdom", he says, "and offer this Jahve of yours the sacrifice you spoke of" [109]. In this way he finally acknowledges that Jahve really exists and can claim Israel as his people. He has second thoughts, however, and sends his army after the Israelites - an earthly military force against the power of almighty God. Pharaoh's host is drowned in the Red Sea, and the Israelites escape to safety [110]. The roles are now completely reversed : Pharaoh has been reduced to impotence by the omnipotent God. "Against such majesty they rose but to fall; the hot breath of your anger burnt them up like stubble" [111]. Here too the dualistic oppositions strike the eye. Jahve and Pharaoh are put opposite each other as major and minor, and havoc is played with the minor term.

b. Do idols exist?

As I wrote earlier, the ferocity of many utterances against idols proves that Israel, even perhaps the greatest prophets, did not consider themselves immune against idolatry. The idols were despised but also feared. But one does not fear what does not exist. There is a distinct possibility that the Israelite religious thinkers really believed that 'the other gods' existed, not so much as supreme divine beings but rather as something like demons. Indeed, many passages of the Old Testament seem to take the existence of other gods for granted [112]. About 835 B.C. the armies of King Josaphat of Judah, together with those of the kings of Israel and Edom, marched against Mesa, the king of Moab. This king, however, sacrificed his eldest son to Kamos, the protective deity of his country, with the result that the invaders had to retire [113]. The effectiveness of his protection clearly implied that, in the view of the biblical author, this Kamos really existed. This is in accordance with the general idea that each people has its own protective deity, Jahve being that of Israel. The consequence could be that an Israelite living outside 'Jahve's domain' had to serve alien gods [114].

Several passages in the psalms state laconically that other gods really exist : "A high god is Jahve, a king high above all the gods' [115]. This does, however, not mean at all that those 'other gods' were admitted into a possible Israelite pantheon, not even as second-rank gods. The idea that "Jahve alone is god" and that "there can be no other" [116] is by no means restricted to the prophets. The formula, moreover, does not restrict Jahve to his own domain, the territory of the Holy Land. Thus King Ezechias of Judah (721-693) prayed : "You alone are God over all the kingdoms in the world" [117]. No other gods are comparable to him [118]. What makes Israel different from all other peoples of Antiquity is that she excludes the alien gods wholly, not only from the official cult but also from the hearts and minds of every believer [119]. They may, perhaps, exist but compared to Jahve they are utterly worthless. Even a categorical statement like "there is none beside me" [120] need not mean a theological formulation of a strict monotheism but, rather, the religious expression of the fact that nobody except Jahve can give any help or hope [121]. Here too the dualistic distance is observed.

Neverthless, we may well ask ourselves how the presence of other gods in the Old Testament should be explained. As I have already pointed out, the introduction of -isms, such as 'monotheism', is not really helpful. This does not mean that Israel was careless about her religious notions. By no means! But the religious mind of this people did not operate alongh the lines of German and Anglosaxon systematic theology. It is, after all, only to be expected that modern scriptural scholars should frequently resort to evolutionary patterns in order to explain the occurence of forms of 'polytheism' in Old Testament writings. According to this line of thought monotheism slowly gained ground till it finally triumphed in the age of the great prophets [122]. This victory, however, never was complete, insofar as many traces of polytheism and paganism can still be found in the Bible [123]. If this viewpoint is correct - and I don't intend to argue against it -, the question remains why the prophetic editors, fervent 'Jahvists' as they were, did not extirpate such remnants lock, stock and barrel. Since we have no reason to suppose that they were careless enough to overlook such explosive utterances, something must have prevented them from eliminating terms of this kind.

Miskotte says that, although the biblical God is great, he is not 'absolute'. There exist influences that cannot be reduced to God and that, at the same time, are not 'nature'; "they surpass 'nature' (as an object of science) immensely". Whereas modern man hardly knows how to cope with them, the Old Testament, in sober reason, holds them for real. Against such nefarious forces God "takes the part of his people, and of mankind" [124]. The biblical authors take advantage here of a dualism that is part even of a non-dualistic creed. They oppose the sublime and omnipotent Jahve, sole object of their veneration, to these prejudicial influences that threaten to monopolize Israel as they had monopolized so many other peoples - influences that are the concretization of (cultic) sexuality, of the adoration of natural forces, of the glorification of earthly rulers, of the divinization of human beings like kings. In exploiting this dualism in the interest of freeing their people from fear of and subjection to these forces, they took a considerable disadvantage into the bargain by referring to these forces as 'gods'. At the same time they extricated themselves by emphasizing that these gods are not 'Godlike', not divine; as 'gods', they are 'non-existent'.

10. Dark powers

a. The 'waters'

Philosophers, Christian ones not excluded, agree that, from a philosophical point of view, matter may be co-eval with God. No argument can be produced that it is, of necessity, co-eval with God. This means that primary matter may also be 'from eternity'. However, rabbinical commentators favoured the idea that, while God exists from eternity, the world, his creation, exists within the temporal order, that is, 'historically'. Even a Jewish thinker like Philo of Alexandria (c.15 B.C.-45 A.D.). who was deeply influenced by Platonic thought, did not accept Plato's thesis that God created the world out of eternal pre-existent matter. In Philo's view God is eternal but matter, as created by God, is not; God first created matter, and from matter the world [125].

Rabbinical authors as well as Philo very likely have the Genesis-text on their side. Writing without any ulterior philosophical motives, the author of Genesis evidently wanted to state that matter is not eternal but created. This follows from his 'in the beginning' which gives all that exists - God alone excepted - a place in the order of time. By saying that "the Spirit of God hovered over the waters" [126] he wanted to express his opinion that Spirit, the divine Spirit, is prior to all matter. König once called this 'the first great idea of the Bible' [127]. This idea is stressed further by the words that God 'created heaven and earth' [128]. Since the Hebrew language possesses no separate word for 'world', the combination 'heaven and earth' signifies 'all created things'. The magnificent psalm 104 leaves not a shadow of doubt that all comes from God. In my opinion the idea of the world (or matter) being co-eval with God is wholly alien to the train of thought of biblical authors. Therefore, there is also no biblical fundament for a dualistic bipartition of God and the world, or for an opposition between them.

But might there not be a notion of chaos, of an initial Chaos, with a capital, as in other mythologies? The first creation story immediately states that the earth was 'tohu wabohu', waste and empty, and that "darkness hung over the 'tehom', the deep" [129]. In all probability this means that the earth was entirely covered with water : "The deep ('tehom') once covered the earth like a cloak" [130]. This 'tehom', or primordial ocean, is something different from 'sea' (= 'yam'), for the 'waters' are ordered to collect in one place that is expressly called 'sea' [131]. There may have been an initial chaos, in the sense of an indiscriminate tangle of elements. Since there is no equivalent for 'chaos' in biblical Hebrew, the author uses the word 'tehom'. But this 'tehom' is not the Chaos of other mythologies; rather this disorderly beginning serves to bring out God's creational power. Here again there is no basis for a dualism of God and primeval matter.

There is also no trace of the idea which we found in Greek and Egyptian cosmology, that, outside the ordered world, the cosmos, there remains a residue of Chaos, of primeval matter that is inimical to the universe and tries to destroy it. The notion that such an unruly element could exist, outside the scope of God's omnipotence, is also wholly alien to biblical theology. Nevertheless, there are indications that the order of the world may be interfered with, by 'tehom' for instance. As a landlocked people the Israelites were viscerally afraid of the 'waters'. This fear lies at the bottom of the story of the Flood. The Flood is a victory of the primeval ocean, the 'tehom'. The waters 'from above' and 'from beneath' combine; the earth, with everything it carries, disappears. At last the water stands 'fifteen cubits higher than the (highest) mountain tops' [132].

But the Flood must not be seen as a disorderly breakthrough of an uncontrollable force from outside creation. It is God himself who unleashes it because of the moral depravity of mankind. The victory of 'tehom' is not complete, since Noah and his family are saved, together with specimens of all animals, even the unclean. But that the story could give rise to great anxiety is proved by the fact that after the Flood God makes a covenant with Noah and his sons and with all living creatures, that is, with the new creation (for this whole episode actually is a second creation). "Never again shall a Flood devastate the world" [133]. The tehom, creature as it is, will be kept firmly under control. If anybody, the present author is able to understand the significance of this. Living in a city that lies well below sea level, he knows that, if the dykes (in this country the crucial symbol of an ordered world) should break, his writing-desk would be covered with six feet of water.

That the waters are feared becomes evident in many places, in the story of Jonah for instance, who is thrown into the roaring sea by a superstitious crew to placate the forces of the deep [134]. Psalm 18 even compares death to a roaring sea : "All above me surged the waves of death, deep flowed the perilous tide to daunt me" [135]. In another psalm the dejected poet likenes himself to one 'who ventured out into mid-ocean, to be drowned by the storm' [136]. Yet another text compares the stricken people of Israel to seafarers in great danger : "High up towards heaven they were carried, then sank into the trough, with spirits fainting at their peril" [137].

In several places horrifying sea-monsters are mentioned. One of them is 'Rahab'. Insofar as the roaring sea is compared to chaos, Rahab may be more or less identical with the deep : "Wounded lies Rahab at your (God's) feet, by the strong arm that has routed your enemies" [138]. In Job it is called 'the rebellious dragon' [139]; it is said there that Rahab and his helpers 'bow beneath God' [140]. "Was it not you that did cut Rahab in pieces, that did pierce the dragon?" [141]. These texts make it abundantly clear that God is all-powerful; even Rahab is nothing to him. But who is this Rahab that has to be subdued? The texts seem to betray a certain subconscious fear of him.

Perhaps we had better take a look first at another sea-monster that has remained better known, Leviathan. This was a many-headed creature : "You (God) did break the heads of Leviathan". It is also said that God 'divided the sea', very likely to detect those monsters down there in the deep [142]. Man is powerless against Leviathan : "Can you (God is speaking to Job) find a hook that will draw him to land, a line that wild hold his tongue fast ... Will you make a plaything of him?" [143]. Of course, this is exactly what almighty God does, he who "has created Leviathan to roam there (in the sea) at his pleasure" [144]. Nonetheless, in spite of this confidence, there seems to hover some fear of 'the great beast of the sea' [145].

With animals like 'dragons', many-headed or not, we are in the sphere of the mythological. We find them in the creation myths of the Middle East, in those of Babylonia (as Tiamat), and in the texts of Ugarit, as opponents of Baal. They try to make the ordering of the world impossible; they have to be fought down in long battles by the gods of heaven. Echoes of this can be found in the biblical references I quoted. But in scriptural theology they no longer represent Chaos; the Bible does not know of an initial Chaos over which God had to triumph, nor of a Chaos that might, eventually, return. The original mythological images, in all probability borrowed from other peoples, are made more harmless, in the text, for instance, where God plays with Leviathan, or they are made more 'historical', when Rahab, for instance, stands for Egypt.

b. Magic

Jacob is undoubtedly right in contending that the mythical elements have been subordinated to history to such a degree that we are confronted with historical fact rather than a myth of creation [146]. One can detect, though, a certain residual fear that certain forces of creation could turn themselves not against God but against mankind. This is no idle fantasy. We are constantly threatened by the occurence of earthquakes, hailstorms, hurricanes, inundations, volcanic eruptions, and other wild forces of nature that seem to run amoc against poor, powerless man.

Fohrer carries conviction when he argues that the attitude of the Old Testament towards existence was, to a large extent, determined by magic, and (perhaps even more) by its manner of dealing with magic. Magic was rampant in and around the Holy Land. "Most dangerous was the Canaanite religion of vegetation and fertility that was built on a foundation of magic. It was for this reason that the conflict between Jahvism and Baalism is such a crucial trait of the pre-exile history of Israel" [147]. The essential difference is not that Jahvism, in contrast to Baalism, did not believe in the existence of demons. On the contrary, both religions were firmly convinced that demons really existed. The real difference is to be found in the way to cope with them.

The most conspicuous example of belief in demons is probably that of the he-goat Azazel, that has become proverbial as the 'scapegoat' [148]. After an elaborate purification ceremony on 'Yom Kippur', or the Day of Atonement, the High Priest of Israel charged the goat with the sins of the people and then turned it loose in the desert. As in Egypt, the desert is considered to be the place where demons roam about freely; the name 'Azazel' is sometimes interpreted as the place to which the goat is sent, sometimes as that of a demoniac power [149].

Another telling example is that of the 'baneful water' [150]. If this is not sheer magic, then at any rate it is very much akin to it. The baneful water is given to a woman to drink whom her husband suspects of adultery. She must appear before a priest who mixes a handful of dust from the floor of the sanctuary with lustral water. Then he pronounces a ban on her and writes it down; he washes it with the water he has cursed and makes the woman drink it. If she is innocent, it will not harm her; but if she is guilty the baneful water will make her very ill. Then again, blood is closely associated with magic.

A very old instance of this we find in the mysterious passage where Moses' wife Sephora circumcises her son with a sharp stone and then touches her husband's feet with the bloody foreskin, saying : "Now we are betrothed in blood" [151]. Very probably this is an apotropaeic (evil averting) act by which Sephora tried to ward off God's vengeance against Moses for not having circumcised his son. Perhaps this pagan woman saw God as a demon. Blood has the same apotropaeic property in the exodus story : the Israelites must sprinkle their doorways with the blood of the sacrificial lamb, so that Jahve would pass by their homes when he went around in Egypt smiting the first-born [152].

This notion of a murderous demon sneaking about in the night can also be found in psalm 91 where it is called 'a nightly terror ... a pestilence that walks to and fro in the darkness' [153]. As late as the era of the New Testament belief is expressed in demons that cause illnesses. The mental confusion to which Saul fell a victim in the later part of his life is explained by saying that an evil spirit 'was upon him' [154]. It is well-known how Saul, on the night before he died at the hands of the Philistines, went secretly to the witch of Endor and asked her to conjure up the spirit of Samuel, who then really appears, this in spite of the fact that the king himself had forbidden such practices [155]. The invocation succeeds; Samuel actually appears. The long reigning King Manasseh (c.692-638) was surrounded by sorcerers; watching auguries and taking omens were normal practices in his days [156].

There is really no end to the number of magical practices in the Old Testament. We would, however, err greatly in supposing that the Bible is a kind of magical handbook or that the religion of Israel was founded primarily on magic. This is a notion that appeals very much to modern people because many of them are wont to equate all forms of religion with magic. Yet if the Scriptures confirm the prevalence of magical practices, they never underestimate the opposition to it. The practitioners of magic incur the anger of the Lord [157]. Consider, for instance, this comment on King Manasseh which, at the same time, is the Leitmotiv of the struggle against magic and sorcery. "The very nations (= of Canaan) which Jahve destroyed to make room for the sons of Israel were guilty of less wrong than they themselves (the Israelites) did, when they were led astray by the example of Manasseh" [158]. The Canaanites were, of course, less guilty than Israel because they did not know the true God.

The theological problem which magic is that it denies the omnipotence of God. It is not so much that there seem to be powers that God would be unable to control, but rather that man has found ways to make good use of them regardless of God's rule of the world [159]. By using magic man takes his fate into his own hands, instead of entrusting it to God. He believes he can remain in control of hidden powers, good or evil, if only he possesses the operative formulas or words and knows the right actions (like the witch of Endor who knew how to raise the spirits of the dead). In fact, a magician or sorcerer sets automatic processes in motion; the desired effect is not brought about by the acting person himself (let alone by God) but by the power of formulas and rites. Even Jahve is forced to acknowledge that power.

In consequence Israelite law forbade all practices of this kind. "Do not consult omens, or pay regard to dreams ... Do not betake yourself to sorcerers, or consult wizzards, to your defilement; you are the Lord's worshippers" [160]. The last words make it clear that magic is not, so to speak, an additional practice, to be invoked in case of need, or a more popular form of religion. On the contrary, it is seen as totally (dualistically) opposed to the wholehearted service of Jahve. The interdiction against boiling a kid in its dam's milk [161] does not arise from pity with the poor thing but from the fact that the Canaanites used the concoction as a magical potion. Mourning-customs that were based on magic, like the tonsuring of heads or the practice of inflicting wounds on oneself, were also prohibited [162]. How seriously Jahvism took this is proved by the fact that indulging in magical practices was threatened with capital punishment [163], for "all such things are hateful to the Lord" [164].

Often, when idolatrous and magical cults were gaining ground among the people with the connivance or even at the instigation of their kings, the priests of the Temple launched a counter-offensive. A very conspicuous example of this priestly influence was the enthronement of the seven-year old prince Joas as king of Judah (c.838-797). The country was then still ruled by the idolatrous Queen Athalia, the murderous grandmother of Joas. The whole action during which Athalia was killed was inspired and ably executed by the High Priest Jojadah who personally took command of detachments of the army and the royal bodyguard. The enthronement was immediately followed by the abolition of the cult of Baal and destruction of his priests [165].

The distinction between the magical and the cultic (that of the priesthood) attitude to existence is very clearly pointed out by Fohrer. The magician serves his own interests or those of his principal; the priest, however, serves the community. Hence, as Fohrer says, the priest is 'rite vocatus', that is to say, he acts as the executive of communal rites, whereas the magician is self-appointed. When a magician inflicts injury on an enemy, he is simply gratifying his own egotistic impulses; the priest, on the other hand, invokes the help of the benevolent deity and wants to placate his ire. The cualistic opposition between these two attitudes could only result in the triumph of one of them. The victorious attitude became the cultic one. What the Jahvistic cult told the people was that in every circumstance of life it had to take recourse to its God. The unity of creed and cult and life was secured by the stipulations of the Law [166]. That the Jahvistic cult and creed were finally victorious is proved by the fact that Jesus did not deem it necessary to take action against magical practices.

c. The 'nomadic ideal'

Fohrer draws our attention also to another conspicuous opposition in the life of Israel that is somehow connected with that between cult and magic. Everyone knows that for Israel, Palestine, or rather Canaan, was the Promised Land. After having fled from Egypt and after having wandered for a long time through the desert, they finally settled in the 'land of milk and honey', and began to cultivate its soil. From nomads they had turned into peasants. We have already seen how, to this agricultural people, the desert had become the habitat of ghosts and demons; they were also very much afraid of the nomadic tribes that lived in the deserts bordering on their land.

But however much this may be true, there is yet another side to this coin. The Canaanite soil had also brought forth the pagan fertility gods, and we know the Israelites were not wholly immune from idolatrous Canaanite influences, to say the least. Perhaps we might express the problem in a modern way and say that the atmosphere of Canaan was somewhat polluted and that it proved necessary to purify it completely. Here the desert presented itself as the purer country, for there Israel, 'in her youth', had been alone with Jahve. In the prophecy of Hosea, God speaks like this : "I will bring her (Israel) back to the desert and there speak to her heart ... She will sing as in the days of her youth, when she came up out of the land of Egypt" [167]. "What memories I have of you", says Jahve to Israel in Jeremiah, "gracious memories of her youth, of the love that plighted troth between us, when I led you through the desert; alone in the barren wastes, you and I. Israel was set apart for the Lord then" [168]. In this way the 'desert' became the 'Idealtypus' of the relationship between God and man. Therefore, it may not surprise us that, in a later age, deeply religious persons, like the Essenes, John the Baptist and Jesus, returned to the desert, in order to be alone with God.

Fohrer calls this the 'nomadic ideal'. He mentions two Old Testament groups that tried to live up to it, the Rehabites and Nazarites [169]. These combated the pernicious influence of 'Canaan' by rejecting its most characteristic elements. The Nazarites were members of a kind of lay order who, like Samson and Samuel, dedicated themselves unconditionally to the service of Jahve. They did not cut their hair [170]. Being 'set apart', they remained as far as possible from the special forms of haircut that were typical of Canaanite worshippers. They drank also no wine [171]. This certainly opposed them diametrically to the Jewish community since the Israelites were fond of wine. Wine was even a very important ingredient of the Passover meal, the greatest religious occasion of the year. But to the Nazarites wine was the fruit of the (polluted) soil of Canaan. It was so typical of Canaan (and, in Nazarite eyes, of all that 'Canaan' represented) that the very first product of the land that Israel beheld, was an enormous cluster of grapes that had to be carried by two men with a pole between them; it was brought by the first men who penetrated into the Holy Land 172).

Still more consistently 'anti-Canaan' was the attitude of the Rehabites. They too formed a lay order founded by Jonadab, the son of Rehab [173]. Jonadab was with the general Jehu, later king of Israel, when this hardfisted man, in 842 B.C., extirpated the Baal cult root and branch, killing in one bloody sweep King Joram of Israel, King Ochozias of Judah, Jezebel, the Queen-Mother, all the descendants of King Ahab, and the Baal-priests to the last man. The Rehabites drank no wine and had no vineyards. They hankered so much after the original purity of the 'desert' that they waived the possession of land and did not cultivate the soil. They did not even build houses and lived in tents. The prophet Jeremiah found this exemplary behaviour 174).

Thus there existed in Israel an at times rather sharp dualism between what Fohrer calls a (in German) 'restaurative' attitude to existence [175], and the general, historical acceptance of 'Canaan', with the risks implied in this acceptance.

11. The origin of evil

a. The tree and the snake

Evil is a crucial part of human condition; as the biblical anthropology that it is, Gen. 1-3 tells us how it originated in the world. There is no trace here of an origin of evil from outside the cosmos, there is also no fundamental flaw in the working of the universe, there is no evil god. In the Garden of Eden man is confronted with two trees, the tree of the knowledge of good and evil, and the tree of life [176]; both stand in the centre of the garden which means that they are highly significant. The tree of life symbolizes immortality; eating of its fruit would safeguard man from the ills of old age. Perhaps this tree is a later addition, for it does not play a role in the Fall.

The crucial tree is that of the knowledge of good and evil. It symbolizes the sovereign judgment over what is good and evil, a judgment that, in the biblical view, is proper only to God. According to Hebrew usage, 'knowledge' means 'to take possession of' or 'to be one with', as 'knowing a woman' means having sexual intercourse with her. Possessing 'knowledge of good and evil' therefore means making oneself into the arbiter of what is good and what is evil. Both trees are, so to speak, 'boundary-posts' saying to man : 'thus far and no farther!' - God having forbidden to touch them. Nevertheless, the first human beings transgress Jahve's prohibition; they ate from the tree, that is to say, they wanted to appropriate judgment in matters and good and evil to themselves. This is what the serpent promised them : "You yourselves will be like God" [177], knowing good and evil [178]. The woman believes that eating of the tree would give insight, and this is what she desires [179]. She presents the fruit also to her husband, and he too savours it.

Does all this mean that the serpent is the real origin of evil? And who, or what, is this 'snake'? He is, of course, no common animal since he can speak with a human tongue and is called 'more subtle than any beast of the field' [180]. The additional words 'which the Lord God had made' make it perfectly clear that the 'serpent' does not imply any independent or even sovereign force of evil; he too is no more than a creature. However, we are not confronted here with a fairy-tale in which animals can talk. Genesis does not suggest that in days long past animals could speak, or that a snake was a being different from what it is now (walking upright, for instance). The author simply uses these traits as a literary device to lend force to his story.

The Book of Wisdom indicates unambiguously who 'the serpent' is : "the devil's envy brought death into the world" [181]. That the serpent is chosen as a symbol of evil is no wonder : everywhere in the world the snake is perhaps the most ill-famed and hated of all animals, bringing sudden death to unsuspecting people. That he knows something of the mystery of life and death - "you shall surely not die", he promises the woman [182] - is, probably, a conclusion drawn from the fact that a snake sheds his hide and thus seems to renew his life; perhaps we might also advance the argument that a snake, creeping along the ground, is in the closest contact with Mother Earth, the source of life par excellence. Furthermore, this animal was especially hateful to Israel because in Canaan there existed an important snake-cult.

We must yet return to the devil as a source of evil. In the context of Gen. 3 the serpent, although bad and with evil designs, plays the role of the seducer. The final moral and existential decision is in the hands, first of the female, than of the male. Theirs was, indeed, a well-considered and freely taken decision, no force being used. The consequence of this is that sin, evil, and death were not the result of an action by a non-human being but of a rational resolve by man. Man is not the deepest source of evil, he is no devil, but, nevertheless, he himself is to blame for the fact that, ever since the Fall, man is morally and existentially in trouble. Thus Genesis rejects any notion that there might be a good god and a bad one.

b. Another origin of evil?

However, having stated this, we must now direct our attention to a very curious passage, also in Genesis, consisting of four verses [183]. "Time passed, and the race of men began to spread over the face of the earth, they and the daughters that were born to them. And now the sons of God saw how beautiful were these daughters of man, and took them as wives, choosing where they would. But God said, This spirit of mine shall not endure in man for ever, he is but mortal clay; his life-time shall be a hundred and twenty years. Giants lived on the earth in those days, and also after that, when first the sons of God mated with the daughters of man, and by them had children; these were the heroes whose fame has come down to us from long ago." Here we find two different races of beings, mingling sexually and producing offspring that is not approved by God. In this way a vision of the origin of evil is expressed that is far more dualistic than that of Gen. 3. Of course, this mysterious pericope has always presented problems to scriptural scholars of all times. Somewhat confused by its intrinsic difficulty, many Fathers tried to explain it - or to explain it away - understanding by 'sons of God' Seth's descendants and by 'sons of man' those of Cain [184]. Gen. 6 : 1-4, however, does not seem to refer at all to earlier quoted pedigrees; apart from that, the question why the offspring of both lines should be 'giants' remains unsolved.

What Saint Augustine, for instance [185], overlooks is that the real opposition is the one between 'the race of men' and 'the sons of God'. 'The race of men' is in the Hebrew original 'ha-adam' (plural), comprising all human beings and making no difference between Sethites and Cainites. The consequence of this is that 'the sons of God' are not human beings. Now in the Bible 'sons of God' - 'sons of Elohim' - usually stands for angels, for members of the divine court. This would mean that angels mated with the attractive daughters of 'the race of men'. It is understandable that a notion like this one has sown confusion in many quarters. The Jewish Genesis commentary in the Soncino edition of the Old Testament tries to get round the difficulty by interpreting 'sons of Elohim' as 'sons of judges and princes' - 'Elohim always implying rulership' [186]. This, however, does not explain why the result should be the birth of giants. And why should a prince not be allowed to marry an attractive girl from another class of the people? Is not this a favourite theme - the Cinderella one - of storytellers? There is simply no way out : the text clearly means that angels - or at least supernatural beings - had 'carnal knowledge' of human girls.

There is in Scripture a tradition of 'fallen angels', of angels who rebelled against God and were, in consequence, banished from heaven [187]. It is possible, perhaps even probable, that these verses about 'the sons of Elohim' are meant as a (very early) part of this tradition. However, their (literary) origin can hardly be anything else than a (Canaanite) myth of supernatural beings consorting with terrestrial females;

Spieser calls this 'undisguised mythology', and, as such, 'atypical of the Bible 'as a whole' [188]. Perhaps the Jahvist, who inserted this into Gen. 6, 'disguised' it somewhat since it is possible that the original pagan myth spoke of 'Elohim' - supernatural beings, or gods -, and that he tuned this down somewhat by making them into 'sons of God'. And it is not so 'atypical' as Spieser thinks, for this is surely not the only fragment of ancient mythology to be found in the Bible. The idea that there could be marital alliances, or sexual encounters, between supernatural and mortal beings was common to Antiquity, and 'must have figured largely in Hebrew folklore' [189].

Although, on the face of it, the text gives occasion to think of sexual desire, of 'angels' lusting after beautiful young females, this need not necessarily be the case. In fact, it is possible to argue that in deciding to marry terrestrial women, the elohim were not primarily motivated by sexual desire. This interpretation would bring us much nearer to what in all probability is the real meaning of this passage: that 'the distinction between the divine and human spheres is blotted out' [190]. This mixing of both spheres is something quite different from the analogy between them that forms the theology of Gen. 1. From the meeting between the elohim and the women a queer race arises, that of 'heroes or demigods', beings 'intermediate between the divine and the human'. In Gen. 6 the offspring of these unions is called 'giants'.

A Hebrew belief that giants indeed existed is attested in many places in the Old Testament. In the words of Skinner, this belief implies that an element of disorder 'is introduced into the creation' [191]. The dualistic element in this passage is that evil, with the ensuing disorder, is not caused by human selfwill but comes from without the world and is brought in by non-human beings. In Gen. 3 the woman sinned because she wanted 'insight' into the very texture of good and evil; there is no erotic element whatsoever. In Gen. 6 there is, however, an erotic background, a 'love-affair' that makes both parties transgress the limits that have been placed on them.

Jahve then interferes to rectify the situation. In his judgment man is energetically reminded that he is only man. As in Gen. 3, he is told that he will not live for ever, that he must die. In the story of the Fall he was not allowed to stretch out his hand to the tree of life; here his life-time becomes restricted to a hundred and twenty years. Both in Gen. 3 and in Gen. 6 man is put at a greater distance from God by being told that he is 'but flesh', but 'mortal clay'. Here too man has reached upwards (to the 'elohim'), but again the result is that he is condemned to being only too human [192].

c. The role of the devil

Contrary to what many people seem to think, the role of the devil in the Old Testament is not very conspicuous. The existence of evil spirits, or devils, was taken for granted. The Hebrew word 'satan', or 'sheitan', originally means 'opponent'; nearly every time it occurs in the Old Testament it is used for human enemies, for ill-disposed and scheming people. Satan, with a capital, that is as a real devil, occurs in Chapters 1 and 2 of the Book of Job. The author uses this text to make it as clear as possible that Satan is not a sovereign power but is wholly dependent on God. Actually he is represented as a rebellious and selfwilled servant in the divine household; in 1 : 6 he appears in order to do homage to his liege lord.

God then gives him permission to put Job to the test, but the latitude he has been given is circumscribed since he may not touch the life of his victim [193]. Here too, the 'tree of life' is guarded by God himself. When David is prompted to take a census, contrary to the will of God, his seducer is called 'Satan' who acts as the declared enemy of Jahve [194]. But neither these passages nor one or two others entitle us to think of Satan in a dualistic sense, as a sovereign force of evil, a kind of bad god and the counterpart of Jahve.

12. Relationships of man

a. 'In the image of God'

In the first creation story it is said that man is created 'in the image of God' [195]. This passage is preceded by a solemn introduction in which God is presented deliberating, so to speak, with his heavenly court ('Let us ...'). The profound significance of this theme is also accentuated by the fact that the loaded word 'image' is repeated three times, in vs. 26-27. Here the author deliberately takes the risk of being misunderstood. It might almost seem as though he were challenging or defying the injunction that Israel should neither make an image of God nor of anyone else either. However, this would be to misinterpret him completely. Man is not said to be an image of God but to have been formed 'in his image' or 'as his image'. The dangerous word 'image' is still more toned down by having added to it, as a kind of prefix, the word 'likeness' ('demut'). For this reason Renckens pleads for a vague translation, something like 'likeness-image' [196]. This would certainly do justice to the intention of the biblical author who would have found the idea outrageous that man is indentical with or similar to God.

Finally, the special place of man in creation is indicated by his formation taking place in the afternoon of the sixth day, obviously as the climax of the works of creation. After this, the Creator could not only state that everything he has made was 'good' (as had been said five times already) but even that it was 'very good'. God's satisfaction with his creational work means that there exists no dualistic distance between God and nature, still less between God and man. Of course, the Fall put man at a greater distance from God but it did not make him lose his privileged position altogether. That God still remains near to him is suggested by the charming passage in which we learn that after the Fall, when the first human beings are on the brink of leaving the Garden, God made 'garments of skin, and clothed them' [197] (although they themselves had already made girdles of fig-leaves to cover their nakedness [198]. Again the author risks the criticism that his metaphors are too bold, in this case by presenting God as a kind of tailor. The image, however, is simply a means by expressing the idea that, in all the great and small vicissitudes of life, God is with mankind.

In a more theological manner this nearness of man to God is expressed by Psalm 8 : "You have placed him only a little below the angels crowning him with glory and honour"; the Hebrew text which uses the word 'Elohim' would even allow the translation 'only a little below God'. Yet the author, only too conscious of the sinful state of mankind, cannot suppress the question : "What is man that you (God) should remember him?" [199]. How, in the fundamentally non-dualistic worldview of Scripture, everything in the order of Creation hangs together, is convincingly demonstrated by Psalm 148. This begins with the words : "Give praise to the Lord", thus indicating the essential function as well as the final orientation of all that exists. This praise has to come, first from the angels, then from the heavenly bodies, even from 'the waters' and the sea-monsters; all natural phenomena, the animals included, must participate in this exordium. Finally, all human beings, princes and commoners, young and old, male and female, must add their voice to the great chorus. What this psalm presents us with is a biblical 'chain of being'.

Another remarkable instance of this basic unity of both orders, the supernatural and the natural, is the story of Abraham and Melchisedech. Abraham is the ancestor and the first patriarch of the people of Israel; he is the special friend of God. He is Jahve's sole adorer, and his God speaks directly to him. From his race the Messiah will be born. Melchisedech is king of Salem which is identified with the later Jerusalem. At the same time he is priest of a supreme divine being called 'El Eljon', the 'most high god'. Abraham doubtless identifies this deity with his own God, Jahve; otherwise he would certainly not have given him 'the tithes of all that he has won'. Thus there is a 'religious bond of common monotheism uniting' Abraham and Melchisedech [200]. Returning from a victorious campaign the patriarch meets this pagan king near Jerusalem; they share a simple meal of bread and wine offered by Melchisedech who pronounces a blessing over Abraham [201]. Apart from other levels of meaning that need not occupy us here, this passage doubtless signifies a peaceful, harmonious meeting between the supernatural order represented by Abraham, and the natural order represented by Melchisedech.

b. Death as an anomaly

So far so good. The relationship between God and man is presented as an harmonious one; the bond that unites Creator and creature is never dissolved. But immediately after the Fall the worst consequence of this primal sin, Death, presents itself. In my opinion the fact that in the original human condition there was no death, does not mean that people would live for ever. For there was also the Tree of Life. After the Fall God took measures to prevent man from savouring the fruit of this tree lest he should live on endlessly [202]. Very likely the suggestion is that, after a life-time in the Garden, man would pass on to eternal bliss without having to go through the gates of Death.

That Death henceforward always would be very near, and that it would often be violent - or should we say that Death as such is a violent thing? -, is the gist of the story of Cain and Abel, the very first incident reported after the expulsion from Paradise. Death is an anomaly; it does not square with Life. This is how the Old Testament puts it : "God did not create Death ... What else meant his creation but that all created things should have being?" [203]. The opposite of Life, therefore, is not Death but non-being. But although the opposition is not really one between Life and Death, there is, nevertheless, a strong dualistic element present here. We are confronted here with an unbridgeable gap between the Life we are intended for, Life without Death, and the Life we all lead, inexorably ending in Death. Man does not accept Death, that is an anthropological truth. This forms one of the most important and primary historical strands. Always and everywhere mankind tries to triumph over Death, or should we say rather, to attenuate it, or even to ignore or to get round this painful fact. Walking in a graveyard we see all around us crosses and tombstones with names on them that tell us : "Don't forget me, I am still here!".

In the foregoing chapter we learned what incredible trouble the Egyptians took in order to secure their survival. But, to a lesser extent, all peoples do the same. All conceivable means are used, one of the most usual being that of giving our own name to our children. Perhaps the most conspicuous, elaborate, and sophisticated means of getting over the fact of Death is history in the sense of 'memoria rerum gestarum', of keeping past events and people alive by reproducing them orally or in writing. But whatever we do, it is utterly hopeless, for we die all of us; we are condemned to death. And with only very few exceptions everyone will be completely forgotten by later generations; no trace will remain.

To the Israelites Death, albeit a painful event, was mainly something that had to be accepted with resignation. They knew how it came about; as the fruit of sin, man would return to the dust from which he had been taken [204]. "As soon as the breath leaves his body, man goes back to the dust he belongs to; with that, all his designs will come to nothing", thus the psalmist states the matter quite soberly [205]. There is in the Bible no trace of the liberation of the spirit by the death of the body - a thought that was dear to Plato. But, at the same time, there is, in by far the greater part of the Old Testament, as yet no inkling of the resurrection of the body that has become so crucial to Christian theology. Certainly some consolation could be found in the fact that, although the individual died, people lived on. More encouraging still was the thought that God is more powerful than Death - "bare to his (God's) eyes is the place of shadows (the realm of the dead")[206] -, and that he would triumph over it in the end : "Death shall be engulfed for ever" [207].

But in spite of this all, Death was felt to be something horrible. It was sometimes seen as a devouring monster : "The grave, and the barren womb, and earth that soaks up the rain, and fire, did they ever say, Enough?" [208]. Sometimes it is even compared to original chaos. "Around me the deadly waters close, the depths engulf me", thus Jonah laments, calling the belly of the sea-monster 'the very womb of the grave' [209]. 'Tyrant Death' it is called [210], not to be welcomed at all : "O Death, how bitter are you ..." [211]. Dying means a radical breach with existence, with all those one has loved. "Lost to memory, like a dead man, discarded like a broken pitcher", says the psalmist [212].

Even God seems to forget the dead. "Men you remember no longer, cast away now from your protecting hand" [213]. At the same time, the deceased seem incapable of reaching out to God : "You have no praise in the world beneath, death cannot honour you" [214]. It is as if there are two worlds, dualistically separated from each other, that of God, of Israel, of living people, and that of the grave, 'my destined home', as Job calls it, even his 'eternal home' [215], a phrase reminiscent of Egyptian thinking. It is a world that stands apart from God. "Not for the dead your wonderful power is shown" [216]; "those who go down into the grave have no promise of you to live for; it is living man that gives you thanks" [217].

c. No blessing for sinners?

Perhaps it was not so much the inevitable fact of dying that caused problems to Israel but rather what came after it. For a very long time Old Testament religion hardly knew an afterlife. There only existed a realm of shadows that may be compared to the Greek Hades; the Israelites called it the 'sheol'. It is a place of oblivion [218]; those who live there are only dust [219]. For them there is no remembering of God; "none can praise you in the grave" [220]. This in itself is a dismal prospect but the real problem was that this fate was the same for good and bad. "Its greedy jaws are open to all alike" [221]. In the hereafter there was no reward for the just; there was no heaven and also no hell. This meant that reward and punishment had to be meted out this side of the grave, during life on earth. Or else God would not be just.

For a long time biblical authors somewhat spasmodically tried to believe that this really happened. Chapter 11 of the Book of Proverbs repeats this endlessly. "The innocence of the upright guides them safely; the treacherous by their own plots are destroyed ... An honest purpose clears a man's path; the wicked are entangled by their own scheming". And it is categorically stated : "Never son of Adam but had the lot his deeds deserved" [222]. The most unambiguous statement of this kind is to be found in Ecclesiastes : "I know well enough that blessings are for those who fear God, who fear his frown. Never a blessing for sinners; never be it said that they live out their full span of days! Reckless of God's frown, they pass like a shadow, and are gone" [223].

But doubts could not fail to creep in. Was this really always true? Without exception? Weren't the exceptions rather numerous? As long as things went well Israel succeeded in suppressing questions like these. But in the period of the Babylonian captivity they persistently cropped up. Of course, Jeremiah knows that Jahve is just - "I know well that right is on your (God's) side" [224] -, and that he is 'a true judge' [225]. But how did it happen that 'the affairs of the wicked prosper', whereas the good suffer? The prophet is so upset by this that he decides to plead against God, to remonstrate with him [226].

Is there a solution, a real, existential solution to this problem? Ecclesiastes, in Hebrew the Kohelet, literally 'the Convoker' (the fiction is that he is King Solomon [227]) doubts it. Although life on earth is the only life man has, and although it is here that the good will be remunerated with happiness and blessings, with children and material goods, he does not recoil from calling this life 'a world of shadows' [228], as though he had read Parmenides or Plato. Nothing is really worth the trouble; "vanity of vanities, all is vanity" [229]. Even wisdom and learning are not worth much and are hardly distinguishable from ignorance and folly [230]. Man must always toil, but he gains nothing from it. "Pitiable indeed I found it, this task God has given to mankind" [231] - this sounds like a piece of wisdom from the mouth of some Greek lyrical poet. Still worse, Kohelet sees 'innocent folk in tears, and none is to comfort them" [232]. "Wrong is done instead of right, injustice instead of justice." But why? Perhaps it is God's purpose to test men [233]. Here is another piece of wisdom that reminds us of similar Greek utterances : "The dead, it seemed, were more to be envied than the living; better yet to be still unborn, never to have known the shameful deeds that are done, out here in the sunlight" 234).

The difference between this and similar Greek poetry is that the Hellenic poet wants to be spared the miseries of life, especially those of old age, while Kohelet is morally disgusted by the rampant iniquity all around him. What the Greek and the Hebrew do have in common, however, is that they are both deeply pessimistic. "All is frustration, and labour lost" 235). This tone of hopelessness betrays that there was something very much amiss in Jewish religious thought in the time of the Kohelet, very probably at some point in the fourth century B.C. (in any case the book is post-exilian). Somebody - I don't remember who - called this book 'the unpaid bill of the Old Testament'; I for one characterize it as a 'failure of nerve'. Small wonder, then, that later Jewish scholarship had its problems with it. The New Testament does not quote it 236). Obviously the rabbinical schools hesitated to consider it canonical. Perhaps its canonicity became universally recognized only after the famous Council of Jamnia at the end of the first century A.D. 237).

Face to face with this great problem, the problem, in fact, of the meaning of life, the Kohelet seems to beg the question. "What need for man to ask questions that are beyond his scope?" 238). Nevertheless, he proposes a decisive answer : "Fear God, and keep his commandments : this is the whole meaning of man" 239). But what commandments does he mean? "Go your way, then, eat your bread with a stout heart, and drink wine to your content; that done, God asks no more of you" 240). Of course, he does not commend gluttony or a materialistic way of life; what he really means is that man has to be content with life as it really is.

d. Job between good and evil

The Book of Job also has the problem of good and evil as one of its central themes but it possesses a far greater dramatic impact. The author of the book is utterly unknown; the time of its origin must, very probably, be put at some time in the fifth century B.C.; this means that it too is post-exilian. It is not unthinkable that there may have been older and shorter versions, while its kernel, perhaps, is the popular but historical story of a man who suffered all kinds of ill simultaneously. It should be noticed that Job is not an Israelite. He lived 'in the land of Us', somewhere 'in the East' [241]. Us must probably be located to the east of Palestine on the borders of Arabia. We might consider Job a wealthy sheik of the steppe. Since he is no Jew no pedigree is given along with his name.

The Book of Job is one of the finest works of world-literature; Job himself has become proverbial. His story is well-known. He is not only rich, he is also a very pious man. Every morning he offers a burnt-sacrifice for his ten children. And then, all of a sudden, his whole wealth is destroyed; all his children are killed at one stroke. He himself is smitten with a foul infection, and there he sits on a dung-hill, scratching his skin with a shard. The only member of his family who is spared is his wife but she keeps nagging him. She is the first to tell him that, in view of his total catastrophe, he cannot possibly be innocent in the eyes of God [242]. For this is the gist of the story. Here we are in the presence of a very just, pious, and God-fearing man. Up to now everything in his life has gone according to the expectations of the sages of Israel. He is blessed in every respect, his riches are immense, his offspring numerous. Then follows the utter destruction of all this. What can this mean in traditional theology other than he has badly sinned against God?

What nobody knows, not even Job, is that behind all this there is, so to speak, a conspiracy between God and Satan. They are putting Job to the test. Satan is convinced that his victim will crack under the strain and finally curse God [243]. This is the first indication that there need not be a moral significance in what happens to us. In my opinion, nearly everyone, not only Jews and Christians, considers the blessings of life as an (of course justified) certificate of his or her good character; the ills are seen as a (less justified) punishment for less noble deeds. Even Job thinks along these lines, and this is the reason why God, in the highly impressive final scene, reproaches him for 'clouding the truth with words ill considered' [244].

Three friends of Job, Eliphaz, Baldad, and Sophar, do their utmost to impress upon him that he cannot be innocent. The idea that somebody could be stricken so severely and, nevertheless, be guiltless, conflicts with the wise views that they have inherited from their forefathers. In their often long-winded remonstrances they hold that Job must have sinned if not publicly, then secretly. There is simply no other way open, for if Job is blameless, God must necessarily be unjust, and this they find a blasphemous thought. To Job too this a blasphemous notion though at times he comes perilously near to it; sometimes he is on the verge of rebellion. "I will protest against God's sentence, demand to know why his judgment is so cruel. Is it well done in you (God) to play the tyrant, to spurn me, the creature of your hands, to smile on the ill designs of the godless?" [245]. The vehemence of these and similar words proves that this problem of good and evil formed a source of cruel torment for Israel. All the time Job keeps repeating that he is utterly blameless.

Then the arrogant Eliu appears who speaking, as he sees it, with superior wisdom, admonishes Job in a long and moralistic speech. Job must not think that he has any rights before God. The Omnipotent is just. The new element that Eliu introduces is that suffering may have a chastening effect; if Job is able to bear patiently with it he will be the better for it. He must, of course, not be rebellious but humble himself before God; then he will have 'justice and a true award' [246]. Thus, at the end of Chapter 37, all the five participants in the discussion are at a loss. Job keeps protesting that he is innocent and, in consequence, does not understand why he must suffer. The three friends feel that Job must have sinned but are incapable of proving this. Eliu puts the problem in a somewhat wider perspective by stating that the just may also suffer. This, however, is not a punishment but a means of coming closer to God.

Now the great question is : will the painful problem be solved in the remaining chapters? Or, to put it in terms of this work, will this fundamental anomaly in the religious thought of Israel be eliminated? Will Jewish theology get rid of this dualistic element and once more become homogeneous and harmonious? On the side of realism there is also considerable gain : the just too may suffer indeed. But the burning question is as follows : if it is true that the just are often badly off, and that the wicked prosper, and if, at the same time, we continue to maintain that God is an unswervingly just judge, where and when will rewards and punishments be meted out?

From the viewpoint of later Christian orthodoxy the final answer in Job does not seem perfectly satisfying. No direct response is given to Job and his adversaries. That the just may suffer is taken for granted by God himself too. The tenor of God's address in Chapters 38-42 is, however, to a large extent determined by the fact that there is still no thought of an afterlife. So the solution must be found within the limits of earthly life. Eliu already pointed the way by stating that suffering may be the test of authentic piety and may even be the earnest of new and greater blessings (which, in the case of Job, do not fail to materialize). However, the poem does not end on this note; in the concluding section God makes no mention of it.

In fact, Job never asked God to explain to him why he has to suffer. His real problem is not that he is sorely afflicted - after all, he is 'patient like Job' - but that serious doubts are thrown on his innocence. He does not implore God to take away his suffering but he wants to be justified publicly. And this is most lavishly granted to him, after the manner of traditional Israelite thought that is, by means of still greater wealth and a large new family [247]. On one point, then, there is a decisive and satisfactory answer : although the just sometimes go through hard times, this does not mean punishment. But still more important is the theological conclusion. God is doubtless just; it would, indeed, be blasphemous to doubt of this. But this does not mean that he is, so to speak, in duty bound to mete out blessings to the pious, and painful things to the evil-doers.

It is for this reason that both of God's great speeches at the end centre, not on his justice, but on his omnipotence. In the eyes of God one may be innocent even if everyone believes the contrary, even if the proof of piety, the prosperous life, is wholly lacking. Thus the outcome of the Book of Job is that there is no correlation between moral behaviour and success or failure in the course of life.

e. A vision of the afterlife

I believe that the Book of Job served as a kind of turningpoint. It turned Israel away from her traditional viewpoint and prepared her for a more effective solution of this painful anomaly. Already in Jeremiah we read of the Valley of Hinnom, or Tophet, just outside Jerusalem, where the Moloch-cult was celebrated. It is a place for the utterly wicked where the silence of death reigns [248]. In the Trito-Isaiah this vale acquires an eschatological significance. He does not mention it by name but it is 'outside the gate (of Jerusalem)' and represents the dark antithesis of the Holy City. There lay "the men that rebelled against me (God) long since; a prey now, to worm undying, to fire unquenchable" [249]. This is perhaps the very first premonition of hell.

The Valley of Hinnom became in the Greek of the Septuagint 'Gê-Hinnom', and this was bastardized in Aramaic as 'Gehenna'. In later Jewish writings the connection with the actual valley was severed; 'Gehenna' became identified with the 'sheol', and was taken to be the lowest part of it, the place where sinners are dispatched and tortured immediately after their death. In this way the sheol was divided into two departments. The higher one was for the just. Thus a different treatment reserved for the good and the bad after death came to be envisaged.

In the last Old-Testament writings, those of the second century B.C., the resurrection of the dead is posited together with a final judgment. The Book of Daniel states : "Many shall wake, that now lie sleeping in the dust of the earth, some to enjoy life everlasting, some to be confronted for ever with their disgrace" [250]. Resurrection would seem, however, to be confined to the Jews alone if, as is highly probable, 'many' applies exclusively to the Jewish dead. During the persecution by Antiochus IV the problem presented itself for the last time in the era of the Old Testament. For could there be any doubt that the Jewish martyrs were utterly innocent, whereas their executioners were cruel monsters? That belief in the resurrection of the dead was firmly established around 160 B.C., is proved by the fact that Judas Machabaeus levied a great sum of silver, and sent it to Jerusalem for sacrifices for the benefit of the dead. For, it was said, "he was a man who kept the resurrection ever in mind; he would have acted foolishly indeed, to pray for the dead, if these would rise no more, that once were fallen. And these had made a godly end; could he doubt that a rich compensation awaited them?" [251]. To pursue this line still further would, however, take us outside the scope of this volume.

f. 'The tenacious inconvenience'

Already in Gen. 3, immediately after the Fall, man is confronted with considerable difficulties - difficulties so great that he often seems to be thrown back on his own resources and on himself. The 'struggle for life' may become so intense that it makes him forget that he is created 'in the image of God'. He may become so absorbed by the problems of his existence that he forgets all about God and lets his religion degenerate into an empty and near meaningless sequence of rituals. "Oh but I (God) am sick and tired of them, your solemn feasts; incense that goes up from your assemblies I can breathe no longer; I will have none of your offerings and sacrifices. I care nothing for the fat victims you slay in my honour" [252]. There are more passages in this vein. Their prophetic authors do not fulminate against the rites themselves but against the idea that it is sufficient to fulfil them, as a kind of magic, without any inner participation. The fact that so many people so easily turned to idols also demonstrates that they must have felt estranged and distant from Jahve. Certainly there existed no open and avowed atheism in Israel. However, an utterance such as the following : "There is no God, says the reckless man" [253], suggests the prevalence of practical atheism or agnostic indifferentism. This means that for some people in Israel (how many of them there were we do not know, but from time to time they must have been numerous) the distance separating them from God became unbridgeable - which is to say that their religious attitude became dualistic.

That the Fall had made existence as such into a problem is suggested by the curious fact that the first human beings suddenly discovered that they were naked. They were created by God in the nude : "Both went naked, the man and his wife, and thought it no shame" [254]. But immediately after the Fall things changed profoundly. The serpent had promised them that, by eating the forbidden fruit, their eyes would be opened [255]. Their eyes were opened indeed, but what did they see? That they had no clothes on! They hastily tried to cover their nakedness by sewing fig-leaves into loinclothes [256]. "I was afraid", says the male, "because of my nakedness, so I hid myself" [257] - as though God could not stand to see him naked! What is really meant is that man's relationship to God has become problematic. That he is 'naked' means that he has made a fool of himself, that he has degraded himself, and that his vision of God is now obscured.

This is a highly significant strand in the biblical anthropology I have already alluded to. Genesis does not mean that nudism is 'paradisiacal' nor that man can regain his original innocence by going about in the nude. Quasi-documentary movies used to present tribes that are still unclothed as 'naked innocence' (or with titles of equal promise). What their makers conveniently forgot was that such tribes, the moment they come into contact with westerners, start clothing themselves, beginning with their genitals, the women first, and then the men. Curiously enough, this reflects the process described in Gen. 3! The primitive peoples of this world seem to consider nakedness not so much as paradisiacal but rather as a condition of backwardness that has to be remedied as soon as they know better.

The awareness of being naked can be very painful; only on very rare occasions it fails to be embarrassing. What makes it so disturbing in most circumstances? Why is it that so many married couples (in the past, it is said, but perhaps even to-day) in making love did (or do) not take off all their clothes? In my opinion only one answer is fully adequate : people believe that they are not beautiful enough. They fear that their body is 'unfashionable' [258]. The real reason why people, nearly always and everywhere, wear vestments (they do so even in very hot climates) is that they want to enhance themselves. Dress, and its correlates make-up, hair-do, perfumes, ornaments, and accessories, serve to hide the defects of the body, to accentuate what is beautiful in it, and, in general, to promulgate and raise the status of the wearer of these clothes. Everyone who, suddenly bereft of his or her attire, has stood naked between some white-suited doctors and a few nurses in starched aprons and caps knows that 'to be naked' means to be reduced to very little.

The need to dress is at the bottom of one of the most important strands in the history of all peoples and all civilizations. That man cannot go naked forces him to spend much of his time, money, energy, and phantasy on his attire; it gives rise to much daily care and labour, to handicrafts and guilds, to factory-work and trade-unions, to shopkeeping and commerce. At the same time, the trouble we have with our clothing is a plain proof that we are constantly struggling with existence. This struggle is never crowned with a definite victory, for even "King Solomon in all his glory was not arrayed like the lilies of the field" [259]. Make-up fades away, clothes get threadbare, soiled or outmoded, gloves are lost, umbrellas crack in the wind. Dress is what the Dutch author Theo Thijssen called 'the tenacious inconvenience' [260]. We are constantly reminded that we fall short of the ideal.

For this is the existential problem behind the fact that we cannot go naked. It means that our relationship to ourselves (and to others) is problematical. We are profoundly dissatisfied with our physical image, that is, with ourselves. There is a strong dualistic element in this, an unbridgeable distance between the high idea we foster of ourselves, or the fine figure we should wish to cut, and the way we really look. Dress, make-up, and ornaments serve to bridge this gap as much as possible. But we never reach the other side, that of the first human beings in the Garden who were stark naked without confronting this problem - the problem, that is, of themselves.

g. The magic circle around marriage

There exists a widespread misunderstanding that, with respect to human sexuality, the Bible is a strictly prohibitive and puritanical book. Actually, Old-Testament authors (and New-Testament ones still less) are not specifically interested in sexual matters. Either they do not devote a single word to this side of human nature, or they report events of this kind - rapes, adulteries, even incest - in such a matter of fact way that the inexperienced Bible reader is inclined to ask : "But does the Bible condone all this?". There is, however, one notable exception but this is just the reverse of being prohibitive. The Song of Songs is one great panegyric on love, on erotic love, on physical love even. For one need not be a psychoanalyst to detect the hidden meaning of so many highly poetic passages.

Of course, there are prohibitions too. Scripture does not take the point of view that everything is permitted to everyone, or that complete freedom in sexual matters is a necessary condition for real human fulfilment. The prohibition orders are mainly to be found in the biblical codes of law, in Leviticus and Deuteronomy, some of them also in Exodus. These codes prefer cataloguing specific cases to formulating general rules. It is not very difficult to determine the one great general rule behind all the detailed applications. The rightful place for sex is marriage; there it is good and lawful, outside it it is wrong - this with the proviso that for a long time Israel accepted polygamy as normal. Homosexuality, pederasty, and masturbation are seldom mentioned but are forbidden; so too is bestiality. More frequent are warnings against visiting prostitutes, more in particular temple prostitutes who brought Israelites into contact with idolatry and alienated them from Jahve. There are a number of strict provisions against incest, a term which usually meant marrying near relatives. Defloration of an unmarried virgin was considered a highly immoral act but adultery was seen as a still graver sexual offence. No wonder, since the institution of marriage was the prop and mainstay of Jewish communal life. Nevertheless, adultery must have occurred often enough; the fact that the warnings are reiterated so often testifies to this.

Thus a magic circle was drawn around marriage. Within it sex was not only permitted, it was good and even holy. Sexual love was the instrument given by God himself to mankind for propagating itself and bringing forth ever new beings 'in his image'. No word in the Old Testament suggests that conjugal sexuality might be bad, repellent, or objectionable. How could that be conceivable when the fruit of sexual love were children? Married couples wanted to have children, many children. Celibacy was of no account, widowed persons tried to remarry, even although for widows this was often virtually impossible. The first aim of marriage was to get offspring; boys were somewhat more welcome than girls. A great number of children was an evident sign of Jahve's favour and a source of the deepest contentment; on the other hand, infertility and childlessness were felt as a punishment by Jahve. It could make women deeply unhappy, especially because they could not understand why this should be their fate.

h. Rifts in the building

But now the first rifts in the building begin to appear. Do we detect a distant trembling of the ground? Many sexual offences, first of all adultery, were punishable by death. Does such heavy punishment betray a certain fear of sexual activities outside the magic circle of marriage? Could it be that Israel considered all forms of extra-marital sex as anarchical and dangerous, and was, therefore, afraid of them? Now there never existed nor do there yet exist human societies that freely permit all forms of sexual activity; there are always some major inhibitions. But in Volume II we saw that Athenian society considered some objectionable forms of sexual behaviour, for instance pederasty, as permissible, sometimes even as commendable. It may have frowned somewhat on male infidelity but it did not punish it.

The reaction of Israel to this kind of thing was far more strict and far more severe. Could it be that she, far more than other peoples, realized that sex, although in itself a good thing, is one of the wild forces of nature and easily becomes uncontrollable, carrying people away from God and from one another? Whether or not this was the case, I do not believe that there is any reason why the Israelite attitude should be dubbed puritanical. After all, within the marriage bond sex might be really enjoyed. This contrasts with the typical puritanical attitude that reluctantly permits sex for the sake of procreation but finds its enjoyment a bad thing.

Let us carry this argument a step farther. For Israel a regular married life and the stern duties of a soldierly existence seemed incompatible. The newly married got a year's leave of service to enjoy the pleasures of marriage [261]. David's general Uriah, when called back by his king from a siege, flatly refused to sleep with his wife : "What, all Judah and all Israel are encamped in tents ... and sleep on the hard ground; should I go home, and eat, and drink, and bed with my wife?" [262]. But there is a still more important incomptability : a man who comes into contact with certain forms of sexuality, however lawful or natural, makes himself unfit to participate in cultic performances. Normally this does not apply to sexual intercourse in marriage. However, when the people made ready to appear before Jahve at the foot of the Sinai, Moses told them to abstain from their wives [263]. Spontaneous sexual events, like nightly pollutions and menstruation made 'unclean'; touching a woman in her period, even touching her garments or sitting on her stool or her saddle, made a person unclean for day; sleeping with such a woman made him unclean for a whole week. She was, so to speak, contagious [264].

Now being unclean does not mean being morally impure or in a state of sin. It means that one is temporarily cut off from participating in cultic celebrations. To modern irreligious people this does not present a problem but for an Israelite it really was a catastrophe. The common cult was the centre of the life of the people, of every family, and of the individual believer. Imagine the father of the family not taking his accustomed place at head of the sabbatical meal! Most of the time it was, however, easy enough to become purified; usually taking a bath sufficed. But exclusion from the ritual proves that sexual occurences of this kind were taken very seriously indeed, even although they were not associated with moral guilt. Modern people will wonder why events like pollution or menstruation were viewed so negatively; aren't they, after all, wholly spontaneous or purely physical? The law-abiding Israelite would not have denied this. He would have urged, however, that it is just their uncontrollable and disorderly character that makes them dangerous. They are alarming manifestations of the wild forces of nature that threaten to carry man away.

i. The anthropological kernel of the question

We now reach the anthropological kernel of the question. How or when did human sexuality originate? Or to put it in other words, was there sex in Paradise? Some people hold that, without sex, it would not have been paradise. There are, or there have been, exegetes who believe that the first sin was a sexual one; the first human beings 'discovered' sexual intercourse. Now, apart from the fact that the text of Gen. 3 does not give the slightest indication of this, apart also from the fact that the woman sins first and alone, this theory would conflict with the attitude the Old Testament takes with regard to sexuality and procreation. After all, the first two human beings were a married couple. So what could be wrong with sexual intercourse?

But, perhaps, this is not all there is to it. We have heard that the first human beings, although naked, were not ashamed of one another. That they were anatomically different did not confuse them; it was self-evident and self-explanatory. There is no mention of sex in either of the creation stories. God orders man to procreate himself but does not specify how. Although the genital zone is fully exposed, attention is, nevertheless, drawn away from it. This is a very curious thing for most of the other myths of creation are built on genital sexuality and frequently abound in crude details. There is nothing of the kind here. This is, of course, no accident; it is obviously intended. Israel wanted a 'clean' creation report. The very first mention of human sexuality only comes after the expulsion from the Garden. "The man had knowledge of his wife, Eve, and she conceived" [265].

There is, however, a connecting link between this event and the 'sexless' creation stories. Immediately after the Fall, "the eyes of both were opened, and they became aware of their nakedness; so they sewed fig-leaves together, and made themselves girdles" [266]. The first result of their new insight was that they became 'ashamed' of one another. That they were anatomically different made them confused; they tried to escape from this by covering their genital zones. This is accentuated by the fact that their girdles consisted of fig-leaves. The Hebrew word for 'fig' ('te'enah') reminded an Israelite of 'rut' = 'ta'anah'; similarity of name meant similarity of nature.

Everything taken together it seems to me that there is a very slight suggestion in the text that, before the Fall, man was innocent of his sexuality. Or should we rather say that the first man and woman were innocent of their genital difference? Nevertheless, there was marriage, divinely instituted; there was the injunction to procreate, to multiply. This was told them in Paradise before the Fall. So we must assume that God wanted man to produce offspring, even in his original human condition. But this does not necessarily mean that these children would be conceived in what we call the usual way.

Of course, speculating on another way of procreating would soon lead to sheer phantasy. We should not forget, however, that nature knows a very great number of procreation-systems many of which are a-sexual. For us, as fundamentally sexual beings, it is well-nigh impossible to imagine a totally different manner of mating and producing offspring. And yet it is not quite unimaginable. In his charming science-fiction movie 'Barbarella', with Jane Fonda in the title-part, the director, Roger Vadim, wholly does away with sex - mirabile dictu in a modern film. It is replaced by a clean ritual of hand-pressing during which curious clucking sounds are produced.

In this age of sex revolutions, one hesitates to suggest that sex need not always be the source of unmixed blessings. Were one to do so, one would doubtless be classified as a Victorian and a prude. Let me, therefore, start with quoting somebody who is a real paragon of modernity, Julian Huxley, the first president of UNESCO. "Why is sex both an inspiring blessing and a primal curse, inflicting guilt as well as joy", he asks [267]. I am certainly not going so far as this author since, in my view, sex is not 'a primal curse'. But neither is it a wholly obvious and natural thing. Let us examine this matter in some detail.

How is it possible that human sexuality so often causes endless misery and leads to exploitation, illness, and even death? Is it not true that wrongly used sexuality occurs on a far larger scale than any other falsely directed human capacity? If sex is 'only natural', purely biological, or simply human, why then do almost all people treat it as a 'tremendum'? Why is life-giving sex so often linked with Death, why is coition called 'la petite mort', why is 'omne animal post coitum triste'? Why is genital sexuality such a cumbersome and complicated thing, why are the results so uncertain (children when we do not want them, no children when we fervently wish to have one)? Why are the consequences of this apparently so simple activity so laborious and irritating : a long pregnancy, a painful confinement, great risks for mother and child, and the care of a helpless young being for a great many years? Why - and this is an highly important anthropological question - are the same organs used for sexual intercourse as for the emptying of the bladder? Finally, and this is the decisive question, why is there, in this respect, no difference between human beings and mammals?

Here Genesis suggests some sort of an answer - an answer that, at the same time, is of the greatest significance for the main theme of my work. This suggestion is that the present form of human (genital) sexuality is something secondary, dating from after the Fall. The consequences of this are twofold. First of all, this means that it fits badly into human existence, and may easily occasion a certain measure of disorder. Man's control of it is not complete; he likes it but also fears it, since it is a wild force of nature. Secondly, it means that human sexuality has to share in the consequences of the Fall. True enough, it is the godgiven instrument to reproduce mankind; at the same time it is an expression of love and of the most intimate unity. But it is also connected with the blackest sides of human nature, with abasement, misery, and death.

It is time now to reach a conclusion. Genesis, in fact the whole Old Testament, starts from the premise that there is a rift between man and his sexuality; he therefore finds himself at a certain distance from it. The rift is not wide, the distance is not great, there is no question of an opposition, let alone of a dualism. On the other hand, there is no complete harmony; man is not really identical with his own sexuality. Starting from this premise, it would not prove difficult to develop utterly dualistic sex-theories and -attitudes, even resulting in a total rejection of sex. In the course of world-history this has happened often enough; more often than not the adherents of these theories appealed to the Bible, sometimes to find in it the arguments they need, and sometimes to reject indignantly its injunction to be fertile and to multiply. Many modern people are convinced that the Old Testament is wholly inimical to sex and to erotic enjoyment. This too shows how easy it would be to widen that distance between man and his sexuality enormously, so much so that even the biblical attitude is presented as dualistic.

j. Why there are men and women

The Old Testament portrays the situation of women - which was not always enviable - also against the background of the original conditio humana. In Gen. 1-3 man and woman are created absolutely equal. The first story offers no problem in this respect. God created man and woman equally 'in his image'. They are blessed together; in fact, God marries them and orders the couple to increase and multiply. We are confronted here with an intriguing question : why is it that there must be men and women? The Dutch scholar Buytendijk opens his famous book on 'The Woman' with the disheartening communication that no discipline has up to now succeeded in explaining why there is a man-woman differentiation in humanity [268]. The apparently so simple answer that otherwise there would be no offspring is not valid because, as I have said already, nature knows many reproduction-systems. With regard to our theme this question is highly relevant since it is not inconceivable that the sex differentiation is one of the great sources of dualistic tendencies. The fundamental notion that man and woman are basically different may give rise to a general sentiment that 'opposedness' is the real tenor of this world.

The answer Genesis gives is that the male-female distinction exists because of the image of God. This means that the origin of this distinction is hidden in God. Although the Bible never expatiates on this mystery, one thing is clear : there exists a kind of structure in God, he is a unity in diversity. This diversity bears some resemblance to the human sexual differentiation. Or, if we stick to our thesis that God is not anthropomorph but that man is theomorph, the human male-female structure is in some ways analogous to a similar structure in God. Now, since in biblical theology, God is pure spirit, there can be no question of masculinity or feminity in him.

The similarity of both structures does not, of course, apply to human anatomy, to the famous 'petite différence' - since this is not found in God -, but to the specifically human side of the anatomical divergency. This is also the reason why, compared to the passage about the origination of man, the creation of the animals is told much more soberly. God also gives them his blessing, and orders them to multiply. But their anatomical diversity is not mentioned nor is it said that they are created 'in the image of God'. Here again, image and the male-female structure belong together but now in the sense of a negation. Israel obviously found it a biologically self-evident fact that there is masculinity and femininity in animals. But with them it is simply and solely a reproduction-system, and no more.

Yet another point must be made in this connection. If God is the origin of masculinity or femininity in man, he is also the ground of their unity. In Plato's 'The Banquet' the play-wright Aristophanes is speculating on the origin of our sexual diversity. He lightheartedly advances the theory that 'man-woman' originally was a unity, 'in form no less than in name', one biologically complete person, that is, with two backs, four legs and arms, with two sets of private members, but with only one head, albeit with two faces. But then the gods became jealous and sliced these persons into two. The sexual urge means that they still long for their original unity [269].

How very different the explanation of the Book of Genesis is! Man and woman are not one being originally but are created different by a loving creative deed of God. They are not nor ever shall be one person. Their humanity will never be complete. Surely human beings long for unity, but not for a unity that was lost. That they are not complete must not seduce them to find this bond of unity in themselves but in God in whom all aspects and forms of the created world are unified. The specifically human side of sexual love is that by means of it man and woman become 'one flesh' [270]. In Hebrew parlance this means that they, by their sexual union, become basically one in this sense that they share one common existence.

On the face of it, the second creation story, in Gen. 2, by J, seems to present a difficulty. Here the creation of man and woman is told in a different way. God creates the male first. In this passage he is acting in a more workmanlike manner, like a potter who fashions a human figure out of wet clay on his potter's wheel. God then breathes the breath of life into the clay figure, and in doing so makes it into a human being of the male sex [271]. The new creature obviously feels himself very much alone; therefore, God resolves to give him a companion. Among the animals, however, man cannot discover a companion who is worthy of him [272]. God now takes a rib from the sleeping male and fashions it into a woman. Awaking, the man at last recognizes the mate he wanted and jubilantly welcomes her [273].

The gist of this story is exactly the same as that of Gen. 1 (by P) : man and woman are absolutely equal in spite of the fact that first the male is created, then the animals, and only then the female. The author chooses this sequence in order to stress his point. It is made abundantly clear that man's equal companion is not to be found among the animals (that, like him, are fashioned from clay). Next, he gives to each of them its proper name [274]. Namegiving means subjection, taking possession of, making something or someone your own.

That God allows the first human being to do this implies that man is destined to administer the earthly estate. It is only in the female that he finds his equal. This is proved by the triumphant cry : "She at last is flesh of my own flesh, and bone of my bone" [275]. This means : she is wholly like me. I always like thinking that he found her extremely beautiful too. True enough, he gives her too a name, but this time it is his own name 'ish' = male, which applied to the woman in the feminine form becomes 'issha'. In doing so he expresses the fundamental notion that man and woman belong to one another, as equal parts of the same union. This occasioned Luther, in his famous German translation of the Bible, to render 'issha' faithfully by 'Mennin' [276].

But what about this rib? Was not the woman created from a man's rib? Doesn't this mean that she is essentially inferior being fashioned as she is from an (apparently superfluous) part of the male body? However, it is often overlooked that the origin of the male is far humbler. He is made from dust, the dust of the dry steppe that is made mouldable by means of spring-water [277]. It is for this reason that he (later) is called 'Adam', for this word reminded an Israelite of 'adamah' = the surface of the earth, from which the male was made. Furthermore, he is created outside the Garden, and then brought by God into it. It is God who presents him with the Garden [278].

The woman, on the other hand, is created in the Garden. She is, so to speak, not an hired manager, like her husband, but a born citizen of Paradise. She is given to the man as a paradisiacal present, and this she will always remain, in spite of the Fall. Her origin is nobler than that of the male for she is made not of dust but of human stock. The choice of a rib is probably related to the idea that it must be a part of the body that is very near to the heart. Of course, the Jahvist had not the slightest intention of giving a lesson in biology. If anyone were to believe that he is in the presence of a crudely primitive attempt to explain the origin of sexual differentiation, verse 21 should be pointed out to him or her. The man is lying in a deep sleep throughout the whole operation. He does not know what is happening but only experiences the happy result. This means that, regarding the man-woman structure, we are in the presence of a mystery, of a divine secret into which man must not probe.

k. Man and woman as 'Adam and Eve'

Doesn't the story of the Fall utterly destroy this optimistic picture? Doesn't Gen. 3 contain a weak spot? Isn't it the woman who sins first, since she, the feebler one, is more open to seduction? Isn't she even portrayed here as a seductress herself, as the 'femme fatale'? The serpent who knew that the first fruit of sin would be Death, chose the woman as his first target because she is the source of life; through her he would deliver the cruellest blow against mankind. She does not give in out of vanity or stupidity, or because of her weakness, but because she wanted insight; she desires 'to know good and evil' [279]. Her husband only plays a secondary role. "She gave some of the fruit to him and he ate with her" [280]. This is certainly not the great scene in which an unsuspecting male is seduced by the arts and wiles of a woman.

Anyhow, this is the last time that man and woman act in the greatest harmony. That their fundamental unity is broken becomes evident as soon as God calls them to account. The man then accuses his wife for what has happened, not omitting to lay part of the blame on God himself : "This woman you gave me, she it was who offered the fruit to me" [281]. Here the first rift between male and female becomes discernible; guilt is driving them asunder. This new divergence between the sexes, ensuing from the Fall, is further developed in God's judgment over them. The man, cast into the role of a farmer, will have to toil heavily. "Through your act the ground is under a curse". However hard he will work, he will harvest hardly more than 'thorns and thistles'. And after a long life of toil he will go back to that same ground - adam of the adamah - from which he was taken.

The judgment over the woman is of a somewhat different character. She is not hit in her work but in her body. Long and arduous will henceforward be the time of her pregnancy; with pangs she will give birth to her children. It is precisely as the source of life that she will suffer. But there is more. She falls back to a secondary position; there is no longer an ideal equality. "You shall be subject to your husband but, nevertheless, you will desire him" [282]. This means that the autonomy the woman looked for is ironically turned into dependence. With this the Jahvist does not mean that the inferior position of women had to be the rule or was a Godgiven situation. On the contrary, it is just the reverse of ideal; as the factual situation it is, it must be seen as a consequence of the Fall.

However, in this same passage something is said of the woman which is not said of the man. Speaking to the serpent God says that he will create a feud between him and the woman, between his seed and hers; she is to crush his head, while he will lie in ambush at her heels [283]. This is a mysterious text; understandably enough there are different interpretations of it. In Christian theology the Virgin Mary is often seen as 'the woman', and Jesus as 'her seed'. But one thing is certain. In the perpetual battle against 'the serpent' = evil, the final victory goes to the woman, not to the man. In this respect, the woman remains what she was intended to be, the source of life.

Immediately after God has finished pronouncing his judgment over serpent, man and woman, the man gives his wife a name. This time it is 'chawwah' = Eve, "because she became the mother of all who live" [284]. Whether or not this text is a later insertion into the text of Gen. 3, it is a remarkable passage since the woman is provided with a name of her own here, whereas the man is still nameless. 'Adam' as a proper name does not occur before Gen. 4:25; there for the very first time it is written without an article. At that point the story of Cain and Abel has already been told, and the pedigree of Cain has been given. Therefore, it then became necessary to distinguish 'the man' = ha adam, from other people. It deserves attention that Eve receives her new name while still in Paradise (albeit it after the Fall), whereas 'Adam' changes from an appellative into a proper name only when the consequences of the Fall are being painfully experienced.

Thus the names 'Adam and Eve', although those of a couple, suggest certain distinctions. De Fraine, for one, supposes that in the name 'mother of all who live' there is an implicit reference to the hereditary character of the punishments [285]. In that case, 'Adam and Eve' would stand, collectively, for all mankind. Modern individualism may tend to find this unpalatable but to the communal sentiment of the ancients it was wholly acceptable. All the same, the fact remains that Eve alone, rather than 'Adam and Eve', is presented as the collective ancestor. Verse 20 seems to say that, for better and worse, whatever has happened and yet will happen, mankind will always remain a unity, and that the source of this unity will be the woman, the maternal womb. Of course, this title of Eve reminds us of Mother Earth who, in ancient thought, also is a mother 'of all that lives'. That this is not a far flung idea is proved by this remarkable biblical text : "Great is the anxiety all men are doomed to, heavy is the yoke each son of Adam must bear, from the day he leaves his mother's womb to the day that he is buried in the earth, that is the mother of all" [286]. Here the two wombs, that of one's mother, and that of Mother Earth, are given as havens, but between these two states man, the child of Adam, is a prey to anxiety.

The distinction between man and woman that is suggested here is expressed as follows by the Dutch author Boelie van Leeuwen : "By our mother we are part of the material world. But by our father we are part of heaven ..., he is the bridge between terrestrial man and his heavenly Father" [287]. Van Leeuwen does not imply that women represent only the material side of life, whereas it is the male who makes spiritual life possible. Everyday experience often proves the exact opposite. What Van Leeuwen really intends to say is that the female sex safeguards the principle of life. Women are at life's origin, they tend and foster it and guard it in all its stages. This really is a great mystery that is entirely entrusted to women, a mystery they understand but which is closed to the male. Current feminist ideology tends to lose sight of the fact that this is a very great privilege which is entirely the preserve of women; man possesses nothing of this kind.

True enough, man also plays an important part in reproduction. But its existential impact on him is not great. More often than not he has no idea of the particular moment when he fathered his child. Anyhow, as soon as there is conception the whole process is beyond him; he has absolutely no part in it. His consort, on the other hand, is inextricably involved; it is an essential part of her life. During the long months of pregnancy and the years of caring for the little one, it is, indeed, synonymous with her life.

An aphorism by the French philosopher George Roditi bears out the truth of Van Leeuwen's saying. "The woman did not acquire the high place that Adam assigns to her in spite of her delayed birth, but precisely because of this delay : she belongs to a second period of life - first the aggressive instincts, first conquest, after that care and preservation. When the male principle is born, the female principle later intervenes and gives a judgment on appeal. Man undertakes, builds, destroys, squanders; woman may acquiesce in this, or she calls him to a halt" [288]. Roditi, of course, means to say that the two principles are complementary. Nevertheless, complementary or not, there is also a clear distinction between them, even an opposedness. We are entitled here to speak of a duality of man and woman. And every duality may, under certain circumstances, develop into a dualism.

1. A prey to anxiety

Man has nothing to compare with the essential female function. "The whole growth and mystery of life was hidden within the female body ... The female was intimately connected with the vast mysterious planetary cycle (we know that the menstruation cycle has the same duration as that of the moon phases - F.). Her very body, like the tide of the sea, was in harmony with all moving things. When we worship a woman, therefore, we bow to the particle of great creating nature which she represents" [289]. This is a biblical notion too, for in the Song of Songs the lover constantly borrows images from nature in order to describe his beloved, and the girl calls herself 'his garden' [290]. But, the author I am quoting, A.N.Wilson, goes on, "the man's body was out of joint with the stars and the moon and wandered upon the earth as a stranger". It is for this reason that a son of Adam is a prey to anxiety.

However true it may be that the male keeps open the line from earth to heaven, in the light of the foregoing passage this looks as though it is a compensation for something else. Only very hard work is his prospect, earning his bread with the sweat of his brow, and at the same time harvesting little more than weeds [291]. This conjures up before our eyes a picture that is very near to that of Death : the Palestinian peasant, with his back nearly broken, standing deadly tired on his dried-out plot covered with stones and overgrown with weeds. Isn't this the exact opposite of being the source of all that lives? If I had to define the difference between man and woman - as it is so subtly presented by the Book of Genesis -, I would do it in the following way. If we were to draw a line between life and death, and if we were to situate male and female along this line, we should then find women somewhat more turned towards life, and men somewhat more towards death. This is, of course, not to say that all men are (potential) murderers out to crush life where they find it, nor that all women are the most tender guardians of all forms of life. Again, experience sometimes teaches us the reverse.

It should, however, not escape our attention that, in the history of this world, soldiers always and everywhere are males. Even when, as it is the case in some countries at the present day, women are liable to military service, they are not to be found in the frontline and in the trenches. The actual fighting is exlusively done by the men. The only instance of female soldiers is that of the Amazons in Greek mythology; this is presented to us by means of myth, as is so often the case, as a purely hypothetical eventuality. Now suppose that women really were soldiers, what would happen then? This is the question put to us by the Amazon myth. There is a general consensus among mankind that, when the men march out to fight, to bruise, to kill, the women have to stay at home and tend what remains of life. To be sure, women may be just as war-minded as men; "in women too the war-god lives", says Sophocles [292]. But when all is said and done, they don't rush at enemy-trenches through murderous machinegun fire with the bayonet fixed on rifle-barrels.

Perhaps some anthropologist will refute me but as far as I know burials are the work of men, and of men alone. Women may lay out the corpse, but it is, so to speak, disposed of by the males. I have never seen or heard of female undertakers; in many cultures the women stay at home while the men bring the deceased to his last resting-place. Only a few weeks ago I was at Konya in Turkey, one of the holy cities of Islam, where some of our party witnessed a burial. The cemetery was thronged with men who passed the coffin over their heads, as though each one of them wanted to touch it. But there was not one woman in sight! And isn't it remarkable too that there are no female butchers? True enough, we find shop-girls in butcher's shops, but the real business of slaughtering in the slaughter-houses is done exclusively by men. The Chilean novelist Isable Allende once spoke of a pork-butcher who "was born with a talent for killing, a rare capacity that is very seldom found in women" [293].

It is a conspicuous fact that in the Old Testament there are no women-priests. This does not constitute discrimination against the female sex. On the contrary, I am rather inclined to view the adjucation of the priesthood to the males as a kind of compensation for the fact that their part in the procreation process is so exiguous. In fact, nowhere are women expressly forbidden to be priests; although other ancient religions recognized female priests, from the earliest times it seems to have been self-evident in Israel that men alone could enlist the ranks of the priesthood. Traditionally, the exercise of ritual functions was entrusted to members of the tribe of Levi; priesthood in Israel was hereditary, transmitted by 'Aaron and his sons' to their posterity. This means that it was passed on along the male line [294].

Now the functions of an Israelite priest were manifold but an elementary and time-consuming part of their work was the performing of sacrifices. In Israel these were multifarious; all kinds of natural products and animals were offered to the Lord. Apart from the drink offerings that went along with the sacrificial meals, there were mainly two kinds of oblations : meal offerings and animal offerings. The meal offerings consisted of cakes and wafers made of unleavened flour and olive oil (the still popular 'matzos'); they were often given by private persons for private reasons, especially by the poor who could not afford an animal. Part of the offering was placed on the altar where it was burnt; the rest belonged to the priest who, with his family, must live off the altar [295].

Then there were animal offerings; the blood of the slaughtered animals was sprinkled around the altar and was supposed to effect atonement [296] as 'blood for the purgation of your souls' [297]. The sacrificial service was, therefore, a bloody affair; the altars and the ground around them must have been constantly besmeared and drenched with blood. I do not mean to say anything depreciatory if I say that the priests were permanently engaged in the work of a butcher. The so-called peace offerings served to restore peaceful communication with God; in them animals of both sexes (but no birds) might be used. A portion of these offerings was burnt on the altar, while another part was destined for the priest and his family; the rest was eaten by the suppliant and his kin in the sanctuary [298]. In the sin offerings, on the other hand, nothing was eaten by the suppliant. Their purpose was to atone for transgressions of the law; even when the transgression occurred wholly by inadvertence guilt was incurred. In some cases part of the flesh was burnt on the altar, the rest belonging to the priests; in others, all of it was burnt outside the sanctuary. Birds (doves) and she-goats and -lambs were used. But often an animal of the male sex (lamb, ram, or bullock) was expressly prescribed [299].

The most important sacifices were the so-called burnt offerings. These were the most purely religious of them all, since the supliant saw them as an act of total self-dedication to God. It is characteristic of this kind of offering that no part of it was eaten, either by the priests or by the suppliant; the totality of the self-dedication was expressed by the wholesale burning of the animal. Sometimes doves and pigeons were immolated, probably by the poor. But obviously the preference fell on cattle or on goats and sheep. These had to be exclusively male, bullock, ram, or he-goat [300].

Reviewing our results we can state that all offerings were consumed or destroyed; nothing was left of them. The usual way to destroy them was by means of fire. When animals were offered the sacrificial ritual was a bloody thing; the precincts of the temple would have reminded one of a public slaughter-house. This went on day after day, from morning to evening. This again is not said in a depreciatory vein. Furthermore, there is the fact that all the more important sacrifices, and all the sacrifices for special cases, were deployed with male animals. The Israelite sacrificial service was an almost exclusively male affair; the priestly performers were male, the principal sacrificial beasts were masculine. Perhaps it will now be understood that there was a very profound anthropological reason to keep women completely out of this.

But there is still more. It is well-known that firstborn sons occupied a privileged place in Israelite families. Such a son was destined to become the head of the family; he was to receive a double share of his father's inheritance [301]. In Canaan the attitude to the firstborn sons was similar; only the Canaanites sometimes sacrificed these sons to their fertility gods in order to win their favour. They believed that they had to prove themselves generous and should, therefore, offer the best they had. It is highly improbable that this cruel custom also existed in Israel. At the same time it was taken for granted that Jahve was equally entitled to the best the Israelites had. But human sacrifices were forbidden to them; they found them repellent. Instead, they ransomed their firstborn sons by offering an animal in payment [302]. More generally, the whole tribe of Levi was seen as the substitute for the firstborn, a tribe that was, as Jahve said, 'to be my own' [303]. Set apart as the Levites were, they were entrusted with the care of the sanctuary [304]. The firstlings of all animals also belonged to Jahve [305]. Those of clean animals were sacrificed; unclean ones could not be offered. Either their neck was broken, or they had to be replaced by a sheep [306].

What deserves our attention in all this is that the firstlings mentioned, whether human or animal, are male; no firstborn girl had to be bought off, no feminine animal was killed. Does this mean that the worth of those of the female gender is so much less than that of the male that no price has to be paid for their lives? Here again I believe that the real anthropological reason for this distinction is of a totally different order. It is that the existential position of women, 'the mothers of all that live', is much more secure than that of men. Over men the shadow of Death is always hovering; the stench of blood is continually on them. The act of redeeming the firstborn son, the future prop and mainstay of the family, serves to solidify, by a ritual act invoking divine assent, the basically insecure position of the males. The motivation given for the redeeming of the firstlings is revealing in this respect. The firstborn sons had to be dedicated to Jahve because he slew all the firstborn of Egypt on the night of the exodus [307]. This ordeal was warded off from the children of Israel because they sprinkled their doorways and lintels with the blood of the paschal lamb (which had to be male) [308]. Once again we find the same connection between firstborn sons, blood, and death.

At this point I must draw the attention of the reader to a curious passage in Gen. 2 that is usually somewhat overlooked since it seems only to be said in passing. "That is why man is destined to leave father and mother, and cling to his wife instead, so that the two become one flesh" [309]. This passage is a comment by the author, the Jahvist, on the second creation story. It struck me that the first half of it - 'the male leaving his parents' - seems to hit the blind spot of commentators and scriptural theologians. They gloss it over in silence, or they treat it as if it were said of the couple rather than of the husband alone. The old explanation that this passage could be a survival of an older matriarchal society is rejected nowadays. Since the learned commentators obviously are at a loss over Gen. 3:24a, I venture my own explanation.

The deeper meaning of this passage is, in my opinion, that the existential position of the male is more insecure and more unstable than that of the female. He is more apprehensive for his safety than a woman and tends, therefore, to cling to a situation that he is familiar with, that of the parental home - a situation, that is, in which he is not yet fully responsible. Although he knows that the married state is his natural destiny, this prospect, nevertheless, makes him feel somewhat uneasy since he then will be the responsible head of a family and will have to cope with unexpected and unpleasant occurrences. It is for this reason that he needs an express command to leave his familiar, and, at the same time, somewhat infantile surroundings. A woman is in no need of this incitement since the care of her husband and children comes far more naturally to her, although she is running far greater risks - death in childbed for instance - than he does.

m. 'The joy of Israel'

This leads me to another point. Our enquiry into Greek literature and philosophy, in Volumes II and III, yielded the conclusion that more often than not women are depreciated by Greek authors and are generally considered by them as an inferior race. In the Old Testament there is nothing of the kind. True enough, there are some quips on quarrelsome or snappy women, but far more numerous are the sneers on ambitious greedy, avaricious, gluttonous, cruel, overbearing, foolish, godless, etcetera males! I ask myself whether, in general, men really have a better press in the Old Testament than women. There is hardly a man, beginning with Adam, without some flaw. Perhaps Abraham is the best of them all, in all his silent obedience to Jahve. Probably he serves as the background against which the others are portrayed. Jacob is a shade or two too cunning; even the great Moses is not without his defects, for he is not only violent (in his hot temper he kills an Egyptian) [310], he later even disbelieves Jahve, for which he is punished [311]. Samson's enormous physical strength is greatly extolled but he is weak as water in the hands of a woman.

In the inscriptions of all surrounding countries kings are always highly praised; often they are described as divine beings. But in Israel kings are severly criticised; there is hardly a king who can stand the test. Solomon, to cite only one instance, is the wisest man on earth but, nevertheless, at the end of his life he is led astray by his countless concubines. Even one of the greatest in Israel, as well as in the history of religions, David, is not spared. It is related in unsparing detail how he seduced the wife of his general Uriah, and, still worse, how he deliberately planned the death of this faithful servant of his. And notwithstanding the fact that he was a great military leader who made the country safe by his resounding victories, he had to tell his son Solomon that God did not choose him to build the great temple. "Blood you have spilt in rivers, and wars you have waged a many; not for you to build me a house, you that have come for me with so much blood on your hands" [312]. More than anything else this makes it clear that the Old Testament fundamentally disapproves of male violence.

In complete contrast to this, Scripture shows us quite a number of women with flawless characters. In Judges we read of Deborah, a kind of Israelite Jeanne d'Arc, who, by her military prowess, enabled Barak to defeat Israel's enemies. "And so for forty years the land was at peace" [313]. Sometimes such women are as violent as the men; the strongfisted Jahel, for instance, who killed the Canaanite king Sisara with her own hands in her tent [314], is a good example of this. But the great woman stouter of heart than the men is, of course, Judith, to whom a whole book in the Bible is devoted. She, 'the joy of Israel', is a curious mixture of masculinity and femininity. When her father-city Bethulia is besieged by the Assyrians, and when the leaders of the town are on the verge of capitulating, this pious widow, with one (female) servant only, leaves the town and descends to the enemy camp. Since she is a highly attractive woman and since she has decked herself out as beautifully as possible, she is received in the most welcoming way and conducted to the tent of the commander-in-chief, Holofernes. This man immediately becomes enamoured of her and takes all possible precautions in order to remain alone with her. But he makes the mistake of getting dead drunk, and when he drops down on his bed, Judith chops off his head with the scimitar she had brought. The gist of this gripping story is, of course, that, in this great emergency in which all Israel was fatally threatened, deliverance was brought by means of a weak, defenceless woman (a widow), while all the men felt utterly helpless.

A non-violent story is that of Esther, the beautiful Israelite girl, who became the concubine of a Persian king, and succeeded, by her influence over him, in averting the wholesale destruction of the Jewish people that was planned by its enemies. Aetiologically this story serves as the explanation of the origin of the Purim feast. But what interests us here is that again a defenceless woman causes the salvation of Israel. Her uncle and guardian Mordechai is aware of this : "Who knows, but you have reached the throne only to be ready for such an opportunity as this?" [315]. Esther herself realizes what a great risk she is taking : "I will break the law by appearing in the king's presence unsummoned, though I must die for it" [316].

Then there is Ruth. To this modest Moabite girl one of the smallest books of the Bible - a kind of short story - is devoted. Like her sister she was married to an Israelite, but he as well as her sister's husband died in Moab; then their mother-in-law, Noemi, decided to return to Bethlehem whence she came. One of her daughters-in-law preferred to stay in Moab but the other, Ruth, accompanied her. In Bethlehem Ruth won the favour of an important townsman, Booz, who was deeply struck not so much by her beauty as rather by her fidelity to her mother-in-law. He married her, and thus she became the greatgrandmother of David, and, thereby, an ancestor of Jesus. She is presented in this story as a shining example of piety. Whereas her sister prefers to stay 'with her own people and the gods they worship', Ruth states that "your (Noemi's) people is my people, your God is my God" [317]. This is all the more remarkable since she is originally a pagan girl, even a Moabite, and Moabites were held in very low esteem by Israel.

In my opinion, what Israel thought of women is magnificently summed up in the great panegyric at the end of the Book of Proverbs. It sings the praise of the housewife and mother. She is portrayed as energetic, untiring, always caring for the members of her household, kindly and hospitable, goodhumoured and sensible. She is a gem for her husband who is loud in her praise [318]. For she is not only a model of femininity, she is also, and perhaps more, a paragon of perfect humanity, and as such she is held up to the men.

n. Why God is male

In this context a very thorny question must also be broached, that of the supposed masculinity of God. This is at present a favourite subject of feminist theology. This often contends that the fact that, in the Bible, God is exclusively pictured as male, is the ultimate cause of male domination over women. Now I am not going to argue with feminist theology. I am quite sure that women in general, not just feminists, have a bone to pick with overbearing and domineering male attitudes. I am equally sure that dominating men, expressly or perhaps more often unconsciously, refer to God's manhood in order to justify their own claim to superiority. To put the matter in terms of my thesis, the masculinity of Jahve may give rise to a dualistic relationship between men and women; actually, this happened often enough.

All this, however, must not make us lose sight of the fact that God, in biblical theology, is neither male nor female. "God I am, not a man (= not human)" [319]. It would be wholly contrary to prophetic insight even to suggest that God might have a physical appearence since he is pure spirit. But that he is neither masculine nor feminine does not mean either that he is 'neuter', an 'it', or a principle or a philosophical idea. In the Bible Jahve is always a person, 'the God of Abraham, Isaac, and Jacob', albeit a person sui generis. Because he is no 'it' and since he is a person, he has to be indicated by a personal pronoun, by 'he' or 'she', that is. This is where the problem starts. Why does the Bible consequently use the masculine pronoun and not the feminine one?

Feminist theology often asserts that this is in accordance with the whole trend of Antiquity : men always and everywhere lorded it over women. And the men who wrote the Old Testament, being the products of this type of civilization, could only imagine a male god as the ruler of all creation. Now we have already seen that in Israel the situation of women was certainly not deplorable. True enough, the husband and father was the one who finally took the decisions but women were not depreciated or considered inferior. Thus there was no compelling necessity to make God exclusively male. It is more to the point that the idea of a female god would have implied for Israel divine sexuality. In all the surrounding religions there were male and female gods, and this always implied sexual relationships. Sexuality, however, ran completely counter to the basic idea of the Jahvistic prophets that God is a purely spiritual being; it was for this reason that the notion of a female god was wholly untenable. This is not since woman was, for Israel, the very picture of lust and desire. But confronted with the religious ideology of the neighbouring nations the prophets had no choice. God had to be masculine.

Still, this is not yet the heart of the matter. If Genesis 1 says that human beings are created male and female 'in the image of God', this means, as I stated already, that the source of manhood and womanhood is to be found in God. People are male and female because of the very nature of God. True enough, God is often pictured as stern and severe but there are also passages in which he is described as tender and caring. This is already the case immediately after the Fall when God makes garments for the first human beings; this means that God would henceforward lovingly care for mankind in its distress. Especially the texts of the Deutero-Isaiah, the book of consolation, bear testimony to Jahve's loving care and motherly tenderness. "Israel, my servant ... I led you by the hand from the ends of the earth, beckoning you from far away, and still I whispered to you ... 'Have no fear, I am with you; do not hesitate, am I not your God? ... It is I, the Lord your God, that hold you by the hand and whisper to you : 'Do not be afraid, I am there to help you. Jacob, poor worm, poor ghost of Israel, do not be afraid' " [320]. Jahve is even more motherly than an earthly mother : "Can a woman forget her child that is still unweaned, pity no longer the son she bore in her womb? Let her forget, but I will not be forgetful of you (Israel)" [321].

Perhaps this feminine side of God is most clearly revealed in Wisdom. True enough, Israel knew a practical wisdom as a natural capatitity that could be developed by education and experience. But there is also a divine wisdom that comes from God; often it is equivalent to 'spirit'. In popular texts and prophetic words alike this wisdom is not human at all but something supernatural that God gives freely to whom he chooses to give it. It is wholly impossible for human beings, even for Israelites, to acquire it by their own exertions. It is a gift of God : "he has poured her (wisdom) on all his creation, upon all living things, upon all the souls that love him, in the measure of his gift to each" 322). This text proves that no man need go without at least some degree of divine wisdom but also that this degree may differ from person to person.

This wisdom is not a part of creation. "From the beginning of time, before the world, he (God) has made me, unfailing to all eternity" 323). "I am the word, she (wisdom) says, that was uttered by the mouth of the Most High, the primal birth before ever creation began" 324). She is God's creative power : "Through me light rose in the heavens ..., none but I might span the sky's vault, pierce the depth of the abyss, walk on the sea's waves; no part of the earth gave a resting-place to my feet" 325). She is the precise counterpart of God, "the glow that radiates from eternal light, the untarnished mirror of God's majesty, the faithful image of his goodness" 326).

Now the decisive point is that this wisdom - this 'chokma' - is feminine. Not only is she constantly referred to as 'she', she is even described as a bride who dwells in God's palace, his favourite, the mistress of his craftmanship 327); she even dwells near God's throne 328). Of course, later religious thinkers, for instance Gnostic ones, were not able to resist the temptation to turn wisdom into a female person, even into a 'paredros' of Jahve. It is, however, wholly inconceivable that such strictly monotheistic writers like the authors of Wisdom and the Book of Jesus Sirach would have been capable of proposing a kind of female God next to Jahve. In the Old Testament 'chokma' is not an individual person but an essential aspect of God, and as such it is feminine.

But if there really exist masculine and feminine, motherly and fatherly aspects of God, this is still no answer to the question why God is consequently portrayed as male in the Old Testament (and in the New). In order to solve this tricky problem we must never forget that the Bible is a story of redemption. Mankind had to be redeemed from the consequences of the Fall, but who would be the redeemer? A female redeemer would be inconceivable for Israel. The idea of redemption by a woman would remind the Israelites irrevocably of temple prostitution in Canaan and Mesopotamia in which visitors of a sanctuary sought liberation and the closest intimacy with the godhead by means of sexual intercourse with a female temple servant or a priestess. For this reason alone the redeemer had to be male. But there is more to it than this.

The Old Testament authors make it abundantly clear that the redemption of mankind would not be an easy process; it would be effectuated through much suffering and pain; as the ultimate expedient even the death of the redeemer would become necessary. This could not be imposed on a woman, not because she was not strong or stalwart enough, but for the basic reason that she always is primarily and essentially the 'mother of all living beings'. It would go against the grain of her being, of her basic function in the world, to bring her into such close contact with death. Furthermore, she is playing her own crucial role in the work of liberation already since she brings forth - not without pain and suffering - new beings dedicated to Jahve. Therefore, the Redeemer had to be male.

A first indication of this is that the animal which, on Yom Kippur, was driven into the desert loaded with the transgressions of Israel, was a he-goat. Then the Deuteroh-Isaiah prophesied the Redeemer in the person of the 'suffering servant of Jahve', who takes upon himself the sins of the people, and is, like a sheep, led away to the slaughter-house [329]. But the most telling incident is Abraham's intended sacrifice of his son Isaac, since this episode directly involves God himself. True enough, the theological implication of this story is that God does not ask mankind to bring him human sacrifices. God tests

Abraham by summoning him to offer his only son Isaac to him. Abraham silently obeys and sets out to the Mountain Moria where the gruesome ritual will take place. At the very last moment Jahve intervenes, forbids him to kill his son, and shows him a ram (a male animal again) to be sacrificed instead of the boy [330].

Christian theology has always considered this passage as a prefiguration of the sacrificial death of Jesus on the Golgotha Mountain. In order to effectuate the redemption of mankind, Christian doctrine says, God did not spare his own, his only son. God, whose relationship with mankind, according to biblical theology, will culminate in its liberation from sin and evil, must necessarily choose the male approach. Perhaps, in order not to suggest that God's freedom is impaired, by using the word 'necessarily', we should rather say that God authorizes the male approach to redemption, the only one that is open to mankind. I believe this authorization to be the fundamental implication of the story of Abraham and Isaac. With regard to redemption, Jahve finds himself, so to speak, siding with the male, since the liberation is only possible by means of death; therefore, he has to be presented as male.

o. Man in his relation to nature

From the viewpoint of biblical anthropology man is not simply 'natural'. He is, indeed, part of nature, as it is proved by his origination from the dust of the steppe. At the same time, however, nature was not able to make him specifically human, for it was God who gave him life, human life, by 'breathing the breath of life into his nostrils' [331] - a thing that God did not do with the animals. That man is more than natural is also proved by God's command that he must cultivate and tend the Garden, and by his namegiving to the animals [332]. This mandate gave him a place of his own in the order of nature, in accordance with the fact that he is the only creature made 'in the image of God'. The Garden is not given to him as his property but he becomes God's 'man of business'; the work he had to do cannot have been exacting, considering the climate and luxuriance of the Garden.

This mandate was not withdrawn as a consequence of the Fall but its execution became more difficult; cultivating and tending the 'adamah' now implied back-breaking toil.

This means that a laborious, if not slightly dualistic, relationship between man and nature came about with the Fall. We might say that, now that the distance between God and man had grown wider, man became even more a part of nature, more 'natural', indeed, than before. However, this close proximity to nature did not make him happier. For nature does not accept him as her own flesh and blood; man always remained somewhat alien to her; he is even somewhat afraid of her. For what she offers him are 'thistles and thorns'.

True enough, God is merciful and he proves this by sustaining mankind by the bounteous gifts of nature. He gives them freely, and he makes the sun shine over the just and unjust equally. The products of nature, of Mother Earth, are available to everyone. At the same time, however, man knows that nature can play very dirty tricks on him; he never can be quite sure that she always will behave tranquilly and benevolently. The Israelites knew that Jahve had effectuated their liberation from Egypt by letting loose all the forces of nature on this country. Israel realized that, although she was able to use the forces of nature to some extent, she would never possess sovereign power over them. "Where were you when I laid the foundations of the earth? ... Was it you or I who shut the sea behind bars?" [333]. It is only by the great mercy of God that the forces of nature do not turn against man : "It is in mercy that I forbear to make Leviathan (the symbol of chaos) a plague for mankind" [334].

Prophetic and apocalyptic texts alike told Israel that the Creator of the world could also become the destroyer of the world. "The Lord means to make the earth a void, a wilderness ... The floodgates of heaven will be opened and the foundations of the world rock" [335]. Texts like these prove that there must have existed a sense of fundamental insecurity; after all, nobody knew whether things would always remain as they seemed to be. This is the kind of feeling modern man experiences when he thinks of the atomic threat; it might suddenly turn against him and destroy him in a final catastrophe.

The wearisome relationship between man and nature is exemplified very clearly by man's attitude to animals. Man still 'gives names' to animals, to his dogs for instance. He also gives names to his cats and his horses and also to other animals. What I mean to say is that he still sees it as his mandate to rule over the creaturely world. In the Garden this meant harmony, a peaceful living together. Medieval painters liked to depict the first human beings surrounded by all kinds of very ferocious but tranquil beasts. In his great prophecy of future peace and harmony Isaiah conjures up this wonderful image : "Wolf shall live at peace with lamb; leopard take its ease with kid; calf and lion and sheep in one dwelling-place, with a little child to herd them. Cattle and bears all at pasture, their young ones lying together; lion eating straw like ox; child new-weaned, fresh from its mother's arms, playing by the asp's hole, putting hand in viper's den" 336).

Doggedly mankind tries to make this prophecy real. We have our domestic animals, we have our pets; even thoroughly urbanized people keep a dog in their three-room flat on the eighth floor. But during the whole course of human history we have only succeeded in domesticating perhaps ten kinds of animals only; by using inexhaustible patience we can tame a few more, mostly for no other purpose than performing tricks in a circus. By far the greater part of the animals happily escape every form of human interference. The utmost we can do is to hunt and catch them.

Our attitude to the animal world is thoroughly ambivalent; it easily becomes dualism - a sort of dualism to which only rarely attention is paid. Perhaps because of being ashamed (for we are in many respects inferior to animals or feel helpless with them) we prefer to ignore it. We are, indeed, animal-lovers but, at the same time, we fear beasts. We may really love certain animals; some people indeed treat them as though they were almost human. Other animals, like snakes, sharks, mosquitoes, or cockroaches, we hate. This ambivalent relationship between the human sphere and the bestial sphere finds an utterly dualistic expression in the fact that we eat animals and that animals eat us. "Man eats the fishes, and the fishes eat us; how is this possible since God blessed them both?", this is what an old fisherman says in a very fine Dutch play [337].

And indeed, in the beginning the case was different. True enough, God gave man command of all living beings, but to this he added a ruling as to what kinds of food should be used. Man might eat all seeding plants (probably mainly cereals are intended) and the fruits of all fruit-bearing trees; the animals were to feed on herbs and grasses [338]. Whatever this text may mean exactly, it seems evident that man and animals were not meant to feed on one another.

After the Flood Jahve reiterates his command to increase and to multiply to Noah and his offspring. But all the animals are now to go in dread of man [339]. Man still must rule over the animal but there is no longer harmony. In the new world-order there is only domination and subjection. This is the consequence of the fact that, before the Flood, the whole earth was full of violence [340]. Henceforward the living and moving part of creation, the animals that is, will serve as food for human beings [341]. There are, however, two restrictions. The blood must not be consumed, for this contains the principle of life, and this belongs to God alone. And secondly, man must keep his hands off his fellow-men for it is expressly repeated that man is created in the image of God [342]. Still, it is does not signify that this reciprocal shedding of blood is to be considered as the normal situation. By no means! Whosoever sheds blood will be held to account for it, whether he be man or beast [343]. This second (and definitive worldorder) is far removed from the first one, that of the Garden, and even from that which was supposed to prevail immediately after the Fall.

p. God's identity

We have now seen that human existence, the 'conditio humana', is not altogether flawless. According to the biblical point of view, the consequence of the Fall is that man is not fully adapted to his surroundings; he has his problems, his existential and incurable problems, with God, his creator, with nature and the animals, with his fellow-beings, and, last but not least, with himself. There are a number of 'loose ends' in his existence - loose ends that never will be tied together. The Bible, however, is not a dualistic book; the cracks and fissures man experiences in the fabric of his life, although they cannot be plastered over, are, nevertheless, still far removed from the hopelessly opposed poles of dualism. Through the whole Bible there runs, when all is said and done, a line to a brighter future.

For the argument of this work two things are of the greatest importance. The first is that human existence is not homogeneous and never will be. The second point is that all of these imperfections can be, and have indeed been, developed into dualistic oppsoitions. Most of all this applies to the distinction between the divine and human modes of existence. At Moses' request Jahve reveals his name, that is to say, his being, his very essence : "I am who (I) am" [344]. There are several modes of rendering this Hebrew text but the essential thing seems to me to be that God reveals himself as the absolute identity, as one who is wholly identical with himself, homogeneous, without shadows and darkness. As the absolute identity God is essentially different from human beings. That his being is not human, not historical, not created, is expressed by the term 'the transcendence of Jahve'. But while the Old Testament time and again stresses this aspect of God, at the same time it is also evident that God is immanent in history, in particular in that of Israel.

However, the idea of the transcendence of God, of his absolute identity, was to mislead later religious thinkers, particularly Gnostics, into stressing the absolute being of God at the expense of his immanence in the world with the result that God becomes unknowable, utterly mysterious, a 'deus ignotus et absconditus'. At this juncture the distinction between divine and human existence becomes authentically dualistic.

What the difference between God and man really means, from an existential point of view, is reflected by another msyterious passage, that in which Jacob wrestles with God. The text informs us that 'somebody' fought with him but it is evident that the person who opposes the patriarch is Jahve. The event takes place at the river Jabbok, a tributary of the Jordan, on the outskirts of the Promised Land, to which Jacob is returning after his fourteen-year stay in Mesopotamia. He has always put his trust mainly in himself and only conditionally in God. Up until now he has relied on his superior slyness to see himself through the difficulties of life, and not without success since it was through cunning that he was able to deceive his father Isaac and his brother Esau. But now, on entering the patrimony of Israel, he is to wrestle with God.

In this struggle he stands his ground well enough. But this nocturnal event - night being the time for mysterious events - changes him profoundly. God tells him that he will be no longer called Jacob but 'Israel'. This means that he now becomes the eponymous ancestor of the Israelite people. There is no consensus among Hebraists as to what 'Israel' may mean but one thing is certain - it contains the name of God (= 'El'). Henceforward Jacob-Israel will be the faithful and unconditional servant of Jahve. There is, however, yet another side to this existential meeting with God. During the fight God touches the hip of Jacob who, from that moment, was to be lame. This 'lameness' signifies that the patriarch has been amputated of a capacity that made him complete in a purely human sense, that is to say, his slyness, his faculty to deceive. He now realizes that a human being standing alone before the face of God is always 'lame'. There is something lacking in our existential make-up. It is not humanly possible to make all the ends meet in life. Confronted with the absolute identity of God man will always stand incomplete [345].

13. Jahve and the king

a. The Gilgal-tradition

In the great historic kingdoms surrounding Israel the ruler was considered either divine himself or the chosen servant of the godhead. Thus in Egypt Pharaoh was a god; in Mesopotamia and in the Persian Empire the kings were the first servants of the gods with special prerogatives. Other peoples, like the Philistines, had a less exalted idea of kingship;

with them kingship was a hereditary political function. Israel's conception of monarchy was utterly different from all this, at least initially. At the end of Moses' great address to his people with which he brought his career to a close and which fills nearly the whole of the Book of Deuteronomy, he told Israel to acknowledge no king other than Jahve. "Our king dwells among us, his favoured people, with the chieftains and all the tribes of Israel assembled around him" [346]. This is the favourite political theory of the prophets which was, eventually, to change Israel into a theocracy. It was for this reason that Gideon refused to be made king by the Israelites who were grateful to him for his victories over the Midianites. "Neither I nor any son of mine shall rule over you; the Lord shall be your ruler" [347].

The same attitude was taken by Samuel, the last of the Judges, in whose opinion too Israel needed no other king than Jahve. This opposition against an earthly form of kingship is sometimes called the 'Gilgal-tradition' - Gilgal (probably near Jericho) being Samuel's favourite place of residence. It is sometimes thought that this prophetic anti-royalist stance cannot have been very strong since Israel was ruled by kings for centuries. However, there always existed a powerful undercurrent of opinion that kingship was incompatible with Moses' original conception of the political organisation of the people.

The initial tribal order was seen as an 'amphictyony', a sacred grouping of the twelve tribes around the sanctuary. This was the place where Jahve could be consulted by the leaders of the people. We find an identical tribal organization around the Apollo-temple at Delphi. However, we need not suppose, as some scholars do, that Israel's sacred tribal order was modelled on the lines of the Hellenic Amphictyony. It is a vexed question whether or not the prophets of Israel who were behind this idea knew anything of the Greek situation. The idea on which this tribal order was built is natural enough since it is based on the numbers three and four. Three is the most sacred (and very probably the oldest) of all sacred numbers; the number four represents the four winds of heaven, that is the whole world. Their product twelve, therefore, represents, exemplifies and comprehends the similarity of the terrestrial and divine orders and the organic connection between them. We find this idea pictured very clearly in Numbers 2. In the desert encampments of Israel the tabernacle tent was placed in the middle; on respectively the eastern, southern, western and northern sides of it (the sequel follows the course of the sun) three tribes were situated. That this notion must have had a strong impact is proved by the fact that Jesus harked back to it by assembling twelve apostles around him (even though since the Babylonian Captivity ten of the twelve tribes no longer existed). Like a second Gideon, he flatly refused to be made king [348]. However, he placed himself in the Gilgal-tradition by declaring to Pilate that he was a king indeed although his kingdom did not belong to this world [349].

b. Theocracy and 'normalcy'

That the original and sacred order of things was to be violated is evinced by the fact that Gideon was succeeded by his son Abimelech - whose name significantly means 'My father is king'. He was able to acquire the dignity of Judge only by murdering his seventy brothers 'over one stone'. Abimelech whom the Book of Judges calls 'king in Israel' had to fight continuously to keep his position. He died ignominiously when trying to force his way into a city where a woman threw part of a millstone on his head. "Thus Jahve punished Abimelech for the wrong he did to his father's name" [350]. This bloody story seems to me the foreshadowing of the history of kingship in Israel, one long relation of division and bloodshed.

There are different traditions as to how Saul became the first real king of Israel (1030-1012). The first of these considers kingship a normal institution approved by God himself. It says that Jahve revealed to Samuel that a certain young man would come to him whom he had to anoint king. Samuel did so and told this young man, Saul, that it was the Lord himself who wanted to have him as the leader of the people. In chapters 9 and 10 (till vs. 16) of Samuel 1 there is not one word of disapproval for the institution of kingship.

The Gilgal-tradition is presented too, for according to this the people approached Samuel asking him for a king. "Give us a king, such as other nations have". Clearly they felt that the loose confederation of tribes, only in times of emergency led by strong leaders called 'Judges', would no longer be able to defend itself against its enemies. Samuel then consults Jahve and is told : "Grant them their wish, it is my rule that they are casting away not yours". He consequently impresses on the people all the nasty things a king would do to them : a monarch will be rapacious and prove to be a tyrant. But all this is to no avail : "A king, we must have a king! We must be like other nations". The (dualistic) difference between the sets of opinion is brought out very clearly here. On the one hand we find the prophetic and theocratic idea of kingship rejected now by the people. Samuel presents Saul to them with these ominous words : "Now you have cast away your God!" [351]. On the other hand, there is an irresistible wish to be just like other nations. The prophets consider this levelling as a downright betrayal of Jahve.

The whole subsequent history of kingship in Israel is treated in the light of this dualistic opposition between theocracy and 'normal' political rule. This last kind of rule is obviously considered basically wrong. The very first king, Saul, has a strong treat of madness in his character; he is an unreliable and violent man. Even the great David is not faultless. His sins with regard to Bathsheba and her husband Uriah are held against him. In his later life there occurs trouble; he has to fight his own son Absalom. Even this deeply religious man proved a bit too 'normal', too down-to-earth, when he wanted to take a census of his people. Counting one's subjects meant, according to ancient opinion, taking possession of them, as if they were the king's own people instead of Jahve's. In consequence, Jahve punished David heavily for this [352].

Of the later kings few find favour with the biblical historiographers. Solomon, however wise he may be, ends in idolatry, the prey of his pagan concubines. Of the rulers of the northern kingdom, Israel, hardly one good word is said. In the royal line of Judah, the southern kingdom, there are a few favourable exceptions, like Hizkiah and Josiah. But the constant refrain is : he defied the will of Jahve, he did what is wrong in the eyes of the Lord, he followed the bad example of his father, and so on. Often the Books of Kings tell us hardly anything of the political history of a reign. The biblical historiographers are obviously not interested in political 'normalcy'; they use another measuring-rod than their modern counterparts. Filled with horror they relate many bloodcurdling scenes of royal cruelties - as though they intended to say : this is what it comes to if you want to be like other nations.

Throughout the centuries the prophets stick to the original idea of Jahve's divine rule. Samuel's precept always remained valid : "The Lord has given you a king. But on this condition, that ... both you and the king follow the guidance of the Lord your God" [353]. As we have already seen, more often than not this condition was not fulfilled : "Kings a many, and with no warrant from me (Jahve)" [354]. The prophet drew the obvious conclusion : "Who but I (Jahve) can aid you? Your king, where is he?" [355]. Again and again Jahve was declared to be the real lawgiver, judge and king of Israel [356]. When, in later centuries, the outlook of Israel widened, Jahve was seen not only as a tribal god but, and even more, as a universal king. "God is king of all the earth ... God reigns over the heathen" [357], "God is king of all the nations" [358]. "Tell the heathen that the Lord is king now", sings the psalmist [359]. In this he is joined by the Deutero-Isaiah : "All shall give God his praise, till the renown of him reaches the islands far away" [360].

14. The antagonism of north and south

a. Precarious unity

In the period after the conquest of Canaan and before Saul became king - roughly between 1200 and 1000 - Israel, as a political entity, was no more than a loose confederation of tribes. Only when the people felt hard pressed by the neighbouring Moabites or the Philistines, for instance, was a common ruler, a Judge, installed. His office was mainly of a military character; it was only temporary and not hereditary. It has been already related how Saul became king; his royal rule had a charismatic origin but was much fortified by his military prowess, in particular against the Philistines. When David succeeded him, his sway extended no further than Judah. The whole north, in fact the greater part of the country, refused to acknowledge the upstart, and remained faithful to Saul's heir, Isboshet [361]. After nearly eight years of continuous strife and fighting, and after Isboshet had been murdered, the north rallied to David who now at last became king over all the tribes [362].

When David conquered one of the last Canaanite enclaves, Jerusalem, he made it into a kind of 'extraterritorial' or 'neutral' city; no specific tribe might claim it as its own property. He then concentrated the cult there, with the Tabernacle (later the Temple), the Ark of the Covenant, and the priesthood. In this way he tried to cement the unity of the tribes by giving them a religious centre that was above all factions. However, the old tribal discord was discernible since David was often called 'king of Judah and Israel', as though two countries were united in his person. The new centralized forms of government that David introduced were not to everybody's liking; the northerners in particular were dissatisfied with them because they felt that these forms impinged on their own time-honoured institutions. At the end of David's reign, when his son Absalom rebelled against him, it was with the support of the greater part of the country and especially of the north. It was only with the greatest difficulty that David succeeded in crushing the rebellion [363].

This painful episode convinced David that his efforts to establish tribal unity had failed; henceforward he found his main support in Judah. It was 'the whole of Judah' that welcomed the king after his victory over the north [364]. Soon enough the northerners became irritated with the king's predilection for Judah. "How is it", they asked, "that our brethren, the men of Judah, have stolen you (David) from us?"[365]. And "there was bitterness between them". This immediately led to a new revolt, this time headed by a certain Sheba, a Saulite, who raised the ominous cry : "David is none of ours; not for us the son of Jesse; go back, men of Israel, to your tents!" [366]. Although David succeeded in suppressing this revolt in its early stages, he fully realized that his united monarchy was dangerously threatened. "This Sheba will do us more harm than ever Absalom did", he sighed [367]. Thus, when David died, it became clear that it would require endless tact to avoid a definitive rupture between north and south.

For a long time King Solomon (ca. 970-928) showed this wisdom. His reign was prosperous and peaceful. But his activities - the building of the Temple, for instance - were expensive, and his hand weighed heavily on the populace. When Solomon was fortifying Jerusalem and constructing the 'Millo', the central part of the new fortifications, Jeroboam, the leader of the corvée workers, 'lifted his hand against him (Solomon)' [368]. Details of this rebellion are not given; Jeroboam soon fled to Egypt where he awaited his chance [369]. The important thing in this context is that a prophet, Ahiah, foretold him that he would become king of the north : "(Jahve) means to wrest the kingship from the power of Solomon and make over ten tribes to you (Jeroboam) ... One tribe (Juda, from which Benjamin hardly could be distinguished) shall remain his". Solomon's idolatrous tendencies were quoted as a reason for this turn-about [370]. In this way the inevitable division of the united kingdom into two was incorporated in the prophetic tradition.

b. Two separate kingdoms

After King Solomon's death, in 928 B.C., Israel as a whole proved ready to accept his son Rehoboam as their king. But when the Israelites expressed the wish that taxation would be reduced, the stupid young fellow gave them a harsh and arrogant answer. This gave Jeroboam, who had returned from Egypt, his long awaited chance. Again the slogan was heard : "Back to your tents, men of Israel! Let David (= the tribes of Juda and Benjamin) look to his own affairs!". Thus the year 928 B.C. became one of the fatal dates in the history of Israel, the year in which the kingdom was split into two separate states, Judah and Israel [371].

During the subsequent centuries there was not much love lost between the two kingdoms. True enough, the notion that the inhabitants of both were descendants of the same Abraham and partook of the same blood, never wholly died away. In many respects the two monarchies were dependent on each other. Nevertheless, there were in this period two separate and sovereign states. The northern king Omri built, ca. 880 B.C., a capital of his own called Samaria, thus renouncing Jerusalem's claim to be the non-tribal capital [372]. Already the first king, Jeroboam, had flouted the Holy City's pretension to be the sole cultic centre. Virtually acting as high priest, he established two new cultic centres in the north, Bethel and Dan, where he set up golden calves and sacrificed to them. And thus 'was great sin caused', says the biblical author [373].

An important difference between Israel and Judah is that in the south there was always a king from the House of David; the line was never broken. In the northern kingdom the dynasty was changed several times; the irregularity of the succession caused very violent events and much bloodshed. The biblical authors have hardly one good word to say of the nineteen kings of Israel. Most of them are depicted as doing 'what was bad in the eyes of Jahve'; the wicked deeds of some of them, like Ahab (875-854), are alluded to vividly. Although the attitude of the historiographers with regard to the twenty kings of Judah is also critical to a degree, the reigns of some of them (Josaphat, Joas, Hizkiah, Josiah) are described in a positive vein.

Finally, it was to be from the royal House of David that the Promised One, the Messiah, would be born, not from one of the northern dynasties. This in particular gave the Davidic dynasty a far more prestigious position than any of the northern royal houses ever possessed; of course, the kingdom and people of Judah also shared in the promised glory of this election. It was the prophet Nathan who foretold David that his dynasty would endure always : "your throne shall remain for ever unshaken" [374]. The very intimate connection between David and his House and the promised Messiah is indicated very clearly by Hosea, about 750 B.C., more than two centuries after David's death. "A long time the sons of Israel must wait, neither king nor prince to rule them, neither sacrifice nor shrine to worship at ... Then they will come back, and to the Lord, their God, betake them, and to David, that is their own true king" [375]. Evidently there is still a 'David' to come. Isaiah makes it clear that this 'David' will be no ordinary king. He tells King Ahaz (735-720) this : "Maid shall be with child, and shall bear a son, that shall be called Emmanuel (= God with us). On butter and honey shall he strife" [376]. Butter and honey are the fare of the gods; they give eternal life. Even Jeremiah who is so fiercely critical of the kings of his days prophesies the coming king as one who will be a king from the stock of David [377].

During the tenth century there was constant warfare between the two kingdoms. "All through Roboam's reign there was war between him and Jeroboam" [378]; such conflicts were to continue without cessation during the following reigns. It was only when Josaphat became king, in 872 B.C., that he and his northern counterpart Omri realized how damaging to both kingdoms this fraternal strife was, surrounded as they were by powerful states. So an alliance was concluded which was cemented by the betrothal of Josaphat's son Jehoram to Omri's daughter Attaliah. A bad consequence of this interstate marriage was that the ambitious Attaliah introduced the Baal cult into Judah; two parties then arose there, the adherents of Jahve and those of Baal. Politically the alliance proved a boon for both kingdoms; sometimes the two kings even campaigned together. Israel, in particular, was now in a far better position to ward off the Moabites and Aram.

After 850 B.C., however, there was a new setback, and then Israel was no longer a match for the growing power of Assyria. At first it seemed that she would be able to breathe more freely since Assyria struck a mortal blow at Damascus, her enemy to the north, and a period of peace and prosperity followed. But in 745 B.C. Tiglath-Pileser III, the great empire-builder, became king of Assyria. By 738 B.C. King Menahem of Israel was paying tribute to him [379]. At this critical juncture his successor, King Pekah, knew of nothing better to do than to besiege Jerusalem (ca. 735 B.C.), with the help of the king of Aram; he even wanted to dethrone the Davidic King Ahaz of Judah and to replace him by a non-Davidic ruler. In this emergency Ahaz appealed to Tiglath-Pileser III; this was not done in vain, for the Assyrian marched on Aram and annexed it (732 B.C.) [380].

In the same year the Assyrian conqueror invaded Israel and annexed Galilee, that is, two-thirds of the kingdom. Pekah was murdered in 732 B.C.; then there was yet another king from yet another family. This king, Osee, tried to get rid of the Asssyrians by asking the help of the Egyptians; his optimistic expectations were much raised by the death of Tiglath-Pileser in 727 B.C. The successor of this king was Shalmaneser V. When this ruler got wind of King Osee's embassy to Egypt, he descended on Samaria and abducted Israel's last king in chains. The city itself valiantly withstood an Assyrian siege for more than two years; it finally fell in 722/721 B.C. It was, however, not Shalmaneser but his successor Sargon who sealed the fate of the northerners once and for all. The population of the province of Samaria was deported to Mesopotamia and Media; the land was resettled with colonists from other parts of the Assyrian Empire [381]. Some of the deported may have managed to keep their identity intact, and to have returned later with the exiles of Judah to Palestine. But the overwhelming majority of the 'ten tribes' merged tracelessly with the indigenous population and, thus, disappeared for ever.

c. Jews and Samaritans

As a result of the colonizing policy of Assyria a new situation developed. Henceforward Palestine consisted of three parts. The northernmost part was Galilee. When the Assyrians annexed it, only a small portion of the inhabitants was marched off; it seems that no great number of foreign colonists was settled in this region. So the ethnic identity of the original population remained mainly intact [382]. More to the south we find the province of Samaria. Here, in the decades subsequent on the fall of the capital, immigrants, and even nomads, from many provinces of the Empire arrived, even from as far away as Media. In the course of time this mixed bag became fairly homogeneous since the newcomers intermingled with one another and with the remnants of the original population. In the far south, after the fall of Jerusalem in 586 B.C., the greater part of the population was left in peace by the Babylonian conqueror. The elite was, indeed, deported but most of them returned after the Babylonian Captivity. So Judah did not experience ethnic changes of importance.

The historic consequence of the ethnic upheaval in the north was the fiercest dualism of ancient Jewish history, that between 'Jews' and 'Samaritans'. We tend to call the post-exilian population of the south 'Jews', from 'Yehudim', in Latin 'Judaei' = 'those from Judah'. The people in the north were the 'Galileans'; they professed the same religion and were, therefore, likewise 'Jews'. True enough, the Galileans were felt to be somewhat different, even a trifle suspect with regard to their faith. However, there was never any question of deep antagonism between Judeans and Galileans.

In between the Samaritans lived. Most of these were originally pagans but gradually they adopted the monotheistic creed of the autochthonous population [383]. In many important respects they did not differ at all from the Jews. They believed in one God, Jahve; they held the sabbath and celebrated the usual feasts; they circumcised their male children; they too expected the Messiah. In spite of all this, they were considered schismatics by the Jews, since they had a temple of their own, on Mount Gerizzim, near present-day Nablus, and since their Bible consisted only of the five books of Moses. This meant that they rejected the historical books as well as the psalms, the prophets and the books of wisdom.

The Jews soon learned to loathe them more deeply than they loathed any other people. "The Jews, you must know, have no dealings with the Samaritans" [384]. This is, of course, a quotation from the New Testament in which it is made abundantly clear how much the Samaritans were abhorred. But already the Books of Kings unequivocally condemn them. "They (the Samaritans) found priests among the dregs of the people, fit to serve hill-shrines (hill-shrines were seen as idolatry - F.), and in the hill-shrines they installed them; but although they worshipped the Lord, they still paid court to their own gods with the usages of their own folk, learned before they ever came to Samaria. And so it is to this day; the old habits still cling" [385].

15. Israel and the Gentiles

"No single characteristic of the Old Testament interpretation of history is more significant than the conviction on the part of various writers that something outside of history is necessary to understand the historical process itself. The meaning of history requires the presence of something that is prior to history and also goes beyond any of the actual achievements of history" [386]. These words of Patterson mean that biblical history should not be read as a work of modern historical scholarship, that is to say, as a relation of events, their causes and consequences, but as the outcome of a relationship between history and 'something else'. What is this 'something else'? God? Perhaps not so much God himself - for the Bible is not a theological treatise - but the presence of God in human affairs, in history that is. Now one of the principal constituent elements in this intimate connection between God and history is that the people of Israel considered itself God's historical agent, or, in other words, his 'chosen people'.

a. The Covenant

Of course, the basic tenet of Israel's faith is that there is only one God; as Israel was only too well aware, she was the only monotheistic people of the ancient world. This notion is highly important with respect to the idea Israel had of herself. Still more crucial, however, is the idea that there existed a special relationship between Jahve and Israel which is expressed by the term 'covenant'. The first great Covenant between God and his people was concluded on Mount Sinai but this had several earlier stages. There is, first of all, the Covenant between Jahve and Noah and his sons. God promised never again to destroy creation by a flood; the pledge of this promise would be the rainbow (= the warrior's bow laid down with the string flat on the ground) [387]. Later God concluded a Covenant with Abraham, the ancestor of Israel. God then promised the patriarch that he would become 'the father of a multitude of nations'; kings would rise from his issue. Not only Abraham himself but all his descendants would be a party to this Covenant. "I will honour this Covenant of mine with yourself and with the race which follows you, generation after generation". This time the pledges were mutual : God would give Canaan to Israel as her inheritance - in return all her male children must be circumcised. This would be 'my covenant in your flesh'. Circumcision meant incorporation into the chosen people; those who were not circumcised must be 'cut off' from Israel [388].

Here we find a marked antagonism to other peoples, the so-called 'gentes' (whose members were called 'Gentiles' = pagans) - to those, that is, who were not circumcised. True enough, circumcision was a fairly general Semitic custom (although practised at a later age and with other intentions than obtained in Israel). But the Egyptians and the Philistines, both of them peoples at whose hands Israel had suffered so much, were not circumcised. In the course of time the word 'uncircumsised' came to be used in a denigrating manner and became virtually identical with 'heathen'. "Giving our sister to one who is not circumcised is ... abominable to us", say the sons of Jacob [389]. Samson complains to Jahve that he is left at the mercy of 'men uncircumcised' = the Philistines [390]. Saul even bids his squire to kill him because he does not want uncircumcised foes (again the Philistines) to finish him [391]. We find a very telling passage in Ezekiel [392] where the prophet is lashing out against all the 'gentes', not even asking himself whether perhaps, some of them might practise circumcision while others did not know this custom. Egyptians, Elamites, those of Meshech and Tubal (kingdoms between Assyria and the Black Sea), Edomites and Sidonians, they are all indiscriminately called 'uncircumcised' (the word occurs eight times in this short passage), meaning thereby enemies of God, all destined to doom.

The word 'covenant' lives on in our languages as 'Testament', a somewhat inaccurate rendering of the Hebrew term 'berit' = covenant, alliance [393]. The fact that we still refer to the Bible as (Old and New) Testament proves how fundamental the idea of Covenant was. Israel's part in the great Covenant, the one concluded on the Sinai, was the observance of the sabbath [394] and the keeping of the Ten Commandments [395]. In return, Israel would be Jahve's own : "you are set apart for me" [396]. Because she was often unfaithful to Jahve, the Covenant had to be renewed more than once. The first time was in the 'fields of Moab', just before the invasion of Canaan [397]. Then, after the conquest, Joshua made the Israelites renew it [398]. After the fall of Samaria the people of Judah pledged itself to Jahve at the instigation of King Hizkiah (720-692) [399]. For the last time the Covenant was renewed under King Josiah (638-608) [400].

b. The idea of election

This notion of 'Covenant' introduces us to the idea of election which was the climactic element in Israel's mental make-up. "Yours is a people set apart for its own God, chosen by its own God, out of all the nations of the earth, as his own people" [401]. This election is not based on the historic importance of Israel : "If the Lord has held you closely to him and showed you special favour, it was not that you overshadowed other peoples in greatness; of all nations, you are the smallest" [402]. No, it is the consequence of God's own volition, an act of his divine love : "It was because the Lord loved you ... that he delivered you ... from the power of Pharaoh" [403]. So the significance of Israel's history is not to be found in the deeds of great kings or in resounding military victories but in a loving act of God.

Jahve will baffle all the plans of Israel's enemies. "Muster then, you peoples, to your overthrow; obey the call, distant lands; summon up your valour, arm yourself in vain! ... All your boasts are belied; God is with us!" [404]. "Envious my foes watch while you (Jahve) spread a banquet for me" [405]. It will be clear that Israel distances herself, in this way, from all other nations. She views herself as standing apart, not standing on a pedestal high above the others, but as being armed with a special divine mandate which no other people may claim as its own. However, Israel did not receive this mandate on behalf of her own salvation but rather for the good of all nations.

Both ideas, that of Jahve's special protection, and that of being a lamp for the nations, figure very prominently in Isaiah. "My servant you (Israel) are, chosen, not rejected ... You shall see your enemies disappointed and put to the blush. What are they? A very nothing ..." [406]. And then : "Those rays of yours shall light the Gentiles on their path; kings shall walk in the splendour of your sunrise ... All the treasures of the Gentiles will be pouring into you ... Who are these that come, swift as the cloud-wrack, as doves flying home to the dovecot? These too (the Gentiles) are your sons" [407]. In Deutero-Isaiah it is in particular the 'Servant of Jahve' who will proclaim God's message to the nations. "My spirit rests upon him, and he will proclaim right order among the Gentiles" [408]; "I have appointed you to be the light of the Gentiles, in you I will send out my salvation to the furthest corners of the earth" [409].

This means that the idea of election was steadily widened till it, in fact, included all other nations - on the condition that they adhered to Israel's God. There is a corresponding broadening and deepening of the notion of Covenant in the great prophets. "A time is coming, the Lord says, when I mean to ratify a new Covenant with the people of Israel and the people of Judah. It will not be the Covenant I made with their fathers ... No, I will implant my law in their innermost thoughts and in their hearts" [410]. The new Covenant will, therefore, be more religious and spiritual than juridical, and more personal than national. Coupled with the widening of the notion of election, this meant that the Gentiles too could become a party to the Covenant.

In view of this tendency to make the Covenant and the election more and more universal (this would become a dominant concept in the New Testament), we would not be justified in asserting that Covenant and election separated Israel so sharply from other nations that the relation must be called dualistic. Nevertheless, it will be evident that these ideas contain the possibility of dualism - a risk that Israel in the course of her long history did not always succeed in avoiding. The ideas mentioned could be narrowed down to such an extent that Israel sometimes seemed to look down in haughty contempt on all others. In our own, highly justified abhorrence of all forms of antisemitism we tend to gloss over the fact that there exists also what one might dub 'anti-goyism'. The (Jewish) Italian novelist Giorgio Bassani, for instance, speaks of "the old atavistic hatred of the Hebrews in their encounters with all that was Christian and Catholic, with the 'goy', that is" [411].

c. 'Never pitying them'

Bible readers, whether or not they are believers, are confronted, in the Book of Joshua in particular, with a disturbing problem. The modern faithful of all denominations feel very uneasy about it. We might call it the problem of 'the wars of Jahve' - a Hebrew book with this title did exist but is lost [412]. One will not only feel unhappy because Jahve is presented as a kind of war lord but still more because the most horrible things are done in his name and even at his express command. Let us put this as bluntly as possible. "Here is the land you are to invade and conquer (Canaan). To make room for you in this land, the Lord your God means to dispossess a multitude of nations at your onslaught ... The Lord will give you victory over them. Your part is to exterminate them, never parleying with them, never pitying them" [413]. A passage like this gives modern readers a queer feeling, especially since it was written by members of a people that was itself to become the victim of so many cruel persecutions, and even of genocide.

With respect to our theme the issue is whether we are confronted here with a case of the most radical dualism. On the one side there is Israel that seems to have a monopoly of divine right, on the other the Canaanite tribes to which even the right of existence is denied. There must be absolutely nothing between these poles, no bonds of marriage, for instance. On the contrary, "overthrow their altars, break their idols, cut down their secret groves, set fire to their carved figures" [414]. What makes this pictute still more horrifying is that this is no theory; this command was, indeed, put into practice. The whole Book of Joshua is full of destruction and extermination. When Jericho was taken, every inhabitant was slain; the invaders spared 'neither man nor woman, neither youth nor age, even cattle and sheep and asses were put to the sword" [415]. When, somewhat later, the city of Ai fell into Israelite hands, "in one day all her citizens perished, men and women, to the number of twelve thousand" [416]. And so on. In city after city, "they put every living thing to the sword" [417].

Our first question must be how radical this radical dualism really is. Part of it doubtless is mere verbiage; 'war propaganda' we might dub it. Often the violence is only verbal. Being violent in words in most cases offers a satisfactory outlet to one's inner fury. Even cold-blooded people, like the English and the Dutch, often use strong language. "If I must see another movie of this kind, I will scream" (I quote from a recent English film review). "I will die unless I know who this man is", "if he falls into my hands, I'll strangle him", which of us is guiltless of expressions like these, without any intention to be taken literally. Semitic peoples are pastmasters in violent language (and less inclined to actual violence than northerners, I have been told).

Calling names is a great art in the Middle East. Jesus, who was a Semite himself, was not above calling the Pharisees 'hypocrites, blind fools, whitened sepulchres, full of all manner of corruption within' [418]. He even told his audience that one who hurts the conscience of a child "had better been drowned in the depths of the sea, with a millstone hung about his neck" [419]. In the psalms we find many examples of harsh language. "Perish the sinner, forgotten be the name of the evil-doer" [420], "Lord, shatter their jaws, ... like spilt water let them run to waste" [421], "put out seven-fold retribution into the laps of our neighbours" [422], "the Lord will pass sentence on the nations, heap high the bodies, scatter far and wide the heads of the slain" [423]. The fact that the execution of such pious intentions is left to Jahve makes it clear that the use of violent language is hardly more than a literary tradition (which did not remain confined to Israel or the Semites alone). It is, however. a tradition that betrays a tendency to dualism.

d. Wholesale destruction as a metaphor

There is in the story of the 'Wars of Jahve' or the 'Holy Wars' a strong metaphorical element. In Joshua and Judges the conquest of Canaan is pictured as one continuous movement, planned strategically and executed accordingly; the final result was the partition of the land by the twelve tribes among themselves. In reality, the conquest went forward by leaps and bounds; there were also many setbacks. We may be sure that many Canaanites perished at the hands of the Israelites but they were by no means exterminated. The most famous city of Israel, Jerusalem, was only conquered a long time after the invasion (ca. 1000 B.C.); in this case no extirpation of the original population, the Jebusites, is mentioned [424]. The first chapter of Judges enumerates about twenty towns, mainly in the north, where the Israelites proved incapable of expelling the Canaanites; they stayed where they were, but were made into tributaries. The Amorrhites succeeded in keeping occupied a large part of the northern hill-country [425]. A highly interesting case is that of Gezer, also in the north. Joshua assigned it to the Levites of Ephraim [426] but the Ephraimites were incapable of ousting the inhabitants [427]. Canaanites and Ephraimites lived side by side there [428]. It was an Egyptian Pharaoh who, in the course of an incursion, took the city that was then, ca. 950 B.C., virtually still in Canaanite hands. He put the inhabitants to the sword and gave the town to King Solomon when his daughter married this Israelite ruler [429].

Instances like these make it clear that we must not read Joshua and Judges like a modern historical work. Von Rad says that the territory invaded by the Israelites was the central mountain ridge, a region that was still largely uncultivated; very probably there was not much heavy fighting here [430]. On this mountain ridge the city of Ai was situated; the Book of Joshua gives us a detailed story of military adventure relating how this stronghold was conquered. After that, as I have mentioned, its twelve thousand inhabitants were massacred. However, not a single inhabitant came to harm for Ai no longer existed in Joshua's days. The excavations of Mrs. Judith Marquet-Krause proved that Ai was destroyed already about 2000 B.C. and was never rebuilt. Could it be that Joshua 8, with the story of Ai, does in fact refer to nearby Bethel? This is sometimes supposed but it is a moot point. Why should the book not mention Bethel if the subject of this story was the capture of that city, and not that of Ai?

A still more intriguing problem is that of the conquest of Jericho. The Book of Joshua circumstantially relates how this stronghold was captured. Here too nobody was spared [431]. In this case another enterprising lady, Kathleen Canyon, proved that, in the period of the conquest, the thirteenth century B.C., Jericho had already lain in ruins since about 1500 B.C. A very small population may have vegetated at the spot but there were certainly not the high walls that came tumbling down at the sound of Joshua's trumpets. For the city was, as the book says, not taken by storm, by scaling the walls, but in a miraculous way. The biblical authors do not try to satisfy the craving for historical exactness that is characteristic of modern man. What they wished to convey is that, for the Israelite invaders, human exertions were of no avail. Without the direct help of Jahve this tiny people never could have conquered Palestine.

This point of view - so utterly different from that of modern historiography - makes for a highly stylized way of relating events. The story is structured and ordered according to the central idea that this is, in fact, a war of Jahve and not of Israel. Taking this prophetic stance the biblical authors did not believe it would really enlighten their readers if they treated them to detailed reports of military events. Instead, they regrouped what they knew of the conquest and did not hesitate to insert a number of legendary elements. This way of handling their material would, they thought, be far more helpful to understand the events rightly, or rather, the meaning of the events. Now it is highly probable that the divine order to exterminate formed an essential part of this stylization of history.

If the wholesale destruction of the Canaanites did not take place and if it is true that Canaanite population groups were to be found in Israel even in much later centuries, it would not be correct to speak of radical dualism - a dualism, that is, leading to the extermination of the inferior pole. On the purely historical plane there existed rather a relative dualism, in the shape of a situation in which the remaining Canaanites were tolerated as second-class citizens. Even Jesus told a Canaanite woman that she did not belong to 'the house of Israel' and was, therefore, not entitled to his help [432].

e. From the ideal to practice

Nonetheless, the fact remains that, in the text I quoted earlier, Jahve explicitly orders Israel to make short work of the Canaanites. In other words, on the ideological or ideal plane there positively is radical dualism. Without a blush the biblical authors ascribed to their God the avowed wish to have the Canaanite tribes exterminated. Of course, just like other ancient peoples the Israelites made no distinction between primary and secondary causes. All illnesses, for instance, came directly from God. Wars in particular were not so much purely political and military events but rather important elements in the divine plan.

Therefore, the Israelites took it for granted that Jahve played a decisive and leading role in their battles; he had to be consulted even as to the tactics to be followed, and he was supposed to support his people during the fighting. Very probably it did not very much bother the Israelites that during their campaigns atrocities were committed. Even modern democratic governments tend to gloss over war crimes when these are committed by their own forces. In Antiquity, when no law of war or Convention of Geneva existed, wars were fought in a cruel way. However, I do not believe that Israel committed more cruelties than other nations, rather less probably.

Once again I do not want to be apologetic. But we must try to understand what was behind the Israelites' ascription of the extermination order to Jahve. A psychologist would very probably say that this is a clear case of projection. The Israelites evidently wished to have no Canaanites about. The fact that Canaanite population groups still lived their midst made them feel uneasy - just like, after the period of the Captivity, the presence of the Samaritans made them nervous.

They projected their wish to be rid of the Canaanites on Jahve as a way of invoking the highest authority for it.

But why were they afraid of these remnants that in no way presented a military or political threat to them? The answer is that those Canaanites were at once their nearest kin and dangerously different from them. Most of these tribes were Semites and spoke Semitic languages and dialects. Before the invasion of Canaan the Israelites themselves spoke an Aramaic dialect but soon after the occupation they began to speak the Canaanite Semitic language, so that Hebrew is rightly called the 'speech of Canaan' [433]. This already is an indication that, culturally, Israelites and Canaanites were more akin than was to Israel's liking. But there is far more to it than this.

There can be no doubt that Israel nursed feelings of great fear of the Canaanite religion, or, rather, of its pernicious influence on her own religious practices. She abhorred this religion, she deemed it nefarious to the highest degree. But at the same time, she felt that the beaten enemy tried to recoup his losses by making the Jahvist religion as similar as possible to his own. This fear certainly was not imaginary or neurotic. On the contrary, as I have already explained, Israel constantly threatened to relapse into superstition and paganism; the foreign gods the prophets most loathed and feared were not the great Babylonian divinities but rather the Canaanite local gods, the 'Baals'. The prophets fought indefatigably and tenaciously against the Baal-cult, its priests, sacrifices and altars, its totempoles, sacred trees and sanctuaries on the hill-tops; debauchery was characteristic of these rites.

Since the prophets fully realized that the presence of Canaanite cult-places and the celebration of pagan rites spelled a lethal danger to the Israelite religion they felt they could not permit themselves to be tolerant. Very probably the Canaanites were no worse or morally more dissolute than other pagan peoples. But they had the misfortune of being nearest to Israel and, therefore, the most direct source of infection. Hence they must, by might and main, be prevented from contaminating the people of Jahve. This fear is the reason why the

Book of Wisdom lashes out so fiercely against the Canaanites (whose abominable name is not even mentioned). "Good reason you (God) had to be their enemy; of what detestable practices they were not guilty ... murderers that would not spare their own children ..., they must have no share in the Covenant. Your will was that our fathers should root them out, these unnatural murderers of their own defenceless children" - the author is thinking of the Moloch-cult here - "and this land so dear to you as no other, should be more worthily peopled by the sons of God".

The author then goes on to explain, in a theological manner, the historical fact that the Canaanites were not exterminated. In doing so, he switches imperceptibly from his 'ideal' and radical stance to a more practical dualism. "Yet they, too, were men, and you (Jahve) wouldst deal gently with them ... Their sentence should be executed by degrees, giving them opportunity to repent" [434]. It is very curious that both the order to root out the Canaanites and the intention to spare them are directly attributed to God. Pious lessons follow on this passage. Justice and mercy should for ever go hand in hand. And if God had been thus lenient with the Canaanites, Israel could justly hope that God would show still greater mercy to her [435].

f. An inconsistency in the biblical presentation

Yet when all is said and done, the problem has not been totally solved. Let us again put the question straight out. The God who told Israel to root out the Canaanites is the same God who said : "Thou shalt not kill" [436]. It was this God who, after the Flood, told Noah and his sons, that is to say, the ancestors of the new humanity : "Whoever shall take the life of his brother-man shall answer for it to me. Man was made in God's image, and whoever sheds a man's blood shall have his blood shed by man" [437]. The killer starts a vicious circle of violence of which he himself will become a victim. Must we, confronted by this apparently contradictory pronouncements, conclude that there is an inconsistency in Jahve? We must rule out this possibility since, from a biblical point of view, it would be blasphemous to ascribe inconsistencies to God. I refer to an earlier section in which I wrote about God's absolute identity - "I am who I am" - which makes him different from all other creatures.

There is no reason to suppose that Jahve allows Israel what he does not allow others. This is not the case. If others are not permitted to kill, Israel isn't either. Already Jacob, the patriarch, reproaches his sons for wreaking vengance on those of Sichem because of the rape of their sister Dinah : "You have made my name abominable to the Canaanites" [438]. In the Book of Judges we read in as many words that it was Jahve himself who spared the nations that Joshua did not exterminate [439].

We must now try to discover the exact value of the warlike history of Israel within the context of the whole Bible. This history is hedged in between images and promises of peace and harmony. At one end we find the immensely peaceful atmosphere of the Garden, where God used to walk in the coolness of the afternoon. This bliss is finally dispelled by Cain's fratricidal murder of his brother Abel which sets the tone for the whole subsequent history of mankind (for all killlings and all wars are fratricidal). At the other end we hear of the future peace and harmony foretold by the great prophets, especially Isaiah. "They will melt down their swords into plough-shares, nation levying war against nation and training itself for battle no longer". Israel, once a warfaring nation, then will be the focus of a new world-history : "A multitude of peoples will make their way to Sion, crying, come, let us climb up to the Lord's mountain-peak, to the house where the God of Jacob dwells" [440].

If we should take the point of view of the prophets - and I believe that we should read the Old Testament with their eyes -, Israel's bloody warfare looks no more than a temporary expedient or a historical interval. With this statement we are coming very close to the kernel of the problem. There is, without any doubt, an inconsistency in the biblical presentation. But it is not an inconsistency in God, it is one in humanity. It seems to me that in the Old Testament God operates on two different plans or levels. On one level Jahve is male and a war-god; on the other level he is purely spiritual and the deepest ground of all peace, harmony and happiness. On the second level he is related to the situation of mankind as it was before the Fall, the ideal human condition that will also be the final one; the first level is related to the historical situation, the prevailing state of the human condition.

The existence of these two levels is exemplified in the history of David. This king is often assisted by God in his military campaigns in a conspicuous way, although these wars are not the 'wars of Jahve' in the proper sense of this expression. For instance, when he was fighting the Philistines in the plain of Refaim, he consulted Jahve by asking him directly : "Shall I attack the Philistines? Shall I be given the mastery?". Jahve answered : "Go to the attack, the Philistines will be at your mercy". David defeated them then and there. Somewhat later, in a similar emergency, he put the same question to God. This time he was told not to attack frontally but to circumvent the enemy. He must wait until he should hear the sound of marching feet in the foliage of the trees. "Then offer battle; it is a sign that the Lord will pass on before you" [441]. On the strength of these and similar occurences one might say that God was fighting David's battles. Nonetheless, this is the same God who forbids David to build a temple for him because his wars were so bloody.

As I have said already, absolute identity is the privilege of God, and of God alone. Because of the Fall, mankind is fundamentally unable to conceive of a seamlessly homogeneous world. Even the greatest prophets of Israel were incapable of merging these two worlds into one; they had to take the inconsistency I have described for granted. Had they succeeded in linking them together they would have put their message beyond the reach of human comprehension. Thus the Bible teaches us that a distinction between an undilutedly theological stance and a historical approach, indispensable as both of them are, is, nonetheless, an inevitable element of the mental make-up of mankind. Therefore, humanity will always have to cope with it. This difficulty is comparable to that of being faultlessly bilingual. If one has a perfect command of some foreign language, his mastery will, though, always be somewhat less complete than that of his native tongue. He will understand certain particularities and peculiarities of this foreign language less well than those of his vernacular. The Old Testament speaks of God in two 'languages'.

Finally, and once again, it must be stated that this inconsistency, this speaking in two 'languages', can easily develop into dualism. The pure spirituality, the 'other-worldliness' of God, can be stressed so heavily that there is no longer any connection between him and our poor humanity. If this happens, then our human 'historicity' will, more often than not, be seen as utter depravity, and human history as Satan's own domain. Then only a few elect, privileged by a special revelation, will be able to escape from the darkness and to proceed to the light.

g. 'The tears of Esau'

Israel's relationship with all other peoples is best exemplified in the story of 'Jacob' and 'Esau'. Why I am right in putting their names in quotation-marks is shown by the answer their mother Rebecca received from God when she consulted him because she felt her yet unborn children (they were twins) 'struggling in her womb' : "There are two nations in your womb; in your body the separation of two peoples has begun ... and it is the eldest that shall be subject to the younger" [442]. The author immediately informs us that this 'Esau' - the eldest - is in fact 'Edom' [443]. 'Jacob', of course, represents Israel. So the struggling of the yet unborn twins signifies the opposition of Israel and Edom.

Who, or what, is 'Edom'? The Dutch exegete Krijger called Edom 'the shadow of Israel' [444]. Just as a man is constantly followed by his shadow, Israel always found Edom at her heels. The country of Edom, of the Edomites, also called 'Seir', is situated between the Dead and the Red Seas; it is a rough mountainous country. The fact that Jacob = Israel and Esau = Edom proves that Israel knew that the Edomites were her nearest kin. This did not prevent her from looking down on her neighbours to the south - this in spite of the fact that Deuteronomy said : "For the Edomites you shall have no repugnance, they are your brothers" [445]. The stories of how the cunning Jacob succeeded several times in deceiving his rustic brother give evidence of this contempt. But here too there is fear. Jacob knew very well that Esau had every reason to hate him. Therefore, when he returned from Mesopotamia he took many precautions to placate his insulted brother [446].

There was much warfare between the peoples of Israel and Edom. This began already when the Israelites, emerging from the desert, were refused passage through Seir by the Edomites; Israel was thus forced to make a long detour [447]. Saul occasionally fought the Edomites but it was David who conquered them [448]; for a time Edom had Israelite governors. After David's death, however, under King Solomon, the Edomites, with the help of Egypt, virtually succeeded in making themselves independent again [449]. Several kings of Judah had to campaign against their neighbour. King Amaziah (797-767) obtained a resounding victory over the Edomites but promptly fell to venerating their gods [450]. Successes like these were always temporary. In the time of King Ahaz (735-732), for instance, the Edomites invaded Judah and made away with a rich booty [451].

What rankled the Israelites most of all was that Edom, as an ally of the Babylonians in 586 B.C., took part in the destruction of the kingdom of Judah [452]. The psalmists and the prophets were furious about this. "Remember, Lord, how the sons of Edom triumphed when Jerusalem fell" [453]; "the same cup you (Edom) too shall drink, and be drunken and stripped bare" [454]; "on Edom, doubt it not, the death-sentence shall fall, the sword of the Lord, glutted with blood, shall execute it" [455]. The whole prophecy of Obadiah is devoted to these 'thieves and midnight-robbers'.

Driven on by nomadic tribes that occupied the southern part of their country the Edomites penetrated into the southern half of Judah which they peopled. After the Babylonian Captivity this region was called 'Idumea'; northward it reached to beyond Hebron. It will not surprise us that relations between Idumeans and Jews were permanently bad. During the wars of liberation the Idumeans rallied with the Seleucids against the Jews. Judas the Maccabee had to fight them - they were still called 'Esau's race' - and defeated them [456]. The final reckoning came with John Hyrcanus, son of Simon the Maccabee, who governed the Jews between 135 and 104. This John forced them into submission and made them circumcise themselves; he was responsible for making, as Flavius Josephus has it, 'their manner of life conform in all other respects to that of the Jews. And from that time they have continued to be Jews" [457].

One of those converted by force was Antipas, a prominent Idumean. His son Antipater was appointed governor of Judaea (55 - 34) by the Romans who obviously considered him a Jew. The son of Antipater was Herod I the Great (37 B.C. - 4 A.D.), a man utterly devoted to the Romans who recompensed him by making him King of the Jews. He had, however, to fight hard for it; he conquered first Idumea and then Samaria and Galilee; finally he captured Jerusalem. The Jews hated him for being an 'Edomite'. His grandson Herod Agrippa I, by virtue of the Romans, ruled over virtually the whole territory of his grandfather. Pilate sent Jesus to him [458]. Somewhat later he became the first persecutor of the Christians [459]. When, in 70 A.D., insurgent Jerusalem was threatened by the Roman army of Titus, the leaders of the city invoked the help of the Idumeans; twenty thousand of them indeed answered the summons and marched to the Holy City [460]. Relations, however, between the Idumeans and the Jews were strained; the main body of the auxiliaries soon departed [461]. During the siege the remainder made overtures to Titus; although the plot was discovered, many of them transferred to the enemy camp [462]. With deep abhorrence the Jewish historian Josephus relates how the Idumeans raged against the Jews, even butchering the chief priests [463]. So, after all, they did not prove to be very 'Jewish'!

From the beginning of their national history till the final downfall of the Temple, 'Edom' was in the eyes of the Jews equivalent with enmity, brutality, and treason. This was all the more painful because

'Esau' and 'Jacob' were brothers, even twin brothers; there is no fiercer hatred, it is sometimes said, than that between brothers. On the surface the picture is perfectly clear, and perfectly dualistic : 'Jacob' is the innocent lamb, and 'Esau' is abominably bad. But there is something more to this. Israel felt uneasy about this relationship. Dr. Krijger asks our attention to a few words in Genesis : Esau, when realizing that his father Esau was not prepared to bestow a blessing on him too, "could not control his voice and wept" [464]. "Israel", says Krijger, "could not forget those tears of Esau. It was felt to be a dark secret." A Chassidic rabbi, Schmelke, of Nikolsburg in Poland, writes : "Tradition teaches us that the Messiah, the Son of David, will not come before the tears of Esau have been dried".

Krijger goes on to say that the real dualism is not that between 'Jacob' and 'Esau' but that it is in both of them. Esau, indeed, contemplated killing his brother [465] but later he was genuinely prepared for a reconciliation. "Esau ran to meet his brother, embraced him, clung to his neck and kissed him, in tears" [466]. Jacob, on the other hand, was perfectly capable of deceit. If 'Esau' had reason enough for tears, 'Jacob' too. The Old Testament certainly draws a sharp dividing line between Israel and the goyim. But there is also a distinction between God, against whom the forces of darkness are powerless, and humanity, and this distinction is far more real and significant [467].

The Old Testament is not really a nationalistic book. It does not begin with the story of Israel but with that of humanity. It derives the whole universal history of mankind from one man, Noah (who was not an Israelite), thus stressing the essential unity of all men [468]. Von Rad says that such a unitarian conception is without precedent in Antiquity [469]. But although this unity is fundamental, diversity is an actual fact, and a painful result of the sinful condition of mankind; this is the meaning of the story of the Tower of Babel [470]. It is in this diversified world of nations that Israel has a place of her own. After having narrated this story the authors henceforward concentrate on the story of Abraham 'and his seed' [471].

Two lines may be followed when we consider Israel's relationship to the 'gentes'. Both of them resemble the Jacob-Esau-relationship. Israel considered herself essentially different from all other peoples, serving, as she did, the one true God. As a small nation, moreover, she felt herself dwarfed by the pagan superpowers that surrounded her. She realized that she lay in the path of the great conquerors, whether the Egyptian Pharaohs en route to the Euphrates, or the Assyrian, Babylonian, and Persian kings marching to the conquest of Egypt. All rode roughshod over the two tiny kingdoms.

But it was not first and foremost the political and military power of their mighty neighbours that Israel feared. Still more was she afraid of their gods and their demons and their cults, which could poison - and often actually did so - her own people. This explains why the prophets, propelled by this double anguish, burst out so frequently and so vehemently against all other nations. In chapter after chapter Isaiah calls down Jahve's wrath over Moab, over Aram, over Tyre, and all their iniquities. Jeremiah did not lag behind. He curses Egypt, Moab, the Philistines, the Ammonites, and finally, in a torrent of words, Babylon. Then Ezekiel in his turn takes over prophesying doom for Babylon, Edom, Ammon, Moab, Tyre, the Philistines, and others, although his special target was Egypt.

These prophecies of doom for almost all other nations certainly constituted a dualistic distinction between Israel and the pagan 'gentes'. But here too, as in the Jacob-Esau-relationship, the prophets look also into the heart of Israel herself. For behind and beyond the Israel-gentes dualism there is another, and still more dangerous one, that between Israel as Jahve's chosen people, and the Israel that did not always want to be so essentially different from others. Probably the prophets were more afraid of this second dualism than of the first; at all events, this fear made their outbursts against the goyim all the more vehement. But they did not spare their own people either. The tone is set by Ezekiel : "Word came to me from the Lord : ... you must confront Jerusalem with the record of her misdoings" [472]. This he, and the other prophets, certainly did! None of them, great and small, ever became tired of confronting Israel with her evil deeds, her infidelity, her idolatry, her wantonness, her luxuriousness, her oppression of the poor. If the gentes had reason for tears, Israel still more!

The solution to the problem that, actually and historically, Israel did not differ so much from other nations, was found by following the second line, that of the reunification of the family of man under the kingship of Jahve. In this movement Israel would be, so to speak, the pathfinder; in fact, Israel, or Sion, would be the propelling force of this urge back to the origins. This would be the final fulfilment of the promise to Abraham : "In you all the nations of the world will find a blessing" [473]. Many of the psalms take up this theme : "The Gentiles may rejoice and be glad; a whole world abide your (God's) judgment, and the Gentiles too obey on earth your sovereignty" [474]. In the Trito-Isaiah we find that great prophecy of the Gentiles trekking to Jerusalem, bringing their gifts to the Lord. They come from far away, from the islands, from the ships on the ocean. Fear will be a thing of the past; the gates of the Holy City will remain open day and night [475]. But all this was for the future, the time of the advent of the Messiah. For the time being the dividing line between Israel and the other remained as it was.

16. Conclusion : the wholeness of the world

a. The way of the Messiah

Life is a mixed blessing. In drawing breath, Goethe said, there is a twofold grace : breathing in is oppressive whereas breathing out is relieving. To this simple statement he added : "So wonderfully life is mixed" [476]. Francis W. Newman wrote that "God has two families of children on this earth, the once-born and the twice-born" [477]. Newman describes 'the family of the once-born' as people who only see the bright side of life. To them God is not 'a strict Judge' but 'the animating spirit of a beautiful harmonious world'. Although "it would be absurd to call them self-righteous ... they are not distressed by their own imperfections" nor, may I add, by those of the world.

William James characterizes them as 'organically weighted on the side of cheer and fatally forbidden to linger over the darker aspects of the universe" [478]. We may draw the important inference from Newman's considerations that the Old Testament is written by and destined for people who are 'twice-born'. Without exception the scriptural authors take a sober and realistic, although not a pessimistic, view of existence. If they picture the bright sides of life with relish, they never underestimate its darker aspects.

The Old Testament is based on the notion that human existence, even nature, is somewhat at variance with itself. I believe that this chapter on the religion of Israel amply proves that, even in this homogeneous system, there are loose ends. Not everything fits together seamlessly. God alone is wholy identical with himself. But man must be content with a world that he is not able to comprehend from a single point of view. If he were capable of this he would be God. The attitude that the Bible takes itself and recommends to its readers is that of being twice-born. Whether or not one likes it, there are two sides to existence, and they can never be completely reconciled to each other.

Is there a way out of this imperfection? There is : it is the way of the Messiah. For in the Messianic kingdom-to-come justice and peace will prevail; the complete harmony of all that exists will be the blissful result. According to the Christians the Messiah has already appeared in the person of Jesus of Nazareth, but for the Jews he is still to come. It is on this issue that Jews and Christians part company. However, with respect to one important fact there exists complete agreement between them. The Messiah will not be able to establish his rule without first passing through suffering and death. In doing so he will definitely reconcile in his person the two aspects of existence.

b. Holiness and wholeness

The Israelites were very well aware that something had gone awry. There is no question, as in the Gnosis, of an initial flaw in creation; God did not make a mistake, and there was no evil power that intervened in the creational process. Man altered his relationship to God of his own free will without realizing that he thus also changed his relationship to his fellow-men and even to nature. The result was that he acquired an eye for the dark aspects of existence. The foregoing paragraphs will have made it clear that, since the Fall, man has to cope with a lot of things that he is unable to control. This lack of control is, I believe, most unambiguously expressed by the biblical laws of purity.

The Book of Leviticus which contains the bulk of these laws repeats many times this general command : "Be holy because I am holy". Somebody - was it not Joseph Pieper? - said that 'holiness is wholeness'. It is for this reason that the oft recurring title of God in the Old Testament is 'the Holy One of Israel'. God alone is 'holy' and he alone is 'whole'. God's holiness is all-embracing but since human beings cannot be 'whole', they can, in consequence, not be holy either, at least not as holy as God. Therefore, the injunction "Be holy because I am holy" does not signify than man can be as whole, as complete, as God. But he must attempt - this is a biblical moral category - to approach God's holiness as much as possible. Since human holiness never can be all-embracing, such an attempt means that man must keep apart from certain aspects of life.

Etymologically, holiness in fact signifies 'being apart'. The wellknown Latin word 'sanctus' is derived from the verb 'sancire' = to fence off, and the Greek word 'temenos' = sanctuary, from 'temnoo = to cut off. The Arab word for 'sanctuary', 'haram', has the same origin. The Hebrew words for 'holy', 'qadosh', and for 'holiness', 'qodesh', are derived from 'qadad' = to put apart, which comes to mean 'to destine somebody or something for cultic service'. These words are closely related to the terms for 'clean' and 'unclean'. 'Clean' is not identical with 'holy', but something or somebody that is 'clean' may become 'holy', that is, fit for cultic service. Things or beings that are 'unclean' can never become 'holy' and are principally unfit for cultic service. Therefore, the Israelites who basically formed a cultic people must keep away from all uncleanness.

Now, if we read the prohibitions and prescriptions of Leviticus, we often wonder why certain things or beings are unclean and make unclean. For instance, one is not permitted to wear a garment made of two different kinds of stuff [479]. Prohibitions like these seem puzzling to us. Why is a man with a disabled foot not allowed to act as a sacrificial priest [480]? Why is a sow or a lizard unclean but not a locust [481]? Possibly some animals and objects are unclean because they played a role in the idolatrous cults of Canaan. This is often said of swine; in fact, eating swine's meat meant apostasy [482]. However, the injunction in Leviticus not to eat the flesh of the pig does not mention this at all but gives a totally different reason : the pig does not chew the cud [483]. This means that there is more to this than abhorrence of idolatry alone.

The American anthropologist Mary Douglas gives a somewhat different turn to the saying 'holiness is wholeness'. She says that holiness is exemplified by completeness [484]. To this she adds : "Holiness requires that individuals shall conform to the classes of things to which they belong. And holiness requires that these different classes of things shall not be confused". Therefore, there was to be no mating of a beast with one of another sort, or a sowing of fields with a mixed crop. The right conception of creation requires that categories are carefully kept apart. This applies still more to the laws regulating the relations of man and animal. "You shall not defile yourself by commerce with a beast nor shall any woman allow any beast to have commerce with her" [485]. Of course, the difference in human categories is also to be respected. "You shall not mate with the daughter of your own son or daughter, you shall not mate with a woman and also with her daughter, you shall not have commerce with a man as with a woman", and many other commands of the same kind [486]. I believe Mary Douglas is right in stating that "holiness is more a matter of separating that which should be separated than of protecting the rights of husbands and brothers" [487].

The close link between holiness and completeness is borne out by the fact that men with personal defects were not allowed to be priests. Those who were blind or lame, or had a deformed nose or a hunchback, or a crushed hand or foot, must not go 'near the altar' [488], although such deformities did not make them unclean. This meant that a man with a broken nose was not prevented from offering a sacrifice to the Lord. The victims of leprosy, however, and other skin diseases were considered unclean [489]; a person with an impaired skin was not 'complete' in Jewish eyes. Even walls or garments with unsavoury spots on them were seen as trespassing on the order of nature [490].

It was in particular with respect to the animal world, at once so near and so alien to mankind, that the right order of nature had to be very carefully respected. This applies most of all to the dietary rules, since it is by eating the flesh of animals that man comes nearest to them. The keeping of cattle and goats was a very common thing in Israel; nearly every household possessed one or more of these animals, and often large herds of them. This means, says Mary Douglas, that 'cloven-hoofed, cud-chewing ungulates are the model kind of food' for the Israelites [491]. All animal meat that did not conform to this model was rejected as unclean, for instance, the flesh of the camel (not the camel himself), because he, although being ruminant, has no cloven hoofs [492].

With regard to other beasts Leviticus follows the threefold scheme of Genesis 1 : each element, the earth, the water, and the air, is inhabited by its own class of animal creatures. In the air the birds fly, they have two legs and possess two wings; in the water fishes swim, they have fins and are covered with scales; on the earth animals walk about on four legs. These are the right kinds of locomotion; every other kind is 'contrary to holiness' [493]. "The winged things that are four-footed you must hold in abomination" [494], the bat for instance. The locust, however, might be eaten because it is not considered a flying animal but a hopping one [495]. An animal living in the water but possessing no fins and scales is unclean [496], for instance crabs and lobsters. Animals that do not walk on all fours but creep or glide, whether with their belly close to the ground, albeit on four feet, or on many feet, are unclean; in this class fall all insects and snakes [497]. A special group is formed by those animals that, although the Creator evidently endowed with hands, nevertheless prefer to use them as forelegs and walk on them; this group includes weasels, mice, and lizards [498].

Mary Douglas concludes her chapter on 'The Abominations of Leviticus' by stating that the dietary laws are "like signs which at every turn inspired meditation on the oneness, purity and completeness of God. By rules of avoidance holiness was given a physical expression in every encounter with the animal kingdom and at every meal" [499]. Quite true, but all the same this attitude betrays a certain ambivalence with respect to the order of nature which is bordering on dualism. On the one hand, Israel knew that the Creator had blessed every living being on earth and told him to multiply; Genesis 1 makes no exceptions. On the other hand, there seem to be two orders of nature, not so much a right one and a wrong one but a right and a less right one.

Curiously enough, there are no dietary taboos regarding vegetable food; it is only in the animal kingdom that distinctions are made. This is doubtless because the fauna is so much nearer to man in the order of nature than the flora. A not inconsiderable part of the fauna was considered dangerous because through pollution it made certain persons and objects unfit for cultic service. This meant that one part of creation was wholeheartedly accepted while another part was viewed with abhorrence. Nothing but these dietary laws could show more clearly that, when all is said and done, Israel did not possess a uniform view of existence. In the first creation story it is said six times that all that God made was good, even very good; nevertheless, Israel banned a number of creatures. For this people, existence was somewhat at variance with itself; this attitude was legalized and even sanctified by its cultic system.

NOTES TO CHAPTER II

1) James Boswell, London Journal 1762/1763, 20.II.1763.
2) Books that Roman-Catholics call 'apocryphal' are called 'pseudo-epigraphic' by Protestants; no Bible edition prints them. The so-called 'apocryphal' or 'pseudo-epigraphic' books doubtless contain much intriguing material with regard to our subject, but since they date from a period after Christ I shall not refer to them.
3) There still exists a small group of Samaritans in and around Nablus in Israel.
4) Very probably Luke never was a Jew and was not circumcised; in Col.4:14 Paul distinguishes him from his Jewish collaborators.
5) It is highly probable that the original version of Matthew was in Aramaic; there is no Latin in the New Testament.
6) Therefore, he called his book : 'Conjectures sur les mémoires originaux dont il paraît que Moise s'est servis pour composer le livre de Genèse'.
7) This combination, perhaps from the pen of the editor, possibly aims at suggesting that Ch. 1 and 2 speak of the same God; it is also possible that J used a story older than E here.
8) For the books of Schapp see the Bibliography.
9) Gen. 1:4-5.
10) Gen.1:14.
11) Gen.1:15.
12) This chapter obviously has a Babylonian background. Astrology and veneration of celestial bodies were rampant in Mesopotamian religion. Although this 'creation story' is most certainly not a historical or cosmological description of what really happened, probably some historical and geographical data have been worked into it. Since the biblical authors did not know at all how the world was created - and this kind of information is not supplied by divine revelation either -, they may have chosen as a kind of blueprint or frame of reference a geological process with which they actually were conversant and that could serve as a model for what they did not know. This model may have been the geological formation Lower Mesopotamia (ancient Sumeria that is). This is a process that shows a striking similarity to the description of Gen.1 : first there is only an enormous lagoon - slowly mud flats and saltings arise - some stretches of land remain permanently dry - plants begin to sprout - animals arrive, first birds, then mammals - finally man appears. This 'model' had the additional advantage that it can be dated, for the first indications of human presence in the delta of the great rivers are from a period of four thousand years B.C. Possibly this can also explain the biblical predilection for a course of time of about four thousand years from the creation to the birth of Christ.
13) Gen.1:1.
14) Is.34:3.
15) Ap.22:5.

16) Wendorff 68.
17) Wendorff 73.
18) Wendorff 31. Antiquity used to count by means of letters, not of numbers, for instance a = 1, a' = 10. The numerical value of the letters then depends on the alphabet used. This means that, when the Jews arrive at a total of years B.C. of 3761, and sometimes of 4163, the Greek text of the Septuagint can have a total of c. 5500 years, and the early Latin translation of 5199. But still other totals are to be found, Wendorff 31. This method of calculating the age of the world was long-lived. In 1654, an Irish prelate, James Ussher, concluded that the world had been created on October 25, 4004 B.C., D.J.Boorstin, The Discoverers. Penguin, 545.
19) Mt.28:19.
20) Ap.7:9.
21) In this passage, and in several others, I am quoting myself verbatim, from my book 'Hoe ontstaat geschiedenis? Een historische antropologie' ('The Origination of History. A Historical Anthropology'). Kampen NL, 1985.
22) Jaki 3/4.
23) Censorinus, De die natali liber XVIII.1. Heraclitus DK 22A13. See my Vol. I 71. See also Cairns 204/205. The title of Cairns' book ('Philosophies of History') must not mislead us. It is not so much about what we usually call 'philosophy of history' but rather about cycle-pattern theories of history.
24) Cairns 204/205.
25) Plato, Tim. 39D, Phaedr. 248E. For a discussion on the possible length of the Platonic Great Year see Cairns 208-211.
26) Cairns 244-250.
27) Gen.3:15.
28) Dan.7:27.
29) Ap.21:9-23.
30) Ap.22:1-5.
31) Goodrich-Clarke 80.
32) The Hebrew word made a detour over the Aramaic 'm.sjicha' and the Greek translation of it 'Chrestos' in the New Testament, to the words 'Messiah' and 'Christ' that occur, in some form or other, in all modern languages.
33) A.S. van der Woude, s.v. 'Messias' in Biblisches-historisches Handwörterbuch II 1197-1204, Göttingen (1964).
34) David was king c. 1000 B.C. The two Books of Samuel are compilations from different sources, some of them contemporaneous with David himself, others from a later date; the final redaction may date from the period of the Babylonian Captivity, c. 550 B.C.
35) 2 Sam.7:13-16.
36) Ps.18:50; see also Ps.2:2, 89:38, 132:10.
37) Is.9:4-6.

38) Is.11:6-9; we find other Messianic prophecies of the same kind in Jeremiah, Micah, and Ezekiel but it is not necessary to go on quoting.
39) The Deutero-Isaiah covers the chapters 40-55.
40) Is.42:1-7; 49:1-6; 50:4-9; 52:13-53:12.
41) Is.42:1.
42) Is.42:2.
43) Is.49:2.
44) Is.50:16.
45) Is.52:14.
46) Is.53:10-11.
47) The later Caesarea Philippi, now Baniyas, on the Jordan, at the extreme northern tip of the Jewish territory.
48) 2Macc.6:1.
49) 2Macc.6:10-7:42.
50) This is at some point between the return of Antiochus IV from his second expedition against Egypt and his death, in the time of the first successes of Judas the Maccabee. For the proofs see Eissfeldt, Einleitung.
51) Dan.7:2.
52) Dan.2:19.
53) Dan.2:29.
54) Dan.2:31-34.
55) Dan.2:38-43.
56) Dan. 2:44-45.
57) Still more clearly the Four Empires correspond with them, while the last and eternal kingdom comes from Heaven.
58) Dan.7:14.
59) Dan.7:5.
60) See Rowley, Darius the Mede, on the status quaestionis.
61) Dan.7:7-8.
62) Dan.7:23.
63) Dan.2:39.
64) Dan.7:9-10.
65) Dan.7:11-12.
66) Dan.7:13-14.
67) Ex.23:21.
68) 1Kings8:10-11.
69) Nelis 89.
70) Wendorff 35/36.
71) Ex.20:2.
72) Ex.12:12 and 20:23.
73) Renckens 25.
74) Patterson 45.
75) Patterson 48.
76) Patterson 71.
77) Sellin, Theologie 45/46.
78) See also Sellin, Theologie 18.
79) Gen.18:1-22.
80) Ex.33:18-23.

81) In her fine novel 'Das unauslösliche Siegel' (1946) the German novelist Elisabeth Langgässer writes : "Da dürfte Moses ihn (Jahve) schauen : das was vergangen war, nicht was zukünftig war".
82) Dt.6:4.
83) Ez.1:26.
84) Humbert 72.
85) Von Rad, Theologie I 150.
86) Ex.20:5; Dt.18:13.
87) Dt.18:13.
88) Ex.20:3; Dt.5:7.
89) Is.44:9-20; Jer.10:1-5.
90) Is.44:9.
91) Jer.2:11.
92) Jer.10:14-15.
93) Is.44:8.
94) Is.45:6.
95) Is.45:21.
96) Jer..4:5 and 14:22; in both cases the same Hebrew word is used.
97) Jer.4:5. The longest tirade against idols one finds in Wisd.13:1-15:19.
98) Ex.22:29.
99) In 'Wilhelm Meister's Wanderjahre'.
100) 1Kings19:18.
101) 1Kings11:4.
102) For instance 2Kings15:27-30.
103) 2Kings18:3-4.
104) 1Kings16:31-33.
105) 1Kings18:19.
106) 1Kings18:21-40.
107) 1Kings18:21.
108) Ex.5:1-4.
109) Ex.12:31.
110) Ex.14.
111) Ex.15:7.
112) See for instance Eichrodt, Theologie I 141-146.
113) 2Kings3:26-27.
114) 1Sam.26:19.
115) Ps.95:3, see also Ps.89:7 and 97:9.
116) 1Kings8:60.
117) 2Kings19:15, see also 19.
118) Dt.4:35.
119) Eichrodt, Theologie I 142.
120) Jes.45:6.
121) Miskotte 179.
122) Rowley, Re-discovery Ch. V, The Growth of Monotheism.
123) For instance Sellin, Isr.-Jüd.Rel.Gesch. Kap. II 3, Das Weiterleben des altsemitischen (hebräischen) Heidentums.
124) Miskotte 179.
125) Seymour Feldman in Enc.Jud. 5 (Jerusalem, 1972), 1066.
126) Gen.1:2.

127) König, Theologie 215.
128) Gen.1:1.
129) Gen.1:2.
130) Ps.104:6.
131) Gen.1:10.
132) Gen.7.
133) Gen.9:8-11.
134) Jon.1.
135) Ps.18:5.
136) Ps.69:3.
137) Ps.107:26.
138) Ps.89:11.
139) Job 26:12.
140) Job 9:13.
141) Is.9:13.
142) Ps.74:13-14.
143) Job 40:20-24.
144) Ps.104:26.
145) Is.27:1.
146) Jacob, Théologie 112.
147) Fohrer, Theol.Grundstrukt. 57.
148) Lev. 16.
149) Shmuel Ahitew s.v. Azazel, Enc.Jud. 3 (Jerusalem 1972), 999-1002.
150) Lev.5.
151) Ex.4:24-26.
152) Ex.12.
153) Ps.91:5-6.
154) 1Sam.19:9.
155) 1Sam.28.
156) 2Kings21:6.
157) 2Kings21:6.
158) 2Kings21:9.
159) See also Fohrer, Theol.Grundstrukt. 60.
160) Lev.19:27-31.
161) Ex.24:26.
162) Dt.14:1.
163) Ex.22:18.
164) Ex.18:12.
165) 2Kings11.
166) Fohrer, Theol.Grundstrukt. 67.
167) Hos.2:16-17.
168) Jer.2:2-3.
169) Fohrer, Theol.Grundstrukt. 60/61.
170) Num.6:5.
171) Am.2:11-12.
172) Num.13:24-25.
173) 2Kings10:15.
174) Jer.35.
175) Fohrer, Theol.Grundstrukt. 61.
176) Gen.2:9.

177) The snake scrupulously avoids pronouncing the proper name of God, 'Jahve', and restricts himself to calling God 'Elohim'; being aware of the immense distance that separates him from God he knows that he is simply not allowed to give God his proper name. That the woman is on the verge of losing the real knowledge she is entitled to, that of things divine, is shown by the seldom remarked fact that she too, in this whole episode, shuns the name of Jahve and also speaks of 'Elohim'.
178) Gen.3:5.
179) Gen.3:6. In this chapter the fruit is not called an apple.
180) Gen.3:1. In her already quoted novel 'Das unauslösliche Siegel' (see note 81) Elisabeth Langgässer says that Satan was not permitted to appear in a human shape although he would have distinctly preferred to do so. The human shape was to be reserved for God's own Son.
181) Wisd.2:24.
182) Gen.3:4.
183) Gen.6:1-4.
184) I must confess that I sang this same song in my book of 1962 'Uit God geboren' ('Born from God'). Now, more than twenty-five years later, I find myself amused to note that, in these 'Reflexions on Gen. 1-11', I fell over backwards in my attempt to explain away that 'sons of Elohim' could mean angels (pp.77-79). In the play of the Dutch national poet Joost van den Vondel, 'Lucifer' (1654), Act I, one of the rebellious angels, Apollion, pays a visit to Paradise to take a look at those new creatures of God, the first human beings. Returning he reports to Belzebub that he felt disturbed when he saw Eve : "I covered my face and my wings in order to restrain my thoughts and my inclinations ... We (angels) do not know a couple of twofold sex, of a maid and a man. Alas, we are the destitute : we have no notion of marrying, of husband and wife, in a heaven without women". He goes on to depict her beauty part by part (not forgetting to mention "what is best glossed over lest it should tempt a Spirit") and concludes in these words : "I scorched my flight-feathers in this delicious fire". Only recently I saw a remarkable movie by the German film-director Wim Wenders, 'Der Himmel über Berlin' ('The Heaven over Berlin'). Here too an angel appears who is bored with the uniformity of heaven and longs for change and colour. At first he sees everything in black and white and is himself invisible, although he has shed his wings. But then he meets a girl, a trapeze-artist in a circus. She too is a kind of (terrestrial) angel, because, during her dangerous act high in the top of the tent, she too wears wings. The still invisible angel visits her in her caravan; when he sees her in the nude he suddenly realizes 'how bautiful the daughters of men are'. When he touches her on the shoulder the image for the first time changes into colour. He now knows that he is in love and decides to become a human being. After a long search he succeeds in finding her again - his world has definitely become colourful now - and has his first

night with her. He then declares that 'our children will be giants'!
185) De Civ.Dei XV, 23.
186) The Soncino Chumash, edited by Dr. A.Cohen. London (1966[6], 1947[1]), 25.
187) Jud.6:2 and 2:4.
188) Spiesz, Genesis 45.
189) Skinner 139. In Tob.3:8 and 6:44 we find the demon Asmodaeus who killed all the bridegrooms of Sara, doubtless because he wanted her all to himself.
190) De Fraine 77/78.
191) Skinner 140.
192) Evidently only man is judged, although the 'elohim' are primarily guilty. However, Genesis is a story, not of angels, but of God and man; the women were guilty too, of course, and, in this Hebrew context, also their fathers who permitted them to marry the 'elohim'.
193) Job 2:6.
194) 1Chron.21:1.
195) Gen.1:26-31.
196) Renckens 97-99.
197) Gen.3:21.
198) Gen.3:7.
199) Ps.8:5-6.
200) Skinner 269.
201) Gen.14:17-24.
202) Gen.3:22.
203) Wisd.1:13-14.
204) Gen.3:19.
205) Ps.146:4.
206) Job 26:6.
207) Is.25:8.
208) Prov.30:16.
209) Job 18:14.
210) Jon.2:6 and 3.
211) Sir.41:1.
212) Ps.31:13.
213) Ps.8:6.
214) Is.38:18.
215) Job 17:13.
216) Ps.88:11.
217) Is.38:18-19.
218) Job 26:5.
219) Ps.30:10.
220) Ps.6:6.
221) Is.5:14.
222) Prov.12:14.
223) Eccl.8:12-13.
224) Jer.12:1.
225) Jer.11:20.
226) Jer.12:1.
227) Eccl.1:1.

228) Eccl.1:2.
229) Eccl.12:9.
230) Eccl.1:18.
231) Eccl.3:9-10.
232) Eccl.4:2.
233) Eccl.3:16-18.
234) Eccl.4:2-3.
235) Eccl.4:16.
236) But to be true, several other books of the Old Testament are not quoted either.
237) Barton 2-7 discusses the problem of canonicity.
238) Eccl.7:1.
239) Eccl.12:13.
240) Eccl.9:7.
241) Job 1:1-3.
242) Job 2:7-10.
243) Job 1:1-12 and 2:1-7.
244) Job 38:2.
245) Job 10:2-3.
246) Job 36:17.
247) Job 42:9-16.
248) Jer.7:30-8:3.
249) Is.66:24.
250) Dan.12:2.
251) 2Macc.12:43-45.
252) Am.5:21-23.
253) Ps.53:1.
254) Gen.2:25.
255) Gen.3:5.
256) Gen.3:7.
257) Gen.3:10.
258) See the book of Bernard Rudofsky, The unfashionable human body. London (1974 (1972[1]).
259) Mt.6:29.
260) Theo Thijssen in his (autobiographical) book 'Het taaie ongerief' (1932) = 'the tenacious inconvenience'.
261) Dt.24:5.
262) 2Sam.11:11.
263) Ex.19:15.
264) Lev.15:16-30.
265) Gen.4:1.
266) Gen.3:7.
267) Julian Huxley, Memoirs I 163. Penguin Book, 1978 (1970[1]).
268) F.J.J.Buytendijk, De vrouw (The Woman). Haar natuur, verschijning en bestaan. Een existentieel-psychologische studie. Utrecht/Antwerpen, 1985[5].
269) Plato, Symp.189E-191D.
270) Gen.3:24.
271) Gen.2:7.
272) Gen.2:21-23.
273) Gen.2:21-23.

274) Gen.2:19.
275) Gen.2:23.
276) We find the same translation 'mannin' in Vondel's already cited (note 184) play 'Lucifer', Act I.
277) Gen.2:6-7.
278) Gen.2:8.
279) Gen.3:4-5.
280) Gen.3:7.
281) Gen.3:12.
282) Gen.3:16.
283) Gen.3:15.
284) Gen.3:20.
285) De Fraine 60.
286) Sir.40:1.
287) Boelie van Leeuwen, De rots der struikeling (The Rock of Stumbling) (1960). This rock is the island of Curacao where the author is born.
288) George Roditi, De geest van volmaaktheid (The Spirit of Perfection), 1987, 56 (original French edition 1984).
289) A.N.Wilson in his novel 'Gentlemen in England' (1985).
290) Song of Songs 5:1.
291) Gen.3:18-19.
292) Sophocles, Electra 1243.
293) Isabel Allende in her novel 'Of Love and Shadow' ('De amor y de sombra', 1984).
294) Num.3:1-14.
295) Lev.2.
296) Lev.1:4.
297) Lev.17:11.
298) Lev.3:7-11:21.
299) Lev.4:23,24,28,32;6:6;14:12,21; Num.6:12.
300) Lev.1.
301) Dt.21:7.
302) Lev.13:2,12;34:20.
303) Num.3:12.
304) Num.8:13-16.
305) Ex.13:2.
306) Ex.13:13;22:29;34:20.
307) Ex.13/14-16.
308) Ex.12:1-32.
309) Gen.2:24.
310) Ex.2:11-12.
311) Num.20:1-3.
312) 1Chron.2:7-8.
313) Judges 4-5.
314) Judges 4:17-24.
315) Esth4:14.
316) Esth.4:16.
317) Ruth 1:15-17.
318) Prov.31:10-31.

319) Hos.11:9.
320) Is.41:8-14.
321) Is.49:15.
322) Sir.1:10.
323) Sir.24:14.
324) Sir.24:5.
325) Sir.24:6-9.
326) Wisd.7:26.
327) Wisd.7:26.
328) Wisd.9:4.
329) Is.53:7.
330) Gen.22.
331) Gen.2:7.
332) Gen.2:15 and 19.
333) Job 38:4 and 8.
334) Job 41:1.
335) Is.24:1 and 18.
336) Is.11:6-8.
337) Herman Heijermans, Op hoop van zegen (In Hope of Blessing) (1900).
338) Gen.1:29-30.
339) Gen.9:1-2.
340) Gen.6:5.
341) Gen.9:3.
342) Gen.9:6.
343) Gen.9:5.
344) Ex.3:14.
345) Gen.32.
346) Dt.33:1-5.
347) Judges 8:22-23.
348) Judges 8:23.
349) Jo.18:33-36.
350) Judges 9.
351) 1Sam.9-10.
352) 2Sam.24.
353) 1Sam.12:13-14.
354) Hos.8:4.
355) Hos.13:10.
356) Is.33:22.
357) Ps.48:8-9.
358) Jer.10:7.
359) Ps.96:10.
360) Is.42:12.
361) 2Sam.2:8-11.
362) 2Sam.2-5.
363) 2Sam.15-18.
364) 2Sam.19:15.
365) 2Sam.19:40-43.
366) 2Sam.20:1.
367) 2Sam.20:6.
368) 1Kings11:26.

369) 2Sam.11:40.
370) 2Kings11:29-30.
371) 1Kings12.
372) 2Kings16:24.
373) 2Kings12:25-33.
374) 2Sam.7:8-16.
375) Hos.3:4-5.
376) Is.7:10-16.
377) Jer.23:5.
378) 1Kings14:30.
379) 2Kings15:19-20.
380) 2Kings16:5-9.
381) 2Kings17:1-7.
382) Hist.Jew.People 135.
383) 2Kings17:24-31.
384) John 4:9.
385) 2Kings17:32-41.
386) Patterson 526.
387) Gen.9:8-17.
388) Gen.17:1-14.
389) Gen.34:14.
390) Judges 15:18.
391) 1Sam.31:4.
392) Ez.32:17-32.
393) A 'testament' actually is a will, in Greek 'diathêkê', but it is also used for 'covenant', for instance in Hebr. 8 and 9.
394) Ex.31:16.
395) Dt.4:13 and 23.
396) Ex.31:3.
397) Dt.29:1.
398) Jos.24.
399) 2Chron.29-31.
400) 2Kings22-23.
401) Dt.7:5-6.
402) Dt.7:7.
403) Dt.7:8.
404) Is.8:9-10.
405) Ps.23:5.
406) Is.41:9-11.
407) Is.60:3-9.
408) Is.42:1.
409) Is.49:6.
410) Jer.31:31.
411) Giorgio Bassani, Gli occhiali d'oro (1958).
412) Num.21:14.
413) Dt.7:1-4.
414) Dt.7:4-5.
415) Jos.6:21.
416) Jos.8:25.
417) Jos.10:28-39.
418) Mt.23.

419) Mt.18:6; Mc.9:42; Lk.17:2.
420) Ps.37:28.
421) Ps.58:7-8.
422) Ps.79:12.
423) Ps.110:6.
424) 2Sam.5:6-8.
425) Judges 1:27-35.
426) Jos.21:21.
427) Judges 1:29.
428) Judges 1:29.
429) 1Kings9:15-17.
430) Von Rad, Heil.Krieg 16.
431) Jos.6.
432) Mt.15:21-28.
433) Is.18:18.
434) Wisd.12:1-11.
435) Wisd.12:19-22.
436) Ex.20:13; Dt.5:17.
437) Gen.9:5-6.
438) Gen.34.
439) Judges 2:23.
440) Is.2:1-5.
441) 2Sam.5:17-25.
442) Gen.25:22-23.
443) Gen.25:33.
444) Krijger 8. I feel deeply indebted to this fine little book.
445) Dt.23:7.
446) Gen.32:1-22.
447) Num.20:14-21.
448) 2Sam.8:13-16.
449) 1Kings11:17-25.
450) 2Chron.25:11-14.
451) 2Chron.28:17.
452) 2Kings24:1; the text says 'Aram' but biblical scholars think that one should read 'Edom' instead, since this tallies better with 'Moab' that is also mentioned.
453) Ps.137:7.
454) Lam.4:21.
455) Is.34:5-6.
456) 1Macc.5:1-5.
457) Flav.Jos., Ant.Jud. XII.258.
458) Lk.23:6-12.
459) Acts 12.
460) Flav.Jos., Jew.Wars IV.224 and 233.
461) Flav.Jos., Jew.Wars IV.345 and 353.
462) Flav.Jos., Jew.Wars XI.378-383.
463) Flav.Jos., Jew.Wars IV.314-318 and IV.267.
464) Gen.27:38.
465) Gen.27:41.
466) Gen.33:4.

467) Krijger 25/26.
468) Gen.10. In this list of peoples Israel is not even mentioned.
469) Von Rad I 165.
470) Gen.11.
471) Von Rad I 168.
472) Ex.16:1-2.
473) Gen.12:3.
474) Gen.67:4-5.
475) Is.60.
476) I found these lines in four stanzas by Goethe and put to music by Carl Loewe (his opus 22). This song opens with the words "Gottes ist der Orient!". However, in a complete edition of Goethe's verse I could not find this poem. The index on opening words did not mention a poem beginning thus. Probably its was part of a larger poem.
477) Francis W.Newman, Soul; its Sorrows and its Aspirations (1852), quoted by James, Varieties 94/95.
478) James, Varieties 96.
479) Lev.19:19.
480) Lev.21:20.
481) See the long list of clean and unclean animals in Lev.11.
482) 2Macc.6:18 and 7:1.
483) Lev.11:7.
484) Douglas 53.
485) Lev.18:23.
486) Lev.18:7-23.
487) Douglas 53.
488) Lev.21:16-23.
489) Lev. 13-14.
490) Lev.14:33-57.
491) Douglas 54.
492) Lev.11:4.
493) Douglas 55.
494) Lev.11:20.
495) Lev.11:21. There remains, however, a difficulty with regard to several kinds of fowl mentioned in Lev.11:13-19, like the eagle, the falcon, the owl, the ibis, and so on, all of them winged and two-legged but, nevertheless, unclean. The problem is, as Douglas 55 says, that the book names them but does not describe them; it is always somewhat uncertain which animals are meant by Hebrew words. There may be several reasons why the birds mentioned are exceptions to the rule, vultures, for instance, because they feed on carrion, the different sorts of owls because they are birds of darkness, storks and ibises because they feed on fish, and in doing so penetrate into another element, the swan because it prefers to glide on the water instead of using its wings. And so on.
496) Lev.11:9-12.
497) Lev.11:27-30.
498) Lev.11:27-30; see Douglas 56.
499) Douglas 57.

CHAPTER III

MESOPOTAMICA AND ANATOLICA

1. The dualism of universal states

In May 1988, during a voyage through Turkey, I traversed the old Hittite country between Cappadocia and Ankara. The modern Turkish capital is only a hundred and thirty miles distant from ancient Hattusa, the great metropolis of the Hittite Empire, now lying in ruins. I was, I realized, in an area once one of the cradles of civilization and the birthplace of all imperialisms, ancient and modern. For it is an highly intriguing historical fact that the region stretching from Central Anatolia south-eastward to the Delta of the Euphrates and the Tigris, along an axis running from south-east to north-west, saw the birth of the first great empires. The very first of them was that of Sumer and Akkad, followed some centuries later by the Hittite Empire; the most powerful empires of this period of history, however, were those of Assyria and Babylonia.

There has been much discussion on the moot question of what exactly imperialism is. In my opinion we should reduce the term to its most simple meaning, that of the building of empire, and by 'empire' I mean a state in which more than one nation or several nations that formerly led an independent existence, are now united under one rule. Toynbee uses to call such states 'universal states'. A sense of unity is predominant in them - so strong that it makes them survive for a very long time [1]; they even believe themselves to be immortal [2]. "This sense of unity is the hallmark of universal states" [3]. To these words this scholar adds that "a universal state is ex hypothesi unique within its own world" [4].

Thus Toynbee furnishes us with the terms that are crucial for the following sections. Empires attribute to themselves a character that is lacking in other, simpler states. Not only do they believe themselves to be immortal - which means possessing a godlike nature - but they are first and foremost 'universal', that is to say, all-embracing. In fact, all empires tend to be world-empires encompassing the whole world; no empire is ever content with its own frontiers. True enough, up to now not one of them ever succeeded in extending its sway to the farthest corners of the world. The obstacles on the path to world-power proved too serious; national resources were not inexhaustible; finally, the vitality of the empire began to wane. The historical upshot is that every empire is only 'unique within its own world', as Toynbee states. In the time and in the region we are considering we find, for instance, the Hittite and the Babylonian-Assyrian Empires subsisting side by side.

Nonetheless, the empire's own world can be large enough to contain innumerable nations and tribes. One look at a map of the Roman Empire in the period of its greatest extension is sufficient to convince us of this truth. But in its own world, large or small, such an empire considers itself unique. This implies that it does not acknowledge other states; they are only there to be engulfed by it. This sense of uniqueness forms the starting-point of our inquiry. My hypothesis is that empires virtually deny the right of existence to other states, or, to put it in more theoretical terms, they consider them non-existent. If this were to prove true, it would mean a case of dualism with far reaching political and historical consequences. For then there would exist a very sharp dividing line between fully authentic states and non-existent ones.

2. Sumer

For countless centuries the great rivers Euphrates and Tigris have flowed seaward through what is now called the Republic of Iraq but was, in olden times, known as 'Mesopotamia', the land between the rivers'. In the neighbourhood of present Bagdad the streams come near each other; from there on to the sea they have built up a low and flat country by depositing layer after layer of mud. Further down the rivers form an inextricable meander of streams and rivulets flowing into the Persian Gulf. The ancient coastline lay more than fifty miles back from where it is now, far to the north of modern Basra; every year twenty meters of the Gulf is silted up, and Mesopotamia, or Iraq, is growing correspondingly larger.

In an alluvial region such as this the first inhabitants generally arrive relatively late, here perhaps around 4000 B.C. The soil is fertile enough but rainfall is rare and the summers are dry and stifingly hot. Those early farmers had to water their land by means of an intricate network of irrigation canals extending from river to river. Such a wide system made cooperation between farms and villages a must; to keep it in working order surveyors were needed, the most important (or ambitious) of whom soon controlled a large area. In all probability it was this necessity of forcing nature to come to the help of the inhabitants that imbued them with a feeling for politics and for power much stronger than in other nations. However, we do not know to what tribe or people those ancient farmers belonged.

At some time in the middle of the fourth millenium B.C. an invasion into Lower Mesopotamia took place. Very probably coming from the east a new tribe arrived, ethnically different from the autochthonous inhabitants; 'blackheaded' they were called. In several stages they extended their sway over the whole country, with Uruk (the Erech of the Bible), Ur, and Eridu as the main centres. The chronology of this period could not be more indeterminate than it actually is; we might, however, venture the opinion that around 3000 B.C. the original population and the invaders had melted into one nation. The fact that writing was invented here ca. 3100 B.C. must have accelerated the transition from a prehistorical to a historical stage [5].

This new nation is referred to as the 'Sumerians'. They themselves called their country 'Kengi(r)' = 'cultivated land'; 'Shumer' is the Akkadian rendering of it that has become the current designation [6].

The Sumerian nation possessed great talents and capabilities; it built up a long-lived and rich culture. The political organization of the country resembled that of later Greece for we find a number of independent city-states, each under a city-king, an 'ensi', of its own. There was no common capital. The city-states fought one another continuously; there were many wars between them. Probably some king or other sometimes succeeded in bringing a large region under his authority but these greater political entities never lasted for a long time [7].

About 2435 B.C. [8] a certain Luzalzaggisi became 'ensi' of the city of Umma. This man was the very first of that long line of brutal and remorseless conquerors that stretches endlessly throughout world-history. First he conducted a campaign against Lagash, captured it, and reduced its palace and temple to ashes. This manner of treating a beaten enemy became the model for all later conquerors and aggressors; in their opinion whosoever opposes their onslaught loses his right of existence. "The men of Umma plundered Lagash and in doing so sinned against Ningirsu, the god", thus the town-chronicler complains. But he adds a prophecy : "The power which they have won will be taken away from them!". Next Luzalzaggisi took Uruk and enhanced his prestige by transferring his residence to this famous city. Ur and Larsa followed; resistance was nowhere stiff.

The victorious king now turned northward and took Nippur. There the priests of the Enlil temple accorded him the title of 'King of the Lands' which means not only that he was already considered the ruler of all Sumer but that he now received divine sanction for his conquests. This trait we shall meet often enough in conquerors : only too often they believe themselves commissioned by heaven to behave as they do. Still more to the north Kish too came under Luzalzaggisi's dominion. The royal chronicles of Sumer tell us that the god Enlil "made straight his (the king's) path from the Lower Sea (probably the Persian Gulf) (over) the Euphrates and the Tigris unto the Upper Sea (probably the Mediterranean)". It is doubtful whether this report refers to an actual conquest for this would have included Syria. Very probably a victorious raid is meant. But even so such a sally was something quite new in Sumerian history [9].

Be this as it may, for the first time in her history all the city-states of Sumer were now united under one ruler. Proudly Luzalzaggisi sums up his titles and his deeds : "(Enlil the god) gave Luzalzaggisi royal power over the country, and threw down the lands under his feet; he conquered from where the sun rises to where it sets". It seems, however, that not all the inhabitants of the former city-states were grateful to him for the hard hand he had used in uniting the country [10].

3. Akkad

To the north of Sumer, and also between the great rivers, lies the country of Akkad. The inhabitants of this region, who arrived there during the fourth millennium B.C., were, unlike the Sumerians, Semites and spoke a Semitic language. Their looks were different too, for they wore their hair much longer than their neighbours and had beards; early sculptured reliefs show them with the fleshy noses and thick lips of the Semites [11]. The political organization of Akkad was similar to that of Sumer, for here too we find city-states, each with a ruler of its own. In one of these towns, Azupilanu, on the Euphrates, an illegitimate child - "my father I don't know" - was born, perhaps around 2435 B.C. He was called 'Sharru-ken', or 'Sargon'. His legend tells us that his mother laid him in an ark of bulrushes and entrusted him to the waves of the river - a curious resemblance to the story of Moses [12]. He was found by a certain Akki who made him his gardener. From then on it is a story of 'local boy makes good', for in due time he became chief cup-bearer to Ur Zafaba, the 'ensi' of Kish [13].

This 'ensi' had very little reason to be grateful to his servant for in some way or other Sargon succeeded in dethroning him. He began by organizing a fine army of archers and javelin-throwers, much more mobile than the solid but unwieldy Sumerian phalanx. The first city he took was Tuttul on the Euphrates, situated at a great distance to the north-west of Kish. This conquest was followed by the capture of Mari, a great commercial centre. From there he pressed on westward to the shores of the Mediterranean. This brought him into conflict with

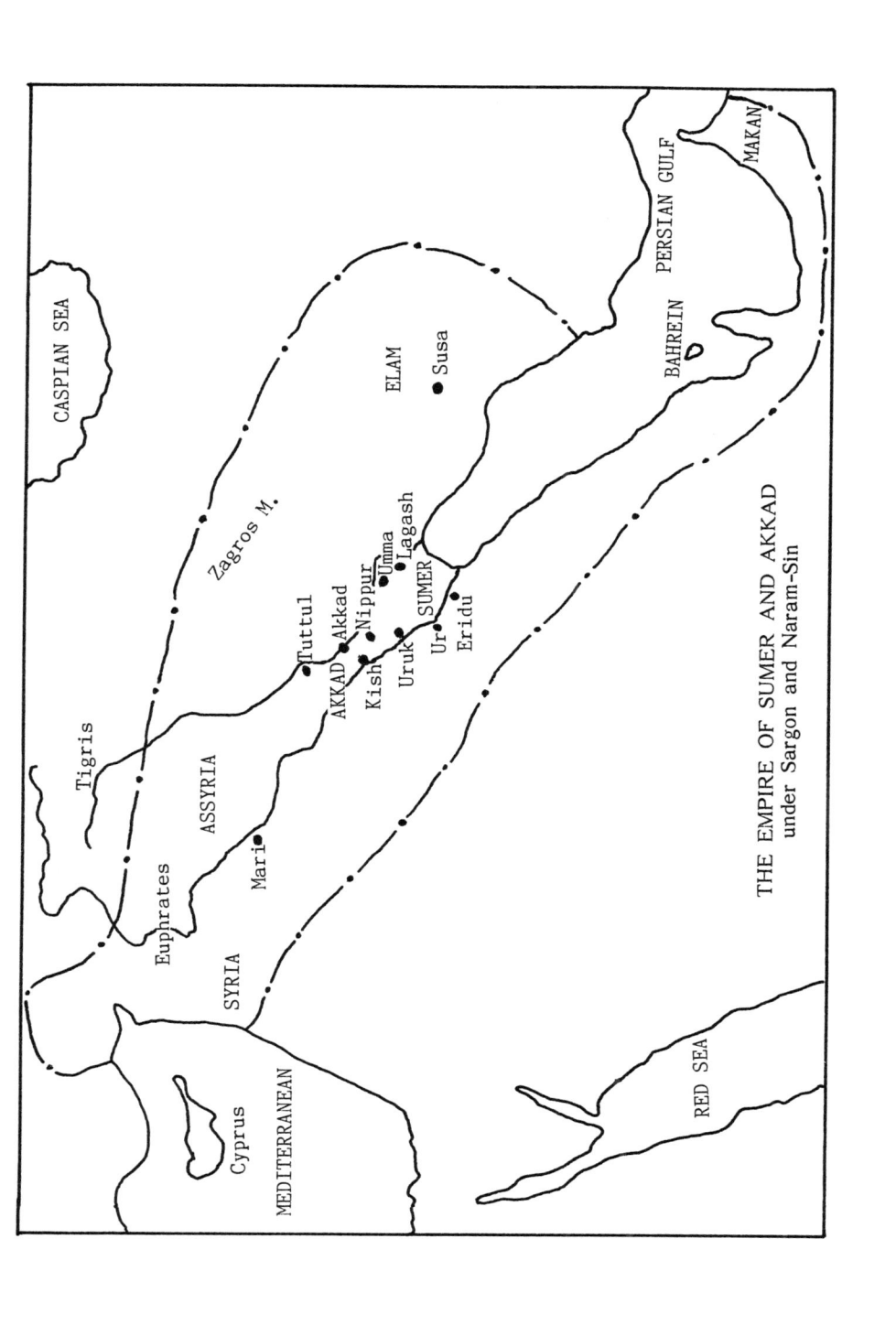

THE EMPIRE OF SUMER AND AKKAD
under Sargon and Naram-Sin

Luzalzaggisi who considered the territory west of the Euphrates as his sphere of influence [14].

Sargon decided to settle his account with his Sumerian rival once and for all but he prepared his next move very carefully. He first taught the Assyrians a lesson and then swerved far eastward to the Zagros Mountains to make it clear to the Guteans that he did not want to see his plans disturbed by this aggressive people. Then at last he swept down on Sumer. Uruk was captured and Luzalzaggisi was taken prisoner. With a collar round his neck he was led away to Nippur like a dog. There Sargon put his humbled rival on show in a cage before the Enlil temple [15]. This too is a constantly recurring feature in the history of conquest : victors usually make short work of their defeated opponents; these too lose the right of existence. All the other cities followed suit, Ur, Lagash, E-Nimmor, and Umma; some of them, however, only fell after a prolonged resistance. The victorious soldiers reached the Persian Gulf and cleaned their weapons in its waters, thus ritually purifying them from the blood with which they had become soiled [16]. Sargon probably even made an appearance on the island of Bahrein. Now all Sumer had come under his sway. The Semitic domination of Sumer would last for two centuries.

4. Sumer and Akkad

Sargon soon left Kish and founded a new residence in Akkad (or Agade). This city has totally disappeared without leaving a trace behind. Perhaps it stood forty miles north of Kish and twelve miles west of present-day Bagdad; maybe modern Der is its successor [17]. Anyhow, the name of this city became attached to the whole northern half of Lower Mesopotamia, Sargon's new realm. After the conquest of Sumer the kingdom was called 'Sumer and Akkad'. Thus the situation originated that I have described in my opening section. Two peoples, utterly different in race, language, and origin, became united - by force, not of their own free will - under a common ruler. This is the very first example of an 'Empire'. Its first dynasty was that of the Sargonids, of Sargon and his successors.

Sargon's rule lasted for a very long time, perhaps even fifty-six years. When he died in 2358 B.C., he was succeeded by his two sons successively, Rimush (2358-2439) and Manishtushu (2349-2334). Both of them, on their accession, had to beat down revolts in many parts of their realm, in particular in Sumer. That not everybody felt happy with their rule is proved not only by these insurrections but also by the fact that both kings were murdered [18]. Then came the most powerful ruler of the Sargonid dynasty, Naram-Sin (2334-2297), a grandson of Sargon. He too began with fighting down a Sumerian revolt. Having successfully put an end to inner troubles he campaigned far and wide. Southward he followed the southern shores of the Persian Gulf till he had incorporated Makan - the present-day Sultanate of Oman - into his kingdom. Eastward, beyond the great rivers, he conquered Elam and planted his standards on the northern shores of the Gulf. Great reliefs in the Zagros Mountains, to the north-west of Elam, prove that there too he triumphed over his enemies. To the north-west of Akkad herself he subdued Assyria and what is now Kurdistan, and, more to the west, Syria, so that he too reached the Mediterranean. Everywhere fortresses were built to keep the conquered populations in check.

There are many signs that, at the height of his power, he could not resist what the Greeks called 'hubris', that is, over-estimation of himself. A stele, found in Susa [19], pictures him larger than life towering high above his own soldiers and his enemies alike; he is standing on two fallen soldiers, we see a third tumbling into an abyss, still others are pictured with broken weapons or we see them clearly wounded to death or crying for mercy. Naram-Sin himself is very heavily armed with axe, spear and bow. The most important feature of this stele, however, is that two horns protrude from his helmet : horns are the emblem of divinity. In fact, he is the first king in these regions whose name in his inscriptions is preceded by the sign for 'godhead' [20]. He wanted to be venerated as 'god of Akkad' identifying in this way with the city-god of his capital; Von Soden calls this an act of 'self-divinization' [21].

"The four corners of the world submitted themselves to him", a text says [22]. For Naram-Sin considered himself not merely king of Sumer and Akkad but, preferably, 'king of the four corners of the world'. This pretension, which he actually embodied in a title, testifies to the enormity of his claims and illustrates the general tendency of empires to become world-wide. To all nations between the 'four corners' and the Empire itself independent political existence is denied; as political entities they are simply considered non-existent.

It is in accordance with this thinking that Naram-Sin baptized his son 'Sharkalisharri' (2297-2272), which means 'king of all kings'; this was not a title but his proper name. But with this son a time of decay and even anarchy began. Ca. 2233 B.C. the Guti, or Guteans, the dangerous aggressors from the Zagros Mountains whom I have already mentioned, swept down on the country like eagles. The city of Akkad went up in flames never to be rebuilt. The rule of the Guteans lasted at least a century; very probably the Sumerians helped them to topple the Sargonid dynasty [23].

About 2130 B.C. an 'ensi', or city-king, of Uruk, Utu-Hegal, succeeded in expelling the 'dragon of the mountains', the Guteans, from Mesopotamia. But it was with the 'ensi' of Ur, Ur-Nammu, that the last great dynasty of Sumer, the 'Third Dynasty of Ur' (2123-2015), began. Sumer was united again; Ur-Nammu's successor, Shulgi (2105-2057), annexed new provinces, for instance Assyria and part of Elam. But although he must forego Syria, he too called himself 'ruler of the four corners of the world'; in the latter half of his reign he too became a god. More than ever before the kings of this dynasty were made gods already during their lifetime.

The last kings of the Third Dynasty bear Semitic names. They had to fight an ever more desperate war on two fronts, against Elam that exerted very heavy pressure on Sumer, and against the Semitic Amorrhites who, from 2100 B.C., steadily made incursions into Lower Mesopotamia. When Sumer's last king was deported by the Elamites, the independent history of the Sumerians virtually ended. We may say there was, ca. 2000 B.C., no longer a Sumerian people. Of course, this was the end of every form of Sumerian imperialism too. An elegy of ca. 1950 B.C. deplores Ur's downfall as a cosmic event. "It was a hurricane", it said, "that destroyed the law, an evil storm wind that changed the times; it brought down good old Sumerian order" [24]. But what the terror-stricken remnants of this ancient people did not and could not realize is that the most important elements of their culture would live on in other civilizations. Not the least conspicuous part of this legacy was the idea of world-dominion.

5. Hammurabi's Babylonian Empire

a. The first master of all Mesopotamia

For a long time it looked as though all imperial dreams were over. Since 2100 B.C. the Amorrhites were on the move again; they came mostly from Canaan and penetrated in successive waves into Lower Mesopotamia. Ambitious sheiks captured cities in the land between the rivers and became city-kings and founders of dynasties. Sumer became a Semitic country in this way. Old tribal feuds were now fought out on an ampler scale between city and city. On the Euphrates, not far from Kish, lay an old and hitherto insignificant town, Babilu. In 1895 B.C. a certain Shumu-abum set up an independent kingdom there and thus became the founder of the First Babylonian Dynasty. The non-Semitic name of this city was altered into 'Babili' which means 'Gate of the Gods'. We are always using the Greek transcription of it, 'Babylon' [25].

The sixth king in this line was Hammurabi (1793-1750). This Semitic name is either spelled as 'Chammu-rabi' and then signifies '(the god) Chammu is great', or as 'Chammu-rapi' and in that case means 'Chammu brings recovery'. He became famous because of his so-called 'Codex Hammurabi', inscribed on a black diorite stele with a height of 2.25 meter. It was discovered at Susa in 1901/1902 and is now on show in the Musée du Louvre at Paris. It is a code of law, or rather a collection of legal case-studies, consisting of a prologue, 282

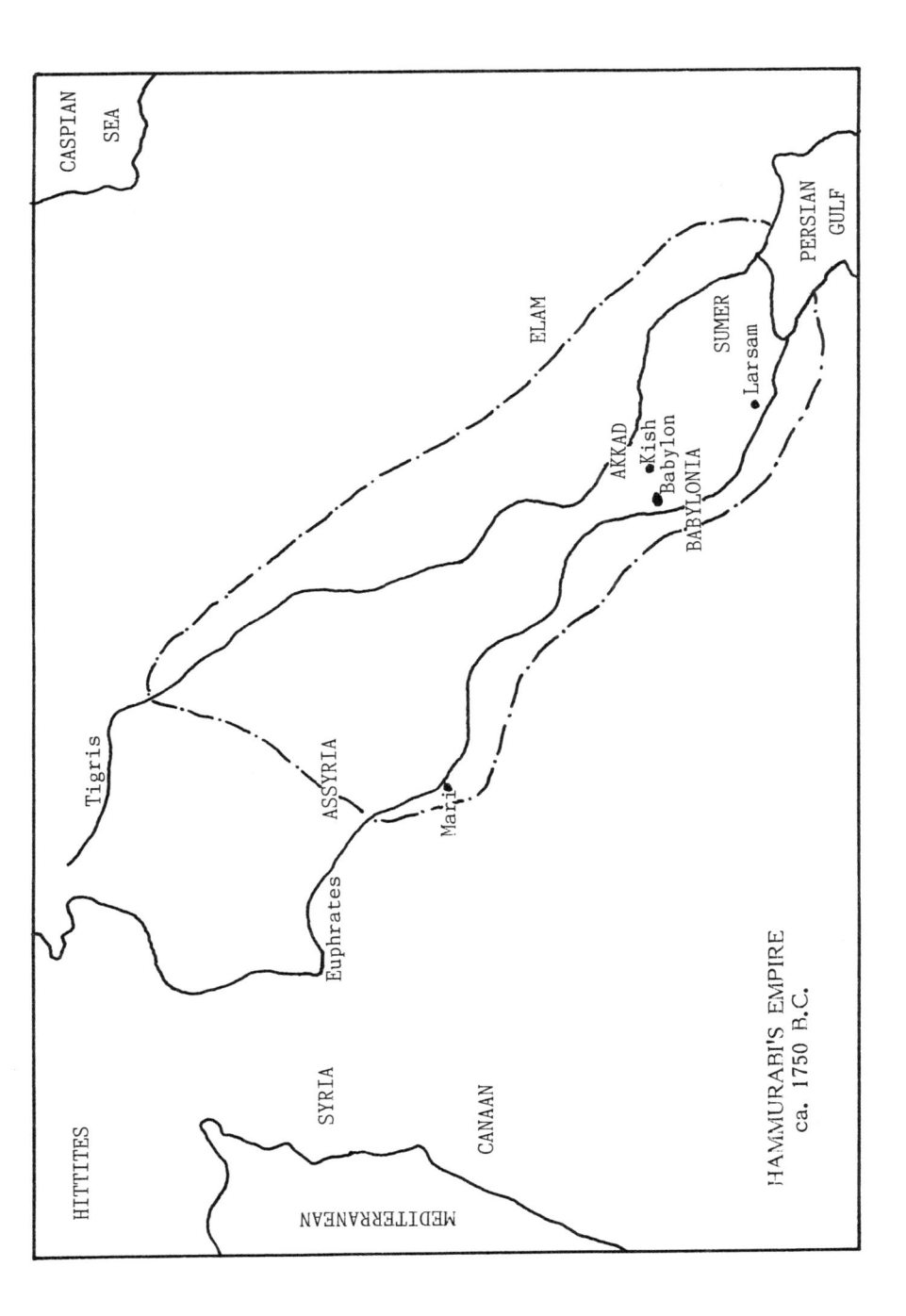

paragraphs and an epilogue [26]. However, what interests us most is his career as a conqueror for he was the first imperial king after the Sumerian period. It is a remarkable fact that great empires often have modest origins. The enormous Roman Empire, finally stretching over three continents, grew out of a tiny town among the hills on the Tiber. When Hammurabi, the founder of the First Babylonian Empire, succeeded his father in Babylon, his power base was not greater than his town although, admittedly, he took it over as a well organized political entity.

His great campaigns all date from the last phase of his reign. Since he had been campaigning for years, he had a well trained army at his disposal. His aggresive intentions did not remain hidden. In 1764 B.C. he found himself confronted by a powerful coalition consisting of Elam, Assyria, and a number of Semitic kings in Mesopotamia. He succeeded in standing his ground but the following year he went on the offensive. He took Larsa, far to the south, in former Sumerian territory. This victory made him the undisputed ruler of what once had been the Empire of Sumer and Akkad. He then turned north following the course of the rivers. In 1761 B.C. he took the important town of Mari, lost it after an insurrection, and then recaptured it in 1759, when he destroyed all the fortifications of the town. After that, he conquered the larger part of Assyria, driving back its king into the mountainous region of the north. He was now virtually master of all Mesopotamia which had never before been united under one ruler. Whether for reasons of political expediency or whether on account of his age, he did not attack Elam and Syria [27].

b. Conquest divinely sanctioned

The divine sanction that was invoked by Sargon of Akkad is not wanting in the case of Hammurabi either; in fact, it was now far more explicit and elaborate. It opens with these significant words, the very first sentence of the Codex Hammurabi : "The exalted Anum king of Annunaki and (Illil) lord of heaven and earth, who allots the destinies of the land, allotted the divine lordship of the multitude of the people unto Marduk the first-born son of Ea". Anu(m) is the god An of the Sumerians, the supreme divinity among their gods. Illil is the Enlil of the Sumerians. Between them they rule over all the gods - the Annunaki being the gods - and over the whole universe. In the fulness of their power they hand over Lower Mesopotamia to Marduk, who is the great god of Babylon. What this means is that there took place a transfer of power, divinely authorized, from the Empire of Sumer and Akkad to the new Babylonian Empire. The solemn wording must not make us forget that it is, in fact, Hammurabi who is installing himself as the successor of the Sumerian rulers; the delegation, of course, was a fiction since the Sumerian Empire had disappeared two hundred and fifty years ago. Throughout all history imperial rulers never would fail to invoke divine authorization for their undertakings.

The text goes on : "(These gods) magnified him (Marduk) amongst the Igigi (= the gods), called Babylon by its exalted name (and) so made it pre-eminent in the (four) quarters of the world, and established for him an everlasting kingdom whose foundations are firmly laid out like heaven and earth". Could anything be more meaningful? The glory of the new supreme god, Marduk, radiates on his city, Babylon, the 'Gate of the Gods'. Its rule will be permanent, even 'everlasting'. This claim of eternity will be heard time and again in the history of empire. Empires stand as firm as the universe and are, in this way, identified with it. It is for this reason that the 'four quarters of the world' turn up again. Somewhat further on it is said that Hammurabi 'stormed the four quarters (of the world)'. Although he never got further than Mesopotamia herself, it is significant as a wish-dream.

"At that time Anum and Illil for the prosperity of the people called me by name Hammurabi, the reverent god-fearing prince, to make justice to appear in the land, to destroy the evil and the wicked that the strong might not oppose the weak, to rise indeed like Shamash over the darkheaded folk to give light to the land". The king presents himself as the beloved son of the great gods from whom he received his proper name, that is, his being. He is identified with Shamash, the sun-god and, at the same time, the god of justice, and is, like him, the guarantee of right and justice for his subjects.

After this introduction there follow several pages of epithets for Hammurabi : "provider of abundant waters for his people, the shade of the land, the dragon amongst kings, the net ensnaring the enemy, the sturdy wild ox who gores the foe, a god among the kings, the favourite of the most high goddess, the shepherd of the people". He ends in this way : "the everlasting seed-royal, the sun-god of Babylon who makes the light to rise on the land of Sumer and Akkad, the king who brings the four corners of the world to obedience, the favourite of Ishtar (the great goddess of Babylonia)". Hammurabi certainly had no mean idea of himself! The important aspect of all this is that the king and his empire stood above anything and anybody else; they were of another order, less 'historical' and more divine, than all other nations and kingdoms. This gave him the right to consider all other nations as devoid of a (political) existence of their own. They could do nothing better than to submit to the 'sun-god of Babylon' [28].

c. The aftermath

There was no worthy successor to this great king. During the long reign of his son Samsuiluna (1750-1712) the Assyrian part of the Empire went lost soon enough. In 1722 B.C. its southern half - that once was Sumer - made itself independent. A later king obtained some minor successes but on the whole there was no redress. The chronicles of the last king of the First Babylonian Dynasty, Samsuditana (1626-1595), tell us that, during his reign, "men of the land of Khatti marched against the land of Akkad (= Babylonia)". These 'men of Khatti' are the Hittites who, coming from the upland plains of Anatolia, far to the west, raided Babylonia. We may take it for granted that they occupied the capital for some time and made an end of the Empire. Probably they even caried away the cult-image of Marduk, thus despoiling the city of its protective deity [29].

Laden with booty the Hittites retired soon enough. Since they were six hundred miles away from their homeland, a permanent occupation of Babylon was clearly impractical. After the downfall of the

Babylonian Empire there followed a vacuum, 'Dark Ages', of which we know next to nothing. Fierce and warlike peoples exerted heavy pressure on Mesopotamia. The Hurrites were a great plague for the Assyrians. In the mountainous regions of Luristan (now western Iran), to the east of Mesopotamia, the Kassites, also called the Cosseans, lived. They are mentioned in Babylonian annals from the eighteenth century B.C. From time to time they raided parts of the Empire but appeared there in force only after the withdrawal of the Hittites. They first occupied northern Babylonia and then, a century later, in 1475 B.C., the southern part of the former Empire. Their rule, that was never to be expansionist, lasted till 1160 B.C. [30].

6. The Hittites

a. The Old Hittite Empire

There is a Time-Life book, by James Hicks, that calls the Hittites 'the first empire-builders' [31]. In my opinion we should leave the priority in matters of imperialism to Sumer. Nonetheless, the soil of ancient Anatolia proved as fertile for empire-building as that between the great rivers. For the Hittites were, indeed, great and successful empire-builders.

An intriguing problem with regard to these Hittites is that their original name very probably was not 'Hittites'. The region where they lived, on the wind-swept plains of Anatolia, in Central Asia Minor - roughly in the vicinity of modern Ankara - was called 'the land of Hatti (or Chatti or Khatti)'; its inhabitants were the 'Hattians'. The invading Hittites were given the name of this nation or this district [32]. Who were they and where did they hail from? They were Indo-Europeans and spoke an Indo-European language. There were other Indo-European speaking peoples in Asia Minor, the Luvians for instance. But as Macqueen says, "the evidence for the original 'homeland' of the Indo-European languages seems to be overwhelmingly against a situation in Anatolia". This same author states that "linguistic evidence points to a Indo-European 'homeland' somewhere in the area that stretches

THE HITTITE EMPIRE
(greatest extension)

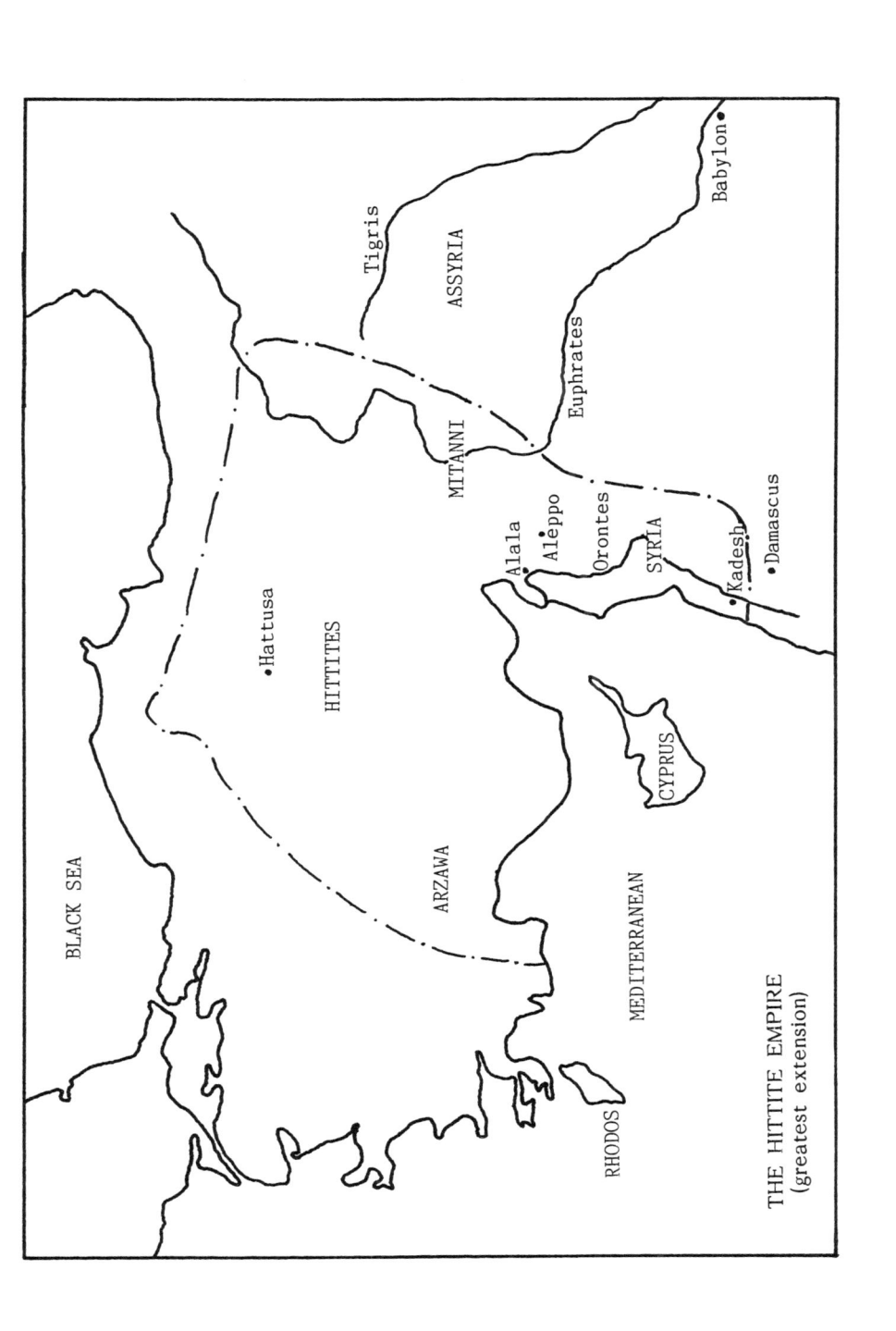

from the Lower Danube along the north shore of the Black Sea to the northern hills of the Caucasus" [33]. We may be sure that the Hittites, whatever they were called originally, arrived in Anatolia from regions to the north of it. But whether it was from the north-west, via the Dardanelles and the Bosporus, or from the north-east, through the Caucasus-passes, need not interest us here [34]. It seems that they were already on the move in the third millennium B.C. In the period after 2000 B.C. they reached Central Anatolia. They succeeded in establishing themselves in 'the land of the Hatti' easily enough, because the local chiefs were constantly fighting one another.

The first report in Hittite language in our possession dates from ca. 1800 B.C. At that time a certain Anittas was king of Kussara. The text says that he was 'agreeable to the weather-god of heaven'; this divine assistance enabled him, it goes on, to make quite a number of conquests. Several cities are cited as captured, among them Hattusa, the capital of the Hattians. He stormed it, destroyed it, cursed it, and let weeds grow at the spot where it stood. Little did he realize that this very Hattusa was to become the great metropolis of the Hittite Empire! At all events, he felt now entitled to call himself 'the great king' [35]. He bequeathed his warlike spirit to later kings. Very little is known of the ensuing period but ca. 1680 B.C. a new name, Labarnas, catches our attention. With this king "Hittite history may be said to begin" [36]. Labarnas risked disregarding Anittas' curse; on the spot where the Hattian capital had stood he began to erect a magnificent city, likewise called 'Hattusa', and no god intervened in his enterprise. The ruins of this city can still be visited; they are near the modern Turkish town of Boghazköy, a hundred and twenty miles east of Ankara.

Several texts relate the imperial deeds of this fearless king. He defied all possible evil consequences by assuming the name of his capital, calling himself henceforward 'Hattusilis', the 'man from Hattusa'. He campaigned far and wide, being on the whole very successful, although he suffered some temporary setbacks. From his heartland he struck out far south, where he reached northern Syria and took Alalah on the

Orontes; Aleppo, however, proved too strong for him. He then turned north-eastward and conquered the territory between Aleppo and the middle course of the Euphrates. A Hurrian invasion interrupted his campaigns but he soon succeeded in driving them back. He then went on campaiging in northern Syria but died in 1615 B.C. of a wound incurred in battle.

The texts I mentioned abound with terms like 'destroying, beating down, fighting like a lion, putting on fire'. He too dubbed himself 'the great king'. "I, the great king, crossed the Euphrates on foot; none (of my predecessors) ever did this ... Sargon also crossed the Euphrates". The mention of Sargon is highly important for this means that Hattusilis consciously resumed the imperial tradition that began with this great Akkadian conqueror [37]. That he truly meant to destroy the independent existence of the peoples and cities he subdued is proved by the fact that he robbed them of their gods and transported them, or more exactly their statues, to Hattusa. These gods represented the national identity of the conquered cities. At his death he left to his successor a kingdom that extended hundreds of miles southward from Hattusa and bordered on the Euphrates and the Orontes.

Hattusilis' successor was his grandson Mursilis I (1610-1580). It was this king who became temporarily master of Babylon. As I have already pointed out, he was not able to keep this city occupied; it was too far from his power base. Another reason for not extending the conquests farther was that royal power was far from stable. The royal princes tried to seize control of affairs; rebellion followed rebellion, and finally Mursilis was murdered by a brother-in-law. After that the kingdom sank into a state of virtual anarchy. The country was redeemed from this situation by King Telebinu who succeeded to the throne ca. 1500 B.C. after chasing away his brother-in-law who was king before him. His outstanding merit is that he issued an elaborate decree regulating the succession; it worked out so well that "the laws thus promulgated seem to have been observed down to the last days of the Hittite Empire" [38]. Although at least five kings followed him on the throne, he was the last important ruler of the Old Hittite Empire.

b. The New Hittite Empire

In the next century, the fifteenth B.C., the Hittites and their kings did not play much of a role in the history of the Middle East. An occasionial success was immediately followed by fresh disasters; enemies threatened from all sides; it even proved difficult to preserve the home territory. But the old vitality had not yet petered out completely. In ca. 1365 a young prince, Suppiluliumas (1365-1345) succeeded to the throne. He had already won his spurs as an army commander by dealing with the enemies in the northern part of Asia Minor [39]. Soon after becoming king himself he felt strong enough to attack a powerful rival, the kingdom of Mitanni. This state, with its Hurrite rulers, was situated to the east of Syria. Its kings rose to power shortly before 1500 B.C. and reigned over a number of vassal-states in the northern part of Mesopotamia. In the unhappy period before the succession of Suppiluliumas, Mitanni had exerted heavy pressure on the Hittite kingdom [40]. After an initial failure the energetic Hittite king succeeded in conquering the capital and crushing Mitannian power. Mitanni was transformed into a vassal-state, in order to act as a buffer-state against Assyria further east [41]. The northern part of Syria, between the Euphrates and the Mediterranean coast, was added to the Hittite domain. Suppiluliumas installed two of his sons as vassal-kings there, one in Aleppo and one in Karkemish.

Suppiluliumas, whom was the real founder of the later Hittite Empire, died ca. 1325 B.C. from the plague; not long afterwards the son who was to succeed him followed him to the grave. A younger son, Mursilis II (1323-1295), now came to the throne, a prince who was cast in the same mould as his father. For the time being he had, thanks to his father, nothing to fear in the east and south; so he could safely turn north and west. To the north of the Hittite country, along the southern shores of the Black Sea, a number of warlike tribes lived. Mursilis II campaigned against them for at least ten years of his reign. Probably he never succeeded in subduing them once and for all, but in any case he kept them at a safe distance [42].

His really great feat was a successful campaign that he conducted against the kingdom of Arzawa, far to the west, already temporarily conquered but now definitely crushed. Since Arzawa was situated in the south-western part of Asia Minor, this meant that the Hittite sway now stretched to the shores of the Aegean, opposite Rhodos. Arzawa was broken up into smaller kingdoms, with nominees of the Hittite king as vassal-princes [43]. It will be clear that the Hittite form of empire differed from that practised by, for instance, the Babylonians; they preferred to surround their country with a wide ring of vassal-kingdoms that were bound to the central power by means of treaties.

As long as things remained quiet in the north and west, the Hittites were able to concentrate their attention on the south. Now one of the unhappy consequences of the Akhenaten period was that of the Egyptian sphere of influence in Palestine, established by Thutmosis III, not much remained. When that great Pharaoh, Ramses II, became king in 1290 B.C., it became clear soon enough that a clash of interests with his Hittite counterpart was at hand. In 1286/1285 B.C. Ramses marched north and met the Hittites near Kadesh on the Orontes in what is considered one of the major battles of Antiquity. This battle is amply documented since Ramses had it pictured at least six times on the walls of his temples - presenting it, of course, as an Egyptian victory [44]. The Hittites claimed the victory for themselves and probably the greater advantage was on their side since they were able to advance further south after this battle, until they were in the proximity of Damascus. Ramses II finally resigned himself to the situation in Syria. In 1269 B.C. the Hittite king Hattusilis III (1278-1250) and Ramses II concluded a treaty in which the Egyptian recognized his Hittite colleague as his equal. The frontier was to remain where it was after the battle of Kadesh; this implied that Egypt now renounced all claims to Syria [45]. To seal the treaty a daughter of Hattusilis III was married to Ramses II.

No wonder that Hattusilis III proudly styled himself 'Tabarna' = 'Great King'. Like earlier Hittite rulers he used to refer to himself as a favourite of the gods (although Hittite kings were not deified during their lifetime). He was addressed as 'the sun' and as 'a hero beloved of the god'. Here is how he thought of himself : "The goddess, my lady, always held me by the hand; and since I was a divinely favoured man, and walked in the favour of the gods, I never committed the evil deeds of mankind" [46]. This already dualistic attitude with regard to the king's subjects was strengthened still more by an elaborate ritual 'designed to protect the king from defilement' [47]. A hair could, literally, be the cause of a servant's death for if a hair was found in the king's wash-water, the unfortunate valet was executed; the water had to be sieved carefully before it was brought to the ruler. When a member of the kitchen-staff violated the rules of cultic purity, not only he but his whole family was sentenced to death [48].

Great as Hattusilis was, or considered himself to be, dark clouds were gathering on the horizon [49]. After his death the northern tribes got aggressive again; Assyria developed into a dangerous rival; in Syria the vassals grew unruly. The end came swiftly. Around 1200 B.C. the great invasion of the 'Sea Peoples' took place. These were Indo-European raiders who overran Asia Minor and Canaan, and were stopped with great difficulty at the frontiers of Egypt. The Hittite Empire was not able to hold them off. Hattusa, the capital, was burnt to the ground, never to be rebuilt. It was, as Goetze said, 'the end of an epoch' [50].

7. The Assyrians

In the foregoing pages Assyria has been mentioned from time to time. It is situated in the northern part of Mesopotamia, in the north-eastern region of modern Iraq where Mosul and Kirkuk are the most important centres nowadays. It is a rugged and mountainous country of which only a small part is habitable and arable. This probably explains why the Assyrian kings were interested in the control of the fertile plains of Babylonia : it was impossible to feed the growing population without the import of corn and barley from the south [51]. The original name of this land was 'Ashur' which we use in the Greek transcription, 'Assyria'. Assyrians were Semites; they wrote a cuneiform script; their language, Assyrian, was akin to that of the Babylonians.

a. The beginnings of Assyria's greatness

The beginnings of Assyria's greatness were modest enough. About sixty miles south of present-day Mosul lay the city of Assur, now in ruins, on the west bank of the Tigris. It is after this city that Assyria is named, for originally it was called 'Subartu'. Nearly due west of Assur, on the western bank of the Euphrates, lay the important city of Terqa, now Tell Ashara. About 1825 B.C. Terqa was conquered by the ruler of Mari, some fifty miles to the south on the same river; in the event the prince of Terqa and most of his family perished. One of the sons, Shamshi Adad, escaped; being a man of an adventurous disposition, he first fled to Babylonia and from there captured the small town of Ekallatum on the east bank of the Tigris, south of Assur.

The great Jachdumlim, king of Mari, made the mistake of paying no attention to this insignificant new kinglet. Ten years after his arrival in Assyria, Shamshi Adad took Assur by surprise; from now on he was king of 'Subartu', as Shamshi Adad I (1815-1782). In 1810 he turned the tables on Jachdumlim, the murderer of his family; this king of Mari and his sons were killed when his mortal enemy stormed his city and captured it. Shamshi-Adad I was not one of the great Assyrian conquerors who created havoc in the whole Middle East. But, with regard to our theme, the important point is that he considered himself the heir of the earlier Mesopotamian rulers with their great pretensions, and transmitted these pretensions to his own successors. In Assur he rebuilt the temple of Enlil which he gave the name of 'House of of the wild bull of the countries'. As we know, Enlil originally was the godhead of the Sumerian town of Nippur; he had been the divine protector of the imperial deeds of the rulers of Sumer and Akkad. That Shamshi Adad now made Enlil into his protective deity meant that he saw himself as the lawful inheritor of Mesopotamian imperialism.

THE ASSYRIAN EMPIRE
(greatest extension)

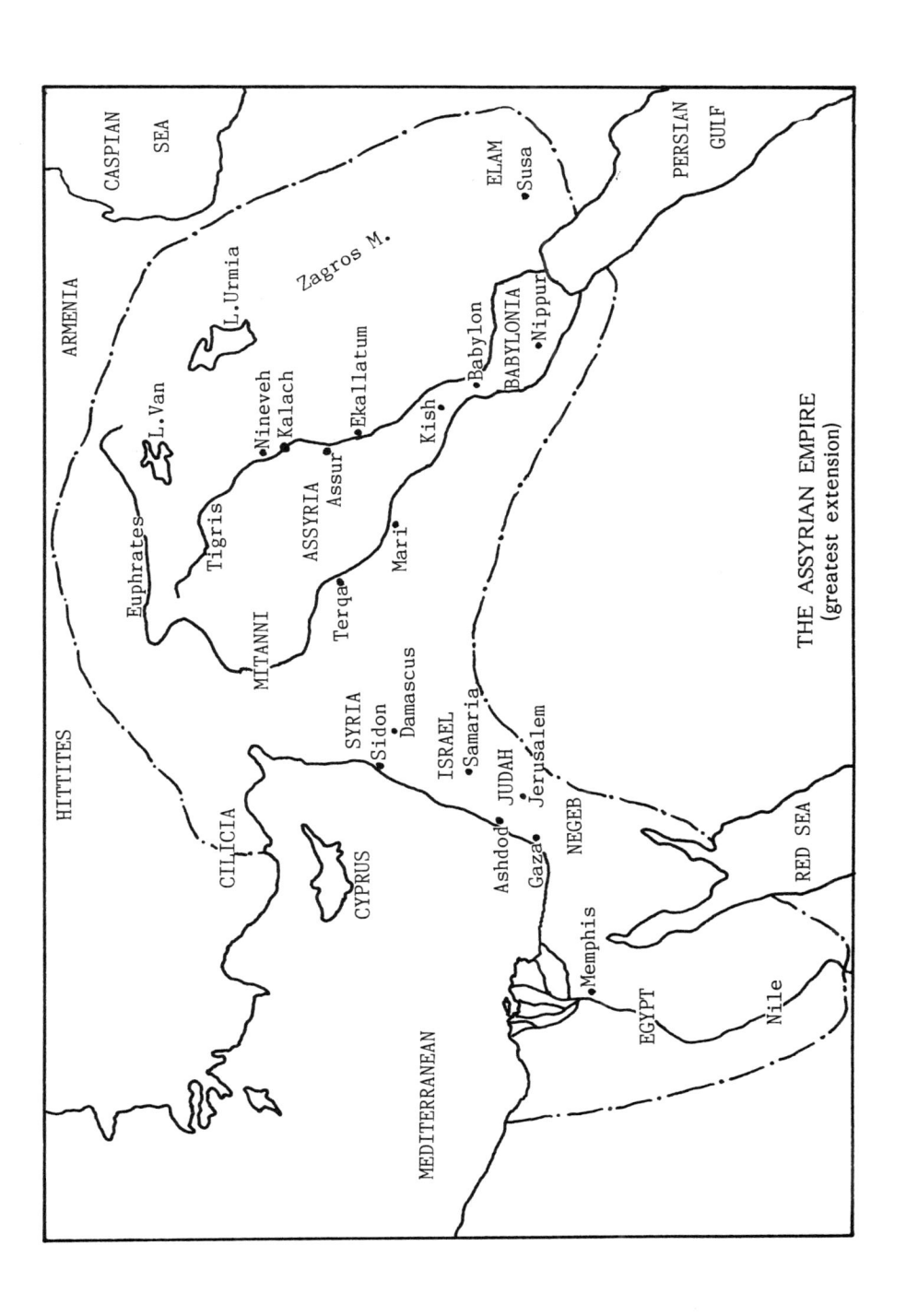

b. The great Assyrian conquests

After the death of Shamshi Adad I in 1782 B.C. it lasted several centuries before Assyria could realize his great pretensions. First Hammurabi became king of Babylonia; he conquered Mari and a large part of Assyria. Later the kings of Mitanni kept the weak Assyrian rulers in check. The great change came with Ashur-Uballit I (1366-1330), the first to call his country 'Assyria' [52]. Centuries of conquest now began. In 1366 Ashur was not a big state, hardly more than 'a few square miles about the city' [53]. Ashur-Uballit succeeded in throwing off the yoke of Mitanni and even annexed part of her territory. He styled himself 'King of Ashur' and 'Great King' and addressed the Egyptian Pharaoh as 'brother' [54].

A short look at the map of the Middle East at the time of Ashur-Uballit's death will convince us that, in 1330 B.C., the Assyrian Empire was still of a modest extent. A successor of this king, Adad-Nirari I (1310-1280), one by one defeated the tribes and nations that permanently threatened his kingdom to the east and south, and then annexed large districts of Mitanni to the west of Assyria proper; thus the whole upper course of the Euphrates came under Assyrian control. He now assumed the proud title 'King of the Universe' and called himself 'Founder of Cities'. The town that profited most of his largesse was Assur where he deployed a great building activity; the reliefs on the walls of the temples he erected are as many testimonies to his victories [55].

Adad-Nirari was followed on the throne by his son Shalmaneser I (1276-1246). In his able hands the Assyrian army became the powerful instrument that struck fear into all the nations of the Middle East. Perhaps the most important event of his reign was that he definitively destroyed what remained of Mitanni. Sensing what was threatening him her last king, Shattuara II, joined forces with the Hittites and the Syrians (or Arameans). With great relish Shalmaneser reports how he defeated the allies, not forgetting to mention that he did this 'at the behest of the great gods'. When he reached the frontier of Mitanni he found the passes blocked and the water supplies cut off. Nearly dying of thirst and fatigue his troops threw themselves on the enemy and routed him completely. The Assyrian king asserts that he waged battle against Shattuara personally, 'at the point of the spear, unto the setting of the sun'. He took 14.400 men prisoner; the capital was captured, and, if we may believe him, he reduced one hundred and eighty Mitannian cities 'to tells and ruins' [56]. What was left of Mitanni after earlier Assyrian inroads was now annexed. Munn-Rankin states that this acquisition gave Assyria control of the trade-routes leading to Syria and Anatolia and "placed at the disposal of its military command a large population with long experience in the art of war" [57].

How Shalmaneser treated rebellious cities is demonstrated by the fate of Arina, a Musri town east of the Tigris. Since it had 'despised the god Assur', he razed it to the ground and scattered salt over its site. "Its dust I gathered and in the gate of my city Assur I poured it out (as a witness) for the days to come" [58]. After a quick triumph in Armenia he annexed eight provinces between Lake Van and Lake Urmia and "brought them in submission at the feet of Assur my lord" [59]. Obviously every conquest was made at the request of the god Assur whose high-priest Shalmaneser was, in addition to being 'the favourite prince' of the goddess Ishtar. He has no rival, he is "the lord to whose feet Assur and the great gods have brought all kings and rulers in submission". He "bursts forth like the flame of fire"; the onset of his arms is 'like the snare of certain death' [60]. He too repeatedly calls himself 'King of the Universe' [61].

After him came his son, Tukulti-Ninurta I (1246-1209), whom the Greeks called 'Ninos'. After succesful campaigns against the rapacious tribes of Armenia and the Zagros Mountains who caused trouble at every succession, he struck out westward into the Hittite country. Victorious, he "carried off 28.000 Hittite warriors from the other side of the Euphrates" [62]. The number may be exaggerated, and these Hittites were perhaps North-Syrians [63]. Nonetheless, this really was a great historical event. For in this context the ill-famed Assyrian deportation policies are mentioned for the first time. The most important event of this reign, however, was the conquest of Babylonia. Very probably the Assyrians felt themselves culturally inferior to their southern neighbours; perhaps therefore they always treated them with a certain deference. But such qualms were foreign to that immoderate man, Tukulti-Ninurta.

At that time Babylonia was ruled by a Kassite (that is, non-Akkadian) king, Kashtiliash IV. The Assyrian began a war against him; he says that he captured his opponent in battle with his own hand. "Stripped and bound I carried him before Assur my lord" [64]. The victor then marched on to Babylon, took it, tore down its walls, and slaughtered a great number of its inhabitants. Then he did something that was disapproved of even by his own subjects [65] : "the treasure ... of Babylon he profanely brought forth", says a later Babylonian chronicle, "and the great lord (god) Marduk he removed from his abode (temple) and carried him off to Assyria" [66]. Babylonia became part of the Assyrian Empire, and the whole of Mesopotamia was now in Assyrian hands. The king's deportation policy and the transfer of the Babylonian godhead prove that, in his view, other peoples were virtually non-existent. In Antiquity a nation belonged to its ground, not only by historical right but even more organically; people and land formed a natural entity under the protection of the local and national deities. Tearing them apart meant that, for the Assyrian rulers, other peoples were nothing at all, in the clearest dualistic vein.

Tukulti-Ninurta had no lack of bragging virtues : 'king of the universe, king of Assyria, king of the four corners (of the world), king of Babylonia, king of Sumer and Akkad (= heir of the oldest imperial claims), king of the Upper and Lower Sea, king of the mountains, king of the plains' [67]. These resounding titles got a hollow ring at the end of his reign. Babylonia wrenched herself from the Assyrian grip; Tukulti-Ninurta was murdered by his own son. Then a long period of decay set in. The roles seemed to be reversed; for some time Assyria was hardly more than a vassal of Babylonia.

Some Assyrian kings were more successful than others in restoring part of the old glory. One of these was Tiglath-Pileser I (1117-

1078). His victorious campaigns greatly eased the pressure to which Assyria had been subjected for so long; crossing North-Syria he even reached the Mediterranean where, sailing in a Phoenician ship, he caught a narwhal [68]. Together with the report that the Egyptian king sent him a crocodile this brings us to another point. Tiglath-Pileser I, who too styled himself 'king of the universe', even counted the wild beasts of the steppe and the woods among his subjects. He was the first Assyrian king to possess a zoo in which lions, wild bulls, and elephants were kept. These animals were not there to be viewed on Sunday afternoons by parents holding children by the hand; they were reserved for the king's hunt. Many fine Assyrian reliefs show, for instance, how lions were set loose from cages, persecuted by the king, and then transpierced with arrows and spears.

Tiglath-Pileser bequeathed this kind of sport to his successors who all relished it. It proved that they exercised power over nature and that even the fiercest animals were no match for them. Tiglath-Pileser boasts of his hunting feats in these words : "Four wild bulls (aurochs), which were mighty and of monstrous size, ... I killed with my iron spear and with my sharp darts ... Ten mighty bull-elephants I slew in the country of Harran ... Four elephants I caught alive ... I have slain one hundred and twenty lions by my bold courage and by my strong attack, on foot; and eight hundred lions I have laid low from my chariot with javelins. I have brought down all (kinds of) beasts of the field, and the birds of heaven that fly, among my hunting spoils" [69].

c. Immense cruelty

Tiglath-Pileser's successors pursued his policy with some measure of success so that each of them could bequeath to his descendants a safer power base; this base was the old cradle-land of Assyria proper with the surrounding regions stretching from the foot of the Zagros Mountains in the east to the Euphrates in the west, and from southern Armenia in the north to the frontiers of Babylonia in the south. This was a sufficient starting-point for a man like Assurnasirpal II (884-859).

who was an indefatigable campaigner and at the same time probably the most cruel of all Assyrian kings [70]. In New York, in the Metropolitan Museum of Art, I saw a picture of him on a relief from his great palace in his capital Kalach; the smile on his face struck me as malevolent and sadistic.

Immense cruelty was, indeed, an integral part of his policy. He was no great conqueror although he too pushed on to the Mediterranean shore and turned Syria into an Assyrian sphere of influence. Ably using his well-organized forces, the first Assyrian army with cavalry, he made it abundantly clear to all tribes and nations surrounding the mother-country to the east, north, and west, that their fate rested once and for all in Assyrian hands. He was "the king who is without a rival among the princes of the four quarters (of the world), ... who has bought into submission those that were not submissive to him, who has brought under his sway the totality of all peoples, the mighty hero who treads on the neck of his foe", etcetera, etcetera [71].

Not without sadism the royal chronicles sum up what he did to those who dared to oppose him. "Two hundred of their fighting men I cut down with the sword, ... with their blood I dyed the mountain red like wool" [72]. "(He) fixed the bodies of his foes on stakes" [73]. "I built a pillar over against the city gate, and I flayed all the chief men who had revolted, and I covered the pillar with their skins, and others I bound to stakes round the pillar; many within the borders of my own land I flayed, and I spread their skins upon the walls, and I cut off the limbs of the officers ... who had rebelled" [74]. From some captives I cut off their hands and their fingers, and from others I cut off their noses and their fingers; of many I put out the eyes" [75]. This utter contempt for human dignity and integrity proves that Assurnasirpal thought and acted in a dualistic way : those who stood between him and absolute power had to be crushed.

To him people were not autonomous beings existing in their own right but only particles of his power. This also becomes evident from his large scale deportation policies. Great masses of men, women and children were displaced and settled somewhere else. Regions that once had a homogeneous population now became mixed in race and language. The magnificent new capital of Kalkhu (Kalach) was populated with deported people [76].

Tiglath-Pileser's son Shalmaneser III (884-859), fortified Assyria's hold on Syria (although he failed to capture Damascus), and exerted great pressure on Israel, the northern kingdom. For the first time in history a non-biblical annal mentions an Israelite king, Ahab, as a member of an anti-Assyrian coalition of eleven princes [77]. On the so-called 'Black Obelisk' in the British Museum we see how King Jehu of Israel pays tribute to Shalmaneser; on another relief we seem him on his knees before the Assyrian ruler with his head to the ground : "Tribute of Iaua mâr Humrî (Jehu son of Omri); silver, gold, etc. I received from him" [78].

A military revolt brought Tiglath-Pileser III (746-727) to the throne, the 'Pul' of the Bible. He made good use of the chaos that prevailed in Babylonia after the death of King Nabu-Nasir in 734; he conquered the country in the years 731-729, and became king of Babylonia as 'Pulu' advancing the claim that he united in his person the respective powers of Assyria and Babylonia. From then on he styled himself 'king of the universe, king of Assyria, king of Babylon, king of Sumer and Akkad, king of the four regions (of the world)' [79]. Another resounding success was the capture of the great Aramean metropolis Damascus in 732 B.C., with the help of new and highly effective siege-engines. This conquest opened the road to the south; the king crossed through Israel and the Philistine country. For the very first time an Assyrian army appeared on the frontiers of Egypt. King Ahaz of Judah presented himself to Tiglath-Pileser in order to do homage to him [80]. Israel had to cede a large part of Galilee to the Assyrians.

The deportation policy was relentlessly pursued. Hundreds of thousands of people were displaced; thirty thousand inhabitants of Syria were settled in Armenia; Armenians went south to Cilicia; Galileans were deported, while pagan foreigners occupied their homesteads. What the king really meant was to make his people 'of one mouth', which means that they must forget their own vernacular - an essential part of their national identity - and learn to speak one common language. In this he succeeded in so far that Aramean, the colloquial speech of the strongest population group, now became the 'lingua franca' of the Middle East [81].

d. Assyria's greatest days

When Tiglath-Pileser's son, Shalmaneser V (727-722), heard that Israel's king had tried to make contact with Egypt, he took this king prisoner and began the siege of Samaria [82]. After an heroic stand of three years this town was captured by Shalmaneser's successor, Sargon II (722-705); he deported what remained of the original population of Israel and resettled the country with foreigners, mainly Babylonians, who later became the Samaritans. Judah regularly paid tribute to Assyria [83]. Both Sargon II and his successor Sennacherib (705-681) campaigned far and wide. In 701 B.C. this last king saw himself confronted with a powerful coalition of kings in Phoenicia and Palestine. The Assyrian ruler had no great difficulty in subduing this alliance; most of the kings readily submitted to him when he marched out against them in force. But Hizkiah, king of Judah, proved of a sterner stuff; the dauntless prophet Isaiah stiffened his will to resist [84].

The royal chronicler of Assyria relates the events in these words : "As for Hizkiah, the Jew, who did not submit to the yoke, forty-six of his strong walled cities, as well as the small cities in their neighbourhood which were without number ..., I besieged and took ... Himself, like a caged bird, I shut up in Jerusalem, his royal city. Earthworks I threw up against him; the one coming out of his city I turned back to his misery ... As for Hizkiah, the terrifying splendour of my majesty overcame him, and the Urbi (Arabs) and his mercenary troops he brought in to strengthen Jerusalem, his royal city, deserted him". The attentive reader will have noticed that one item of news is lacking in this report : that Jerusalem was captured. The Assyrian army had to withdraw suddenly, very probably because of the outbreak of a plague-epidemic. Nevertheless, Hizkiah had to cede part of Judah to Assyrian vassals in Gaza and Ashdod and henceforward paid tribute [85].

Sennacherib's second historical feat was to make a definite end of always insurgent Babylon. In 689 B.C. he took the city, razed it to the ground, deported the population, and burnt down its temples. Canals were dug right through the town, which was then flooded with water. "That in days to come the site of that city, and (its) temples and gods, might not be remembered, I completely blotted it out with (floods of) water, and made it like a meadow" [86]. In Assyrian mythology the name of the god Marduk (originally a Babylonian divinity) was replaced by that of Ashur. It seems that even many Assyrians took it ill of their king that he thus insulted the great god. In any case, he was murdered in 681 B.C. [87].

The new king, Esarhaddon (681-669), was a son of the former. Under his sceptre the Assyrian Empire reached its greatest extent for Egypt was now conquered. Small wonder that he was so successful, for "I entered into Nineveh, my royal city, joyfully, and took my seat upon the throne of my father in safety. The south wind blew, - the breath of Ea, the wind whose blowing is favourable for exercising kingship. There awaited me favourable signs in heaven and on earth, a message from the soothsayers, tidings from the gods and goddesses". He did not fail to mention that he had exterminated those people who had other plans for the succession 'to the last man' (literally : 'as one') [88]. Probably he felt uneasy about what his father had done to Babylon, or rather to Marduk; after the city had been lying fallow for a number of years, he decreed that it should be rebuilt. He circumvented the will of his father by declaring that everything had been the will of Marduk himself. The original plan was that the city would be left desolate for seventy years but the god reversed the order of the cuneiform signs for 'seventy', being in the sexagesimal Akkadian system 60 and 10, and thus came out on only eleven years [89].

The campaign against Egypt, Assyria's great rival in the Palestinian-Syrian sphere of influence, took place in 671 B.C. Passing the Negeb desert was a laborious affair for the Assyrian army; once in Egypt it had to fight three pitched battles in fifteen days. But then, after a siege of only one and a half day, the Assyrians made a triumphant entry into Egypt's proud capital Memphis. The badly wounded Pharaoh, Taharka, who, by the way, was a Nubian, fled and left his whole family in the hands of the conqueror. The booty that fell to the victors was enormous; everywhere Assyrian governors and officials were appointed [90].

No wonder that this Esarhaddon too used the most resounding titles for himself : 'king of the universe, king of Assyria, mighty warrior, first among all princes ..., creature of Ashur and Ninlil, beloved by Sin and Shamash, favourite of Nabû and Marduk, beloved object of Queen Ishtar's affection, heart's desire of the great gods; the powerful, the wise, thoughtful and knowing ... It was I that marched triumphantly relying on their might, from the rising to the setting sun, and had no rival, who brought in submission to my feet the princes of the four quarters (of the world)" [91]. No mention is made of the fact that the subject countries were not infrequently seething with revolt. Anyhow, he had to use the most exquisite cruelty to hold them down. "That the might of Ashur, my lord, might be manifested to (all) peoples, I hung the heads of Sanduarri (king of Kundi in the Taurus region) and Abdi-Milkutti (king of Sidon) on the shoulders of their nobles and with singing and music paraded them through the public square of Nineveh" [92].

Assyria's last great king was Assurbanipal (669-627). There exists a wonderful relief, now in the Musée du Louvre but originating from the royal palace at Nineveh, that pictures this king larger than lifesize on his chariot. His charioteer and his groom are much smaller than he, while the servants who accompany the chariot are hardly taller than its wheels. Probably he came to deplore his father's decision to rebuild Babylon since he had to beat down a revolt there.

The last historical victory of Assyria was the conquest of Elam, to the east of the river Tigris. After having campaigned against this country for thirty years on end he brought it down at last. "I captured Susa, the great metropolis, the abode of their gods ... At the command of Ashur and Ishtar I entered into its palaces, and dwelt there amidst rejoicing." All that he found in these palaces and temples was carried off to Assyria. "The sanctuaries of Elam I destroyed to non-existence. Its gods (and) goddesses I scattered to the wind(s) ... The sepulchres of their earlier and later kings, who did not fear Ashur and Ishtar, my lords, (and who) had plagued the kings, my fathers, I destroyed, I devastated, I exposed to the sun. Their bones I carried off to Assyria" [93]. Here again the dualistic tendency of these reigns becomes evident : everybody who resisted the imperial kings, godheads not excluded, was reduced to 'non-existence', a term that occurs literally in the text. The downfall of this ancient power had an unexpected consequence. Once Elam had disappeared there was no buffer-state left to prevent the Persians from reaching Mesopotamia.

Assyria's immoderate imperial pretensions and her senseless cruelties laid the foundation for her downfall which arrived quicker than anybody would have thought. In 612 B.C. a coalition of her enemies, led by her most inveterate foe, Babylonia, entered Nineveh. The last Assyrian king was buried under its ruins; the last Assyrian city fell in 608 B.C. Thousands and tens of thousands of Assyrians paid with their lives for the sins of their kings. Nineveh was destroyed so completely that two centuries later Xenophon and his Greek army could pass over its grounds without having the slightest idea of the greatness that lay buried beneath their feet. Thus ended the greatest empire the world had ever seen.

8. The New Babylonian Empire

The sudden downfall of the Assyrian Empire did not mean the end of Mesopotamian imperialism. Although for four long centuries Babylonia had had to be content with a subordinate role in the power game, she had never forgotten her own imperial claims. After so many rulers of alien stock, King Nabopolassar (626-605) was, apparently, an indigenous Babylonian, a 'Chaldean'. He profited, of course, from the downfall of Assyria to make his own country once again independent. His son, Nebuchadnessar II (Nabuchodonosor) (605-562) was, however, to be the

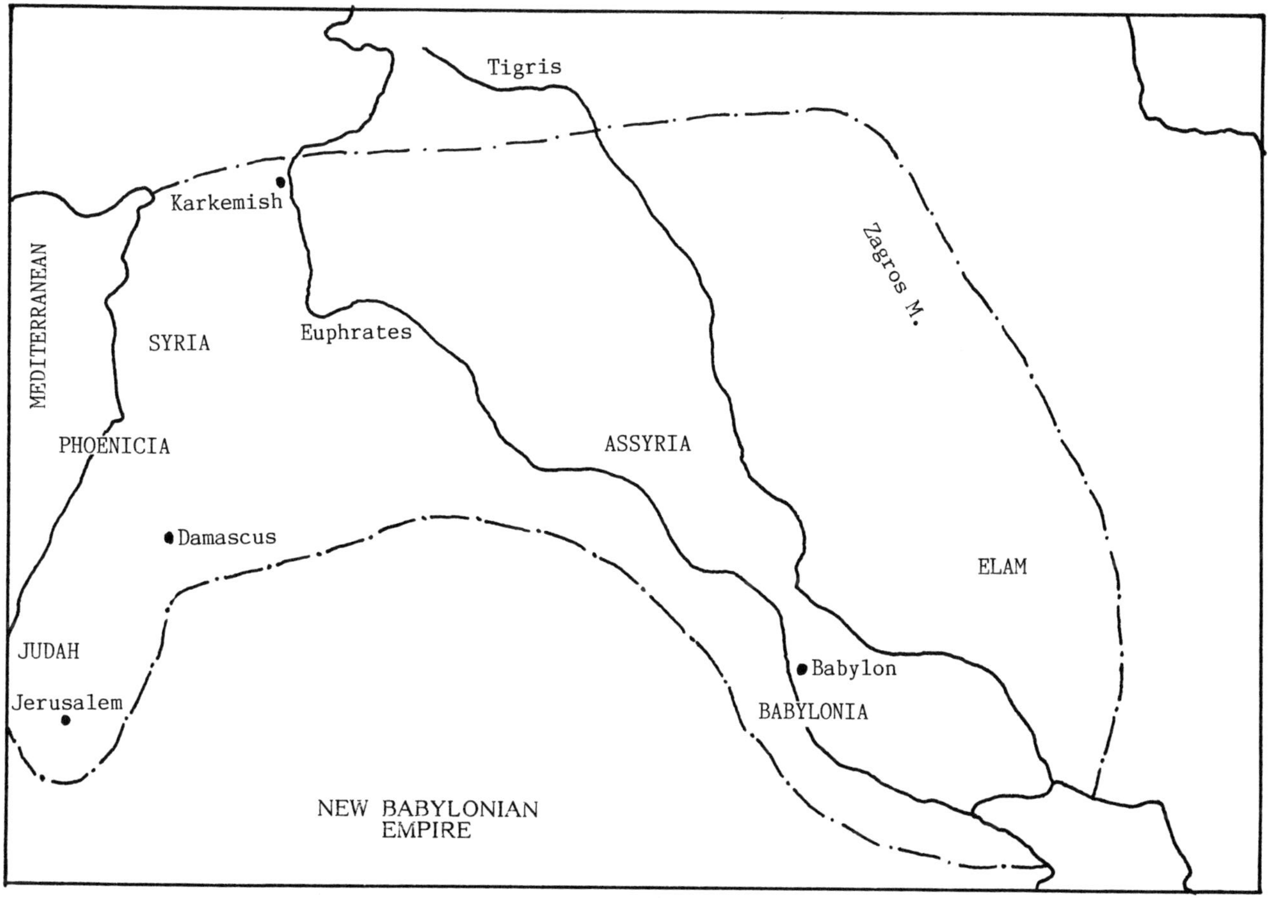
Tigris
Karkemish
Zagros M.
MEDITERRANEAN
SYRIA
Euphrates
PHOENICIA
ASSYRIA
Damascus
ELAM
JUDAH
Babylon
Jerusalem
BABYLONIA
NEW BABYLONIAN EMPIRE

real founder of the New Babylonian Empire. In 606 B.C., while still crown-prince, he countered Egyptian attempts to annex Syria. He defeated the Egyptian army in the battle of Karkemish in 605 B.C. and was hotly pursuing it southward when he had to hasten back to Babylon because of the death of his father. Once he was king, he continued to campaign in Syria and Palestine, although he never succeeded in penetrating Egypt herself.

A relief in the Wadi Brissar, in the Lebanon Mountains, shows him fighting a lion and cutting down a cedar. The accompanying text says : "I performed what no other king did; I broke through the steep mountains, I split rocks, I opened passages, and thus I smoothed a way for the transport of cedars, tall and strong, of incomparable beauty and of exceptionally dark quality" [94]. His successes against Egypt had evil consequences for the last remaining Jewish state, Judah, which was virtually a vassal of Egypt. This forced Nebuchadnessar to take action against it. In 597 B.C. he besieged and captured Jerusalem; King Jojakin and a great number of nobles were deported to Babylon. Babylonian sources of the following years mention 'Ja-u-kin' as receiving rations [95]. Zidkiah now became king as a vassal of Babylonia.

This monarch was unwise enough to play the Egyptian card again, despite the stern warnings of Jeremiah, a prophet with acute political insight. Of course, Nebuchadnessar returned in force, beat the Egyptians back, and blockaded Jerusalem. After a siege of one year and a half, starvation forced the garrison into capitulation. The Holy City was thoroughly looted, Solomon's temple and a great part of the city went up in flames, the walls were levelled to the ground, and Zidkiah's sons were slaughtered before his eyes, while he himself was blinded and transported to Babylonia together with a great many nobles, artisans, and craftsmen, one of the exiles being the prophet Ezekiel. Judah now became a Babylonian province [96]. The last city in the Palestinian-Phoenician region to capitulate was Tyre in 573 B.C. after a siege of thirteen years.

Nebuchadnessar's New Babylonian Empire comprised all the former Assyrian conquests, with Elam, the Zagros Mountains, and the whole of

Mesopotamia, and, in addition, Syria, Phoenicia, and Palestine. Egypt, now once again a sovereign state, was alone excepted. However, a great thunderstorm was already gathering on the northeastern horizon. A new power, that of the Medes was rapidly rising. Their empire already stretched through Armenia to far into Asia Minor. Somewhat later, however, the centre of power suddenly shifted from the Medes to the Persians. In 539 B.C. Cyrus, the first great king of the Persians, pushed west and like a flash of lightning appeared in Babylon. The sudden fall of the Babylonian Empire and the onslaught of the Persians opened a new chapter in world-history.

9. Kingship

In the preceding sections it was maintained that a dualistic distinction existed between the Anatolian and Mesopotamian Empires on the one hand, and all nations outside them on the other. To every people not incorporated in an Empire the right of existence was virtually denied. Opposing the onslaught of imperial power or rebelling against it usually had the worst possible consequences. The Empire not only annexed the territory of a conquered state but arrogated its deities to itself. Often the whole nation was destroyed without much ado, as happened to the Israelites of the northern kingdom who were deported to Mesopotamia and vanished there into the autochthonous population. We must now address ourselves to the question of whether or not a sharp dualistic distinction between the king and his subjects (which, as we have seen, was so characteristic of Egypt) was equally the case within the framework of an Empire.

a. The Hittite kings

The extreme care taken to protect a Hittite king from impurity, which I referred to earlier on, provides us with a good starting-point for our discussion. Originally a Hittite king was not an Oriental despot at all, but the greater the extension and the power of the Hittite Empire became, the more powerful also the king grew. In the later stages of the Empire he was seen as the deputy of the gods on earth. Although he was not considered a god during his life, he was deified after his death [97]. "The land (of the Hittites) belongs to the weather-god. Heaven and earth (and the) people belong to the weather-god. He made the Labarna (title of the king) his regent, and gave the whole country of the Hittites to him. Thus the Labarna will rule the whole country with his (the god's) hand" [98]. Every year the king reported to the gods on the course of his reign.

This exalted position of the later Hittite kings set them apart from all others. The king was protected from his surroundings by very elaborate rules of purity. I have already given several examples. The kitchen-staff had to take an oath every month that they would not bring tainted water to the king. The royal shoemaker only used leather that came from the royal domain - on pain of death. All this makes it abundantly clear that a Hittite king was a being utterly different from all others. The king, as the intermediary between gods and men, had to be pure, since every form of impurity would fatally endanger his functioning as a divine deputy; this, in its turn, would mean a lethal threat to the well-being of his people.

But where did this danger arise from? The answer is simple : from everybody and everything that was not royal, that did not belong to the inner royal circle. Now Mary Douglas who, in her already cited book 'Purity and Danger', emphasizes this point, says that there is danger wherever the normal ordering of things is impaired. Disorderliness is a serious threat to the fabric of society. 'Dirt', for instance, is a form of disorderliness, for it is 'matter out of place' [99]. We all hate dirt; therefore, housewives continually clean their homes, and road-sweepers clean the streets. It is a deeply felt complaint against modern cities that they are 'dirty'. A very telling example of this abhorrence is that hair in the king's wash-basin that even led to the unhappy servant's death. But this capital punishment was in accordance with the demand for absolute purity. The king must under no condition come into contact with 'matter out of place'.

With regard to our theme the decisive point is that everything and everybody outside the royal circle was 'out of place'. All human beings and all objects outside that circle belonged to a world of disorderliness, and were, therefore, a constant threat to the relationship between the king and the gods. The nearest the king came to the ordinary world was by eating food. In doing this, he associated, even to some extent identified himself with that ordinary world. In order to make this inevitable contact as innocuous as possible food and kitchen-staff had to be purified constantly. Another revealing instance of the scrutinous avoidance of 'dirt' and irregularity is that no member of the royal bodyguard might slip away to urinate as long as the king was near [100].

b. Legendary kings of Sumer

From the earliest times Sumerian kings were viewed by their subjects as very special persons outside the common run of men. This is already the case with the rulers in the Sumerian King List that gives the names of the kings in the period before 2500 B.C. Some of them became the legendary heroes of epic tales, like Lugalbanda who is the main character of two of them, or like the famous Gilgamesh to whom and to whose epic we shall have to return. Lugabanda later was deified; his successor, Dumuzi, is the protagonist of an important Sumerian epic. He too made his way into the Sumerian-Akkadian pantheon, and as god of the blossoming spring he was extremely popular. It is possible that in Syria, Phoenicia, and Israel he was known as 'Adoni', and with the Greeks as 'Adonis'. As late as the sixth century B.C. the prophet Ezekiel witnessed the women of Jerusalem, who called him 'Tammuz', lamenting his death [101]. The month 'Tammuz' in the postexilian Jewish calendar still bears his name; Kramer says that "the fasting and lamentation which mark its seventeenth day no doubt hark back to the Sumerian days of the distant past" [102].

c. The historical Mesopotamian kings

The beginnings of historical Mesopotamian kingship were modest enough. It seems that "the oldest political institution in the country was the assembly of all free men; that they left power to deal with urgent matters in the hands of a group of elders; and that in times of emergency they chose a 'king' to take charge for a limited period". This is what Frankfort calls 'Primitive Democracy' [103]. Thus the initial political system was based on general discussion and communal action. But, as Frankfort goes on to explain, "communal action required unanimity, and this could be reached only by means of persuasion. Hence the need for action and leadership fostered a parasitical growth of personal power which ultimately destroyed the original system of government" [104].

Schmökel considers the idea of 'primitive democracy' 'as a peculiarity of some American scholars' [105]. The fact, however, that the Sumerian King List describes kingship as having descended from heaven does not necessarily plead against the definition of the king as 'no more than primus inter pares, a leader elected in time of war' [106]. But 241.000 years after the establishment of divine kingship, "the Flood swept over (the land). After the Flood had swept over (the land, e.g. carrying away all that existed) and kingship had descended from heaven (a second time), Kish became the seat of kingship". In the meantime, the royal insignia, the sceptre, tiara, and pastoral staff, 'lay before Anu' (i.e. were guarded by the gods) [107]. The heavenly origin of kingship must probably be seen as the theological justification of its later form.

This divine origin must not make us think that Mesopotamian kings were regarded as gods, like their Egyptian counterparts. True enough, the names of some kings are preceded by the cuneiform sign for divinity. We find this for the first time in the case of Naram-Sin of Akkad, and after him before the names of the kings of Ur and Isin, and some others. However, the names of the greatest and best-known of the kings, Hammurabi, and the famous Assyrian and Neo-Babylonian kings, go without it [108]. In consequence, we must not see the kings as gods [109]. But of course the king was a great favourite of the godheads. "To Eannatum, the ensi of Lagash, whom Ningirsu (a god) had conceived of (in his mind), Inanna (a goddess), because she loved him, gave the kingship of Kish in addition to the ensiship of Lagash" [110]. Luzalzaggisi was the first to style himself 'king of the land' which means that he ruled the whole country with all its city-states. This acquisition of new power too is presented as a divine favour. "When Enlil, king of all countries, had given the kingship of the land to Luzalzaggisi ..., on that day he (Enlil) pacified for him the road from the Lower Sea (the Persian Gulf) to the Upper Sea (the Mediterranean)" [111]. Here we have the theological justification of Sumerian imperialism, the oldest in the world. "To Sargon, king of the land, Enlil gave no rival; Enlil gave him the whole territory from the sea above to the sea below" [112]. This imperial claim is expressed in the often mentioned title 'king of the four corners of the world'; 'king of the universe' is a shade more grandiose still.

The kings of Mesopotamia were not bound to the gods in that very special and well-defined relationship that prevailed in Egypt between Pharaoh and gods like Amon-Ra or Osiris. However, a Mesopotamian prince too is a 'son of the gods', of several gods at a time. Thus Hammurabi calls himself 'son of Sin', as well as 'son of Marduk', 'son of Dagan', and 'son of Enlil' [113]. That the king was the beloved of the gods "was said to materialize in the successes of the ruler in war and in the prosperity of the country in peace" [114]. Royal statues stood in temples and were the objects of veneration, in particular after the death of the king; for the modern mind it is not easy to comprehend that, as Frankfort explains, some of these statues were divinities to whom offerings were brought, whereas the kings they represented were not divine [115].

The difference between Egyptian and Mesopotamian kings is most clearly demonstrated by the fact that Mesopotamian rulers were not, like the Pharaohs, an integral part of nature. Kingship in Mesopotamia was primarily a social institution, with highly important theological and religious implications, but not a constitutive factor of the fabric of nature [116]. While in Egypt the death of the king endangered the natural system, in Mesopotamia "the natural process remained under the control of the gods; and the king could only attempt to bring about favourable conditions by retaining the divine favour" [117]. However, the task of a Mesopotamian ruler with regard to nature was important enough. It was his special function to maintain the harmony between human society and nature, although he did this in a less direct way than his Egyptian counterpart. He performed his task "only by watching over the service of the gods and attuning the life of the community to such portents as were vouchsafed him as revelations of the divine will" [118]. Hence Assurbanipal could confidently state that "in my reign there was fulness to overflowing, in my years there was plenteous abundance " [119]. However, the ruler was no mere executor of divine commands. He was also capable of influencing the decisions from on high, to some extent, for instance by the use of magic. Thus Hammurabi, in great tranquillity of mind, stated : "I am the sun of Babylon who causes light to rise over the land of Sumer and Akkad" [120].

This makes it quite clear that a Mesopotamian ruler was not a common human being. Far from it! He is (dualistically) opposed to all his subjects, even to the highest officials of court and state, for he belongs to a superhuman order [121]. Of course, as Frankfort remarks, the ambiguity of his situation - for like Pharaoh he was human and superhuman at the same time - must have posed problems for those who surrounded him. This scholar illustrated his point with a quotation from the diary of Samuel Pepys who, on July 19, 1662, wrote that it lessened his esteem of his king (Charles II) that the monarch, sailing down the Thames in his barge, did not prove capable of stopping the downpour. In my country, the Netherlands, we know a natural phenomenon called the 'Orange sun'. This refers to a popular belief which sometimes is expressed even in journalism, that when the Queen (of the House of Orange) appears in public, in particular during royal festivals or visits, the sun is sure to shine - as though it were the Queen who causes this.

The consequence of the special significance of a Mesopotamian king is that he had to be present at, or even preside over, a number of rituals that must be performed in order to ensure the undisturbed course of nature. One of the most important and the most elaborate of these was the New Year's Festival which lasted twelve days in all. It was enacted at the end of the winter when the fields still lay bare; it coincided with the revival of the apparently dead nature. In all its long and intricate ceremonies the king played a conspicuous part; often he was the main executant.

The nearest the king came to being a god himself was during the mysterious ceremony that is known as the 'Sacred Marriage'; this was celebrated not by all Mesopotamian kings but by a number of them. It took place during the New Year's Festival, probably in the night following its tenth day [122]. In it god and goddess unite; their sexual union takes place when the powers of nature still lie low and coincides with the moment that the earth, the Great Mother, becomes fertile again [123].

Since the Sacred Marriage originated in ancient Sumer, way back in the fourth millennium B.C., the goddess originally involved was Sumerian Inanna, the 'lusty, lustful, and deeply venerated deity of the city of Uruk' [124]. In later Mesopotamian kingdoms with a Semitic language she was known as 'Ishtar', the love goddess. It is an intriguing question who took her place during the ceremony in the bridal room but this is not known. The bridegroom of Inanna was the legendary deified Sumerian king Dumuzi who, in some way or other, became her lover. As I already explained, Dumuzi became the Semitic Tammuz. Later, in Babylonia, he was superseded by the more important Marduk.

It was the king who represented the god during the wedding ceremony with the accompanying sexual mating. A Sumerian poem in which King Iddin-Dagan is presented as the partner of Inanna brings out this godlike character of the ruler very clearly; in it the king is called 'Great Ruler of Heaven' which is an epithet of Tammuz. "Around the shoulders of his beloved bride he has laid his arm, around the shoulders of pure Inanna he has laid his arm. Like daylight she ascends the throne on the great throne dais; the king, like unto the sun, sits besides her ... The blackheaded people (= the Sumerians) are ranged before her", or rather, before both of them [125]. Here we have the dualistic opposition squarely before our eyes : the king and his subjects obviously belong to different orders of beings.

10. Dualistic aspects of Mesopotamian and Anatolian religion

a. The Sumerian religion

In the foregoing paragraphs we met, as inhabitants of Mesopotamia, first Sumerians and then Semites. With respect to religion the influence of the Sumerians was immensely powerful; it was not to remain restricted to Mesopotamia alone. The pattern they designed of the world of the gods, the ideas they had of the relationship between gods and men, their notions of how the gods were to be venerated and placated, can be recovered, without important alterations, in the religion of the later Babylonians and Assyrians. As Kramer says, these ideas "became the basic creed and dogma of much of the ancient Near East" [126]. We can detect elements of their cosmology and theology even in the Old Testament. A good example of how far in time their influence reached is that the very last king of Babylonia, Nabuna'id (Nabonidus), who lost his throne to the Persians in 539 B.C., preferred to venerate Nanna-Sin as his favourite god. This deity was the moon-god of Ur and Harran, way back in history three thousand years [127].

How did the universe originate? According to Sumerian cosmology, everything started with a primeval sea; the question where this sea came from does not seem to have entered the mind of the Sumerians. It simply was there; Kramer dubs it, in Aristotelian terms, 'first cause and prime mover' [128]. In a more authentically Sumerian image, the sea is 'the mother who gave birth to heaven and earth' [129]. In this sea, or from this sea, heaven and earth rose, heaven being the vaulted firmament, and earth a flat disc [130]. Not improbably the combination of heaven and earth - one word in Sumerian, 'anki', meaning something like 'universe' [131] was seen as a mountain, with the earth as its base, and the firmament as its top [132]. Anyhow, both heaven and earth were conceived of as gods; 'An', or 'heaven', was a male god, and 'Ki', or 'earth', a female one.

All the gods of Mesopotamia are given human forms, and are, therefore, anthropomorphic. An and Ki mated and brought forth 'lil', that is air, or breath, or wind, called by Kramer 'atmosphere' - to the Sumerians also a god, one of the greatest, Enlil. Enlil abducted his mother Ki, turning his back on his father An. We are presented here with a sharp distinction between the 'great above' - where the sky-gods reside - and the 'great below' - where the chthonic deities dwell, those of the earth and the underworld [133]. To Enlil many great names are given, such as 'the father of the gods', 'king of heaven and earth', 'the king of all the lands'. His temple stood in Nippur [134]. He too has a female companion, Ninlil, the air-goddess; from their union Nanna, the moon-god, also called 'Sin' [135], was born. The moon-god and his wife Ningal brought forth the sun-god Utu. Their daughter was the famous Inanna, the goddess of love and sexuality, the Ishtar (Astarte) of the Semites, still present among us in the form of 'Esther'. Finally there is the god Enki, the 'lord of the earth', the 'lord of below', later considered identical with the Akkadian god 'Ea'. He is the god of wisdom and the ruler over the subterranean sweet-water ocean that feeds all streams, springs, and sources of the Mesopotamian plain. Enki is the practical executor of the world-ordering plans of Enlil [136]. Perhaps we might say that he is the god of culture and civilization. Although there are many minor deities, the 'Anunnaki' and the 'Igigi', the gods and goddesses I mentioned by name are the main divinities of the Sumerian pantheon.

We must now return for a moment to Enlil who has a plainly dualistic character. This is very important since he is the principal god of the Sumerians. Samuel Noah Kramer, who doubtless is one of the greatest experts on Sumerian history and civilization, protests that Enlil is a benevolent deity. "It was he who established plenty, abundance, and prosperity in the land." He categorically denies the view held by other scholars that Enlil could also be a god of destruction and misfortune [137]. True enough, Sumerian hymns often exalt Enlil's beneficent actions : "Without Enlil, the great mountain, no cities would be built, no settlements founded ... In field and meadow the rich grain would fail to flower, the trees planted in the mountain forest would not yield their fruit" [138]. At the same time we get a first glimpse of the darker sides of Enlil's character in the myth of Enlil and Ninlil. Disobeying the prohibition of her mother, beautiful young Ninlil goes bathing in a canal. Overcome by her beauty Enlil rapes her. However, the gods, furious at this shameful deed, banish him from Nippur. The girl, having become pregnant, gives birth to the moon-god Nanna [139]. True enough, this poem is often interpreted as a fertilization myth. Enlil is equated with the fertile wind carrying pollen, and Ninlil with the grain [140]. Yet even so, the role assigned to Enlil is not a deeply moral one.

More doubts of Enlil's wholly friendly nature crop up when we read in the 'Ershemma song', addressed to Enlil, that he is 'bad weather of enormous power' [141]. In a song lamenting the destruction of the city of Agade we hear that Enlil was extremely irate : he "kicked the houses of the town of Unug into the dust, like a powerful bull' [142]. In another hymn, the 'Ibbisin song', an almost endless series of disasters are attributed to An and Enlil : "bad weather devours everything like a hurricane ..., the canals give bitter water, on the fields only grass is growing ..., mothers do not care for their children ..., kingship is taken away from the land of Sumer ..., the course of Euphrates and Tigris is changed", and so on, and so on [143]. This leads to the inevitable conclusion that the Sumerians located the origin of evil squarely with the gods. If, in their eyes, all good things came from above, the bad things too came thence.

After their coming into being the gods were not so satisfied with their existence as might reasonably be expected. They found it a troublesome burden to procure their daily subsistence. They complained but Enki, the god who was qualified enough to find a solution, was sleeping. His mother, the sea, roused him from his stupor and asked him 'to fashion servants of the gods'. He then tells her how to do this : she must mix clay (with water, probably), and 'bring these limbs into existence'. Alas, on the tablet from which I am citing the actual description of this fashioning is lacking. It appears, however, that six different types of human beings were modelled (for man, of course, will be the servant that is meant). It is by no means clear what these types of man look like, except for two of them, the eunuch and the barren woman. Then Enki himself makes yet another type of man, a weak and feeble creature.

Another poem, called 'sheep and grain', makes it abundantly clear that man exists in order to serve the gods. He must raise cattle and grow grain to satisfy their needs. If the gods bestow the benefits of civilization on him they do this to serve their own interests [144]. It must be perfectly clear, therefore, that human existence is subordinate to that of the gods. It is not really autonomous but stands in relationship of servile dependence to the life of the divinities. At the same time, what is wrong in human life, for instance, barrenness or impotence, is directly ascribed to the will of the gods, even to their clumsiness or spitefulness. Like their Greek counterparts, Sumerian gods do not love mankind. They expect man to serve them, mainly by observing the ritual of the cult. This is what people did indeed, to the best of their ability.

Summarizing we must state that the relationship between gods and men in Sumeria was relatively dualistic : although they could not do without one another, the gods kept themselves coolly and haughtily at a great distance from their creatures whom they considered inferior beings and used as servants.

b. The Hittite religion

There is in Hittite religion an element that we also discovered in Greek theology : their pantheon is not homogeneous. Generations of gods succeed each other, only too often fighting ferociously among themselves. We read about this in a poem that modern experts call 'Divine

Kingdom' [145]. Once upon a time Alalu was king in heaven; Anu stood before him as his cup-bearer. But after nine years Anu rebelled and triumphed over Alalu. Now Anu was king in heaven; Kumarbi stood before him and served him as his cup-bearer. But after nine years Kumarbi rebelled and triumphed over Anu. He bit off and devoured Anu's private parts. However, Anu got his revenge for the consequence of Kumarbi's deed was that he generated the weather-god Teshup. Although Kumarbi tried to devour his son, Teshup was nevertheless safely born with the help of magic. Anu then conspired with Teshup to destroy Kumarbi; the text is defective here but in the end Kumarbi was defeated and the weather-god became 'king in heaven', the main god of the Hittites.

The sequel is told in the 'Song of Ulikummu' [146]. Kumarbi was not able to swallow his defeat. The best means, he thought, of hurting the weather-god was to create a rival for him. He succeeded somehow in impregnating an enormous rock and got a son from this strange mother whom he called 'Ulikummu'. Kumarbi expected that this son, the stone god, would not only be capable of trampling down Teshup like salt but even of shaking the gods from heaven. Before all others the sun-god perceived what kind of being was growing up. But the gods, although they tried to make an impression on Ulikummu by means of music and the lures of love, were unable to do so (no wonder, for he was made of stone). Then a great fight arose, between Ulikummu on one side, and Teshup, assisted by thunder and lightning and seventy lesser gods, on the other. The original text is defective here but very probably the weather-god was defeated. This meant that cosmic order itself was now seriously threatened. But Ea, the god of wisdom, was equal to the situation. He gave the advice to separate heaven and earth by cutting them apart with a great brass knife. Fortified by this device the gods took heart and attacked Ulikummu who still stood bragging that he would chase all the gods from heaven. In all probability the poem ended with the final defeat of Ulikummu.

Two elements in this fascinating myth are of the utmost importance to our theme. The first is that the gods are none too sure of their supremacy. If there is no stability in human life, divine existence is equally unstable. This means that there is a fatal flaw in world-order, represented by the dualistic opposition between the gods themselves. The second element is that the gods can only feel safe if they succeed in keeping the earth at a very great distance. The fatal threat that Kumarbi embodies is that he can dispose of chthonic and terrestrial forces and turn them against the gods. It is a sign of divine prudence that these forces - natural and human forces - are kept away from the gods as far as possible.

This theme of a murderous conflict between the gods of above and below returns in the myth that explains the origin of the Purulliyas-festival. We know the name of its author : he was a certain Killas, a priest. When the weather-god and the serpent Illuyankas were in a certain city, the serpent insulted the god who then summoned all the other gods to help him punish the offender. A banquet was organized to which the serpent too was invited. He came with his sons but, becoming drunk, he was bound and killed by the weather-god. There is yet another version of this myth. In this the serpent triumphed over the weather-god and carried away his heart and eyes. The mutilated god then made his son marry a daughter of his victor. The dutiful son persuaded his wife to give him the heart and the eyes of his father; having received them he restored them to the weather-god. With his power thus fully restored the god, accompanied by his son, went to the sea-shore and killed the snake there [147]. Here we are in the presence of a pitiless feud between the celestial forces and the chthonic powers; the heavenly god can only triumph with the greatest difficulty. The story is clearly dualistic for there is no quarter given; in the end the opposite pole is destroyed. Since the weather-god, in the second version, descends to the sea-shore, we are perhaps allowed to think of the serpent as a sea-snake, a kind of Hittite Leviathan.

Between gods and men not much love is lost. According to Furlani, the relationship between these categories of beings was identical to that between king and subject, or between master and slave. In accordance with this notion the Hittites called themselves 'slaves' of the godhead. Like an earthly king the divinity issues laws and prescripts which must be faithfully followed by man; infraction constitutes a sin and will be punished accordingly. The gods assign to every man a task in life; whatever he thinks of it he must conscientiously fulfil it. Just as to an earthly ruler tributes have to be brought to the gods, consisting mainly of food offerings since the deities are fond of a good meal. He who fails to obey the divine commands or to pay the desired respect to the gods will be relentlessly pursued by them. Everything in Hittite life had something to do with the gods; indeed, everything and everyone, human beings included, belonged to them. Man's whole existence was one long service to the heavenly powers [148].

c. Babylonian religion

Thanks to the endless patience of scholars who pieced it together from a great number of fragments on broken clay-tablets, we now possess a long poem in Akkadian (the language of the Assyrians and Babylonians) called 'Enuma Elish'. These fragments date from different periods, some even as late as the second century B.C. However, it is assumed that the original version dates back to ca. 1200 B.C. Its theological aim is clearly that of establishing Marduk as the main god of the Mesopotamian pantheon [149].

Originally, there was nothing at all, only the amorphous mass of the primeval ocean. From this indefinite chaos two divine powers sprang, the first being Apsu, the second Tiamat. Apsu was male, the god of the sweet waters on which the earth is swimming; he fed all rivers and springs. Tiamat, on the other hand, was female (sometimes even bi-sexual), and was the goddess of the salt ocean. The texts speaking of Tiamat have a negative ring, as if she were a monster. At one point she is compared to a mutilated camel. Between them Apsu and Tiamat represent the first generation of gods. The second generation was that of Lachmu and Lachamu, two divinities of whom we know next to nothing. After a very long time a third pair appeared, that of Anshar and Kishar. Anshar is 'the totality of heaven', and Kishar 'the totality of earth'. This means that the two spheres have now been separated from each other. Then, again after a great number of years, the mightiest gods of the pantheon appear, although the texts are none too clear about the way these generations come into being. This fourth generation consisted of a triumvirate, Anu, the ruler of heaven, Ea, the ruler of the waters, and Enlil, the lord of the earth.

From this triumvirate Enlil is virtually spirited away; the texts seldom mention this ancient Sumerian supreme god. The reason is a political one : he had to be replaced by the Akkadian Marduk. The rise of this son of Ea to the highest position in the pantheon was coincidental with that of Babylon to imperial rule. The fierce battles for supremacy Babylon had to fight are reflected in Marduk's exertions for attaining supreme power. But, of course, there is more to it than this politico-historical background.

The younger gods do not show as much respect for the original divine pair Apsu-Tiamat as might reasonably be expected. Apsu complains to Tiamat that he can not sleep because of the noise they make and decides to destroy them. Ea comes to know of this and succeeds in killing Apsu by means of a magic weapon. From then on he himself is lord of the waters. In his new ocean-palace he then fathers Marduk. The young god cuts a remarkably fine figure : "His eyes were four; his ears were four; when his lips moved, fire flashed out". This leads to the obvious enough conclusion : "Among the gods his stature was preeminent".

But although Apsu is dead now, Tiamat is still alive and kicking. She sees her rest disturbed by the winds Anu has created and which rage over the deep. Therefore she resolves to give battle and fashions eleven monsters to assist her in her fight against the junior gods. In order to meet this threat the assembly of the gods appoints Marduk as king, offering him the sceptre, the throne, and the royal insignia. Protected by an amulet and a magical plant, Marduk challenges Tiamat and succeeds in killing her. From her dead body he now models heaven and earth and all that they contain including mankind [150].

This myth clearly expresses a certain fear that the cosmos may not be as stable as it should be. There is a dualistic division between the older and the younger generations of gods, that is to say, between unspecified matter and the cosmic forces of order. Primordial matter is seen as dangerous; it is monstrous itself and brings forth monsters. Its intentions are bad. With the greatest difficulty and only in successive stages it is brought under control by the cosmic powers. It has to be kept firmly in its place; obviously there is a residual fear that the chaos might return. Very probably for the Babylonians this fear was occasioned by the irregular behaviour of their great rivers. The fact that this poem was recited every year at the New Year's Festival proves that the Babylonians felt the need of constantly ordering the chaotic powers to stay where they were.

'Enuma Elish' also narrates how everything, and more in particular man, was created. This was an idea of Marduk who wanted to assure the repose of the gods by creating servants for them. Ea acquiesces in this plan but orders his son to create man from the blood of one of Tiamat's helpers. The others may go scotfree as long as one of them is sacrificed to this end. Now Kingu, one of the auxiliaries, is killed; from his blood Marduk fashions man. This remarkable story not only proves that humanity is not only there to make the life of the gods easy and carefree but still more that it is a kind of hostage for the good behaviour of the powers of Chaos. Man, Tiamat, and her helpers are all of the same blood, and, in consequence, essentially different from the race of the heavenly gods.

One of the Babylonian poems rose to great fame, second only to the Iliad and the Odyssey. It is the Gilgamesh-epos, translated now into many languages. It was discovered in the ruins of Assurbanipal's palace at Nineveh, scattered into innumerable fragments. Restored as a unity it turned out to be written on twelve clay-tablets. It was popular already in Antiquity; fragments were and are being unearthed in sundry other places. At least four Sumerian stories are its predecessors; the work was translated into Hittite and Hurrian. It owes part of its present-day popularity to the fact that it contains a description of the Flood. We may take it for granted that both the Genesis story of the Flood and that in Gilgamesh refer to an inundation in Lower Mesopotamia of an unknown extent and with the most catastrophic consequences.

When the poems opens, Gilgamesh, who is simply a human being, the ruler of Uruk, is behaving badly; he is constantly oppressing the people of his city. The gods hear the people complaining to them; at their request the goddess Aruru models from clay a man of the wilderness, whose name is Enkidu. His hair grows long and wild and covers his whole body, his food is grass, he does not consort with human beings but rather with wild beasts. Here we meet, for the first time in world-literature (or in anthropology), a so-called 'feral man'. 'Feral men' are human beings of both sexes; they are not raised by their parents but grow up in the wilderness among the animals and obviously feel one with them. Having been discovered and brought back to human society they usually do not succeed in adapting themselves to their new and unaccustomed surroundings; more often than not they cannot even learn to speak a human tongue. The case of Enkidu who feels perfectly at ease with animals and can speak with them proves how much mankind has always been intrigued by the phenomenon of 'feral men'. Behind it a (dualistic) opposition is lurking, that between our civilized life with its severe restrictions, its loneliness even in the midst of nature, and the lost (but longed for) harmony and understanding with all other creatures.

Enkidu is discovered by a hunter and his existence reported to Gilgamesh. The king immediately realizes that Enkidu is intended as a rival, the bushman being his exact counterpart. The fact that Enkidu is a special creature of the gods makes it clear that the deities do not fully condone the human, that is, the civilized way of life. Gilgamesh decides to make Enkidu powerless by a very human trick : he sends a temple-harlot to him who is ordered to seduce the wild man. In a few vividly descriptive lines the poet narrates how Enkidu runs right into the trap. The consequences are terrible : he is suddenly alienated from the animals; even the gazelles flee from him. Here again a dualistic element turns up, that of the distance between man and his own sexuality. The poem considers human sexual power as something negative; it makes one lose his or her innocence, and puts man at a greater distance from nature (this in spite of the fact that sex is so often proclaimed to be 'only natural').

There is no other solution for Enkidu than to follow the prostitute to the city, where he learns to eat human food. This means that he is now fully incorporated into normal human life. He then meets Gilgamesh with whom he enters into a great wrestling-match that makes the walls of the town shake. Finally, Enkidu is overcome, but the two combatants shake hands and become friends. In fact, Gilgamesh is constantly acting as the wily opponent of the gods for he has now succeeded in thwarting their designs. He even becomes an ally of the heavenly gods, for both friends set out to destroy a horrifying, fire-breathing monster that is the warden of the cedar-forest. Even Gilgamesh has to place himself under the protection of the sun-god Shamash in order to achieve his aim. As we may expect the hero kills the dragon. This means that he is fighting the battle of the celestial gods against the chthonic powers, apparently not wholly subdued yet.

Since Gilgamesh has now become somewhat godlike himself, the goddess Ishtar falls in love with him and wants to marry him. But Gilgamesh who represents human autonomy over against the gods makes light of her entreaties. He complains that she is a fickle woman having used up too many lovers already. The reader must realize what an affront to the gods it meant for people in Antiquity to reject their favours. Of course, Ishtar's father Anu is furious about this insult and sends a bull, especially created for this purpose, to punish Gilgamesh. But assisted by his friend, the hero succeeds in tearing out the heart of the animal. This constitutes yet another defeat of the high gods, and the friends feast over it.

Of course, the gods have their revenge. They make Enkidu ill, and after a sickbed of twelve days he dies, deeply mourned by Gilgamesh. Having now become afraid of death himself, the hero decides to consult his ancestor Utpanishtim. His name signifies 'I found life' which means that the gods have granted him immortality. Gilgamesh, wanting to learn his forefather's secret, sets out to the nether world. What he really wants to achieve is to triumph over one of the most fundamental oppositions in human existence, that between life and death. After many adventures and after having crossed 'the waters of Death', Gilgamesh finally finds Utpanishtim whom he asks for the secret of his immortality. By way of an answer this man tells him the story of the Flood.

The gods, being no great admirers of mankind, rather arbitrarily decided to extirpate the human race by means of a Flood. But Ea, the god of wisdom, considered this sheer folly, and he warns Utpanishtim of what is impending. Following the god's instructions, Utpanishtim constructed a boat, an ark, which saved him from the inundation in which all other living beings perished. When all was over, Enlil raised Utpanishtim and his wife to a state of divinity, making them into 'gods like us'. This is why he is immortal.

Understandably enough, this story does not satisfy Gilgamesh. But now Utpanishtim challenges him to stay awake for six days and seven nights on end. Gilgamesh fails dismally by falling asleep. He now realizes that, although being godlike and partially divine, he still is basically human. This means that he has to accept his lot, which is to be mortal; in other words, he is only human and no god. "Death sits in my bedchamber, and wherever I set my feet is Death"; these lines bring out the dualistic difference between the eternal gods and mortal man. Add to this that the Babylonians did not know of an afterlife; no heaven awaited them.

Gilgamesh now returns to Uruk but Utpanishtim, at the request of his wife, gives him a farewell present. It is not the gift of immortality but a magic plant that will revigorate him when he grows old and make him young again. However, to acquire this plant he must dive into the ocean since it grows on the bottom of the sea. This means that it is in the possession of the chthonic powers, and, therefore, part of the primeval material of which the world is made. The high gods of heaven withheld this gift from mankind. In the happy possession of this plant Gilgamesh travels back to his city. But somewhere along the road he discovers a pool in which he takes a bath. Now a snake smells the scent of the plant, swallows it, and immediately sloughs his skin. Gilgamesh showed himself unable to wrest the secret of eternal youth from the gods, just as he was unable to discover the secret of immortality. The secret of eternal youth, symbolized by the magic plant, remains where it came from, with the chthonic powers personified by the snake.

Gilgamesh regains Uruk; all that is left to him is this city. He consoles himself with admiring and pointing out its beauty. There is also a shorter poem, not a part of the great epos, that relates the death of Gilgamesh. It contains the revealing fact that Enlil did not destine the hero for eternal life but for exercising (earthly) kingship. The upshot of this poem is, perhaps, not so much that man is not immortal - which is a homespun truth - but rather that he is not without some special form of immortality. Although man must die, his works - symbolized by the magnificent city of Uruk - live after him.

NOTES TO CHAPTER III

1) Toynbee, Study VII 41.
2) Toynbee, Study VII 7.
3) Toynbee, Study VII 44.
4) Toynbee, Study VII 57.
5) Schmökel, Land Sumer 50.
6) Von Soden 534.
7) Von Soden 541.
8) Scholars have reached no agreement among themselves with respect to the dates of the earlier part of ancient Western Asian history. There are different systems. Since they are all of them defended with equal fervour, an author must stick to one of them. I preferred the dates of Von Soden and those of the tabellaries at the end of Prop.Weltgesch. I.
9) King, Sumer and Akkad 197/198.
10) Schmökel, Land Sumer 65-67; Woolley 47-50.
11) King, Sumer and Akkad 40-46.
12) Ex.2:3.
13) Beek 73.
14) Beek 73; Woolley 50.
15) Beek 73; Schmökel, Land Sumer 67.
16) Friendly communication by Prof. van der Toorn.
17) Beek 73.

18) Von Soden 549.
19) Now in Musée du Louvre at Paris.
20) Beek 76.
21) Von Soden 557.
22) Woolley 54.
23) Von Soden 553; Schmökel, Land Sumer 69.
24) Schmökel, Land Sumer 76-80.
25) Von Soden 568-570 and 576.
26) Beek 80.
27) Von Soden 587/588.
28) Text in Baylonian Laws II 8-13.
29) King, Babylon 210/211.
30) Brinkman s.v. 'Kassites', Reallex.d.As. 5 5/6; Beek 84-86.
31) Jim Hicks, De eerste imperium-bouwers. Time-Life Book B.V. Dutch transl. 1983^4 (1974^1)(Am. original 1974).
32) Gurney 17/18.
33) Macqueen 25.
34) Macqueen 26.
35) Klengel 57/58.
36) Gurney 21.
37) Macqueen 42; text in Klengel 62/63.
38) Gurney 25.
39) Macqueen 45.
40) Redford s.v. 'Mitanni' in Lex.d.Äg. 25 (1980), 149-152.
41) Macqueen 45.
42) Macqueen 47; Gurney 33.
43) Gurney 33.
44) Goetze 253/254.
45) Goetze 258/259.
46) Gurney 65.
47) Gurney 65.
48) Klengel 111/112.
49) Gurney 38.
50) Goetze 266.
51) Beek 16.
52) Beek 90.
53) Olmstead, Assyria 41.
54) Olmstead, Assyria 42.
55) Munn-Rankin, Ass.Mil.Power 274-279; Smith 270-275; Weidner s.v. 'Adadnarâri' in Reallex.d.Ass. 1, 27-29.
56) Luckenbill I 39/40, nr. 116.
57) Munn-Rankin, Ass.Mil.Power 291.
58) Luckenbill I 39, nr. 114.
59) Luckenbill ib.
60) Luckenbill I 38/39, nr. 113.
61) Luckenbill I 46, nr. 130 and 131, 47, nr. 134, and 48, nr. 139.
62) Luckenbill I 57, nr. 164.
63) Smith 284; Munn-Rankin, Ass.Mil.Power 291.
64) Luckenbill I 60, nr. 172.
65) Beek 90.

66) Luckenbill I 49, nr. 141.
67) Luckenbill I 50, nr. 42.
68) Wiseman 461.
69) Luckenbill I 86, nrs. 247 and 248.
70) Schmökel, Ur, Assur, Bab. 126.
71) Luckenbill I 139, nr. 437.
72) Luckenbill I 142, nr. 440.
73) Luckenbill I 140, nr. 438.
74) Luckenbill I 147, nr. 445.
75) Luckenbill I 147, nr. 445.
76) Luckenbill I 171, nr. 484.
77) On the monolith of Kurkh, now in the British Museum; Luckenbill I 233, nr. 611 : '10.000 soldiers of Ahab, the Israelite'.
78) Luckenbill I 211, nr. 590.
79) Luckenbill I 291, nr. 808.
80) 2 Kings 16:7-11.
81) Schmökel, Ur, Assur, Bab. 129; Von Soden 96-98.
82) 2 Kings 17:3-6 and 18:9-11; there is only one heavily mutilated text of Shalmaneser's reign which does not mention Israel. affairs.
83) Luckenbill II 2, nr. 4.
84) 2 Kings 18-19.
85) Luckenbill II 120, nr. 240; see Her. II 141.
86) Luckenbill II 152, nrs. 340 and 341.
87) Von Soden, Nahe Osten 105.
88) Luckenbill II 202/203 nr. 506.
89) Luckenbill II 243, nr. 643.
90) Olmstead 383.
91) Luckenbill II 203, nr. 507.
92) Luckenbill II 212, nr. 528.
93) Luckenbill II 310, nr. 810.
94) Beek 129.
95) Von Soden, Nahe Osten 125; 2 Kings 24:8-17.
96) 2 Kings 25.
97) Klengel 109-111.
98) Goetze, Kulturgeschichte Klein-Asiens 88, cit. Schenkel 111.
99) James 129.
100) Klengel 111.
101) Ez.8:14.
102) Kramer, Sum. 45; the king list is printed 328-331.
103) Frankfort 215.
104) Frankfort 216; Saggs, Greatness 359/360.
105) Schmökel, Kult.Gesch.d.Alt.Or. 85 : 'keine ernst zunehmende Spur einer 'primitiven Demokratie' im alten Sumer'.
106) Saggs, Greatness 360.
107) Kramer, Sum. 328; Schmökel 85.
108) Frankfort 224.
109) Saggs, Greatness 360/361.
110) Votive inscription on a boulder, ca. 2400 B.C., Kramer, Sum. 310.
111) Frankfort 227/228.

112) Votive inscription on a clay-tablet, Kramer, Sum. 324.
113) Frankfort 300; he does so in the preamble of his code.
114) Oppenheim. Anc.Mes. 98.
115) Frankfort 302-306.
116) Frankfort 231.
117) Frankfort 307.
118) Frankfort 309/310.
119) Luckenbill II 292, nr. 769.
120) Driver/Mills II 12, code V 4-9.
121) This does not apply to the early Assyrian kings.
122) Frankfort 318.
123) Frankfort 331.
124) Kramer, Sacr.Marriage 57.
125) Frankfort 296.
126) Kramer, Sum. 112.
127) Schmökel, Kult.gesch. 188.
128) Kramer, Sum. 113.
129) Kramer, Sum.Myth. 39.
130) Kramer, Sum. 113.
131) Kramer, Sum. 112.
132) Kramer, Sum.Myth. 39.
133) Kramer, Sum.Myth. 41.
134) Kramer, Sum. 119.
135) Probably a Semitic name, Kramer, Sum. 122.
136) Kramer, Sum.Myth. 41/42.
137) Kramer, Sum. 119.
138) Cit. by Kramer, Sum. 121.
139) In the myth 'Enlil and Ninlil : the Begetting of Nanna', a poem of 152 lines. Kramer quotes quite a number of lines from what he calls 'this delightful myth', Sum.Myth. 43-47. Why is a tale of a rape 'delightful'?
140) Jacobsen 103/104.
141) Sum.Akk.Hymnen 77.
142) Sum.Akk.Hymnen 187.
143) Sum.Akk.Hymnen 189-192; Kramer, Sum. 123.
144) Kramer, Sum.Myth. 53/54 and 68-73. Kramer warns that the interpretations of the texts remain tentative.
145) Schöpf.Mythen 160-162.
146) Schöpf.Mythen 163-171.
147) Furlani 87-89.
148) Furlani 118-123.
149) Schöpf.Mythen 122.
150) Schöpf.Mythen 121-151; Saggs, Greatness 409-416.

CHAPTER IV
PERSICA

1. The coming of the Persians

From ca. 1200 B.C. Indo-European tribes calling themselves 'Aryans' pushed southward from the limitless steppes of Asia, the one driving on the other. They included, amongst others, the Dorians who destroyed the Creto-Mycenaean civilization in Greece, the Thracians and the Phrygians who settled on both sides of the Bosporus and the Dardanelles, and the Philistines who occupied the coastal strip of Palestine - to which country they gave their name -, thus keeping the people of Israel away from the sea. Much farther to the east, along the shores of the Caspian Sea, Iranian tribes moved southward. As a kind of vanguard of these tribes the Persians, marching south along the Zagros Mountains, finally reached the southern part of present-day Iran. The name of this country is that of its invaders, for 'Iran' signifies 'land of the Aryans'. Later other Iranian tribes, principally the Medes, followed in the wake of the Persians, but saw their road to the west blocked by powerful states such as Assyria, Babylonia, and Elam. These western Iranians found homesteads, more comfortable than those of the Persians, in the north-western provinces of modern Iran. The process that is described here lasted many centuries [1].

2. The Median Empire

Medes, or 'Madai', are mentioned for the first time in the annals of the Assyrian prince Shalmaneser III who died in 824 B.C.; this entry probably dates from the year 836 B.C. An Assyrian note on 'Persians', or 'Parsua', is somewhat older still. A century later, in 713 B.C., the Assyrian royal annals state that forty-two Median chiefs had to furnish horses for the Assyrian army by way of tribute. It is roughly from this date on that Greek historiography has to take cognizance of the Medes; Herodotus mentions a certain Deioces who, according to him, united and ruled the Median nation [2]. This may have occurred in 709 B.C. but whether this Deioces is the same person as the chieftain Daiakku who is mentioned in Assyrian annals is another question. At any rate, Median unity was a fact under Deioces' son, whom Herodotus calls 'Phraortes' but whose real name was Khshathrita. Allegedly he governed his people for at least twenty years after ca. 675 B.C.; he also subdued the Persians, and thus became the founder of the Median Empire, with Ecbatana, now Hamadan, as its capital [3].

The Medes, having learned the art of war from the Assyrians, turned it against their masters. When the Babylonians revolted against Assyria, the Medes, under their king Cyaxares (625-585), became their closest allies; they assisted the Babylonians in 612 B.C. with a strong force when the latter took Nineveh, the great capital of the Assyrian Empire. Cyaxares' lust for foreign adventures was not spent yet; he pushed on and conquered the whole north-eastern part of Asia Minor, including the former Hittite heartland, and finally reached the frontiers of the kingdom of Lydia that occupied the north-western regions along the Aegean and the Black Sea. There was persistent fighting between the Medes and the Lydians; if Cyaxares intended to add Lydia to his conquests, he finally had to admit that she had proved too strong for him. An eclipse of the sun, says Herodotus, showed him that he was on the wrong track; probably the Babylonian king Nebuchadnessar II (who did not want Media waxing too powerful) acted as an intermediary. The river Halys became the definitive frontier. In 584 Astyages, Cyaxares's successor (585-550), even married a Lydian princess [4].

THE MEDIAN EMPIRE

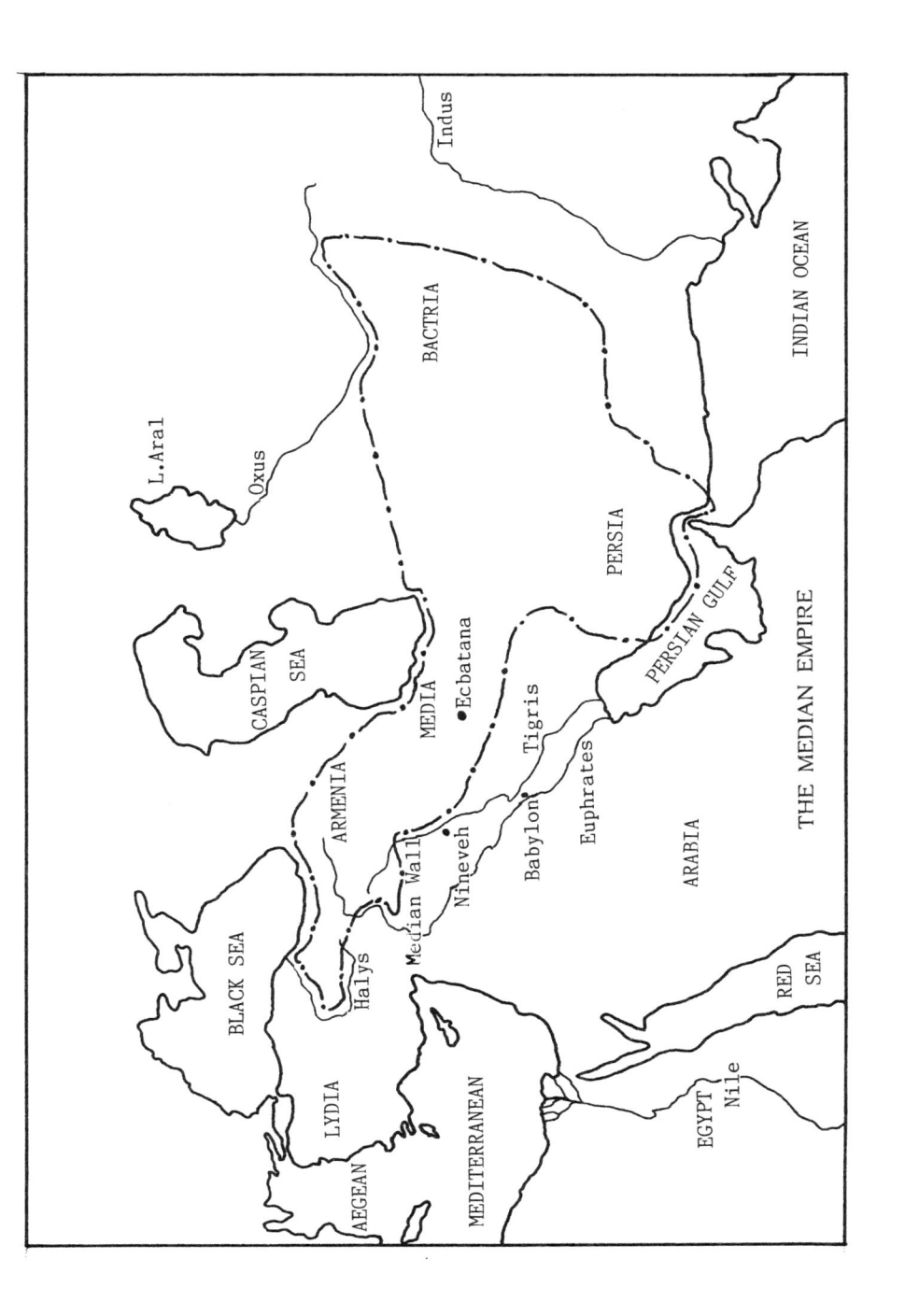

The New Babylonian Empire, that filled the vacuum caused by the downfall of the Assyrians, always viewed Median power with some distrust. In order to keep them away from Mesopotamia King Nebuchadnessar II built a wall between the northern courses of the Euphrates and the Tigris, called 'the Median Wall'. During the Babylonian Captivity of the Jews the prophet Jeremiah pinned his hope on the Medes : "Here is a people on the march from the north country (= Media) that shall attack Babylon and turn her land into a desert" [5]. It was, however, not the greatly feared Medes who brought down 'Babel' but the Persians.

3. The Persian Empire

Perhaps under Median pressure, or of that of other inimical tribes, the Persians left the surroundings of Lake Urmia where they had originally settled and migrated in a south-easterly direction until they established themselves in the south-western part of Iran to the northeast of the Persian Gulf. In the Assyrian annals their land is called 'Parshash' or 'Parsumash'; the Greeks gave it the name of 'Parsis' from which our 'Persia' has been derived. The inhabitants themselves referred to it as 'Fars' and called themselves 'Farsi', the most authentic Persians. In this region Persepolis, their capital, went up; this name too we have adopted from Greek historiography. The events described in these lines may have happened about 700 B.C. [6].

a. The founding of the Empire by Cyrus

In the sixth century B.C. the Persians were only the vassals of the Medes. But in 559 B.C. Kurush II, son of Cambyses I and grandson of Kurush I, became king of Persia; with him one of the greatest conquerors of world-history ascended the throne. We know him by the Greek form of his name as 'Cyrus'; he came from the royal house of the Achaemenids that was to govern Persia for more than two centuries. Nearly immediately after his succession he turned against his suzerain, King Astyages of Media, whose troops began to mutiny at the approach of the Persians; Ecbatana soon fell into the hands of Cyrus. Thus the roles were reversed, for from now on the Medes had to serve the Persians. Cyrus treated King Astyages, his prisoner, with great clemency, proving in this way that the harsh and cruel politics of the Assyrians and Babylonians belonged to the past.

At this point King Croesus of Lydia (560-546) who also ruled over the Greek cities on the Aegean coast marched out against Cyrus. The sudden and unexpected downfall of the Median Empire had brought the Persians to the Lydian frontier in the east, and, at the same time, made an end of Lydia's alliance with Media. Croesus was married to a Lydian princess, a daughter of King Astyages. Perhaps he had an eye on Cappadocia, the most western part of the Median Empire. Cyrus, however, who had succeeded to all Median imperial claims, of course considered Cappadocia, with Armenia, as part of the new Persian sphere of influence. So, when Croesus crossed the Halys and entered into Cappadocia, Cyrus took this as an act of aggression. His reaction was swift. He marched his well-trained army westward over a thousand miles, chased his opponent from Cappadocia with one stroke, and drove him back into Lydia where he captured Sardes, the capital, in 547 B.C. [7]. Cyrus' conquest of the Lydian kingdom also brought the Greek cities on the coast under his sway.

The Persian king now went east again for he had great plans. Retracing his footsteps he crossed the whole lenghth of his empire, till he reached what had been the most eastern provinces of the Median Empire, Hyrcania and Parthia. Insatiable as he was he pushed on and on, always farther east, continually annexing new provinces far beyond the Oxus (now the Amu Darja). In modern terms this meant that Afghanistan, some of the southern republics of Soviet-Union, and by far the larger part of Pakistan were incorporated in his empire. In the east it stretched nearly to the Indus, and in the north-east it reached the middle course of the Jaxartes (now the Syr Darja). Fortress-towns were founded in these regions to safeguard the newly won territories from inroads by tribes from the steppes of Southern Russia.

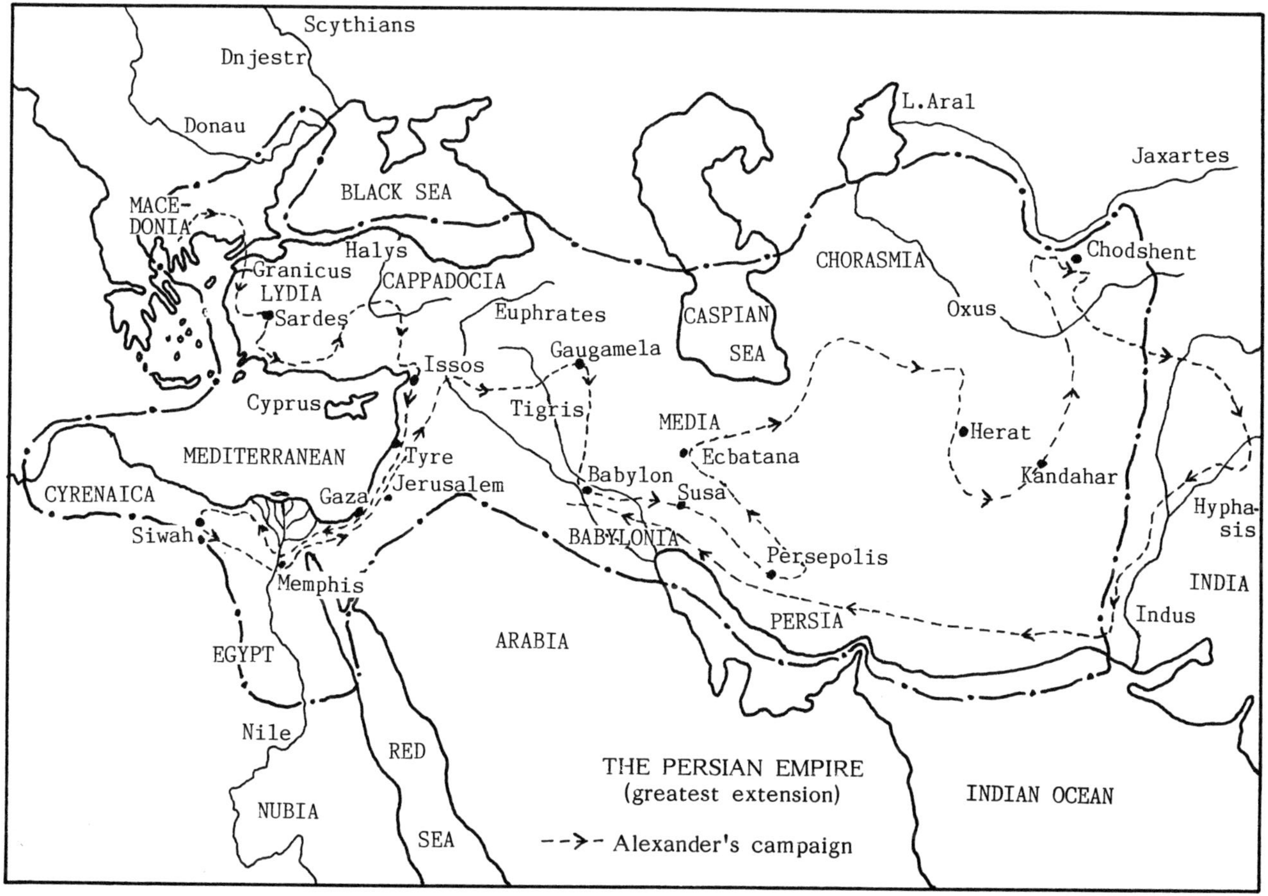
Scythians
Dnjestr
Donau
MACE-
DONIA
BLACK SEA
Halys
Granicus
LYDIA
Sardes
CAPPADOCIA
Euphrates
Issos
Cyprus
Gaugamela
Tigris
MEDITERRANEAN
Tyre
Jerusalem
Gaza
CYRENAICA
Siwah
Memphis
EGYPT
Nile
NUBIA
RED
SEA
ARABIA
Babylon
BABYLONIA
Susa
MEDIA
Ecbatana
Persepolis
PERSIA
CASPIAN
SEA
CHORASMIA
L.Aral
Oxus
Herat
Kandahar
Chodshent
Jaxartes
Hypha-
sis
INDIA
Indus
INDIAN OCEAN
THE PERSIAN EMPIRE
(greatest extension)
Alexander's campaign

With his eastern and western wings now safe, Cyrus swooped down on what he probably considered his main enemy, Babylonia. The once great Babylonian Empire met a lamentable end; with its downfall the agelong history of Mesopotamian imperialism came to a surprising conclusion. Babylonia's last king, Nabonidus (556-539), was not much of a ruler. He was mainly interested in archaeology. What was worse, he neglected the worship of the national god Marduk, being biased in favour of Sin, the city-god of Harran, the town where he resided most of the time. So when Cyrus was approaching Babylon in force, he did not meet much opposition; he even found allies in Babylonia, for instance the priesthood of Marduk. In 539 B.C. he entered Babylon without having had to fight; only the citadel kept up a token resistance for a few days.

Once again Cyrus made it perfectly clear that the hard times of oppression and cruelty were over. This was all the more important since he now found himself in the heartland of the old, stern imperialism. King Nabonidus, although made a prisoner, got the status of privileged guest at the Persian court; when he died a year later, Cyrus joined in the mourning. Making good use of the circumstance that a large part of the Babylonian population hailed him as their liberator, the king installed himself as 'king of Babylon', and assumed the time-honoured title of 'king of the land'. As such he presided over the next New Year's Festival when he bowed to Marduk and clasped the hand of his statue, legalizing his kingship in the way all his predecessors had done. Finally, he gave the exiled Jews the freedom to return to their land, thus making it clear that the deportation policies were abolished. Forty thousand Jews took the way home under the guidance of a high Persian magistrate. The Jews were so grateful to him that they gave him a Messianic title and called him 'the Anointed of the Lord' [8]. The fact that Cyrus generously assisted in the reconstruction of the temple of Jerusalem shows that the destruction of religious identity had made place for tolerance and respect.

The fall of Babylon also delivered her dependencies into the hands of Cyrus, who in this way became master of Syria, Palestine, and Phoenicia; as a consequence his empire now stretched to the frontiers of Egypt. The fact that he could dispose of the great fleets of the Phoenician cities boded little good to the Greeks. In his later years the indefatigable king again went campaigning on his north-eastern frontier; in 530 B.C. he fell fighting against the Massagetes somewhere to the south of Lake Aral. He was succeeded by his son Cambyses II (530-522) [9].

Cyrus was not only a great conqueror but also a wise and magnanimous ruler. With him a new era in the art of government opened. Not without reason his country-men called him 'Father'. But we must not make the mistake of believing that he was not an imperial ruler. On the contrary, he assumed all the resounding imperial titles, like 'Great King' and 'King of Kings'. This is what he said of himself : "Marduk has visited all lands in search of an upright prince after his own heart, whom he took by the hand. He named his name 'Cyrus of Anshaw', and to the kingdom of the whole world he called him by name" [10]. In fact, he gave the old imperialism a powerful new upthrust by making himself the inheritor of all the imperial claims up to then, although he put the imperial rule on a new footing. His own claim was certainly not more modest than that of his Mesopotamian and Hittite predecessors; he too aspired to the kingship of 'the whole world'.

b. Cambyses conquers Egypt

Cambyses began his reign by executing a plan that was already in his father's mind, the conquest of Egypt. After having crossed the Sinai desert he defeated Pharaoh Psammetichus III, the last independent ruler of Egypt for innumerable centuries, in a battle near Pelusium (525 B.C.). The unfortunate king was sent away to Susa. The Persians then entered Memphis, the capital; from then on Cambyses considered himself Pharaoh of Egypt and began acting as such. Like his predecessors on the Egyptian throne he styled himself 'son of Ra' [11]. When this country was turned into a Persian satrapy, the last great kingdom of the Ancient Middle East disappeared from the scene.

In Memphis Cambyses sat ceaselessly devising plans for the conquest of the world. Expeditions were to be sent out against the mighty city of Carthage whose dominions extended over the whole western half of the Mediterranean. But the Phoenician admirals showed no inclination to send their fleets against a town that was originally a Phoenician colony. However, the Persians succeeded in extending their sway over Cyrenaica and Barca, the eastern half of what is now the Republic of Libya. The many Greeks who lived there thus became subjects of the Great King [12] - a second group of Greek colonies that is, along with those on the Aegean coast. Greek reports say that Cambyses also wanted to conquer Nubia but that he failed dismally. However that may be, part of Nubia was actually annexed [13]. Then news arrived that a usurper had seized power back home in Susa. Cambyses immediately began to retrace his steps but died suddenly in 522 B.C. when he was marching through Palestine. Rumour would have it that he found his end by his own hand, which would be in accordance with other rumours that he was mentally deranged or epileptic [14].

c. Darius I and the Scythian menace

His successor, Darius I (521-486), was not his son nor even a near relative. Since he too was a scion of a branch of the Achaemenid house, and because the army remained loyal to this dynasty, he succeeded in occupying the throne after killing the usurper. He must have felt that his claim to the throne was somewhat shaky - there was, indeed, quite a number of rivals -, for in order to fortify his claim, he had himself pictured on one of those enormous rock-reliefs at Bisutun (between Hamadan and Kermanshah). There we see him standing on the dead body of the usurper; eight other pretenders stand tied on a rope behind him. Another important aspect of this relief, to which we shall return later, is that Darius is protected by a god, Ahura Mazda, whose seat, the sun disc, stretches its wings over the whole scene. The accompanying text, in old Persian, Babylonian, and Elamite, expressly states that Darius is an Achaemenid king, the ninth in succession [15].

Such a solemn declaration was all the more necessary since his many rivals were only too apt to take the attitude that he himself was a false pretender. Darius had to spend two whole years in beating down a number of uprisings, perhaps the most dangerous of these taking place in Babylonia. It is said that in nineteen battles he defeated nine kings [16]. But finally he mastered the opposition; he could now devote his energy to more grandiose schemes.

Perhaps he asked himself if Persian imperialism had already reached the farthest limits of its possibilities. Doubts may have assailed him when he looked about him in 513 B.C. An attack on India was out of the question; the logistical problems of an enterprise like this must have seemed insuperable. The deserts of Arabia and Africa did not look more attractive. Cambyses had already given up all plans to subdue Carthage; Darius did not revise this decision. The only remaining possibility was a sally in a northerly direction, in the Balkans that is [17]. Such a campaign may have seemed useful to the king, even necessary. His empire possessed natural frontiers on many sides; from the extreme north-east they were, clock-wise, the Caucasus, the Oxus region and the Indus, the Indian Ocean, the Arabian desert and the Sahara. Darius can hardly have been afraid of the Greeks. Till they surprised him with a revolt in 500 B.C. he believed the Asiatic Greeks were firmly under control; of their European counterparts he knew next to nothing.

But he may have felt uneasy about the Scythians. This great and warlike people, living in the regions to the north of the Black Sea - in what is now the Ukraine -, had made a very deep incursion into Western Asia in 633 during which they had defeated the Medes, conquered a large part of Asia Minor, crossed through Syria and Palestine, and had even temporarily threatened Egypt. Darius must have considered them a potential danger. It is probable that this king, in the context of the great consolidation of his empire and as the heir of the Median princes, wanted to eliminate the security risk that the

Scythians constituted; he would make sure that this people was ready to recognize Persian overlordship in Asia. It is possible to view the campaign against the Scythians as the last phase of the steps that had to be taken in order to secure the interior and exterior peace of the empire [18].

In the Aegean region some minor acquisitions had been made already. Cyprus had been annexed by Cambyses; the islands of Samos, Chios, and Lemnos had voluntarily accepted Persian rule in 525 B.C. In about 513 B.C. Darius crossed the Bosporus on a floating bridge with a large army, marched on to the Lower Danube, reached the other shore on a second boat-bridge, and may even have penetrated Southern Russia as far as the Dnjestr. The general direction of the campaign seems to have been directed at the Scythians; however, they escaped him. Nevertheless, the results of the European campaign were impressive enough : Thrace and Macedonia, together with a number of Greek cities on the shores of the Sea of Marmora and the Black Sea, became part of the Persian Empire. In this way a third group of Greek cities was incorporated into it. Darius now was the undisputed master of the greatest empire the world have ever seen. His rule stretched from the Lower Danube to the Indus, and from the Nile to the Syr Darja [19].

Not without reason Darius caused this inscription to be engraved on his tombstone at Naqsh-i-Rustam : "I am Darius, the Great King, the King of Kings, king of countries containing all kinds of men, king in this great earth far and wide, son of Hystaspis, an Achaemenid, a Persian, son of a Persian, having Aryan lineage". He then sums up all the countries outside Persia proper over which he ruled, 'by the favour of Ahura Mazda' [20]; they number twenty-nine.

d. The Great Kings and the Greeks

There is no reason to assume that Darius was interested in Greece proper. This loose collection of petty states, constantly fighting among each other, would have meant nothing at all to him. But in 500 B.C. the Greek cities on the coast, under the leadership of Milete, revolted against Persian rule. It took the Persians seven years to beat down this rebellion 21). A highly important consequence of this revolt was that it brought the Persians into contact with the European Greeks. Two Greek cities, Eretria and Athens, had sent military assistance to the Ionian Greeks; Athenian infantry took part in the capture of Sardes, the capital of the Lydian satrapy to which the Greek coastal strip belonged. Darius saw this assistance as a provocation, as an unwanted intervention in Persian affairs.

In my Volume II I have treated the Persian attempts to conquer Greece at great length. Three campaigns, in 492, 490, and 480 B.C., all failed dismally. Darius I died in 486 B.C. to be succeeded by his son Xerxes I (486-465), who took the initiative for the greatest campaign of them all, that of 480 B.C. Although the Persians on this occasion penetrated into Hellas as far as Athens, and although they returned in strength in 479 B.C., they did not prove able to maintain themselves there. Defeated as they were in the battle of Plataeae in 479 B.C., they withdrew to Asia Minor never to return.

Immediately after their hard-won victory the Greeks went over to the offensive. In long years of war the Greek cities of Asia Minor were liberated and restored to their freedom. Although the Greeks suffered some setbacks from time to time, on the whole they were very successful. In the course of the Graeco-Persian war the Persians lost all their possessions in Europe. When peace was concluded at last in 448 B.C., they also had to give up the Greek coastal strip along the eastern shores of the Aegean. Since the Persian navy had to leave the Aegean Sea, the whole of the Aegean basin was now removed from Persian control. The permanent in-fighting between the Greek city-states that I described in Chapter II of my Volume II gave the Persians the opportunity to intervene in Greek affairs again, more with gold, however, than with an armed force.

In order to win the financial and military assistance of the Great King the principal Greek antagonists proved only too ready to deliver their brothers on the opposite shore into the hands of the Persians. In 413 B.C. Sparta concluded a treaty with the Great King stipulating that the coastal strip would belong to Persia once again. Because of internal dissensions the Persians were not able to make good use of this license immediately. This became possible only in 386 B.C. In that year one of the many general Hellenic peace treaties was concluded, making an end of the endemic wars for a couple of years. This treaty is called 'the King's Peace' since it was concluded under the aegis of the Persian king Artaxerxes III (390-337). This king got his reward : the Greeks acknowledged his right to rule over the Asiatic Greeks.

After the death of Xerxes I in 465 B.C. there was a succession of weak kings plagued by intrigues. The heavy hand of the empire pressed hard on the peoples of the empire, taxes were high, and, as a consequence, revolt followed revolt. Many satraps ruled as if they were independent kings, Egypt fell away, Syria and Phoenicia followed suit. Complete disintegration seemed near.

With the advent of Artaxerxes III the course of events changed drastically. Ghirshman says that he, "although without doubt cruel and brutal, possessed a will of iron and the authority of a statesman". This author then goes on to say that "his accession was steeped in the blood of all his brothers and sisters, to the number of several dozen. Was this too high a prize to pay for re-establishing the unity of the Empire ...?" [22]. Curious question! As though there could exist any motive that could justify a slaughter like that! The king trampled down one rebellion after the other and reconquered Egypt. Order was restored everywhere. It was the Indian summer of the empire. In 337 B.C. Artaxerxes was murdered. His successor, Darius III Codomannus, the last king to sit on the throne of the Achaemenids, was a relative of his. It was the extreme misfortune of this ruler to be confronted by one of the greatest conquerors of world-history, Alexander the Great, king of Macedonia.

e. Alexander's campaign

Initially the young king, who since 338 B.C. was also master of Greece, seems to have fostered no intention to destroy the Persian Empire. We may safely assume that he considered this a task far beyond the limited resources of his country, the more so because the Greeks were only lukewarm in supporting his cause. This must have been disappointing to him for he was deeply imbued with the Panhellenic ideal. What he wanted was to cross over to Asia at the head of a united Greek army in order to liberate the Greek cities of Asia Minor once and for all. Perhaps even then he believed that the only way to safeguard the independence of these cities was the definitive destruction of the Persian Empire.

The twenty year-old Alexander flashed upon the Persian Empire like sudden lightning in the sky of a summer evening. Darius III expected nothing of this kind. When he heard that the Macedonian was coming, he ordered that he should be bound and brought before him 23). In 334 B.C. Alexander crossed the Dardanelles and entered Asia with a relatively small force. First of all he paid a visit to Troy that closely resembled a pilgrimage (the Iliad was his bedside book), and then met the army of western satraps at the river Granicus. His victory revealed his brilliant capacities as a military commander for the first time. For the time being he had nothing to fear. Marching southward, roughly following the Aegean coastline, he liberated the Greek cities one by one, conquering the Lydian capital Sardes and freeing proud Milete. He then made an enormous detour through the interior of Asia Minor and conquered the ancient Hittite heartland. Swinging southward again he reached the Mediterranean near Tarsus.

In spite of the heavy blows he had already dealt the Persian Empire, he does not seem to have been completely at ease about the situation. The Persian navy, still disposing of a number of excellent harbours in Phoenicia, was perfectly able to intervene in Greek waters and foment revolt in Greece, or to cut off Alexander's supply lines. This consideration caused the king to enter Phoenicia. Here a large Persian host, commanded by the King of Kings in person, joined battle with the Macedonians at Issus in 333 B.C. Riding one of his daring charges Alexander routed the Persians. Darius fled but his family and his whole baggage train fell into the hands of the Macedonian. When the Great King, by means of a personal letter, offered an alliance, Alexander answered that Darius had to acknowledge him as his sovereign. This meant that, at least in Alexander's thinking, the Achaemenid dynasty had already lost its right to the throne. However, in practice the Persians were still able of hitting back very hard.

The conquest of Phoenicia and Palestine took a whole year, for Tyre resisted the Persian onslaught for nine months and Gaza for two. Without having had to strike a blow Alexander then entered Egypt where he was hailed as a liberator. During a visit to the Ammon temple in the Siwah oasis in the Sahara the oracle told him in private that he was the son of a god and that he was destined to dominate the whole world. Already his victory at Issus had given his ambitions a far greater dimension; from then on he aimed at conquering the whole Persian Empire. The Ammon oracle declared him a king by divine right; although in this respect he deviated from Greek tradition, it must have seemed logical to him since he had already been recognized as divine. It was clear by now that all the imperial rulers of the last three thousand years had found a worthy successor, one who would not even be content with the greatest empire as yet in the history of the world.

After having recrossed Palestine and Syria Alexander entered Mesopotamia; in 331 B.C. at Gaugamela on the Tigris, he found an immense Persian army in wait for him, again under the leadership of the king himself. Nothing daunted by its elephants and its chariots armed with scythes (the tanks of the Persians), Alexander attacked and put his royal opponent to flight once again. In fact this was the end of the war; the Persian Empire had virtually ceased to exist. Greeted with flowers Alexander made a triumphal entry into Babylon; somewhat later he took Susa, the Persian capital. Hearing that Darius was held prisoner by one of his eastern satraps Alexander followed his trail only to find his imperial opponent murdered. The old saying of the conquered conquering the conqueror came true now, for from this moment Alexander no longer behaved like a Greek king. He decked himself with the royal purple of the Persian rulers and demanded of his courtiers (but not of the Macedonians who stubbornly resisted) that they make the 'proskunêsis', the obeisance with forehead to the ground.

One look at the map will convince the reader that, immense though Alexander's conquests were, the still free part of the empire was as large or even larger than the already conquered western half. Alexander campaigned for years here, going through exotic adventures. Constantly at grips with ferocious tribes that did not easily yield to him, the king fought his way through what is now Afghanistan and reached the southern slopes of the Hindu Kush. He left quite a number of Alexander-cities, all called 'Alexandreia', behind him - like Kandahar in Afghanistan that still bears (a variant of) his name; Herat, also in Afghanistan; and Chodshent, in the Soviet republic of Uzbekistan - , founded as garrison-towns to keep the locals in check. He then went southward along the upper course of the Indus and even crossed it hoping to advance as far as 'the end of the world'. His ambitions really knew no limits any longer but at the Hyphasis, now the Beas, in India, his soldiers definitely refused to go one step farther. He returned and followed the course of the Indus southward; near the Indian Ocean he turned westward again through what is now Pakistan and Iran.

Back in Susa in 324 B.C., he began to put into execution plans for uniting the Greek and oriental world. In this he displayed another imperial feature, the wish that all his subjects should be cast in one mould. Ten thousand Greek and Macedonian soldiers were married to Iranian girls, twenty-four of his generals to as many eastern women, and his greatest general, Hephaestus, to Darius' sister. To crown it all, he himself gave his hand to Statira, the dead king's daughter (which would connect him with the legal Achaemenid line).

The way he tried to organize his newly won empire shows that he owed a great deal to the Persian tradition of government, far more so than to the Macedonian. The provinces of the empire - the satrapies - were left intact, many of them with Persian satraps; Macedonians, Greeks, and orientals were all equal in his eyes. What he aimed at was a mixed civilization - which we now call Hellenism - unified, as far as this was possible, by speech, culture, and custom. Who knows how the course of world-history would have run if Alexander, still only thirty-one years old, had not died suddenly at Babylon in 323

B.C. At that moment he was scheming to execute the plan from which Cambyses had had to desist, the conquest of Carthage.

There was no one to succeed him, no adult son of the same ability, no general with even a spark of his genius. His commanders started to fight among themselves; the final result of their in-fighting was that, after 301 B.C., three separate kingdoms had come into being, Macedonia, Egypt, and Asia. There is no need now to describe the vicissitudes of these monarchies. It is sufficient to state that Alexander's great imperial dream had already evaporated in its infancy.

For the time being no great empire remained; the idea of imperialism seemed to be dead. But in the offing we see a new nation preparing itself for a new imperial role. Far, far to the west, in Italy, in the region of Latium, stood a tiny city, hardly more than a collection of villages among the hills; the sturdy and hardfisted peasants who lived there, the Romans, would become the taskmasters of the ancient world, and the real successors to all the imperial rulers from the dawn of Sumerian history to the death of Alexander the Great.

4. The origins of dualism

"Iran is the classical country of dualism", thus runs the very first sentence of Duchesne-Guillemin's little book on Iranian religion [24]. This surely is the honest conviction of many people, scholars and others; in their opinion the religion of Iran is the historical origin of all dualisms; from this every later form of (religious and philosophical) dualism is thought to have been derived. Only a few weeks ago a friend asked me why I had not opened this series with an account of Iranian dualism. He himself doubtless would have done so, he somewhat disapprovingly remarked. What he, an historian, meant is that a phenomenon like dualism must have an origin in time.

I feel that, at this stage of my investigation, it has become necessary to make a statement on the basic idea behind this work. I for one do not believe that dualism has an historical origin. To look for such an origin is an idiosyncrasy of historians, and of many others whom they have taught to think like them. What historical scholarship wants to do is to locate persons and events in time as exactly as possible. Fixing an event on the time-line is a kind of verification; it comes near to falsification when this does not prove possible. From such a chronologically defined point the historian traces long lines of development; for instance, that of democracy since its establishment in Athens ca. 500 B.C.

Historically minded people - and who is not thus minded - feel rather at a loss when an event or a phenomenon cannot be chronologically dated. This, for example, is the case with myth; it even is crucial to myth that it has no definite origin. It seems to have always been there and to have undergone no essential change in the course of time. This conflicts with Burckhardt's famous dictum that historians still adhere to : "The essence of history is change" [25]. The professional historian depreciates myth precisely because it is timeless and changeless, utterly unhistorical that is; to him it is identical with something that is not true, at best with phantasy. Nevertheless, I do not believe that we must search the realm of mythology in order to detect the origin of dualism. Basically this concept is not a mythical one, although many myths doubtless exhibit dualistic traits. I have already passed in review many instances of this and more are to follow.

It is becoming more and more apparent that dualism, far from being confined to the sphere of religion and philosophy, occurs in every conceivable field of life, in history and politics, in literature and art, in social relationships and in personal life. Wherever we are looking, we see people grappling with or suffering from or trying to accomodate themselves to unbridgeable oppositions. So we are in the presence of a general human phenomenon; since it fundamentally forms part of our human make-up we are entitled to dub it anthropological. The origin of dualism is not to be found in history or in mythology, in religion or in philosophy, but in the human condition.

However, I must now caution the reader against a serious misunderstanding. To vary a famous saying of Karl Marx, I am not of the opinion that the history of mankind is the history of dualism.

The fact that in my texts up to now I have skipped so many important and interesting subjects is sufficient proof of this. In my view dualism is not an all-pervading and omnipresent phenomenon. Seen from an essentially anthropological point of view dualism is something secondary. What people long for is first and foremost harmony, togetherness, a perfectly smooth and unruffled existence, 'Meeresstille und glückliche Fahrt'. At the same time, however, they often prove incapable of attaining this ideal.

No human life is without its oppositions; no human society can manage without them. As I already explained in the preface to Volume I, we try to comprehend the world not only by combining phenomena but also by opposing them. Most of the time such oppositions are harmless, we use them many times a day : summer and winter, hot and cold, old and young, far and near. However, this habit of opposing phenomena can lead to the general proposition that although harmony is our ideal, 'opposedness', nevertheless, is the rule and, in consequence, an essential part of the world-order. Or should we say, perhaps, that there exists something that makes the world-order somewhat less orderly, something that makes it difficult for us to understand the world as order?

Now, this notion of 'general opposedness', if we look at it from an anthropological angle, must have a concrete cause. At this point of my investigation I do not yet venture to give a decisive answer - if there exists one, - but I tend to believe that it is to be found in the man-woman-structure. If man's philosophy of life begins with the consideration of man himself, then his basic starting-point would obviously be the fact that human beings are anatomically different and that this distinction leads to deeply differing functions in life. Hence he would tend to draw the conclusion that the whole order of the world must, in consequence, be twofold, and, furthermore, that there are higher and lower orders of existence which are difficult to reconcile with one another.

Since this sentiment of being anatomically and sexually, and, therefore, anthropologically distinct is so deeply ingrained in mankind, and, unconsciously, makes itself constantly felt in our habits of life, it is easily carried over into other fields of human existence, with the consequence that we may experience 'opposedness' nearly always and everywhere. Now, if we continue to assume that harmony and wholeness form the real tenor of our life, and that dualism is not only a secondary but also a disturbing factor, we might infer from this that dualism, like beauty, is in the eye of the beholder. Oppositions doubless abound; they are, as already stated, necessary to understand the world; but irreducible oppositions are man-made. They exist because some people, for whatever reason, want them to exist. In my opinion there are, indeed, some people who seem to have an innate tendency to intensify normal oppositions into unbridgeable ones, not only in philosophical thought or in religious conceptions but also in daily life and in the most common relationships. Perhaps this is also valid for nations and civilizations.

Why some people think or act dualistically while others do not must be decided according to each case. In my Volume III I mentioned that Plato, as a young man, was confronted with deep disappointments, even frustrations. It is not inconceivable that these experiences reinforced a latent tendency to dualism. A case in point would be that of Adolf Hitler, a dualistic thinker and politician if there ever was one. I sincerely believe that the difficult relationship between his parents encouraged and stimulated his innate disposition to dualism. If this is correct, then Hitlerite dualism too had its origin in the man-woman structure.

With all this in mind, in particular that dualism as such has no historical origin - with the consequence that Persian religious dualism is not the font of all dualisms -, we may now turn to this highly intriguing phenomenon.

5. Dualistic aspects of pre- and non-Zoroastrian religion.

I consider myself lucky that my subject does not force me to present a complete picture of non-Zoroastrian Persian religion. To do this would have saddled me with almost insuperable difficulties. First of all, it is fairly impossible to avoid anachronism when speaking of these questions. Ancient sources are scarce; many highly important texts date from the post-Achaemenid period. One may feel tempted to update certain elements from later texts considerably in order to get a clearer and more complete picture - fortifying oneself with the reflection that these sources contain much older materials. I bypass the fact that the religions of the eastern and western Iranian tribes were by no means wholly identical.

Furthermore, we must bear in mind that Zoroastrianism did not completely replace or destroy the older forms of religion. The old popular form of religion subsisted side by side with the new and more 'official' cult. This circumstance diminishes the risk of anachronism to a certain extent since there exists a fair amount of continuity between older and more recent forms of non-Zoroastrian religion. Actually, Zoroaster, with his religious reform, did not start from scratch but adopted some elements from the older religion; he reacted strongly against others. It is sometimes difficult to say what is authentically Zoroastrian and what is not. Yet another problem is that we must distinguish between what is authentically Zoroastrian thinking and what was added by his immediate followers.

Nevertheless, in spite of all these obstacles something must be said of the older type of religion, not only because it formed the context of Zoroaster's thinking but still more because it contains many clearly dualistic elements. Religious dualism occurred in Iran long before the great prophet. Several older and more recent authorities are of the opinion that this dualism originated in the physical nature of the country. Arriving in Iran from the steppes of Central Asia the invading tribes found a land marked by strong oppositions. In Iran there are forbidding mountain ranges but also fertile plains, and these habitable stretches alternate with burning waterless deserts. While the summers are usually stiflingly hot, the winters bring severe cold. We may, therefore, agree with Mary Boyce that "these sharp contrasts tended ... to foster a dualistic way of thought, a tendency to see the opposition in things, which was to find such a profound and sharply defined expression in Zoroastrianism itself" [26]. In order to limit the danger of anachronism as much as possible I shall restrict myself to the period ending with the downfall of the Achaemenid Empire. I shall, therefore, steer clear of religious developments in Hellenistic, Parthian, and Sassanid times.

a. Three great gods : Vayu, Mithra, and Zervan

Since they left archaeological traces behind them, we may be sure that Iran had inhabitants long before the Indo-European Persians arrived; their oldest village dates from six to eight thousand years ago. These non-Indo-Europeans had religious notions, as we can conclude from their tombs and rock reliefs, especially in the western part of the country that was nearest to the religiously more developed Mesopotamian region. Gabriel says that these oldest Iranians had 'very primitive religious ideas' [27]. However that may be, their religion was polytheistic to the core. The same applies to the Indo-European Aryan tribes that penetrated into Iran during the second millennium B.C. These Persians too were polytheistic, with the proviso that their gods were different from those of the autochthonous population.

According to Widengren, already the oldest texts show elements of a cosmology that we can understand better by enlisting the aid of later material [28]. As is to be expected - since both peoples are of common stock, the original religion of the Aryans, in many respects, shows a close resemblance to that of the Indians. A supreme god (a 'Hochgott', says Widengren) common to both peoples is Vayu, the god of the wind. He is, so to speak, the life-breath of the world, and, as such, the beginning of all things; he is like a pillar that connects heaven and earth. Widengren says that he is thought of as the driving force of the universe; this in its turn is considered to be the body of the gods or 'as a cosmic primeval being from whom the androgynous godhead is born' [29].

Vayu is good and bad at the same time. "The wind is blowing

where it will". Like the wind itself, Vayu is ambivalent; he is at once benevolent and destructive. He is, indeed, unpredictable; for this reason he is a god of fate [30]. "I want to venerate success and good luck", the believer prays to Vayu, who overlooks 'all other creatures' (his prayer, of course, does not mention the failure and the bad luck that are also in the power of this god [31].

With regard to our theme it is of intense interest that Vayu evidently has two aspects, a good one and a bad [32]. These aspects are intrinsically so different that it is possible to speak of 'two beings who are independent of each other' [33]. In some texts both Vayu's even confront one another [34] : "The bad Vayu is the abductor and destroyer, wheras the good Vayu is the opponent, and, at the same time, the one who combats the evil Vayu" [35]. There obviously are, as in Faust, two souls in his breast. The good Vayu is a god of justice, the supreme judge, and the sovereign ruler [36]. Girls pray and sacrifice to him in order to find a good husband and to have fine children [37]. On his dark side, however, he is the god of death, "he who leads away a man when he is bound" [38].

Another important god is Mithra. Generally speaking he is a god of justice and order. As such he protects the righteous but, at the same time, punishes the wicked. He is a kindly god, the very personification of friendliness. But for those who trample on the faith he is a 'wrathful Lord' [39]. The Iranians liked to conceive of him as a war god who fought for them against their (self-evidently wicked) enemies [40]. There are, however, also verses which suggest that even to his worshippers Mithra was not so invariably benevolent as they wanted him to be [41]. Several poems suggest that he unites in himself quite a number of dualities : day and night (the sun and the moon), the light and the dark, good and evil. "You are the best one and the bad one, o Mithra, for the lands. You are the best one and the bad one, o Mithra, to mankind" [42].

Since he is good and bad at the same time, Mithra is able to dispense different gifts to people : richness, power, and progeny, but also sickness and death, impotence and bad seed [43]. It all depends on this god. When he likes somebody he may give him or her all possible good things. Those who invoke him he favours most but he is not interested in people's motives and does not decide on moral grounds [44]. Here again we find the dualistic opposition between the interests of the godhead and those of mankind; the deity does not really care for the well-being of mortals. In conclusion we may state that Mithra too is a divinity with a double aspect.

A third great god, Zervan, or Zurvan, presents us with a double problem, one of a scholarly nature, and another regarding the composition of this section. The question is whether this really is an old pagan godhead known to Zoroaster's contemporaries. If, on the other hand, he only became inmportant in a later period, that of the last Achaemenids, should he, then, get a place in a description of early Zoroastrianism? When we are informed that this divinity is also called 'zaman' or 'zamanah' and that these names are used when Zervan is identified as 'Absolute Time' ('absolute' meaning that distinctive time-sequences, like day and night, are not yet thought of [45]), then we feel inclined to believe that such an abstract appellation must be of a later date. Scholars of the preceding generation, like Nyberg and Widengren, saw in him a god who was much venerated in the old days, as a god who united in himself various, as yet undifferentiated, oppositions, such as good and evil [46]. In a more recent work, however, Mary Boyce states that it is unlikely that Zervan is an ancient god [47].

To the prophet himself and his immediate followers he seems to have been insignificant : Zoroaster's own poetry does not mention him, and he plays only a very small role in early Zoroastrian liturgy [48]. This would, in itself, be a sufficient reason for not discussing Zervan's place in or in relation to Zorostrianism. However, there may have existed a religious movement in Iran called 'Zervanism' which was derived from orthodox Zoroastrianism. This was a favourite idea of Zaehner; although by no means all Iranologists followed him in this respect, there still are recent scholars who share his opinion. However that may be, although the main impact of this movement, if it did exist, was felt after the period with which we are concerned in this chapter, that ending with the arrival of the Macedonian conquerors, there is, nonetheless, a strong possibility that it originated already in the Achaemenid times, Therefore, I shall have to return to it later.

b. Ormuzd and Ahriman

The position of Ormuzd and Ahriman in the Iranian pantheon is, of course, a highly intriguing question. In western opinion they are often, however erroneously, understood to be the main entities, even the dual divinities, of Zoroaster. What they meant to the prophet must be explained later. For the moment we must ask ourselves whether, and in what shape, they occurred in the old pagan religion. First of all, we must realize that 'O(h)rmuzd', or 'O(h)rmazd', is a more recent form of 'Ahura Mazda' [49]. According to Nyberg, 'Ahura Mazda' is not a proper name (if this god had a proper name, what it was will always remain a mystery) [50]. The most probable interpretation of these two epithets is that 'Ahura' means 'Lord' and 'mazda' 'wise'. The god's double name, therefore, would mean 'the wise Lord' or 'Lord Wisdom'. Later the two epithets became a composite, sometimes written as one word, 'Ahuramazda'; still later versions like 'Ormuzd' are derived from it [51].

Ahura Mazda belongs to the supreme gods and was generally venerated in the Iranian world [52]. He too was a god of heaven, specifically of the day-time heaven, whereas Mithra was the god of the nocturnal sky. Ahura Mazda, therefore, is a god of light. As such he is 'widely looking', and, in consequence, omniscient. Because the heavenly vault and its luminaries, in particular the sun, follow a fixed course, this god is also the principle of order, of the cosmic order as well as that of human life [53]. 'Ahriman' too is a later (Pahlevi) form of an older name, this time of 'Ahra (or Angra) Mainyu'; this signifies 'evil spirit'. In later Iranian texts we find it also spelled as 'ahreman' or 'ahrmen'. In Greek this became 'Areimanios' [54] and in Latin 'Arimanius'; most of us, however, will know him as 'Ahriman'. In Zoroastrian thought Angra Mainyu is the irreconcilable opponent of Ahura Mazda. Yet, however important he was to Zoroaster, he seems to have played no great role in the ancient pagan religion. But this too was marked by dualism. Whereas, in Boyce's words, the Zoroastrian dualism was of an ethical nature - the opposition between good and evil -, in the older way of thought it was 'theistic' - the opposition between 'the gods of the sky, dispensing prosperity and happiness here and hereafter, and those of the underworld, to whom men sacrificed in order to avoid their dark and joyless abode' [55].

6. Persian kingship

Iranian kingship, Achaemenid rulers not excepted, were elected by an electoral college [56]. This college represented the army as well as the whole nation (the nation was seen as identical with the army). In practice the choice was restricted to the members of one family; the ruling prince of course tried to secure the election of his favourite son as much as was in his power. The election was not a purely political affair since it took place under the aegis of the sun-god. When there were several equivalent candidates, as was the case after Xerxes' death, the electors had recourse to a divine sign to be given by a horse, the sacred animal of the god. Widengren says that this is the real background of Herodotus' famous story that Darius I, among seven pretenders, was designated as king by the neighing of his mare. Usually this is explained as the effect of a banal trick performed by his groom [57]. Anyhow, although a Persian king was not a god, he was under the special protection of the celestial powers, as this author says.

We may even go further and state that the king was the image, or representation, of the god on earth. Like the Japanese emperor, he traced his descent from the gods [58]. For this reason the king was holy and unassailable. This means that he was not at all an ordinary person and lived very far removed from the common run of mankind. He was seen as the brother of the sun and the moon and had his real home among the stars. In consequence, the king, like the celestial gods, is a cosmic ruler. Warlike kings were more like the sun-god; peaceful princes represented the moon-god. The king himself is born in fire; he rushes down from heaven in a pillar of fire. His clothes and tiara were studded with stars, an obvious sign of his personal relation to the cosmos.

The real function of the king was to provide happiness. His ascension to the throne was a happy event for the prisoners for then they were all liberated. We have already seen that Persian kings did not kill their royal prisoners-of-war but treated them as honoured guests [59]. The king's principal task was not to act as an army commander or to promulgate laws but to procure rain - without rain no fertility and no crops. In the ritual of the Iranian New Year's Festival the king triumphs over all evil forces; the whole creation is renovated then, and sufficient rainfall is ensured [60].

Contrary to what modern people believe a Persian king did not fight battles. True enough, he accompanied the army on important missions but the real work was done by his generals. His proper function was to secure good luck for his soldiers. It was for this purpose that King Xerxes overlooked the Straits of Salamis in 480 B.C. from a high throne on the shore of Attica, and that Darius III stood on a hill in his chariot during the great battles against the Macedonians watching the course of events. When defeat was certain he turned about and sped away. But, says Widengren, this was no cowardice for, in spite of everything, he had to continue existing as king.

All this will have it made it sufficiently clear that a Persian king was a being apart, totally different from the rest of his people, even from the highest courtiers and officials - so much so that we are perfectly entitled to speak of a dualistic distance. As a being descended from heaven and as a favourite son of the sun, the king was believed to wear a nimbus; for this reason it was dangerous to look straight into his face [61]. The supreme ruler never moved about on foot but passed along on horseback or in a waggon. Only at great festivals the king took his meal together with his guests; normally he ate alone - a custom that was still followed by the last Shah of Iran, Mohammad

Reza Pahlavi. When guests were present, the king sat behind a curtain. The biblical Book of Esther relates how dangerous it was to approach the king uninvited and unannounced. "All servants of the king - Xerxes in this story -, and all inhabitants of the provinces of the king know that every man or woman who uncalled for approaches the king has to expect only one thing : capital punishment" [62].

There was only one correct way of approaching the king : to throw oneself flat down before him. The Achaemenid kings borrowed this custom from Mesopotamian royal ritual. This is what the Greeks called 'proskunêsis'; they abhorred it because they believed it to be an evident proof of the servile attitude of the Asiatics. This, however, is not how the Persians themselves saw it; for, as a courtier explained to Themistocles, by bowing so low for the king he was honoured as the representative of the god who is the preserver of all things [63]. To this Greek statesman a meeting with the Great King seemed 'a dreadful ordeal' [64]. It will not surprise the reader that Achaemenid kings acted as sacrificial priests. As such the prince had to wear a white robe; his customary attire, however, was purple since he was the nominee of the army assembly. By way of compromise he wore a purple tunic with a broad white middle belt.

7. What we know of Zoroaster

The great prophet of Iran was Zoroaster, or Zarathustra [65]. This second form of his name was immortalized by Nietzsche in his famous book 'Also sprach Zarathustra'. But however famous the prophet may still be, the fact of the matter is that we know next to nothing of him. His very existence has been doubted; even to-day there are scholars who believe him to be a mythical figure. Yet not every scholar has withstood the temptation to make this very vague figure into a Zoroaster in his own image. He has been alternatively seen as an innovator or a conservative, as a social reformer or a reactionary, as a peasant or a nobleman, as a shaman or a philosopher. What is the truth about him [66]?

We find, says Widengren, authentic material about Zoroaster in the Avesta, specifically in the oldest part of this collection, the so-called 'gathas' which are poems composed by the prophet himself. Usually it is assumed that Zoroaster came from East Iran [67]. It is perhaps possible to be somewhat more precise and restrict ourselves to Chorasmia, in the extreme north-east of the country, the region south of Lake Aral [68]. The dates of his life are problematic. As Molé puts it, they form part of 'the Zoroastrian legend'. All the Greek sources we have - the Greeks were intrigued by Zoroastrianism - situate the prophet six thousand years before Plato (or five thousand years before the Trojan War) [69]. In Herculaneum a papyrus fragment was discovered that gives the names of Plato's students at the Academy towards the close of his life. One of these names belongs to a Babylonian (a 'Chaldean'); according to Nyberg the members of the Academy heard from this man what they knew about Zoroaster [70].

The date mentioned - 'six thousand years before Plato' - gives us a first glimpse of Zoroastrian mythology. 'Six thousand' is, of course, a mythical number. It suggests the well-known theory of 'aeons' or 'ages of the world' that occurs in many cosmogonies. However, the number of the aeons and the number of years in each aeon may differ considerably. In Zoroastrian mythical chronology we find a total duration of the world of twelve thousand years - one thousand years for every constellation in the zodiac, or for every month in the year [71]. History is divided into four parts or aeons. In the first three thousand years Ahura Mazda creates all things, but since they remain in a transcendent state they are immobile. In the second three thousand years creation begins to materialize; it is also the time of primeval man. The malicious Evil Spirit discovers what Ahura Mazda is doing and creates a dark counter-world. Ahura Mazda finally succeeds in making him powerless. In the third period of three thousand years the Evil Spirit completely recovers and overruns Ahura Mazda's luminous world. Primeval man perishes. Good and bad are mixed together; this is the world we live in. In the last aeon of, once again, thirty centuries, the world will be transfigured; the luminous world will be restored to utter perfection [72].

Zoroaster is given a place in this scheme by situating him in the beginning of the second aeon; Ahura Mazda created him when the material world began its yet blameless existence. When the third period, that of the 'mixture' began, Ahura Mazda sent him to the earth to help the people reinstate order. In this version Zoroaster would be the reincarnation of primeval man. That the Chaldean sage I mentioned combined Zoroaster with Plato in a chronological scheme means that, in his ideology, Plato was the reincarnated Zoroaster, and one of the saviours who, like all his spiritual sons, would purify the world [73].

There is also a more down-to-earth specification of Zoroaster's life-time, for Iranian tradition has it that he lived '258 years before Alexander' [74]. True enough, we do not know for certain which date of Alexander is meant. His birth? His accession to the throne? The beginning of the war? The destruction of Persepolis in 330 B.C.? Or could this refer to the first year of the first Seleucid king? Whatever the case, this piece of information would situate the prophet in the sixth century B.C. which would be in accordance with some Greek sources that say that he met Pythagoras [75]. Yet not every scholar is ready to accept this as the truth of the matter. Indeed, however satisfying such a precise indication may seem to the modern historical mind, it is very probably an artificial construction. It was postulated by priests of the Sassanid period who did not really reckon from Alexander backwards but took the reign of Cyrus as their starting-point. These scholar-priests thought that King Cyrus was the father of Darius I (which, as we have seen, is not correct); they identified him with the Kavi Vistaspa, the protector of the prophet, a legendary king to be met with in the Avesta.

In doing so they annexed Cyrus for the Zoroastrian religion since the year of the conquest of Babylon, 539 B.C., was seen as that of Zoroaster's greatest triumph : the conversion of Cyrus - or rather of the Kavi Vistaspa - to his faith. It was also thought that the prophet was at that moment thirty years of age; this would mean that he was born in 570 B.C. Counting forward in time from that year, and not insisting too much on chronological precision, one might say that this was, indeed, more or less, '258 years before Alexander' [76]. Yet modern scholars are convinced that this date of 570 B.C. is not correct. Duchesne-Guillemin thinks that the only thing we may be certain of is that Zoroaster did not live later than 600 B.C. [77]. Widengren goes still farther back, contending that we should be content with a date some time between 1000 and 600 B.C., at any event earlier than Cyrus or Darius I [78]. A still earlier dating is that of Boyce who says that "it seems natural to conclude that the prophet - lived sometime between, say, 1400 and 1200 B.C., at a time when his people were perhaps still dwelling in northern Central Asia, before moving south in their turn to fix their abode in Khwarezm (= Chorasmia)" [79]. Modern scholarship, therefore, leaves us with a range of eight centuries for the lifetime of Zoroaster!

The prophet calls himself a 'zaotar' [80], that is 'a priest', and, at the same time, a composer of hymns and a sacred poet. In fact, he composed a great number of hymns, the 'gathas', which I have already referred to. He was married and had at least two children, a son and a daughter, and very probably more than one daughter. Soon after he had begun to preach his new doctrine he was forced to flee; he found a new refuge with King Vistaspa [81]. This king was the chief of a nomadic tribe that was wandering between Lake Aral and the Oxus basin [82]. And this is nearly all the factual knowledge we possess of the life of this famous personality [83].

What we know of Zoroaster's doctrine [84] we must glean from the Avesta. This is not really a book but a loose collection of writings; the editions of Westergaard (1852-1854) and Geldner (1886-1895) which made the Avesta available to Europeans give the work more coherence than it actually has. The collection comprises hymns, formulas, stories, and laws. We possess no manuscripts older than the thirteenth century. However, these documents do not offer us the original book as it still existed in the ninth century, since it is estimated that three quarters of it has been lost. The thirteenth-century manuscripts reproduce the edition existing in the time of the Sassanid kings; this recension was probably completed during the reign of King Shapur II (310-379); it contains materials from different earlier periods. It is, of course, quite a problem to distil the oldest texts out of this mass but scholars are convinced that the gathas date back to the days of Zoroaster himself and contain his ipsissima verba. The rest is often dubbed 'the younger Avesta" [85].

8. Zoroaster's doctrine

a. The Wise Lord and the Holy Immortals

The core of Zoroaster's message is that there is only one god to be venerated, Ahura Mazda [86]. He is the 'Wise Lord'. 'Ahura Mazda' is not really a proper name but rather, says Lommel, the expression of his being. In fact, the god himself tells the prophet that he has twenty names, the twentieth being 'mazda' [87]; he then goes on to cite many more names that describe qualities of his being [88]. The believer who 'murmurs them day and night' will never suffer evil [89]. Ahura Mazda is the Creator, he himself being uncreated. This is his most conspicuous quality. However, he did not create alone for he had helpers; neither did he create everything, for he did not bring forth what is evil. He is good and he is holy, he is the father of all and everything. At the end of time he will be the great Judge [90].

On the face of it we may seem to be in the presence of sheer monotheism. Since Ahura Mazda is the beginning and end of everything - which means that he encloses the whole development of the world - and since all that is good is on his side, with all good people who adhere to Zoroaster's doctrine [91], we might even speak of monism. But when we take in the whole divine scene at a glance we also perceive a number of spirits. Ahura Mazda is, to use an old Iranian word, 'spenta', which, literally, signifies 'working'; what this means is that he is causing effects. Because the godhead himself is holy these effects can be nothing else but holy and good. This word 'spenta' may be translated in different ways [92]. Widengren says its specific meaning is 'holy' [93] in contrast to what is not holy, in man for instance; however, it is far more important that what is not holy is personified as an anti-divine spirit. This is where dualism makes its appearance on the scene.

The divine (good) 'spenta' is realized in a number of spirits that are called 'amesha spentas - a word that might be rendered by 'Holy Immortals' or 'Bounteous Spirits'. From the standpoint of systematic theology it is not easy to say what these 'spentas' are exactly - attributes of Ahura Mazda or aspects of his being. Or are they independent beings? One should remember that they are also his gifts to man. Zoroaster himself was not too specific about them. Founders of religions would never qualify for chairs of systematic theology. Shortly after his death his followers tidied his system somewhat. In doing so they came down to seven 'amesha spentas' or 'Holy Immortals'.

The principal one of these is the Holy Spirit or the Spenta Mainyu; the other six are the Good Mind, Truth (Ahsa), Right-Mindedness, the Kingdom, Wholeness, and Immortality. Ahura Mazda is the father of all seven spirits but his fatherhood must not be understood in the crudely biological sense of the Greek and Egyptian theologies. Zoroaster's idea of paternity resembles that of the Bible; it is to be taken in a spiritual sense and means 'creation'. As Zaehner expresses it, the spirits 'are thought into existence'. According to this scholar, "the Holy Spirit, Truth, and the Good Mind stand nearest to God and are rightly regarded as his hypostases". Zoroaster's adherents even identified the Holy Spirit with Ahura Mazda himself, although the gathas do not do this [94].

b. The Evil Spirit

Spenta Mainyu, however, is one of two twin spirits, the other being 'Angra Mainyu' or 'Ahra Mainyu'. Originally 'angra' or 'ahra' may have meant 'enemy' or 'inimical' but it is usually translated as 'bad' or 'evil'. So Angra Mainyu is the 'Evil Spirit'. That Spenta Mainyu and Angra Mainyu are twins is said in as many words in one of the gathas : "In the beginning those two spirits who are ... twins were known as the one good and the other evil, in thought, word, and deed" [95]. It seems highly probable that Zoroaster, with his concept of two opposed spirits, is borrowing from the older tradition of Iranian mythology that, as we have seen, is evidently dualistic. Perhaps Vayu was his example, the godhead that is divided into good and evil halves [96].

Zoroaster's system doubtless was monotheistic but not seamlessly monistic; his was not even a homogeneous world. For although there was one good god, the source of all goodness, there was also an evil divinity, Angra Mainyu. This divinity is not a creature or a son of Ahura Mazda; the prophet obviously judged it impossible that evil could come from good. Angra Mainyu too, the Hostile Spirit, exists from the beginning, he too is an uncreated being [97]. In one of the gathas, as we have seen, it is said that the two spirits are twins [98]. If taken literally this word 'twins' would present us with a very great problem. Many a scholar has been haunted by it. For twins have, of course, the same father. But is it possible, even conceivable, that Ahura Mazda, being the father both of the Holy Spirit, Spenta Mainyu, and of the Evil Spirit, Angra Mainyu, would be the origin of the Destructive Spirit, the Evil One? Apart from the fact that Zoroaster very probably did not consider the Wise Lord the 'father' of the Holy Spirit, the expression 'twins' should not be taken too literally, at least not in the prophet's own poetry.

Later followers - who perhaps may be called 'Zervanites' -, did so; in their ideology Ahura Mazda and Ahriman were twins, born from the same womb. Their father was Zervan or Time. But this was considered a heresy by orthodox Zoroastrians. It is, for this reason, that Zoroaster and his early adherents posited a common origin for good and evil [99]. In the original Zoroastrian gatha 'twins' must mean that good and evil are co-eval; they are both from the beginning and uncreated. The prophet needed this conception in order not to make good into the origin of evil. The consequence of this is, of course, that the universe is basically dualistic. This is brought out by the same gatha I quoted already : "When these two spirits met, they created both life and non-life". There are, therefore, two worlds, one of goodness and truth, the other of wickedness and lies, which is equivalent to 'non-life'.

The term 'twins' used for the Good and the Evil Spirit does not so much denote that they must have the same father but points, rather, to their relationship with one another. Their being 'twins' would then signify that they are co-eval but not equivalent. Now, if Angra Mainyu chooses to be bad by his own free will, Spenta Mainyu must be good by his own choice too. That this interpretation is the correct one follows from Zoroaster's own words : "Of these two Spirits the evil one preferred to do evil, the Good was chosen by the good spirit" [100]. This bears some resemblance to what is said of the origin of evil in the Book of Genesis. There too evil is the consequence of a free choice made by the first human beings. The great difference, however, is that in the Bible this choice is made in a human setting and is, for this reason, entirely human, making mankind responsible for the existence of evil in the world. Zoroaster's choice is made in the divine sphere, before and outside human history. This reminds us of the Gnostic notion that the presence of evil in the universe is the result of some kind of derailment in the cosmogonic process. Anyhow, in this way Zoroaster succeeded in combining his monotheistic (or monistic) starting-point with his dualistic views.

c. The dual entities

This choice between good and evil is equally open to human beings. Those who opt for the Good and side with Ahura Mazda will receive the bounteous gifts of the god as his spentas. Those who prefer to be bad will have all kinds of evil on their hands. What will bestowed on both classes of people may be systematized somewhat since the gathas present a series of dual (or dualistic since they are utterly irreconcilable) entities. This double series emanates from the Spirits of Good and Evil. For instance, 'obedience' ('shraosha' in Iranian) is coupled with 'disobedience'. Who is obedient is ready to follow the divine precepts. There are more dual concepts of this kind but according to Lommel only six of them, in the thinking of the gathas, govern the world. Only these are the constitutive elements of cosmic order [101].

First of all, there is the Good Mind and the Bad Mind [102]. To the Good Mind belong good opinions, praiseworthy thoughts, and ennobling ideas, but also the actions follow from them. The Evil Mind leads to bad thoughts, evil speech, and blameworthy deeds. Next there is the dualistic pair of Truth and Lies. These also occur in popular religion as Asha and Drug (or Druj). This last word, an Indo-European one, meets us again in some Germanic languages, in German as 'Trug', 'Betrug', and 'betrügen', in Dutch as 'bedrog' and 'bedriegen', the equivalent of the English words 'deceit' and 'to deceive' [103]. The essence of Drug is that it is utterly opposed to Truth; it is the Lie, Falsity, Insincerity, everything that is crooked and not fair and square. 'Drug' is the source of all possible social evils, in particular of the fact that people bring each other into court because they feel cheated or the victims of fraud [104]. Truth will finally triumph over Drug : "Drug will disappear ... in the North (= the region of darkness) you (Drug) will disappear; you shall not be able to destroy the corporeal world of Asha" [105]. And also ; "Truth will triumph over Bad Lie, over the obscure one from whom all darkness comes" [106]. The last text proves that Asha and Drug are inexorable enemies fighting one another till at last the definitive victory goes to Truth.

Still another pair is Dominion and Misgovernment. It is evident that Zoroaster with his spenta-concept of 'Kingdom' (or 'Empire) meant, in the first place, political and administrative rule. When, however, he asks for good government he is not only thinking of kings and satraps but also of housefathers and landowners. In his opinion only those who are ready to exercise good dominion may be allowed to rule. Bad managers are the implacable enemies of the good. "Whosoever robs these (the bad) of their dominion or of their life, he is going the path of right insight" [107]. Good Dominion depends on and is caused by the Good Mind. All the good spentas are interconnected, just like the bad ones. The following pair is Docility (or Devotion to Duty) and Rebellion (or Arbitrariness). These two follow from the former pair. Docility does not mean servility; it is rather the capacity, or the virtue, that enables a person to do his or her duty silently, with inner contentedness. For rulers and ruled alike it implies modesty, readiness to serve, humility and willingness to work. On the opposite side we find rebellion, wilfulness, arrogance, resistance, and pride [108].

The last two pairs can best be presented as couples. On the one hand, we find Well Being and Not Dying; on the other, Misery and Death. All the English words I am using are - as the reader will understand - only approximative renderings of the corresponding Iranian terms. 'Well-Being' means 'totality, completeness, wholeness'. 'Health', as Lommel rightly remarks, is to us a physical condition whereas in Zoroaster's thought it is a spiritual force and even a celestial presence. In his ideology illnesses are disturbances of the physiological order caused by evil substances that are subject to the devil rather than to material causes [109].

Not Dying or Not-Being-Dead is an attempt to render 'Amurtat'. One need not be an accomplished linguist to recognize in this word the negation 'a' and 'murt' = mort, morte, muerte, meaning 'death' in the Romance languages; English keeps it in 'mortal' and Dutch in 'moord' = murder. 'Amurtat' is not the same as 'Life'. In Zoroastrian thought Life is rather the physical substance that is dissolved at the moment of dying. According to Lommel, 'immortality' comes nearer to the meaning of 'amurtat'. 'Not Dying' is an active force that unites a human being with the divine sphere. Zoroaster says that it empowers the believer to participate in the 'long life'. This 'long life' differs fundamentally from life on earth, which is, by definition, short [110].

Finally, we must remain aware of the fact that these spentas are not identical with the qualities or virtues that are summed up by the apostle Paul as the fruit of love or enmity [111] - although they often remind us of the Zoroastrian oppositions. The spentas are not so much qualities but rather beings, spirits, or geniuses.

d. The need to choose

Every human being must make a conscious choice for what is just and good. This means that we must be pious, honest, and veracious, enemies of the Lie and of the Liar. Man must be honest in his dealings with his fellow-men; he must, for instance, duly pay the wages that are promised [112]. Since the Iranians formed an agrarian people, cultivation of the earth and stock-breeding were very important to Zoroaster's ideology. Viniculture, gardening, and irrigation were all very praiseworthy and noble occupations; if performed in the right spirit, with the Good Mind, they become perfect expressions of Well-Being. Zoroaster in particular stressed the significance of the cow. Tending cattle with care and in a loving way proved that a person was on the right side. Caring for people and caring for cattle were put on the same line. "Whoever is good for the truthful ... or who diligently looks after his cow, he will dwell on the meadow of Truth and of the Good Mind" [113].

It seems that, for Zoroaster, the farmer was the really pious man. Those who did not raise cattle could not be good. Indeed, their fate looks hopeless, since the prophet states categorically : "He who is no peasant will not leave a good memory behind him, however much he may exert himself". Zoroaster who had a craving for oppositions is creating one here between those who tend the soil and those who do not. Nothing can be worse than violence against cattle; sacrifices of cows were seen as violence. The prophet was a decided opponent of animal offerings. He spoke of the high-priest and of the sacrificial priest (the epithet 'sacrificial' bears here a negative connotation) as those who deliver the cow to murderous lust [114]. Very probably he did not want cows to be slaughtered for their meat; they might only be kept for milk and as draught-animals. However, this does not mean that Zoroaster propagated a vegetarian way of life [115].

The whole universe is split up into two halves, that of Spenta Mainyu, and that of Angra Mainyu; these two are involved in constant warfare. Human life forms no exception to this. Here too we find a permanent battle. The same sharp dividing line that runs through the cosmos that divided the good from the bad in this life. Not only must the just fight what remains of evil in themselves; they must also come to grips with it wherever they find it. It was the holy and stern duty of Zoroastrians to combat Lies and Untruth. Neglecting this duty meant that one was on the wrong side and a liar himself. In social life the good must keep apart from the wicked as much as possible. This moral separation had a strongly dualistic character since it divided society into two halves which were to have no intercourse with each other; on the contrary, constant warfare between them was the catchword.

At the moment of death the good will be definitely separated from the bad. "Those who are bad will be forever at home in the house of Drug" [116]. But the just will attain Eternal Bliss after having passed the Cinvat-Bridge [117]. They will then arrive in the 'House of Song', of eternal praise, that is [118]. It will be self-evident that only those may pass that bridge who, during their stay on earth, made the good choice and acted accordingly. It is at this point that Zoroaster's dualism shows its most stringent character.

e. Ahuras and daevas

In ancient Iran, as in India, there existed two kinds of supranatural beings, 'ahuras' and 'daevas'. In the Iranian pantheon only three gods, the 'supreme lords', (the 'Hochgötter'), were called 'ahura'. The usual word for 'god' is 'daeva' which we meet again in the well-known Latin word 'deus'. It is Indo-European in origin and means 'shine, be bright' [119]. Apart from the three 'ahuras' there were many more gods or 'daevas'. Although the ahuras were also daevas, the fact that there were so many daevas who were not ahuras caused a distinction between both appellations. They came to denote two kinds of divine beings who were not equivalent, with the daevas belonging to a somewhat lower level. Probably they were seen as gods of nature or of the nether world. Vayu is a complicated god; in his good aspect he is a supreme god, although his less benevolent aspect makes him a daeva [120].

It is nearly impossible to follow the development of the 'daeva'-belief in Iranian religion. To all intents and purposes it seems to have been a road downward. Originally there seems to have been no dualistic distinction between supreme gods and lesser ones, although the daevas were somewhat second-rate spirits. In the course of the centuries, however, the Iranian religion became more and more dualistic; Duchesne-Guillemin even speaks of 'a dualistic reform' which he ascribes to the Iranian priesthood, that is to say, well before Zoroaster [121]. The distinction between ahuras and daevas did not escape this tendency; more and more daevas came to be identified with demons who did not belong to the pantheon; one of these demons is 'Drug'. Probably these demons originally led an independent existence apart from ahuras and daevas, but then they became confounded with the latter. So the final meaning of the word 'daeva' was the exact opposite of its original significance [122]. At the same time this implies that a dualistic distinction between good and bad supernatural beings had originated.

When Zoroaster came, he found two mutually opposed series of spirits in existence. Yet for him, Ahura Mazda alone could be thought of as god, or God. This was the monotheistic foundation of his religious system. But this did not mean that he banished all the other supernatural beings. By no means! He allotted all of them a place of their own. He virtually ignored Mithra who, to him, was only a part of Ahura Mazda's creation; in the gathas he is mentioned generically among 'the other ahuras' [123]. All divine beings bcame 'spentas', entities or qualities, 'aspects' of the one supreme god or of the lower spirits at his service. Then there were the daevas who, to the prophet, were synonymous with idols as well as with devils. This means that, in the original Zoroastrian ideology, demons or devils had a place of their own. As the fierce opponent of the popular religion, Zoroaster seems to have equated its adherents with idolators, even with devil-worshippers [124]. "But you, daevas", he says, "you are all of you descendants of the Evil Mind, and whosoever sacrifices to you belongs to Drug and Pride" [125].

It is an ascertained fact that Zoroaster believed in the existence of evil spirits, the inveterate opponents of all that was good and holy; they constantly tried to attack and to destroy Ahura Mazda's creation [126]. There were countless numbers of them. Of course, in the view of the prophet these devils were spirits, but human beings could identify themselves with devils to such a degree that they too, after their death, became devils. Wicked people who sinned deliberately and constantly were already devils during their life-time; "once dead such a one becomes a spiritual daeva". Zoroaster calls such people 'harlots of the devil' [127]. Among those who are devil-worshippers, the Avesta cites persons who commit paederasty [128]. Sorcerers and witches were also people with a devilish nature, just like those for whom the night was the appropriate time to commit their wicked deeds : 'thieves and robbers and other vermin that shun the light' [129]. Even some animals, especially noxious insects, but also scorpions, snakes, and mice possessed a devilish nature. To Zoroaster they really were 'non-beings' [130].

f. Body and soul

It is wholly in accordance with the dualistic separation between good and bad, between benevolent and evil spirits, between good and wicked people, that there also existed, in Zoroaster's ideology, a marked difference between body and soul (or spirit). This distinction, however dualistic it may be, is not necessarily one between the good and evil parts of the human constitution. As Lommel explains, both spirit and body can be good as well as bad. There are, therefore, two different dualisms discernible in this field. However opposed spirit and body may be, this does not mean that spirit is necessarily good and body just as necessarily bad. The good spirit and the good body are, nonetheless, opposed entities. Yet even more opposed is a good spirit and a bad body, while the sharpest opposition is that between a bad spirit and a bad body [131].

Body and soul are two different modes of being; this means that man exists in two different ways. These two modes ran parallel to one another and, at the same time, to the bipartition of the universe into spiritual and material or corporeal parts. The good spentas I already described are not only aspects or servants of the great god but are also present in man in his good qualities. The corporeal part of the universe is the vault of heaven with the celestial bodies (we too call the sun, the moon, and the planets 'bodies'), while on earth matter is represented by the human body, and further by fire, metal, water, plants, and the domestic animals [132]. What is good in this world is the domain of the prophet and his pious adherents.

In total contrast to all the elements that constitute goodness in the world, we find the wicked (who, in the prophet's opinion, are hardly human) and their retinue of ills such as illnesses, death, natural catastrophes, false doctrines, and tyranny, and, in addition, wild and dangerous animals, like the snake and the wolf; we have already seen that to Zoroaster the animals he did not like were 'non-beings'. In the prophet's eyes bad men resembled ferocious animals; they really were 'feral men', the offspring of dragons and wolves [133]. Just as the cow was the good animal par excellence, the wolf was the typical representative of all that was evil in the human and animal world [134]. Isn't it curious that the favourite nickname of Adolf Hitler, the one he gave to himself, was 'wolf'?

g. Life and Death

One of the most telling oppositions in Zoraster's ideology is that between Life and Death. Life is good, and a living body is good. Death is caused by the Evil Mind and his servants, the devils. As soon as a human person dies his body no longer is a body but a corpse. And as a corpse it is bad, the property of the devil. We know from the Old Testament that a person who came into contact with a corpse defiled himself and needed to be purified. But what a Jew had to do then was child's play compared to the purifications the Zoroastrian had to undergo. A corpse was so to speak, the material form of Death. As such it profaned everyone and everybody with which it came in touch, not only human beings. Burying it would mean defiling the earth (which is good), throwing it into a river would desecrate the water (which is equally good) [135]. As a consequence the disposal of a dead body presented quite a problem.

h. The end of the universe

Zoroaster's doctrine of the end of the universe is a highly important part of his teaching. There is in the gathas, as Boyce says, 'a sense of urgency, of the end of things being at hand'. Here again the prophet is deviating from the pagan past since in the ancient religion "the generations were seen as succeeding one another remorselessly like the waves of the sea". This "strong sense ... of striving towards a common end, a foreseeable goal, has been held by some to be the most remarkable characteristic of his teachings" [136]. It will be evident that destruction will be dealt out then to all evil and all evil-doers. Angra Mainyu will be sent where he belongs, to Hell.

The righteous will enjoy the same kind of existence as the Immortals themselves; they will not grow older, never be sick or tired again. They will be in Heaven in their bodies; senses and spirit will be equally contented [137]. In fact, Heaven will be the recreated earth, with mountains transformed into flat plains, resplendent with an endless diversity of plants. Those who are to live in this Paradise will enjoy the company of the divine beings, even of great Ahura Mazda himself [138]. "Then Ohrmazd (and all divine beings) and men will be (together) in one place" [139]. Boyce adds that in this way, "Zoroaster offered men a reasoned explanation for all that they had to endure in life, seeing this as an affliction brought upon them by the Hostile Spirit, and not imputing it to the Creator, who was to be worshipped, the sufferings of his creatures on earth" [140].

9. Zoroaster's dualism

We must return once more to the question of Zoroaster's dualism. His doctrine of the end presupposes a doctrine of the beginning. I have already mentioned that spiritual existence, in the chronological order, has precedence over the material world. The very first era of the universe, that of the first three thousand years, is that of spirituality. The first of all supernatural beings is, of course, Ahura Mazda. But in this period we also find the Right Mind and the Bad one. Zoroaster expressly states that they too are 'initial spirits' [141]. This means that Angra Mainyu was not a product of cosmological development but was present from the beginning of the first cosmic age. We would say, therefore, that

Ahura Mazda and Angra Mainyu were contemporaneous. It is our essentially historical mind which makes us express this with a chronological term.

Very probably, however, the prophet himself, had he understood our way of seeing this, would have laughed at this queer idea of modern man. I believe that the idea of a temporal order did not enter his mind at all. Of course he thought in temporal sequences but not in synchronisms or in chronological terms, that is, in terms of temporal logic (as we do). Instead, he would explain that there is a spiritual order, and in this order Ahura Mazda takes precedence over Angra Mainyu, simply because the Good is superior to Evil. Since Ahura Mazda and Angra Mainyu are not equivalent entities, either in the spiritual or in the temporal order, there is no absolute dualism in original Zoroastrianism, that is to say, in the religious ideology of the prophet himself. The first principle of the universe is monistic, but just below this (highly abstract) level, dualism emerges. This dualism is relative for, in some form or other, it is dependent on Ahura Mazda who, in the end, will have the last word.

Ahura Mazda's adherence to the Good implies that Evil has no attraction for him. His goodness is essential, so much so that, in Nietzsche's famous words, he is 'jenseits vom Guten und Bösen', beyond Good and Evil. In consequence, his basic function is to guarantee the the unity of the world. But all others, from the daevas down to human beings and even animals, must choose. "The two initial spirits have proclaimed their natures : the one is good, the other bad, in thought, word, and deed. Of these the Right Mind chose the Law, but this the Spirit of Drug did not do" [142]. Man, the prophet tells his followers, is free in his choice; indeed, it is to be feared that there are people, even many people, who prefer to be wicked. In this they follow the example of the daevas who became 'devils'. Even the cow had to choose between the good herd and the bad one; the animal made the intelligent choice.

Good and Evil, the good and the bad, will fight one another as long as the world lasts. But at the end of time the universe will pass through the ordeal of fire. The flames of Hell will consume all those who live the wicked way; their plight will be eternal. Ahura Mazda will establish on earth the 'second existence' over which he himself - will reign. There, as we have seen, the faithful will enjoy the eternal bliss of Paradise.

10. Zoroaster's religious community

Mary Boyce begins her account of what she calls 'the prehistoric period of the faith' - that from Zoroaster to the Achaemenid kings - with these ominous words : "The early history of Zoroastrianism is wrapped in deep obscurity" [143]. We may be sure of the fact, however, that Zoroaster founded a religious community of believers. We may be equally sure that they had a hard fight on their hands against the adherents of the popular religion; many allusions in the gathas testify to this. The prophet's reform was radical; he wanted to abolish many venerable elements of the ancient creed and ritual. Of his first circle of adherents we know next to nothing; they must have been convinced that the founder of their community was a divine person himself [144]. They took it for granted that he would come back in the end; in fact, they thought that he still lived somewhere guarded by 99.999 spirits. In the fulness of time a holy girl will be fecundated by his sperma; her eschatological name will be : 'She who beats down all', and her son 'will triumph over all enmity of daevas and men' [145].

Nyberg believes that the original Zoroastrian community must be located in the region between Lake Aral and the Jaxartes [146]. From there the creed spread to the south and the west by missionary effort alone. It is utterly unknown when it reached western Iran but from that time on we have historical reports of it. It is highly probable that Zoroaster meant his religion to be a world-wide one; however, as Mary Boyce states, when it entered recorded history, this great vision had been lost; by then it was a purely Iranian phenomenon. This scholar gives as a reason for this that the early missionaries preferred to work among their co-nationals because of the absence of a language barrier and still more because of their national pride. The ancient Iranians were basically a people of conquerors, despising all others, the 'anarya', or non-Aryans [147]. Thus the dualism in Iranian national sentiment bedevilled one of the non-dualistic elements in original Zoroastrianism.

In the time of the Achaemenid kings, in the sixth and fifth centuries B.C., that is, it was an important religious phenomenon in western Iran too. However, it never became general, for the old popular religion continued to exist side by side with Zoroastrianism; the relationship was uncomfortable. It is a vexed question with regard to this period in the history of religions whether or not the great Achaemenid kings were orthodox Zoroastrians. What seems to argue against this assumption is that none of them ever mentions Zoroaster's name in their texts. However, Ahura Mazda's name figures pre-eminently in the inscriptions on their monuments; he evidently is their great god too. On the other hand, Darius never speaks of Ahriman or of the spentas. Of none of the kings do we find any unambiguous confession of adherence to the Zoroastrian faith [148]. This does not mean that the Achaemenid rulers knew nothing of Zoroastrianism, or, on the assumption that they did, that they were indifferent to it or even opposed it. Mary Boyce shows that they must have been very near to Zoroastrianism, if not in words, then in their deeds [149]. Possibly they adhered to a simplified and somewhat tuned down form of the new creed. Perhaps, as supreme rulers of a great empire with an enormous diversity of peoples, creeds and cults, they did not deem it wise to take a too radical stance in religious matters,

11. Prayer and ritual

There exists no religion without some communal act of worship. The Zoroastrian community forms no exception to this; its members met to adore their supreme god. The 'unrecorded centuries' yield only the scantiest information about early Zoroastrian cult and practices. However, we may be certain of the fact that the believers wore the 'Zoroastrian badge', very probably introduced by the prophet himself. They wore - and still wear - a cord wound round their middle and tied in a knot on the back. It is called the 'kusti'. While praying they tie and untie it repeatedly. After initiation at the age of fifteen every Zoroastrian, male and female, is entitled to wear this kusti. On the skin they wear a snowy white shirt, the symbol of holiness and purity.

Prayer is an important part of the Zoroastrian's religious duties. Before praying they wash face, hands, and feet; then they untie the kusti and hold it before them in their outstretched hands. The prayers are directed to Ahura Mazda, and then they close with curses directed against the Evil Spirit; at this point the ends of the kusti are angrily moved, as though they were whipping him. During the last words of the prayer the kusti is once again tied round the waist. In the early days there were seven annual festivals marked by religious services which were attended at daybreak. There never have been any bloody sacrifices, in particular the slaughter of cows and bulls [150].

12. Syncretism and heresy

For a long time Herodotus was the chief informant for Europeans on Zoroastrianism. Yet although he travelled widely in Asia Minor, he seems never to have visited Iran. Apart from some minor misunderstandings, what he has to say of this religion is a fairly accurate description [151]. But he also alludes to some religious phenomena that do not tally at all with orthodox Zoroastrianism. "The Persians", he says, "sacrifice to a great many gods"; the priests did this in a wholly un-Zoroastrian way by slaughtering animals. He does not even mention so much as the name of Zoroaster. What does this mean? In any case, it proves that at the end of the fifth century B.C., orthodox Zoroastrianism was far from general. Perhaps it was losing ground.

Many scholars are of the opinion that on its road westward through Iran, Zoroastrianism underwent a process of syncretism which must have started at a very early stage. Elements of the ancient Iranian religion were incorporated into the new system. Boyce says that the

Persians, being a great imperial people, "set their own imprint on it in a number of lasting ways". One of the best-known of these is the fire-service. Zoroastrians gathered around a great fire built on an altar-stand; this cult is mentioned already under the first Achaemenids [152]. It is possible that the fire-cult was introduced as a counterweight against the building of temples. Fire, the most abstract element conceivable, seemed to orthodox believers a far purer image of the godhead than the statues and icons that were venerated in these temples. Since such fires were raised inside temple precincts and were kept continuously burning, a priesthood was needed to attend them. Yet although Zoroastrianism in the fifth and fourth centuries B.C. occupied a privileged position in the Persian Empire, favoured as it was by the rulers, we know very little of its organization [153].

Apart from the fact that Zoroastrianism incorporated some religious elements that originally were foreign to it, it was threatened by a full-blown heresy that was called 'Zervanism'. Although, as I have already stated, its full blast was felt only in the period after that of the Achaemenids, there can be no doubt that it began to develop during the reigns of the later rulers of that dynasty. There is a rhyming Dutch proverb that says : "Every heretic has his letter" [154]; this means that a heretic is always able to find some support for his views in the orthodox writings themselves. This also applies to the Zervanites. The word 'zervan', signifying 'time', indeed occurs in the Avesta; in its younger sections it even mentions a minor deity called 'Zervan'. Although he was no more than a very subordinate divine being, this personification meant that time was beginning to be hypostatized as 'Time'.

The Zervanites pounced on a gatha verse that I have already quoted : "Truly, there are two primal spirits, twins, renowned to be in conflict". Twins, so they reasoned, must have a common father. Then they drew the inescapable conclusion that Ahura Mazda and Ahriman (as the Evil Spirit had come to be called) had a common father, 'Zervan' = Time. Although, as Mary Boyce says, originally this was only an intellectual (scholastic, as she dubs it) speculation, it later grew into an important heresy. True enough, in the Zervanite creed too Ahura Mazda was the Creator, Zervan leaving the care of the world to him. Since the Zervanites venerated Zoroaster's great god as fervently as the orthodox, they too considered themselves faithful Mazdaites, and, as is often the case with heretics, they even saw themselves as the most orthodox of the orthodox. However, Ahura Mazda was no longer the only uncreated god. The purity of Ahura Mazda was endangered too, for both he and Ahriman were blood-brothers according to the Zervanites. In relation to orthodox Zoroastrianism this implied that the distance between good and evil had become narrower. No longer are "good and evil ... utterly separate and distinct by origin and nature" [155].

It is important to note that the idea modern Europeans have of Zoroastrianism is deeply influenced by Zervanism. There is no indication whatsoever in genuine Zoroastrianism that the prophet's two opposed spirits were Ahura Mazda and Ahriman. Still less were Spenta Mainyu and Angra Mainyu both engendered by the Wise Lord. Boyce regards popular European versions of Zoroastrianism as "an adaptation from Zervanism - a heresy, that is, evolved by unbelievers from a heresy". That this mutilated version of orthodox Zoroastrianism became so attractive she attributes to the fact that modern people tried to reconcile it with their monism. What must have misled them is the Zervanite notion that good and evil have a common origin. However, this is a radical misinterpretation of Zoroaster's pure and undiluted dualism [156].

APPENDIX TO CHAPTER IV

ON SECRET MALE SOCIETIES

As I have already explained in Volume I, dualism is often accompanied by a number of secondary phenomena - for instance, vegetarianism. Another instance of the tendency to dualism is the occurrence of closed or secret societies with a doctrine of their own and more often than not specific ways of life. I classified such societies as 'esoteric' because their members hold themselves apart from the common run of mankind and keep their secrets to themselves in order that they should not be profaned by the uninitiated. In fact, the very first chapter of this series was devoted to the Pythagorean movement that, albeit not really a secret society, was still a closed one professing a special creed, its members living according to rules of life and conduct wholly their own. It is possible that in ancient Iran too there existed societies of this kind. However, we are confronted with a problem here. Among the experts of Iranian life and history Widengren is the only one to contend that this was really the case in Iran; he found little or no support for this supposition with his colleagues. For this reason I present his story with all proper reservation.

The societies Widengren is referring to were associations of males; their members were young soldiers. They were called 'mairya' which is a general term for 'young man'; these associations were in fact open to everyone if only he was young. Widengren says that the members did not exactly represent the most valuable sections of the nation; even robbers were found among them [157]. The members were usually referred to as 'two-legged wolves' - a name that forebode nothing good and sets them dualistically apart from peaceful people. This unfortunate impression was fortified by the black colour of their banner - remember that the cultic robe of the king was white! Their emblem was a dragon; sometimes the banner itself was even fashioned in the shape of a dragon. Now a dragon is a chthonic animal, often the deadly enemy of the celestial divinities who were represented by the king [158]. This emblem and the black colour show that they were rabid enemies of Ahura Mazda, the high god of heaven [159].

The favourite god of these secret societies was Mithra. We have already seen that this godhead was double-sided. It was, of course, his dark side that the associates honoured most, since they led, as Widengren expresses it, a 'photophobic existence', especially after the oncoming of the Zoroastrian religion of the light [160].

Their appearance was wholly in accordance with their dark character. They dressed in black; originally they probably fought naked; later, however, they fought with uncovered breast (to show their heroism). They covered the nether parts of their body with a leather belt. In many societies like these, with an evidently 'macho' character, leather is a favourite material, worn if possible directly over the naked body. It very probably suggests to the wearer a nearness to animals since he is wearing their skin. They wore their hair long and plaited which, in all probability, made them look particularly ferocious [161].

Their way of life put them apart from and even in total contrast to normal human society. They repudiated marriage but not sex, for the 'mairya' were accompanied by 'jahika's' or 'jaki's', harlots, that is. Very probably they lived together and shared one or more girls between them [162]. Black magic was rampant among them; all of them had magic powers at their disposal; the best 'mairya' were also the best magicians. They acquired their magic potential in an horrifying way, namely by cannibalism. It is especially for this reason that they were called 'wolves'. Having assembled in a cemetery they dug up the freshly buried corpses and devoured in nightly carousels. In this way they appropriated to themselves the life force of the people they ate and in doing so doubled their own [163].

It will be evident by now that we are confronted here by a clear case of dualistic opposition to society. It is even a case of absolute dualism since the mairya considered themselves independent of human society in every respect. The animal characteristics they adopted are proof of this, but even more so the fact that they did not respect the dead. Honouring the dead is probably the most ancient custom of society.

That the mairya were hated and feared goes without saying. They acted as the declared and inveterate enemies of Iranian society. This was already the case before Zoroaster came but the enmity was intensified by the progress of the new religion. Widengren points out that in Zoroaster's days the population saw this dark and mysterious society as something alien and inimical. It would be intriguing to know what made the mairya into such fierce opponents of all that everyone considered normal and good. However, we simply do not know enough of ancient Iranian history to give a satisfying answer. There exists a possibility that the mairya, for some reason or other, identified themselves with tribes that, in Iranian national tradition, were seen as the arch-enemies of the Aryans [164].

NOTES TO CHAPTER IV

1) Altheim 137/138; Girshman 73-75.
2) Her. I 101.
3) Her. I 102 and 98; Altheim 139/140; Girshman 75 and 95/96.
4) Her. I 74; Girshman 113.
5) Jer.50:4.
6) Girshman 91.
7) Girshman 129/130; Altheim 159/160.
8) Is.44; 45:1-4.
9) Girshman 131-133; Altheim 160.
10) In a Babylonian text cited by Girshman 133/134. 'Anshaw' being the old Elamite name for the Persian heartland of 'Parshumash', Cameron 179.
11) Olmstead 90.
12) Her. III 13 and IV 165.
13) Her. IV 25 and 97.
14) Her. III 62.
15) Ghirshman 139/140.
16) Ghirshman 141.
17) Mostly verbatim from my Vol. II 4.
18) My Volume II 6/7, partly verbatim.
19) My Volume II 4/5, partly verbatim.
20) Ghirshman 153. This text is reproduced from a tablet found at Susa with some variations from the text on the tomb.
21) See Vol. II 7-10.
22) Ghirshman 201.

23) Ghirshman 209.
24) Duchesne-Guillemin, Orm. et Ahr. 1.
25) Burckhardt 70-72.
26) Boyce, Hist.Zor. I 18/19.
27) Gabriel 14.
28) Widengren, Rel.Ir. I 8.
29) Widengren, Rel.Ir. 11.
30) Widengren, Hochgottgl. 189.
31) Yasht 15.1 ('yasht' means 'veneration'). This incantation is repeated eleven times in all (ed.Wolff 267-271).
32) Widengren, Hochgottgl. 194.
33) Widengren, Hochgottgl. 196.
34) Widengren, Hochgottgl. 196.
35) Datastan i Denik 30.4; this is a Pahlavi text, not from the Avesta, cit. Widengren, Hochgottgl. 197.
36) Widengren, Hochgottgl. 202.
37) Yasht 15.40 (ed. Wolff 272).
38) Yasht 15.42 (ed.Wolff 273).
39) Yasht 10.69 (ed. Wolff).
40) Boyce, Hist.Zor. I 30.
41) Boyce, Hist.Zor. I 31.
42) Yasht 10.29 (ed. Wolff 203).
43) Yasht 10.108-111 (ed. Wolff 215).
44) Widengren, Hochgottgl. 105.
45) Widengren, Hochgottgl. 279.
46) Widengren, Rel.Ir. 151.
47) Boyce, Hist.Zor. I 199, n. 4.
48) Boyce, Hist.Zor. I 81.
49) Zaehner 72.
50) Nyberg, Rel.alt.Ir. 21.
51) Nyberg, Rel.alt.Ir. 95-97.
52) Nyberg, Rel.alt.Ir. 95.
53) Nyberg, Rel.alt.Ir. 98/99.
54) Lommel 18.
55) Boyce, Hist.Zor. I 84.
56) This passage is sticking closely to Widengren's very clear exposition, Rel.Ir. 151-155.
57) Her. III 84-87. I confess that I myself explained this to my pupils often enough as a trick.
58) Xen., Kuroupaid. VII.224.
59) Widengren, Rel.Ir. 55-57.
60) Widengren, Rel.Ir. 47/48.
61) Widengren, Rel.Ir. 57.
62) Esth.4:11.
63) Plut., Them. 27.3.
64) 'Auto to deinon', Plut., Them. 27.2.
65) His name is spelled in the Avesta as 'Zarathustra', in Pahlavian as 'Zartusht' or ' Zartuxsht', and in Persian as 'Zaratusht' or 'Zardusht', Molé 369.
66) Molé 271.
67) Widengren, Rel.Ir. 60.

68) Duchesne-Guillemin, Rel.anc.Ir. 139.
69) Duchesne-Guillemin, Rel.anc.Ir. 135; Nyberg, Rel.alt.Ir. 27.
70) Nyberg, Rel.alt.Ir. 27.
71) Nyberg, Rel.alt.Ir.28. Nyberg o.c. 29 thinks that an older scheme with a total duration of nine thousand years is glimmering through this more recent one. Herzfeld I 5 supposes that the older scheme is Aryan while the newer one has a Babylonian origin. The 9000-years scheme would refer to Aryan racing with its nine rounds; the Babylonian 12.000-years scheme is then based on the senary arithmetical system that was common in Mesopotamia. Attempts to harmonize the two systems are supposed to be discernible.
72) Nyberg, Rel.alt.Ir. 28/29.
73) Nyberg, Rel.alt.Ir. 29/30.
74) Herzfeld I 1.
75) Duchesne-Guillemin, Rel.anc.Ir. 137.
76) Boyce II 68/69.
77) Duchesne-Guillemin, Rel.alt.Ir. 137.
78) Widengren, Rel.Ir. 61.
79) Boyce, Hist.Zor. I 190 and II 3.
80) Yasna 33:6.
81) Yasna 46:12.
82) Widengren, Rel.Ir. 60-66; Duchesne-Guillemin, Rel.Anc.Ir. 140-144.
83) Molé 273 is despairing of even the slightest possibility to reconstruct Zoroaster's life. A biography of the prophet based on the gathas is a desperate undertaking, he says; "une Vie de Zoroastre reste, dans l'état actuel de notre documentation, une pure utopie". According to him, all that we believe to know is sheer legend; he seems to doubt even the historical existence of Zoroaster.
84) Scholars use the names 'Zoroaster' and 'Zarathustra' indiscriminately. Lommel, however, says that he reserves the appellation 'Zarathustrian' for all those elements in his religion that are based on the prophet's own words, and 'Zoroastrian' for all that are found in the writings of later followers who appeal to the prophet for their convictions, Lommel 8.
85) Lommel 1/2; Duchesne-Guillemin, Rel.anc.Ir. 31 sqq.
86) It is one of the many moot questions of Iranian religion whether Zoroaster 'invented', so to speak, Ahura Mazda, or wether he is an older god.
87) Yasht 1.7-8.
88) Yasht 1.12-15.
89) Yasht 1.16-18.
90) Widengren, Rel.Ir. 74-76; Lommel 10-13.
91) Widengren, Rel.Ir. 76.
92) Lommel 17 sqq : 'klug'; Zaehner 45 sqq 'bounteous'.
93) The Russian word for 'holy' = 'svat' is related to it.
94) Zaehner 45/46; Widengren 784/75.
95) The words 'in thought, word, and deed' occur literally in Art. 10 of the Scout Law : " A scout is pure in thought, word, and deed".

96) Zaehner 42; Widengren, Rel.Ir. 74.
97) Boyce, Hist.Zor. I 192.
98) Yasna 30:3.
99) Boyce, His.Zor. I 193.
100) Yasna 30:5.
101) Lommel 88.
102) Lommel 36-40.
103) Lommel 43.
104) Lommel 47.
105) Yasht 3:17.
106) Yasht 19:96.
107) Yasna 46:4.
108) Lommel 62.
109) Lommel 66.
110) Lommel 66-68.
111) Gal.5:19-24.
112) Yasna 44:19.
113) Yasna 33:3.
114) Yasna 31:10 and 44:10.
115) Lommel 249.
116) Yasna 46:11.
117) Yasna 46:10.
118) Widengren, Rel.Ir. 87.
119) Boyce, Hist.Zor. I 23.
120) Duchesne-Guillemin, Rel.anc.Ir. 190.
121) Duchesne-Guillemin, Rel.anc.Ir. 190.
122) Lommel 90.
123) Boyce I 195 and 267.
124) Lommel 91.
125) Yasna 32:3.
126) Boyce, Hist.Zor. I 97.
127) Videvdat 8:32.
128) Videvdat 8:26 and 32.
129) Yasht 8:44, 15:56, 6:4.
130) Lommel 98/99.
131) Lommel 101/102.
132) Lommel 111.
133) See the long tirade in Yasht 3:7 sqq.
134) Lommel 113/114.
135) Lommel 116.
136) Boyce, Hist.Zor. I 233.
137) Boyce, Hist.Zor. I 245.
138) Boyce, Hist.Zor. I 246.
139) A Pahlevi text quoted by Boyce, Hist.Zor. I 246.
140) Boyce, Hist.Zor. I 246.
141) Yasna 45:2.
142) Yasna 30:3.
143) Boyce, Hist.Zor. I 249.
144) Nyberg, Rel.alt.Ir. 269.
145) Yasht 13:141-142; Nyberg, Rel.alt.Ir. 305.

146) Nyberg, Rel.alt.Ir. 313.
147) Boyce, Zor. 47.
148) Duchesne-Guillemin, Zor. 34-49.
149) Boyce, Zor. 55-57.
150) Boyce, Zor. 31-38.
151) Boyce, Zor. 60.
152) Boyce, Zor. 60-66.
153) Her. I 131, 132, 140; Boyce, Hist.Zor. II 183.
154) "Iedere ketter heeft zijn letter.""
155) Boyce, Zor. 67-70.
156) Boyce, Hist.Zor. II 233.
157) Widengren, Hochgottgl. 324.
158) Widengren, Rel.Ir. 25.
159) Widengren, Hochgottgl. 343.
160) Widengren, Hochgottgl. 346 and 350.
161) Widengren, Rel.Ir. 25; Hochgottgl. 343.
162) Widengren, Rel.Ir. 24; Hochgottgl. 330 and 337.
163) Widengren, Hochgottgl. 336/337.
164) Widengren, Hochgottgl. 344/345.

BIBLIOGRAPHY

1 ORIGINAL SOURCES

A COLLECTIONS

ANCIENT RECORDS OF ASSYRIA AND BABYLONIA. Ed. David Luckenbill. Chicago, 1926 (cited as Luckenbill I and II).

THE AVESTA. Die heiligen Bücher der Parser, übersetzt von Fritz Wolff. Strassburg, 1910. (Photomechanischer nachdruck Berlin, 1965).

THE BABYLONIAN LAWS. Edited with translation and commentary by G.R.Driver and John C.Miles. Vol. II. Oxford, 1955 (also cited as Driver/Mills II).

THE BIBLE. The Bible, mainly the Old Testament, is cited according to the individual books. There exist, of course, innumerable editions of it, and also translations in every modern language. As my standard translation into English I used that by John Knox, The Holy Bible. A Translation from the Latin Vulgate, in the light of the Hebrew and Greek originals. London (1958^3, 1955^1). The great advantage of this translation is that it reads so well. However, it is not based on the Hebrew text. For this reason, I checked the Knox version with the original Hebrew and with other translations. Among those I mention only The Soncino Chumash, edited by Dr. A.Cohen. London (1966^6, 1947^1).

THE EGYPTIAN COFFIN TEXTS. 7 Vols. Ed. Adriaan de Buck and Alan H.Gardiner. Chicago, 1935-1961 (cited as Coffin Texts).

PYRAMID TEXTS (cited as Pyr.text).
    1. The Ancient Egyptian Pyramid Texts. Translated into English by R.O.Faulkner. Oxford, 1969.
    2. Kurt Sethe, Übersetzung und Kommentar zu den altägyptischen Pyramidtexten. 6 Vols. Glückstadt/Hamburg.

DIE SCHÖPFUNGSMYTHEN. Ägypter, Sumerer, Hurriter, Hethiter, Kanaaniter und Israeliten. Darmstadt, 1977 (typografischer Nachdruck der originellen Ausgabe, 1964^1).

SUMERISCHE UND AKKADISCHE HYMNEN UND GEBETE. Eingeleitet und übersetzt von A.Falkenstein und W. von Soden. Bibliothek der Alten Welt. Zürich/Stuttgart (1953) (cited as Sum.Akk.Hymnen).

URKUNDEN DES AGYPTISCHEN ALTERTUMS. Herausgegeben von Georg Steindorff. IV. Berlin, 1955 (cited as Urk. IV).

URKUNDEN DER 18. DYNASTIE. Bearbeitet von Wolfgang Helck. IV. Berlin. 1956 (cited as Urk.Buch 18.Dyn.).

B INDIVIDUAL AUTHORS

CENSORINUS
Censorini De die natali liber. Ed. Nicolaus Salmann. Leipzig, 1983. Traduction : Le jour natal. Par Guillaume Rocca-Serra. Paris, 1980.

JOSEPHUS, FLAVIUS
Antiquities. Loeb Classical Library. 7 Vols. (cited as Flav.Jos., Ant. Jud.).
The Jewish War. Loeb Classical Library 203 and 210. Translated by H. St.J.Thackeray (cited as Flav.Jos., Jew.Wars).

HERODOTUS
Historiai. Loeb Classical Library. 4 Vols. Translated by A.D.Godley (cited as Her.).

PLATO
The Banquet. Loeb Classical Library. Vol. 166. Translated by W.R.M. Lamb (cited as Symp.).
Phaedrus. Loeb Classical Library. Vol. 36. Translated by H.N.Fowler (cited as Phaedr.).
Timaeus. Loeb Classical Library. Vol. 234. Translated by R.G.Bury (cited as Tim.).

PLUTARCH
Themistocles. Loeb Classical Library. Vol. 47. Translated by B.Perrin (cited as Them.).

SOPHOCLES
Electra. Loeb Classical Library. Vol. 21. Translated by F.Storr.

XENOPHON
Cyropaedia. Loeb Classical Library. Vol. 51. Translated by Walter Mills (cited as Xen., Kuroupaid.).

II SECONDARY WORKS

A WORKS OF REFERENCE

GROLLENBERG, Lucas, Atlas van de Bijbel. Amsterdam-Brussel, 1955.

BAINES, John and MALEK, Jaromir, Atlas van het Oude Egypte. Amsterdam-Brussel, 1980 (original edition : Atlas of Ancient Egypt, Amsterdam, 1980).

BEEK, M.A., Atlas van het Tweestromenland. Overzicht van de geschiedenis en beschaving van Mesopotamië van de steentijd tot de val van Babylon. Amsterdam-Brussel, 1960 (cited as Beek).

Biblisches-historisches Handwörterbuch. II. Göttingen (1964).

Bijbels Woordenboek. Roermond and Maaseik. 1954-1957[2] (revised edition).

Dictionnaire de la civilisation égyptienne. Par George Posener. Paris (1959) (cited as Dict.Civ.Eg.).

Encyclopaedia Judaica. Jerusalem, 1974[2] (1972[1]) (cited as Enc.Jud.).

Lexikon der Ägyptologie. Herausgegeben von Wolfgang Helck and Eberhard Otto. Wiesbaden, 1972-1988 (cited as Lex.d.Ag.).

Paulys Real-Encyclopädie der classischen Altertumswissenschaft. Neue Bearbeitung von Georg Wissowa. IIA. Stuttgart, 1921 (cited as PW IIA).

Reallexikon der Assyriologie und Vorderasiatischen Archäologie. 5 Vols (not yet complete). 5/6. Lief. Berlin-New York, 1980 (cited as Reallex. Ass.).

B MONOGRAPHS

ALDRED, Cyril, 1. Akhenaten. Pharaoh of Egypt. A New Study. London, 1969[2].
    2. The Egyptians. London (1961).

ALTHEIM, Franz, Das alte Iran. Propyläen Weltgeschichte. II. Berlin-Frankfurt-Wien (1962).

BAIKIE, James, A History of Egypt. From the earliest times to the XVIIIth dynasty. Vol. I. London, 1929.

BARTON, George Aaron, A Critical and Exegetical Commentary on the Book of Ecclesiastes. Edinburgh (1947, reprint of the edition of 1908).

BAUMGARTNER, Elise J., The culture of Prehistoric Egypt. I. London, 1947.

BEN-SASSON, H.H., A History of the Jewish People. Edited by -. London, 1972² (1969¹).

BENVENISTE, Emile, The Persian Religion according to the chief Greek Texts. Paris, 1929.

BLUMENTHAL, Elke, Untersuchungen zum ägyptischen Königtum des Mittleren Reiches. I Die Phraseologie. Abhandlungen der sächsischen Akademie der Wissenschaften zu Leipzig. Philologisch-historische Klasse. Band 61, Heft 1. Leipzig, 1970.

BOSWELL, James, London Journal 1762-1763. Penguin Books 2538. 1966.

BOYCE, Mary, 1. A History of Zoroastrianism. 2 Vols. Leiden, Vol. I, 1975. Vol. II, 1982². Handbuch der Orientalistik. Erste Abteilung. 8. Bd. 1. Abschnitt. Lieferung 2. Heft 2A.
    2. Zoroastrians. Their Religious Beliefs and Practices. London, 1979.

BUYTENDIJK, F.J.J., De vrouw. Haar natuur, verschijning en bestaan. Een existentieel-psychologische studie. Utrecht-Antwerpen, 1969[16].

CAIRNS, Grace E., Philosophies of History. Meeting of East and West in Cycle-Pattern Theories of History. New York (1962).

CAMERON, George E., History of Early Iran. Chicago (1936).

DOUGLAS, Mary, Purity and Danger. An Analysis of the Concept of Pollution and Taboo. Ark Paperback. London, 1984 (1966¹).

DUCHESNE-GUILLEMIN, Jacques, 1. Ormazd et Ahriman. L'aventure dualiste dans l'Antiquité. Paris, 1953.
    2. La religion de l'ancien Iran. Paris, 1962.
    3. Zoroastre. Etude critique avec une traduction commentée des Gâthâ. Paris (1948).

EICHRODT, Walther, Theologie des Alten Testaments. Teil I Gott und Volk. Göttingen (1962⁷)(1957¹).

EISSFELDT, Otto, Einleitung in das Alte Testament. Tübingen, 1964³, neue bearbeitete Auflage. Theologische Grundrisse, herausgegeben von Rudolf Bultmann.

ERMAN, Adolf, 1. Aegypten und aegyptisches Leben im Altertum. Neu bearbeitet von Hermann Ranke. Tübingen, 1923.
2. Die Religion der Aegypter. Ihr Werden und Vergehen in vier Jahrtausenden. Berlin-Leipzig, 1934.

FOHRER, Georg, Theologische Grundstrukturen des Alten Testaments. Berlin-New York, 1972.

FONTAINE, P.F.M., Hoe ontstaat geschiedenis? Een historische antropologie. Kampen (NL), 1985.

FRAINE, J. de, Genesis uit de grondtekst vertaald en uitgelegd. De boeken van het Oude Testament. Deel I, Boek I. Roermond and Maaseik, 1963.

FRANKFORT, H., 1. Ancient Egyptian Religion. An Interpretation. New York, 1948.
2. Kingship and the Gods. A Study of Ancient Near Eastern Religion as the Interpretation of Society & Nature. Chicago, 1948.

FURLANI, Giuseppe, La religione degli Hittiti. Storia della religioni. Vol. 13. Bologna, 1936.

GABRIEL, Alfons, Die religiöse Welt des Iran. Entstehung und Schicksal von Glaubensformen auf persischem Boden. Graz (1974).

GARDINER, Sir Alan, 1. Egypt of the Pharaohs. An Introduction. Oxford, 1961.
2. Egyptian Grammar. Third edition, revised. London (1973) (1927[1]).

GHIRSHMAN, R., Iran from the Earliest Times to the Islamic Conquest. Pelican Book A 239. Penguin Books, 1965 (French edition 1951).

GOETZE, A., The Hittites and Syria. Cambridge Ancient History II.2. Cambridge, 1975.

GOODRICH-CLARKE, Nicholas, The Occult Roots of Nazism. The Ariosophists of Austria and Germany 1890-1953. Wellingborough (1985).

GURNEY, O.R., The Hittites. Pelican Book A 259. Penguin Books (revised edition 1962) (1952[1]).

HAYES, William C., Most Ancient Egypt. Edited by Keith C.Seele. Chicago & London (1965).

HEGEL, Georg Friedrich Wilhelm, Vorlesungen über die Philosophie der Weltgeschichte. Mit einer Einführung von Theodor Litt. Universal-Bibliothek 4881-85/85a-b. Stuttgart (1961).

HELCK, Wolfgang, Zur Vorstellung von der Grenze in der ägyptischen Frühgeschichte. Hildesheim, 1951.

HERZFELDT, Ernst, Zoroaster and his World. Princeton, 1947.

HICKS, Jim, De eerste imperiumbouwers. Time-Life Books B.V. 1983^4 (1974^1) (American original 1974).

HORNUNG, Erik, Grundzüge der ägyptischen Geschichte. Darmstadt, 1978.

HUMBERT, Paul, Études sur le récit du Paradis et de la chute dans la Genèse. Neuchâtel, 1940.

HUXLEY, Julian, Memories I. Penguin Books, 1978 (1970^1).

IONS, Veronica, Egyptian Mythology. London, 1973^3 (1965^1).

JACOB, Edmond, Théologie de l'Ancien Testament. Neuchâtel-Paris (1955).

JACOBSEN, Thorkild, The Treasures of Darkness. A History of Mesopotamian Religion. New Haven-London, 1976.

JAKI, Stanley L., Science and Creation. From eternal cycles to an oscillating universe. Edinburgh and London (1974).

JAMES, William, The Varieties of Religious Experience. A Study in Human Nature. With an Introduction by Arthur Darby Nock. The Fontana Library 2520 L. (1971) (1901-1902).

KEES, Hermann, 1. Das alte Ägypten. Eine kleine Landeskunde. Wien-Köln-Graz, 1977.
  2. Der Götterglaube im alten Ägypten. Leipizg, 1941.
  3. Totenglauben und Jenseitsvorstellungen der alten Ägypter. Grundlagen und Entwicklung bis zum Ende des mittleren Reiches. Leipzig, 1926.

KEMP, Barry J., Old Kingdom, Middle Kingdom and Second Intermediate Period, c. 2686-1552 B.C. Ancient Egypt. A Social History. Ed. B.G.Trigger, B.J.Kemp, D. O'Connor and A.B.Lloyd. Cambridge, 1983.

KING, Leonard W., 1. A history of Babylon from the Foundation of the Monarchy to the Persian Conquest. London, 1915.
2. A History of Sumer and Akkad. An account of the early races of Babylonia from prehistoric times to the foundation of the Babylonian monarchy. New York (1910, reprinted 1968).

KLENGEL, Evelyn and Horst, Die Hethiter. Geschichte und Umwelt. Eine Kulturgeschichte Kleinasiens von Catal Hüyük bis zu Alexander dem Grossen. Wien-München (1970).

KÖNIG, Eduard, Theologie des Alten Testaments kritisch und vergleichend dargestellt. Stuttgart, 1922.

KRAMER, Samuel Noah, 1. The Sacred Marriage Rite. Aspects of Faith, Myth, and Rituals in Ancient Sumer. Bloomington-London (1969).
2. The Sumerians. Their History, Culture and Character. Chicago, 1963.
3. Sumerian Mythology. A Study of Spiritual and Literary Achievement in the Third Millennium B.C. Philadelphia, 1944.

KRIJGER, A., De tranen van Esau. Verklaring van een bijbelgedeelte. Kampen (1986).

KRISTENSEN, W.Brede, Leven uit de dood. Verzamelde bijdragen tot de kennis der antieke godsdiensten. Amsterdam, 1947.

LOMMEL, Hermann, Die Religion Zarathustras nach der Avesta hergestellt. Tübingen, 1930.

MACQUEEN, J.C., The Hittites and their Contemporaries in Asia Minor. London, 1975.

MÉTIN, Albert, La transformation de l'Egypte. Paris, 1903.

MISKOTTE, H., Als de goden zwijgen. Over de zin van het Oude Testament. Amsterdam, 1956. German translation by Hinrich Stoevesandt, Wenn die Götter schweigen. Über den Sinn des Alten Testaments. München, 1966³ (partly rewritten by the author).

MOLÉ, Marijan, Culte, mythe et cosmologie dans l'Iran ancien. Le problème zoroastrien et la tradition mazdéenne. Paris, 1963.

MONTET, Pierre, 1. Eternal Egypt. London (1964).
2. Géographie de l'Égypte ancienne I. Paris, 1977.

MORENZ, Siegfried, 1. Ägyptische Religion. Die Religionen der Menschheit. Bd. 8. Stuttgart (1960). 2. Die Begegnung Europas mit Ägypten. Sitzungsberichte der sächsischen Akademie der Wissenschaften zu Leipzig. Philologisch-historische Klasse. Bd. 113. Heft 5. Berlin, 1968.

MORET, A., Le Nil et la civilisation égyptienne. Bibliothèque de l'humanité. Synthèse historique. L'évolution de l'humanité. Première section II.I. Paris, 1926.

MUNN-RANKIN, J.J., Assyrian Military Power 1300-1200 B.C. Cambridge Ancient History II 2 (1975).

NELIS, J., Daniel. Roermond-Maaseik, 1954.

NYBERG, H.S., Die Religionen des alten Irans. Leipzig, 1938 (original Swedish edition Uppsala 1937).

OLMSTEAD, A.T., 1. History of Assyria. Chicago/London (1968[3]) (1923[1]). 2. History of the Persian Empire (Achaemenid Period). Chicago (1948).

OPPENHEIM. A. Leo, Ancient Mesopotamia. Portrait of a Dead Civilization. Chicago-London (1964).

PATTERSON, Charles H., The Philosophy of the Old Testament. New York (1953).

RAD, Gerhard von, 1. Der heilige Krieg im alten Israel. Zürich, 1951. 2. Theologie des Alten Testaments. Bd. I Die Theologie der geschichtlichen Überlieferungen Israels. München 1950.

RENCKENS, Herman, De godsdienst van Israel. Roermond and Maaseik, 1963[2].

ROEDERER, Günther, Die ägyptische Götterwelt, eingeleitet und übertragen von -. Zürich-Stuttgart (1959).

ROWLEY, H.H., 1. Darius the Mede and the Four Empires of the Book of Daniel. A Historical Study of Contemporary Theories. Cardiff, 1959[2] (1939[1]). 2. The Re-discovery of the Old Testament. London (1945).

SAGGS, H.W.F., The Greatness that was Babylon. A sketch of the ancient civilization of the Tigris-Euphrates valley. London, 1962.

SANDER-HANSEN, C.E., Der Begriff des Toten bei den Ägyptern. Det Kgl. Danske Videnskabsernes Selskab. Historisk-Filologiske Meddelser. Bind XXIV, Nr. 2.12. København, 1942.

SCHARFF, Wilhelm, 1. In Geschichten verstrickt. Zum Sein von Zeit und Ding. Wiesbaden (1976², photomechanical reprint of 1959¹).
2. Philosophie der Geschichten. Wiesbaden, 1975² (photomechanical reprint of 1959¹).

SCHMÖKEL, Hartmut, 1. Kulturgeschichte des Alten Orient. Stuttgart, 1961.
2. Das Land Sumer. Die Wiederentstehung der ersten Hochkultur der Menschheit. Stuttgart, 1956².
3. Ur, Assur und Babylon. Drei Jahrtausende im Zweistromland. Stuttgart (1955).

SELLIN, Ernst, 1. Israelitisch-jüdische Religionsgeschichte. Leipzig, 1933.
2. Theologie des Alten Testaments. Leipzig, 1936.

SETERS, John van, The Hyksos. A New Investigation. New Haven and London (1966).

SKINNER, John, A Critical and Exegetical Commentary on Genesis. The International Critical Commentary on the Holy Scriptures of the Old and New Testaments. Edinburgh, 1951 (1930², 1910¹).

SMITH, Syndey, Early History of Assyria to 1000 B.C. London, 1928.

SODEN, Wolfgang von, 1. Der Nahe Osten im Altertum. Propyläen Weltgeschichte II. Berlin-Frankfurt a.M.-Wien (1962).
2. Sumer, Babylon und Hethiter bis zur Mitte des zweiten Jahrtausends v.Chr. Propyläen Weltgeschichte I. Berlin-Frankfurt a.M.-Wien (1961).

SPIEGEL, Joachim, 1. Die Idee vom Totengericht in der ägyptischen Religion. Leipziger ägyptologische Studien. Heft 2. Glückstadt (1935).
2. Das Werden der Altägyptischen Hochkultur. Ägyptische Geistesgeschichte im 3. Jahrtausend vor Chr. Heidelberg (1953).

SPIESER, E.A., Genesis. Introduction, Translation and Notes. The Anchor Bible. New York (1964).

TOYNBEE, Arnold, A Study of History VII. London, 1955² (1954¹).

WENDORFF, Rudolf, Zeit und Kultur. Geschichte des Zeitbewusstseins in Europa. Opladen, 1953³.

WIDENGREN, Geo, 1. Hochgottglaube im alten Iran. Eine religiösphänomenologische Untersuchung. Uppsala-Leiden (1938).
2. Die Religionen Irans. Die Religionen der Menschheit. Band 14. Stuttgart (1965).

WILSON, John, The Culture of Ancient Egypt. Phoenix Books. The University of Chicago Press, 1962 (first published as 'The Burden of Egypt').

WISEMAN, D.J., Assyria and Babylonia c. 1200-1000 B.C. Cambridge Ancient History II.2 (1975).

WOOLLEY, Leonard, Vor 5000 Jahren. Ausgrabung von Ur (Chaldäa). Geschichte und Leben der Sumerer. Stuttgart w.d. (sechste Auflage) (übersetzung aus dem Englischen von Heribert Hassler; original title : Ur of the Chaldees, A record of seven years excavation. Penguin Book A 27. 1950 (1929¹).

ZAEHNER, R.C., The Dawn and Twilight of Zoroastrianism. London (1961).

GENERAL INDEX

Aaron, 93, 140
Abdi-Milkutti, 231
Abel, 113, 136, 178
Abimelech, 158
Abraham, 69, 88, 112, 113, 144, 147, 150, 151, 163, 168, 183, 184
Absalom, 159, 161, 162
Abydos, 56
Academy of Plato, 283
Achaemenid(s), 259, 263, 264, 269, 270, 276, 278, 280, 282, 299, 300, 302
Acts of the Apostles, 60
Adad-Nirari I, 223
Adam, 116, 134, 136, 137, 138, 139, 144
Adoni(s), 236
Aegean (Sea), 16, 220, 258, 260, 263, 265, 266, 268
Afghanistan, 260, 270
Africa(n), 8, 9, 264
Agade see Akkad
Agnostic(icism), 122
Aha, 9
Ahab, 92, 105, 163, 228, 255
Ahaz, 164, 165, 181, 228
Ahiah, 162
Ahitew, S., 195
Ahra Mainyu see Angra Mainyu
Ahriman, 279, 288, 300, 302, 303
Ahura Mazda, 263, 265, 279, 280, 283, 284, 286-287, 288, 289, 294, 297, 298, 299, 300, 301, 302, 303, 305, 308
Ai, 173, 174
Akh, 46, 56
Akhenaten, 28-36 passim, 55, 85, 220
Akkad, 204, 208-209, 209-212, 213, 214, 215, 222, 228, 237, 239, 243

Akkadian, 206, 218, 225, 230, 236, 241, 242, 247, 248
Akki, 208
Alalah, 217
Alalu, 245
Aldred, C., 21, 22, 32, 33, 34, 35, 54, 55, 56
Aleppo, 218, 219
Alexander the Great, 267, 267-271 passim, 284, 285
Alexandria, 96
Allende, Isabel, 140, 199
Altheim, F., 306
Amarna, 29, 32, 33, 34, 35, 36, 56
Amasis, 19
Amazons, 139
Amenemet I, 26
Amenope (Book of Wisdom of), 20
Amenophis II, 55
Amenophis III, 28, 29, 35
Amenophis IV see Akhenaten
Ammon(ites), 184
Ammon Oracle, 269
Amorrhites, 173, 211, 212
Amu Darja see Oxus
Amun (Amon), 30, 32, 33, 36, 39-40, 238
Amun-Re, 30
An, 214, 242, 243
Analogia entis, 64
Analogy of being see Analogia entis
Anatolia(n), 204, 215, 216, 217, 224, 234, 241
Anglosaxon, 95
Angra Mainyu, 279-280, 292, 296, 297, 298, 303
Animism, 85
Anittas, 217
Ankara, 204, 216, 217

321

Ankh, 31, 48
Ankhes-En/paten, 36
Anshar, 247
Anshaw, 247
Anshaw, 262
Antef, 27
Anthropology, anthropologist, anthropological, 8, 66-67, 70, 89, 105, 113, 123, 128, 140, 143, 151, 250, 272
Anthropomorphism, anthropomorphic, 87-89, 132
Antiochus III, 78
Antiochus, IV, 78, 79, 82, 122, 123
Antipas, 182
Antipater, 182
Anu, 245, 248, 251
Anum, 213, 214, 242
Apocalyptic authors, writings, 74, 75-84
Apsu, 247, 248
Arab(ic), 22, 29, 187, 229
Arabia(n), 118, 264
Aral, Lake, 283, 285, 299
Aram, 164, 165, 184
Aramaic, 60, 79, 121, 176, 191, 192
Aramean(s), 223, 228, 229
Arina, 224
Aristotle, Aristotelian, 13, 54, 241
Aristophanes, 132
Ark of the Covenant, 161
Armenia, 224, 228, 234, 260
Artaxerxes III, 267
Aruru, 250
Aryan(s), 257, 265, 276, 306, 308
Arzawa, 220
Ashdod, 229
Ashur (god), 225, 230, 231, 232
Ashur-Uballit I, 223
Asia, 22, 257, 264, 265, 268, 271, 275, 285
Asia Minor, 16, 216, 219, 220, 221, 234, 258, 264, 266, 301
Asiatic(s), 8, 9, 17, 18-19, 21, 22, 24, 282
Asmodaeus, 197
Assmann, J., 31, 32, 36, 55, 56
Assur (city), 222, 223, 224
Assur (god) see Ashur
Assurbanipal, 231, 239, 249

Assurnasirpal II, 226-228
Assyria(n)(s), 22, 24, 7, 145, 164, 165, 168, 184, 204, 209, 210, 211, 213, 215, 216, 219, 221, 221 -232, 233, 237, 247, 256, 257, 258, 259, 260
Assyrian Empire, 205, 223-232, 232, 258
Astarte (see also Ishtar), 86, 242
Astrology, 68, 191
Astruc, Jean, 61
Astyages, 258, 259, 260
Aswân, 2, 4, 15
Atbara, 2
Aten, 29, 31, 32, 33, 34, 36, 85
Athalia, 103, 164
Atheism, atheist(s), atheistic, 91, 122
Athenian, 126, 266
Athens, 266, 272
Attaliah see Athalia
Attica, 281
Atum, 38
Augustine, saint, 108
Avaris, 24
Avesta, 283, 284, 285, 295, 302, 307
Ay, 33
Azazel, 100
Azupilanu, 208

Baal, 86, 92, 93, 99, 103, 105, 164, 176
Baalism, 100
Babel, 183
Babili, Babilu see Babylon
Babylon, 184, 212, 213, 214, 215, 218, 225, 230, 231, 233, 234, 239, 248, 259, 261, 262, 269, 270, 284
Babylonia(n)(s), 68, 77, 79, 80, 82, 99, 166, 176, 181, 184, 191, 204, 215, 226, 228, 229, 230, 232, 233, 237, 240, 241, 247, 249, 257, 258, 260, 261, 263, 264, 283, 306, 308
Babylonian Captivity, 62, 78, 116, 158, 166, 175, 181, 192, 259
Babylonian Empire, 80, 81, 205, 212-216, 232-234, 259, 261

Bagdad, 206, 209
Baikie, J., 5, 52
Barta, W., 31, 55, 56
Barton, G.A., 198
Baruch (Book of), 59
Basra, 206
Bassani, G., 171, 201
Bathsheba, 159
Baumgartner, E.J., 52
Beas see Hyphasis
Bedouins, 18
Beek, M.A., 253, 254, 255
Behrens, P., 52
Belzebub, 196
Benjamin (tribe), 78, 162
Berckenrath, J. von, 54, 55
Bethel, 163, 174
Bethlehem, 146
Bethulia, 145
Bible, 20, Ch. II passim, 191, 206, 289
Bietak, M., 54
Bisutun, 263
Black Obelisk, 228
Black Sea, 168, 217, 219, 258, 264, 265
Blue Nile, 2
Blumenthal, E., 27, 55
Boghazköy, 217
Book of the Dead, 51
Boorstin, D.J., 192
Booz, 146
Bosporus, 217, 257, 265
Boswell, J., 58, 191
Boyce, M., 275, 278, 280, 285, 296, 299, 300, 301, 302, 202, 307, 308 309, 310
Brahma-days, Brahma-year, 71
Brinkman, J.A., 254
British Museum, 228, 255
Brunner-Traut, E., 54, 55
Burckhardt, J., 272, 307
Buto, 12
Buytendijk, F.J.J., 131, 198
Byblos, 19

Caesarea Philippi, 193
Cain(ites), 108, 113, 136, 178
Cairns, G., 72, 73, 192
Cairo, 2, 28
Cambyses I, 259

Cambyses II, 262, 262-263, 264, 265, 271
Cameron, G.E., 306
Canaan(ite)(s), 16, 69, 86, 100, 102, 103, 104, 105, 107, 108, 142, 145, 150, 160, 161, 168, 169, 171, 173, 174, 175, 176, 177, 178, 188, 212, 221
Canon (of the Bible), 59, 60
Canyon, K., 174
Cappadocia, 204, 260
Carmel, Mount, 92
Carter, H., 28
Carthage, 263, 264, 271
Caspian Sea, 257
Cataracts of the Nile, 15
Cathars, 13
Caucasus, 217, 264
Censorinus, 71, 192
Central Africa, 3
Chaldean(s), 232, 283, 284
Charles II, king of England, 239
Chassidic, 183
Chatti see Hittites
Cheops, 28, 30
Chilean, 140
Chios, 265
Chodshent, 270
Chorasmia, 283, 285
Christan(s), 34, 59, 63, 64, 73, 80, 81, 91, 96, 114, 118, 120, 136, 151, 171, 182, 186
Christian X, king of Denmark, 27
Christianity, 60, 84
Cilicia, 228
Codex Hammurabi, 212, 213
Colossans, Letter to the, 191
Cinvat-Bridge, 293
Convention of Geneva, 175
Copenhague, 28
Coptic, 6
Council, First Vatican, 59
Council of Trent, 59
Cossaeans, 216
Covenant, 167-169, 170, 177
Creto-Mycenaean, 257
Croesus, 260
Curaçao, 199
Cush(ite)(s), 15, 52

Deuteronomist (D), 61, 62
Deuteronomy (Book of), 61, 125, 157, 181
Devil(s), 110
Diadochi, 80
Dinah, 178
Dnjestr, 265
Domitian, 60
Douglas, M. 188, 189, 190, 203, 235
Dorians, 257
Dual shrines, 11
Dualism, dualistic, 5, 6, 8, 9, 11, 13-15, 17, 24, 25, 26, 29, 32, 35, 37, 39, 54, 45, 46, 48, 50, 53, 57, 64, 68, 71, 75, 81, 82, 87, 89, 90, 91, 94, 95, 96, 97, 102, 103, 108, 109, 110, 111, 112, 115, 120, 123, 124, 131, 138, 147, 152, 153, 155, 159, 166, 170, 171, 172, 175, 180, 193, 184, 204, 205, 221, 225, 227, 232, 234, 239, 241, 242, 244, 246, 248, 250, 252, 271-274, 275, 278, 280, 281, 288, 289, 292, 294, 295, 297-298, 300, 303, 304, 305
Duality(ies), 8, 10, 11, 12, 13, 14, 15, 25, 33, 36, 38, 39, 45, 53, 67, 137, 277, 279, 289
Duchesne-Guillemin, J., 271, 284, 307, 308, 309, 310
Dumuzi, 236, 240
Dutch, 124, 137, 154, 172, 196, 290, 302
Dyad, 13

Ea, 230, 242, 245, 248, 252
Eannatum, 238
East African, 2
Eaton-Krauss, M., 56
Ecbatana, 258, 260
Ecclesiastes (Book of), 116, 117
Ecclesiasticus (Book of), 59, 149
Edom(ite)(s), 94, 168, 180-183, 184
Egypt, Ch. I passim, 69, 78, 84, 93, 99, 100, 101, 103, 104, 143, 152, 156, 162, 165, 181, 184, 193, 220, 221, 229, 230, 231, 233, 234, 238, 239, 262, 264, 267, 271
Egyptian(s), Ch. I passim, 78, 81, 85, 93, 97, 114, 115, 116, 165, 173, 220, 223, 226, 233, 237, 238, 239, 262, 287
Eichrodt, W., 194
Eissfeldt, O., 193
Ekallatum, 222
Elam(ite)(s), 168, 210, 211, 231, 232, 233, 257, 263, 306
Elijah, 92, 93
Eliphaz, 119
Eliu, 119
El Nikrash, 54
Elohim, 85, 108, 109
Elohist (E), 61, 62, 191
Emmanuel, 164
Endor (witch of), 101, 102
English, 22, 172, 291
E-Nimmor, 209
Enki, 242, 243, 244
Enkidu, 250-251
Enlil, 207, 209, 214, 222, 238, 242, 243, 248, 252, 253
Ephraim (tribe), 173
Erech see Uruk
Eretria, 266
Eridu, 206
Erman, A., 7, 52, 55
Esarhaddon, 230-231
Esau, 156, 180, 181, 182, 183, 184
Esoteric, 75, 79, 80, 304
Essenes, 104
Esther, 146, 242
Esther (Book of), 282
Ethbaal, 92
Ethiopia(n), 1, 2
Euphrates, 22, 23, 184, 204, 205, 207, 208, 209, 212, 218, 219, 222, 223, 224, 226, 243, 259
Europea(n)(s), 264, 265, 266, 301, 303
Eve, 136, 137, 196
Evolution (theory), evolutionism, evolutionary, 63, 66, 70, 71, 85
Exodus (book of), 61, 84, 125
Exodus (event), 69
Ezechias, 94
Ezekiel (prophet), 233, 236
Ezekiel (Prophecy of), 89, 168, 184, 192

Ezra (Book of), 59

Fall, 63, 66
Faust, 277
Fayyûm, 4
Feith, 41
Feldman, S., 194
Feminist, 137, 147
Feral men, 250
Flood, 97, 98, 237, 249, 250, 252
Fohrer, G., 103, 104, 105, 195
Fonda, J., 129
Fraine, J. de, 137, 199
France, 61
Frankfort, H., 10, 14, 46, 47, 52, 53, 54, 237, 238, 239, 255, 256
Fröhlich's Syndrome, 35
Fundamentalist(s), 63
Furlani, G., 246, 256

Gabriel, A., 276, 307
Galilee, Galileans, 165, 166, 182, 228
Gardiner, A., 16, 52, 54
Gaugamela, 269
Gaza, 229, 269
Gehenna, 121
Geldner, 285
Genesis (Book of), 19, 60, 60-63, 84, 85, 86, 87, 88, 89, 96, 105, 107, 108, 109, 110, 122, 128, 130, 131, 132, 133, 136, 139, 143, 183, 189, 190, 197, 249, 289
Gentes, Gentiles, 168, 170, 184, 185
Gerizzim, Mount, 166
German, 1, 34, 64, 95, 134, 194, 196, 290
Germanic, 290
Gezer, 173
Gideon, 157, 158
Gilgal, 157, 158, 159
Gilgamesh, 236, 249-253
Ghirshman, R., 267, 306, 307
Giveon, R., 54
Gnosis, gnostic(s), 64, 155, 186, 289
Goethe, J.W., 91, 185, 203
Goetze, A., 221, 254, 255
Golgotha, 151
Goodrich-Clarke, N., 192

Gospel of John, 60
Gospel of Matthew, 69
Gospels, 60, 76
Grand Tour, 20
Granicus, 268
Great Year, 71-72, 72, 74
Greece, 71, 207, 265, 266, 267, 268
Greek(s), 17, 19, 20, 21, 46, 59, 60, 69, 73, 81, 88, 97, 115, 116, 117, 121, 139, 144, 157, 192, 201, 210, 212, 221, 224, 232, 236, 244, 258, 259, 260, 263, 264, 265, 266, 267, 268, 269, 270, 279, 282, 283, 284, 287
Griffiths, J.C., 54
Gurney, O.R., 254
Gutean(s), 209, 211

Halys, 115
258, 260
Hamadan, 258, 263
Hamitic, 8, 9
Hammurabi, 212-213, 213, 214, 215, 223, 237, 238, 239
Harran, 226, 241, 261
Hatshepsut, 56
Hatti see Hittites
Hattians, 217
Hattusa, 204, 217, 218, 221
Hattusilis I, 217-218
Hattusilis III, 220-221
Hayes, W.C., 2, 52
Hebraists, 156
Hebrew(s), 19, 23, 60, 68, 76, 79, 90, 93, 97, 106, 108, 109, 110, 112, 117, 133, 155, 168, 171, 187, 192, 203
Hebron, 181
Hegel, G.F.W., 43, 51, 56
Heijermans, H., 200
Helck, W., 53, 54, 56
Heliopolis, Heliopolitan, 37-39, 39, 49, 55
Hellenism, Hellenistic, 78, 270, 276
Hephaestus, 270
Heracleopolis, 25
Heraclitus, 71, 192
Herakhty see Horakhty

Herat, 270
Herculaneum, 283
Hermopolis, 37, 39, 55
Herod Agrippa I, 182
Herod I the Great, 182
Herodotus, 17, 20, 54, 255, 258, 280, 301, 306, 307
Herzfeldt, E., 308
Hesiod, 80
Hicks, J., 216, 254
Hieraconpolis, 9, 12
Hindu Kush, 270
Hinnom, Valley of, 121
Hitler, A., 274, 296
Hittite(s), 204, 215, 216, 216-221, 223, 224, 234-236, 244-247, 249, 258, 262, 268
Hittite Empire, 204, 205, 216-221, 234
Hizkiah, 160, 163, 169, 229
Holistic, 64
Holofernes, 145
Holy Roman Empire, 80-81
Homo sapiens, 66, 70
Hor-akhty, 26, 29, 30, 31
Hornung, E., 52
Horus, 7, 9, 14, 15, 24, 27, 53
Hosea, 104
Humbert, P., 89, 194
Hurrites, Hurrian, 21, 216, 218, 219, 249
Huxley, J., 129, 198
Hyksos, 21-22, 23, 24, 31
Hyphasis, 270
Hyrcania, 260
Hystaspis, 265

Iddin-Dagan, 240
Idumea(n)(s), 181, 182
Igigi, 214, 242
Iliad, 249, 268
Illil see Enlil
Illuyankas, 246
Imperialism, 204, 212, 216, 232, 238, 261, 262, 264
Inanna, 238, 240, 242
India(n), 71, 264, 270, 276, 293
Indian Ocean, 264, 270
Indo-European(s), 216, 221, 276, 290, 293
Indus, 260, 264, 265, 270

Intermediate Period (First), 25
Ionian, 266
Ions, V., 56
Iran, Iranian(s), 216, 257, 259, 270, 271, 275, 276, 277, 279, 281, 283, 284, 289, 290, 291, 292, 293, 294, 299, 300, 301, 304, 305, 305, 306, 308
Iranologists, 278
Iraq, 205, 206, 221
Irish, 192
Isaac, 147, 150, 151, 156
Isaiah (prophet), 229
Isaiah (Prophecy of), 60, 76, 77-78, 90, 121, 148, 150, 153, 160, 164, 170, 178, 184, 185, 193
Isboshet, 161
Ishtar, 2156, 224, 231, 232, 240, 251
Isin, 237
Islam(ites), 91, 140
Island of the Blessed, 47
Israel (modern state of), 19
Israel (northern kingdom), 77, 92, 94, 105, 127, 159, 161, 162, 163, 164, 165, 228, 229
Israel (patriarch), 156
Israel (people of), Ch. II passim, 234, 236, 255, 257
Issus, 268, 269
Iustitia originalis, 67

Jabbok, 155
Jachdumlim, 222
Jacob (patriarch), 19, 144, 147, 148, 155, 156, 168, 178, 180, 181, 183, 184
Jacob, E., 99, 195
Jacobsen, Th., 256
Jahel, 145
Jahvism, Jahvists, Jahvistic, 95, 100, 103
Jahvist (J), 61, 62, 63, 87, 109, 134, 136, 143, 101
Jaki, S.L., 192
James (Letter of), 59
James, W., 186, 203, 255
Jamnia, Council of, 117
Japanese, 280
Jaxartes (Syr Darja), 260, 265, 299

Jeanne d'Arc, 145
Jebusites, 173
Jehu, 195, 228
Jeremiah (Prophecy of), 59, 90, 91, 104, 105, 116, 121, 164, 184, 192, 259
Jericho, 157, 172, 174
Jeroboam, 162, 163, 164
Jerusalem, 112, 121, 122, 161, 162, 163, 164, 166, 173, 181, 182, 184, 185, 229, 233, 236
Jesus Christ, 69, 76, 86, 104, 136, 146, 151, 158, 172, 175, 182, 186
Jew(s), Jewish, 59, 60, 64, 69, 74, 78, 90, 91, 96, 104, 118, 120, 121, 122, 125, 146, 166, 182, 186, 189, 191, 192, 193, 229, 233, 236, 259, 261, 296
Jezebel, 92, 105
Joas, 103, 163
Job, 99, 110, 115, 118-120
Job (Book of), 98, 110, 117-121, 121
Jojadah, 103
John the Baptist, 104
John Hyrcanus, 182
Jojakin, 233
Jonadab, 105
Jonah, 98, 114
Joram, 105, 164
Jordan, 156, 193
Josaphat 94, 163, 164
Joseph (son of Isaac), 19
Josephus, Flavius, 182, 202
Joshua, 169, 173, 174, 178
Joshua (Book of), 171, 172, 173, 174
Josiah, 62, 160, 163
Juda (tribe), 78, 162
Judaea(n)(s), 166, 182
Judah (kingdom), 62, 76, 77, 78, 92, 94, 103, 105, 127, 159, 161, 162, 163, 165, 166, 169, 170, 181, 228, 229, 233
Judas the Maccabee, 78, 122, 182, 193
Judge(s) (in Israel), 157, 158, 159, 160
Judges (Book of), 145, 158, 173, 178

Judith, 145, 146
Judith (Book of), 145
Juppiter, 90

Ka, 43-46, 47, 56
Kadesh, 220
Kákosy, L., 56
Kalach, 227, 228
Kalkhu see Kalach
Kamos, 94
Kandahar, 270
Kaplony, P., 43, 56
Karkemish, 219, 233
Karnak, 39
Kastiliash IV, 225
Kassites, 216, 225
Kees, K., 6, 52, 54, 56
Kemp, B.J., 25, 55
Kengi(r), 206
Kermanshah, 263
Khatti see Hittites
Khnum, 44
Khshathrita, 258
Khwarezm see Chorasmia
Ki, 242
Killas, 246
King, L.W., 253, 254
King's Peace, 267
Kings (Book of), 160, 166
Kingu, 249
Kirkuk, 221
Kish, 207, 208, 209, 212, 238
Kishar, 247
Klengel, E. and H., 254, 255
Kn-ꜣImn, 55
Kohelet see Ecclesiasticus, 116
König, E., 97, 195
Konya, 140
Kramer, S.N., 236, 241, 242, 255, 256
Krijger, A., 180, 183, 202, 203
Kristensen, W.B., 57
Kumarbi, 245, 246
Kundi, 231
Kurdistan, 210
Kurkh, 255
Kurush I, 259
Kussara, 217

Labarnas, 217

Laberna, 235
Lachamu, 247
Lachmu, 247
Lagash, 207, 209, 238
Lamentations of Jeremiah, 59
Langgässer, E., 194, 196
Larsa, 207, 213
Latin, 187, 191, 279, 293
Latium, 271
Lebanon Mountains, 233
Leeuwen, B. van, 137, 138, 199
Lemnos, 265
Levi (tribe of), Levites, 140, 142, 173
Leviathan, 99, 152, 246
Leviticus (Book of), 61, 125, 187, 188
Liberal(s), 34, 87
Libya(n)(s), 16, 21, 22, 263
Loewe, C., 203
Lommel, H., 289, 291, 295, 307, 308, 309
London, 58
Louis XV, 61
Louvre, Musée du, 212, 231, 254
Lower Egypt, 2, 4, 7, 8, 10, 11, 12, 14
Lugalbanda, 236
Luke, 60, 191
Luristan, 216
Luther, M., 59, 134
Luvian(s), 216
Luzalzaggisi, 207, 208, 209, 238
Lydia(n)(s), 258, 260, 268

Maat, 24, 25, 26, 30, 38, 42
Maccabees (Books of the), 59
Macedonia(n)(s), 22, 80, 265, 267. 267-271, 279, 281
Macedonian Empire, 80, 82
Macqueen, J.C., 216, 254
Makan, 210
Manasseh, 101, 102
Manetho, 9, 22
Manishtushu, 210
Marduk, 214, 215, 225, 230, 231, 238, 240, 247, 248, 249, 261, 262
Mari, 208, 213, 222, 223
Marmora, Sea of, 265
Marquet-Krause, J., 173

Marriage, 125-126
Marx, K., 272
Marxists, 34
Mary (mother of Jesus), 136
Maspero, G., 44
Masagetes, 262
Matthew, 191
Medes, Median, 234, 257, 258-259, 259, 260, 264
Media, 165
Median Empire, 80, 81, 258-259, 260
Median Wall, 259
Medinet Habu, 16
Mediterranean (Sea), 16, 92, 207, 208, 210, 219, 226, 227, 238, 263, 268
Melchisedech, 112, 113
Memphis, 10, 29, 36, 37, 55, 231, 262, 263
Memphite theology, 10, 14, 40
Menahem, 164
Menes, 9, 10
Menkhepure, 11
Merenptah, 16
Mesa, 94
Meshech, 168
Mesopotamia(n), 75, 77, 81, 82, 150, 156, 165, 181, 191, 205, 206, 209, 211, 212, 213, 214, 216, 219, 221, 222, 225, 232, 234, 237, 238, 239, 240, 241, 242, 247, 250, 259, 261, 262, 269, 276, 282, 308
Messiah, 68, 76-77, 112, 163, 166, 183, 185, 186
Messianic, 193, 261
Métin, A., 52
Metropolitan Museum of Art, 227
Micah (Prophecy of), 192
Middle East, 172, 219, 222, 223, 229, 241, 263
Middle Kingdom, 25, 40
Midianites, 157
Milete, 19, 265, 268
Millo, 162
Miskotte, H., 95, 194
Mitanni(an), 219, 223, 224
Mithra, 277-278. 294, 305
Mit-Rahineh, 10

Moab(ite)(s), 94, 146, 160, 164, 169, 184
Mohammad Riza Pahlavi, 281, 282
Molé, M., 283, 307, 308
Moloch, 121, 177
Monad, 13
Monistic, 57, 64, 289, 298
Monolatry, 85
Monotheism, monotheist(ic), 28, 29, 84, 85-86, 91, 95, 112, 149, 166, 289, 294
Montet, P., 19, 20, 52, 54
Mordechai, 146
Morenz, S., 39, 40, 47, 48, 51, 54, 56, 57
Moret, A., 52
Moria, Mountain, 151
Mosaic, 87
Moses, 20, 23, 54, 59, 61, 88, 89, 93, 101, 127, 144, 155, 157, 191, 194, 208
Mosul, 221, 222
Munn-Rankin, J.J., 224, 254
Mursilis I, 218
Mursilis II, 219-220
Musri, 224

Nablus, 166, 191
Nabonidus see Nabuna'id
Nabopolassar, 232
Nabû, 231
Nabuchodonossor II see Nebuchadnessar II
Nabuna'id, 241, 261
Nabu-nasir, 228
Naguib, 22
Nakedness, 123-124, 128, 129
Nanna, 243
Nanna-Sin, 241, 242
Naqsh-i-Rustam, 265
Naram-Sin, 210-211, 237
Narmer, 9, 11
Nasser, Lake, 4
Nathan, 163
Naucratis, 19
Nazarites, 104, 105
Nebhepetre Mentuhotep I, 25
Nebuchadnessar II, 79, 232-233, 258, 259
Nefertiti, 29, 34, 35, 56

Nekhbet, 9, 12
Nelis, J., 193
Netherlands, the, 239
New Kingdom, 25, 31, 39
New Testament, 59, 60, 74, 140, 150, 166, 169, 170, 191, 192
Newman, F.W., 185, 186, 203
New Year's Festival, 23, 30, 240, 249, 261, 281
New York, 227
Nietzsche, F., 282, 298
Nikolsburg, 183
Nile, 1, 2, 3, 4, 6, 7, 8, 15, 18, 19, 23, 37, 42
Nineveh, 230, 231, 232, 249, 258
Ningal, 242
Ningirsu, 207, 238
Ninlil, 231, 242, 243
Ninos see Tukulti-Ninurta
Nippur, 207, 209, 222, 242, 243
Noah, 98, 154, 167, 177, 183
Noemi, 146
Nomads, 3, 8, 18
Northern Africa, 1, 2
Norwegian, 57
Nubia(n)(s), 15, 17, 18, 22, 23, 231, 263
Numbers (Book of), 61, 158
Nun, 37, 38, 39, 40
Nyberg, H.S., 278, 279, 283, 299, 307, 308, 309, 310

Obadiah, 181
Ochozias, 105
Odyssey, 249
Old Kingdom, 10, 25, 40
Old Testament, 27, Ch. II passim, 241, 296
Oldenburg, R., 55
Olmstead, A.T., 254, 255, 306
Olympia, 86
Olympiad(s), 69
Oman, 210
Omri, 163, 164, 228
One and the Many, the, 38-39
Oppenheim, A.L., 256
Orange (House of), 239
Ormuzd, 279-280, 297
Orontes, 218, 220
Osee (king), 165

Osee (prophet), 92, 163, 165
Osiris, 6, 7, 10, 14, 33, 46, 48, 49, 238
Otto, E., 13, 15, 54, 56
Oxus (Amu Darja), 260, 264, 285
Pahlavi, Pahlevi, 279, 307, 309
Pakistan, 260, 270
Palestine, Palestinian, 16, 17, 18, 103, 118, 139, 165, 174, 220, 229, 230, 233, 234, 257, 262, 263, 264, 269
Panhellenic, 268
Panium, 78
Pantheistic, 64
Paradise, 63, 67, 73, 74, 13, 124, 128, 129, 134, 136
Paris, 212, 254
Parmenides, 91, 116
Parthia(n), 260, 276
Passover, 104
Patterson, Ch.H., 87, 167, 193
Paul (apostle), 191, 291
Pekah, 164, 165
Pelusium, 262
Pentateuch, 59, 60-62, 85
Pepys, S., 239
Persepolis, 259, 284
Persia(n)(s), 22, 24, 78, 146, 184, 232, 234, 241, Ch. IV passim, 306
Persian Empire, 78, 80, 81, 82, 156, 259-271
Persian Gulf, 206, 207, 210, 238, 259
Pharaoh, 6, 10, 11, 12, 17, 18, 21, 22, 24-28, 28, 30, 31, 37, 40, 44, 81, 93, 156, 169, 173, 184, 220, 223, 231, 238, 239, 262
Pharisees, 172
Phidias, 86
Philistine(s), 16, 101, 156, 160, 161, 168, 179, 184, 228, 257
Philo, 96
Phoenicia(n), 92, 226, 229, 233, 234, 236, 262, 263, 267, 268, 269
Phraortes see Khshathrita
Phrygia(n)(s), 257
Pieper, Joseph, 187
Pilate, 158, 182
Plataeae, Battle of, 266

Plato, 20, 54, 71, 96, 114, 116, 132, 192, 198, 274, 283, 284
Platonic, 96, 192
Plutarch, 307
Poland, 183
Polytheism, polytheistic, 84, 85, 86, 95, 276
Presocratic, 13
Priestly Code (P), 61, 62, 63, 68, 85, 87, 89
Protestant(s), 59, 191
Proust, M., 73
Proverbs (Book of), 19, 115, 146
Psammetichus III, 262
Ptah, 40, 45
Ptolemaeans, Ptolemaic, 8, 78
Pul(u) see Tiglath-Pileser III
Purim Feast, 146
Purulliyas Festival, 246
Pyramid Texts, 11, 38, 47
Pythagoras, Pythagorean, 13, 20, 284, 304
Pythagoreanism, 71

Rabbinical, 69, 96
Rad, G. von, 89, 173, 183, 194, 202, 203
Rahab, 98, 99
Ramses II, 16, 28, 220
Ramses III, 16
Rationalism, rationalist(ic), 91
Re (Ra), 11, 29, 30, 31, 38, 45, 262
Rebecca, 180
Redford, D.B., 254
Red Sea, 93, 180
Refaim, 179
Reformers (Protestant), 59
Rehab, 105
Rehabites, 104, 105
Renckens, H., 86, 111, 193
Revelation of John, 60, 69, 74
Rhodos, 220
Rimush, 210
Roboam, 164
Roditi, G., 138, 199
Roman(s), 22, 60, 69, 78, 80, 90, 182, 271
Roman-Catholic(s), 59, 182, 191

Roman Empire, 205, 213
Romance languages, 291
Rome, 69
Rowley, H.H., 193, 194
Rudofsky, B., 198
Russia(n), 260, 265, 308
Ruth, 146
Ruth (Book of), 146

Sacred Marriage, 240
Saggs, H.W.F., 255
Sahara, 1, 2, 3, 5, 264, 269
Salamis, Straits of, 281
Salem, 112
Samaria (province), 165, 167, 182
Samaria (town), 163, 165, 169, 229
Samaritan(s), 59, 166, 175, 191, 229
Samos, 265
Samson, 104, 144, 168
Samsuditana, 215
Samsuiluna, 215
Samuel, 101, 104, 157, 158, 159, 160
Samuel (Books of), 192
Sander-Hausen, C.E., 49, 57
Sanduarri, 231
Sara, 197
Sardes, 260, 266, 268
Sargon I (king of Akkad), 208-210, 213, 218, 238
Sargon II (king of Assyria), 165, 229
Sargonids, 209, 210, 211
Sassanid, 276, 284, 285
Satan, 110, 118, 180, 196
Saul, 101, 158, 159, 160, 161, 168, 181
Sauneron, S., 42, 56
Säve-Söderbergh, T., 55
Schapp, W., 64, 191
Schenkel, W., 14, 54, 255
Schmökel, H., 237, 253, 254, 255, 256
Schoske, S., 54
Scout Law, 308
Scythian(s), 264, 265
Sea Peoples, 16, 221
Secularization, 51
Sed Festival, 11, 12, 23
Seir, 180, 181
Seleucid(s), 78, 80, 82, 182, 284
Sellin, E., 87, 193

Semitic(s), 8, 9, 21, 85, 168, 172, 175, 208, 211, 212, 213, 222, 240, 241, 242, 256
Semnah, 17
Sennacherib, 229-230
Sephora, 101
Septuagint, 121, 192
Sesostris I, 17, 26
Sesostris III, 27
Seters, J. van, 54
Seth(ites) (biblical), 108
Seth (Egyptian), 6, 7, 14, 15, 23, 24, 53
Seti I, 7
Sex(ual)(ity), 36, 38, 108, 109, 125-131, 148, 150, 251
Shalmaneser I, 223-224
Shalmaneser III, 228, 259
Shalmaneser V, 165, 229
Shamash, 214, 231, 251
Shamshi Adad I, 222, 223
Shapur II, 285
Sharkalisharpi, 211
Shattuara II, 223, 224
Sheba, 161, 162
Shu, 38
Shulgi, 211
Sichem, 178
Sidon(ian)(s), 168, 231
Simon the Maccabee, 182
Sin, 231, 238, 261
Sinai, Mount, 16, 88, 127, 167, 169, 262
Sion, 178, 185
Sisara, 145
Siwah, Oasis, 269
Skinner, J., 109, 197
Smenkh-ka-Re, 35
Smith, S., 254
Socialist, 34
Socrates, 73
Soden, W. von, 210, 253, 254, 255
Solomon, 92, 116, 124, 145, 159, 162, 173, 181, 233
Son of Man, 81-82
Song of Songs, 125, 138
Sophar, 119
Sophocles, 140, 199
Soviet-Union, 260

Sparta, 266
Spenta Mainyu, 287, 289, 292, 303
Spiegel, J., 50, 56, 57
Spieser, E.A., 109 , 197
Statira, 270
Subartu, 222
Sumer, 191, 204, 205-208, 208, 209, 209-212, 212, 213, 214, 215, 216, 222, 225, 228, 236, 239, 240, 243, 255
Sumerian(s), 206, 207, 208, 209, 210, 211, 212, 213, 214, 222, 236, 237, 238, 240, 241, 242, 243, 244, 248, 249, 271
Suppiluliumas, 219
Susa, 210, 212, 262, 263, 269, 270, 306
Syr Darja see Jaxartes
Syria(n)(s), 78, 207, 210, 210, 213, 217, 218, 219, 220, 221, 223, 224, 226, 227, 228, 230, 233, 234, 236, 262, 264, 267, 269

Tabarna, 220
Tabernacle, 62, 161
Taharka, 231
Tammuz, 236, 240
Tarsus, 268
Taurus, 231
Tefnut, 38
Teje, 29
Telebinu, 218
Tell Ashara, 222
Temple of Jerusalem, 62, 86, 103, 161, 162, 182, 261
Terqa, 222
Teshup, 245
Thames, 239
Thebes, Theban (Egyptian), 17, 21, 25, 37, 39-40, 55
Themistocles, 282
Theomorphism, theomorphic, 87-89, 132
Theophany, 89
Thijssen, Th., 124, 198
Thrace, Thracian(s), 257, 265
Thutmosis I, 22
Thutmosis III, 28, 220
Thutmosis IV, 15

Tiamat, 99, 247, 248, 249
Tiber, 213
Tiglath-Pileser I, 225-226
Tiglath-Pileser III, 164, 165, 228-229
Tigris, 204, 205, 207, 222, 224, 231, 243, 259, 269
Titus (Roman emperor), 182
Tobiah (Book of), 59
Tophet, 121
Toynbee, A., 53, 204, 205, 253
Trojan War, 20, 283
Troy, 268
Tubal, 168
Tukulti-Ninurta (Ninos), 224-225
Turkish, Turkey, 22, 140, 204, 217
Tut-Ankh-Amun, 28, 35-36
Tuttul, 208
Two Ladies, the, 12-13, 15
Two Lands, the, 7-15, 53
Tyre, 184, 233, 269

Ugarit, 99
Ukraine, 264
Ulikummu, 245
Umma, 207, 209
UNESCO, 129
Universal states, 204
Unug, 243
Upper Egypt, 2, 3, 7, 8, 10, 11, 12, 14
Ur, 206, 207, 209, 211, 237, 241
Uraeus, 12, 30
Uriah, 127, 145, 159
Urmia, Lake, 224, 259
Ur-Nammu, 211
Urnil, 1, 2
Uruk (Erech), 206, 207, 209, 211, 240, 250, 252, 253
Ur Zafaba, 208
Us, 118
Ussher, J., 192
Uto, 12
Utpanishtim, 251, 252
Utu, 242
Utu-Hegal, 211
Uzbekistan, 270

Vadim, R., 129
Valhalla, 47

Valley (of the Nile) see Upper Egypt
Van, Lake, 224
Vayu, 276-277, 288, 293
Vegetarian(ism), 292, 304
Velde, H. te, 56
Vistaspa, 284, 285
Vondel, J. van den, 196, 199

Waddell, W.G., 54
Wadi Brissar, 233
Wadjet, 12, 53
Wenamum, 19
Wenders, W., 196
Wendorff, R., 192, 193
Wenig, S., 54, 55
Westendorf, W., 56
Westergaard, 285
White Nile, 2
Widengren, G., 276, 278, 280, 281, 283, 285, 304, 306, 307, 308, 309, 310
Wildung, D., 54
Wilson, A.N., 138, 199
Wilson, J., 1, 3, 5, 8, 16, 52, 54
Wisdom (Book of), (Egyptian), 20, 106, 177
Wisdom (Book of) (Hberew), 59, 149
Wiseman, D.J., 225
Woolley, L., 253, 254
Woude, A.S. van der, 192

Xenophon, 232, 307
Xerxes I, 266, 267, 280, 281, 282

Zaehner, R.C., 287, 307, 308, 309
Zagros Mountains, 209, 210, 211, 224, 226, 233, 257
Zandee, J., 50, 57
Zarathustra see Zoroaster
Zervan, 278, 288, 302, 202
Zervanism, 278-279, 303-303
Zervanites, 288, 302, 303
Zeus Olympios, 78, 86
Zidkiah, 233
Zoroastre, 275, 278, 279, 280, 282.286, 286-297, 297-299, 299, 300, 301, 303, 306, 308
Zoroastrian(s), 280, 283, 284, 288, 291, 292, 294, 296, 298, 299, 300, 301, 302, 305, 308
Zoroastrianism, 275, 276, 278, 280, 299, 300, 301, 302, 303
Zurvan see Zervan
Zodiac, 71, 283